TURTLES

CITY AT WAR, PT. 2 ▸ VOLUME 23

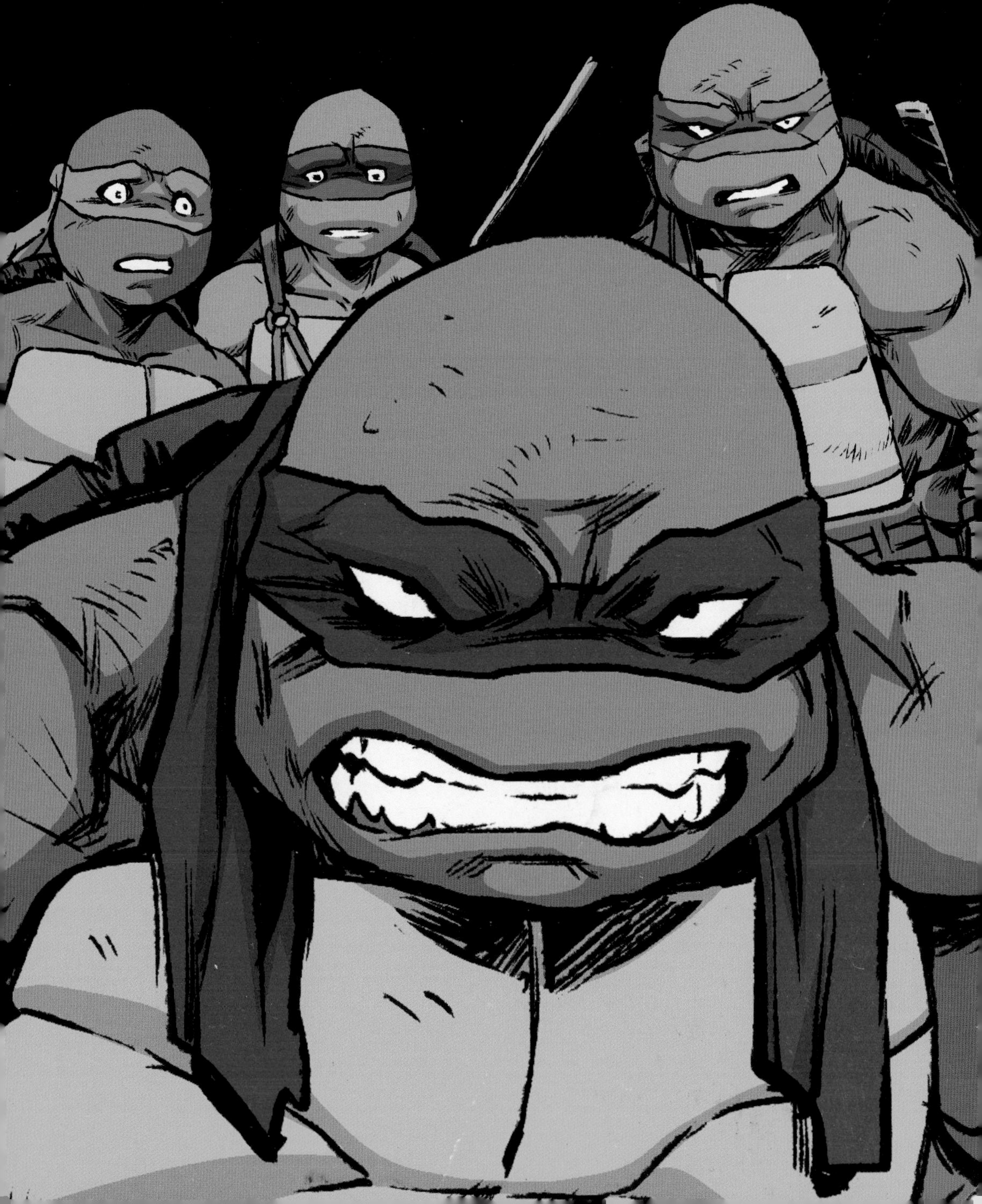

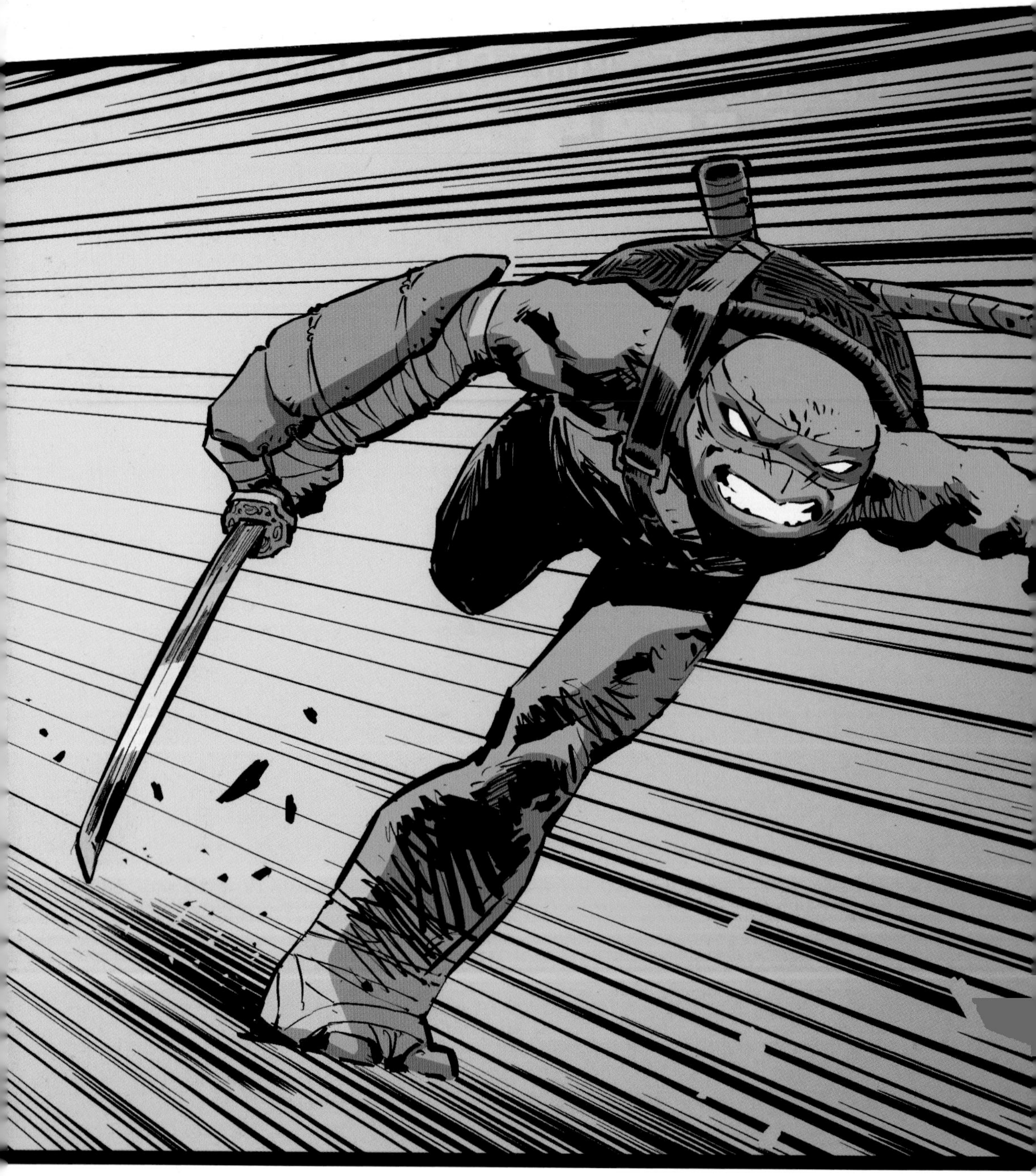

Story by Kevin Eastman, Bobby Curnow, and Tom Waltz **Script by Tom Waltz**

nickelodeon™

Special thanks to Joan Hilty & Linda Lee for their invaluable assistance.

For international rights, contact **licensing@idwpublishing.com**

ISBN: 978-1-68405-625-5

23 22 21 20 1 2 3 4

IDW®
www.IDWPUBLISHING.com

Chris Ryall, President & Publisher/CCO • **Cara Morrison**, Chief Financial Officer • **Matthew Ruzicka**, Chief Accounting Officer • **David Hedgecock**, Associate Publisher • **John Barber**, Editor-in-Chief • **Justin Eisinger**, Editorial Director, Graphic Novels and Collections • **Jerry Bennington**, VP of New Product Development • **Lorelei Bunjes**, VP of Technology & Information Services • **Jud Meyers**, Sales Director • **Anna Morrow**, Marketing Director • **Tara McCrillis**, Director of Design & Production • **Mike Ford**, Director of Operations • **Rebekah Cahalin**, General Manager

Ted Adams and Robbie Robbins, IDW Founders

Facebook: **facebook.com/idwpublishing** • Twitter: **@idwpublishing** • YouTube: **youtube.com/idwpublishing**
Tumblr: **tumblr.idwpublishing.com** • Instagram: **instagram.com/idwpublishing**

Originally published as TEENAGE MUTANT NINJA TURTLES issues #96–100.

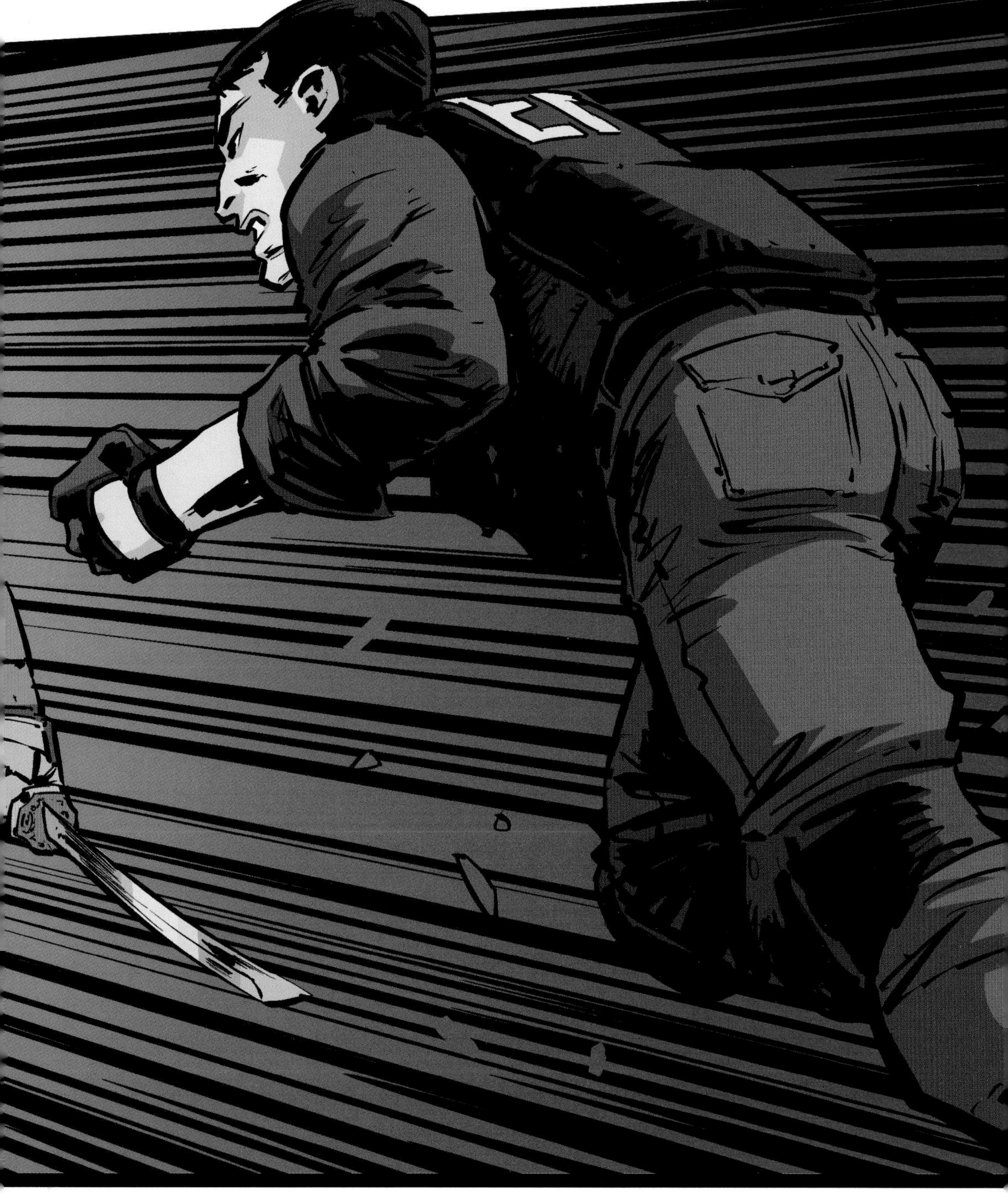

Art by Michael Dialynas and Dave Wachter

Additional Art by Mateus Santolouco, Adam Gorham, Dan Duncan, and Cory Smith

Colors by Ronda Pattison

Additional Colors by Bill Crabtree

Letters and Production by Shawn Lee

Series Edits by Bobby Curnow

Cover by Sophie Campbell

Collection Edits by Justin Eisinger & Alonzo Simon

Based on characters created by Peter Laird and Kevin Eastman

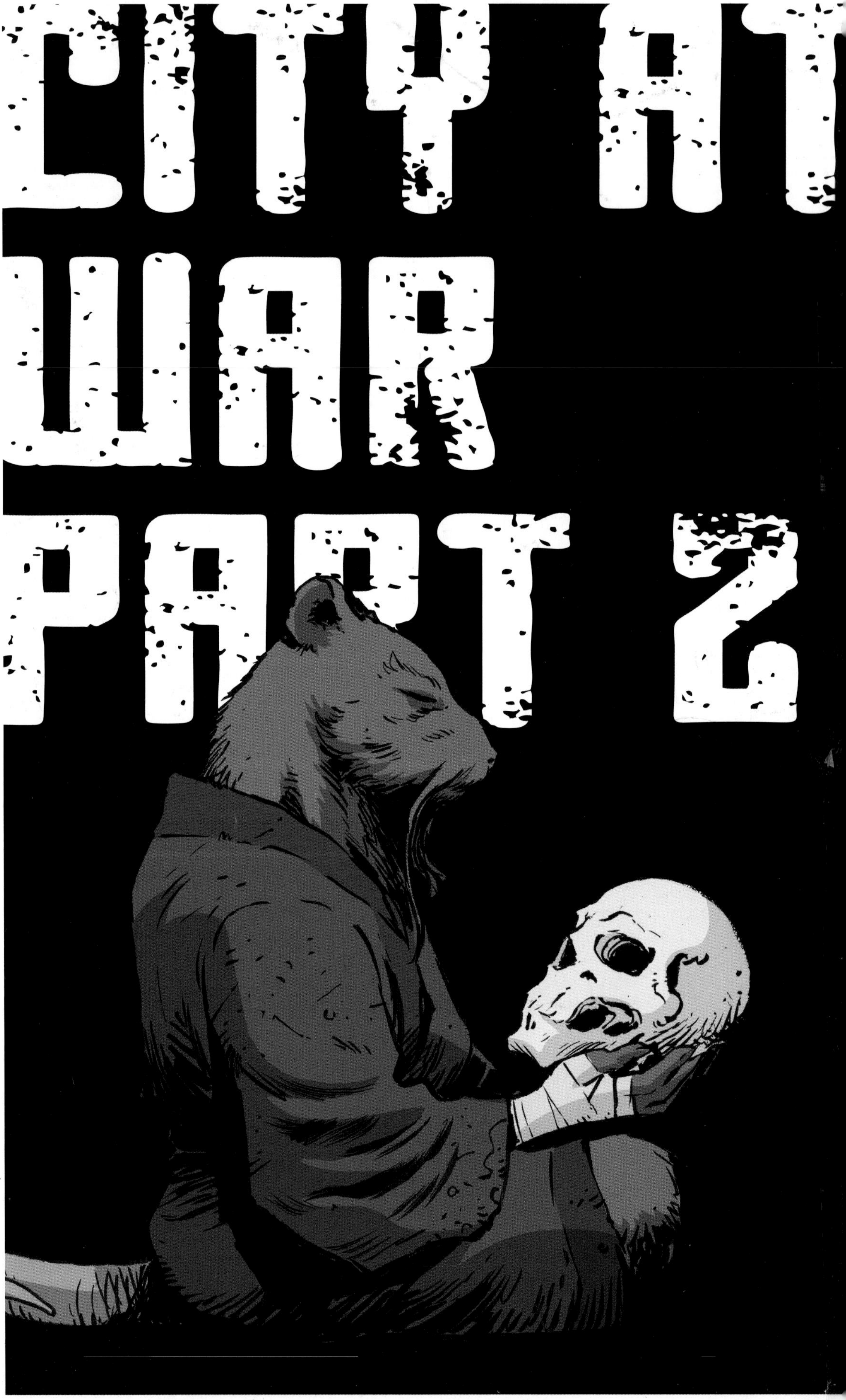
CITY AT
WAR
PART 2

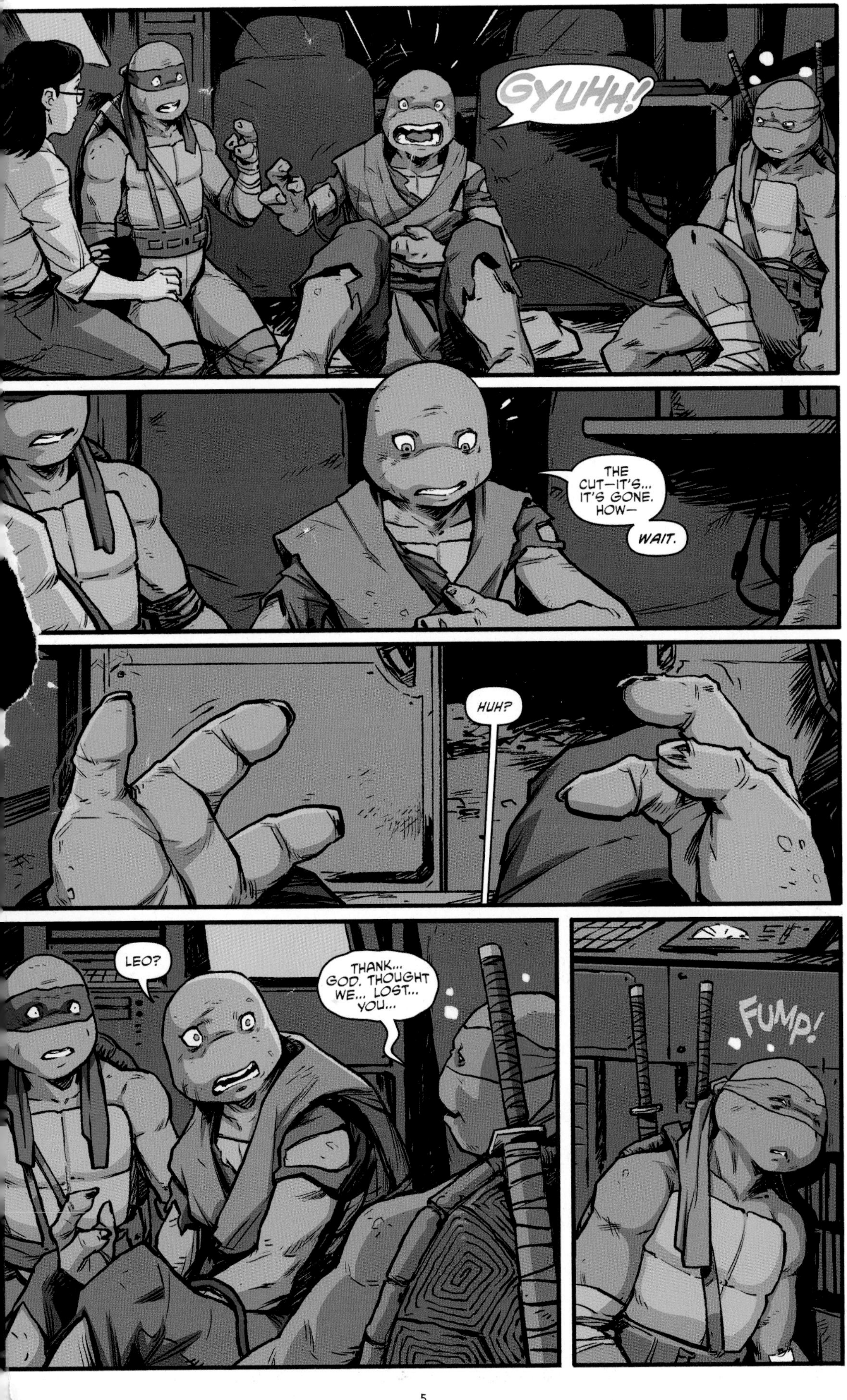
GYUHH!
THE CUT—IT'S... IT'S GONE. HOW—
WAIT.
HUH?
LEO?
THANK... GOD. THOUGHT WE... LOST... YOU...
FUMP!

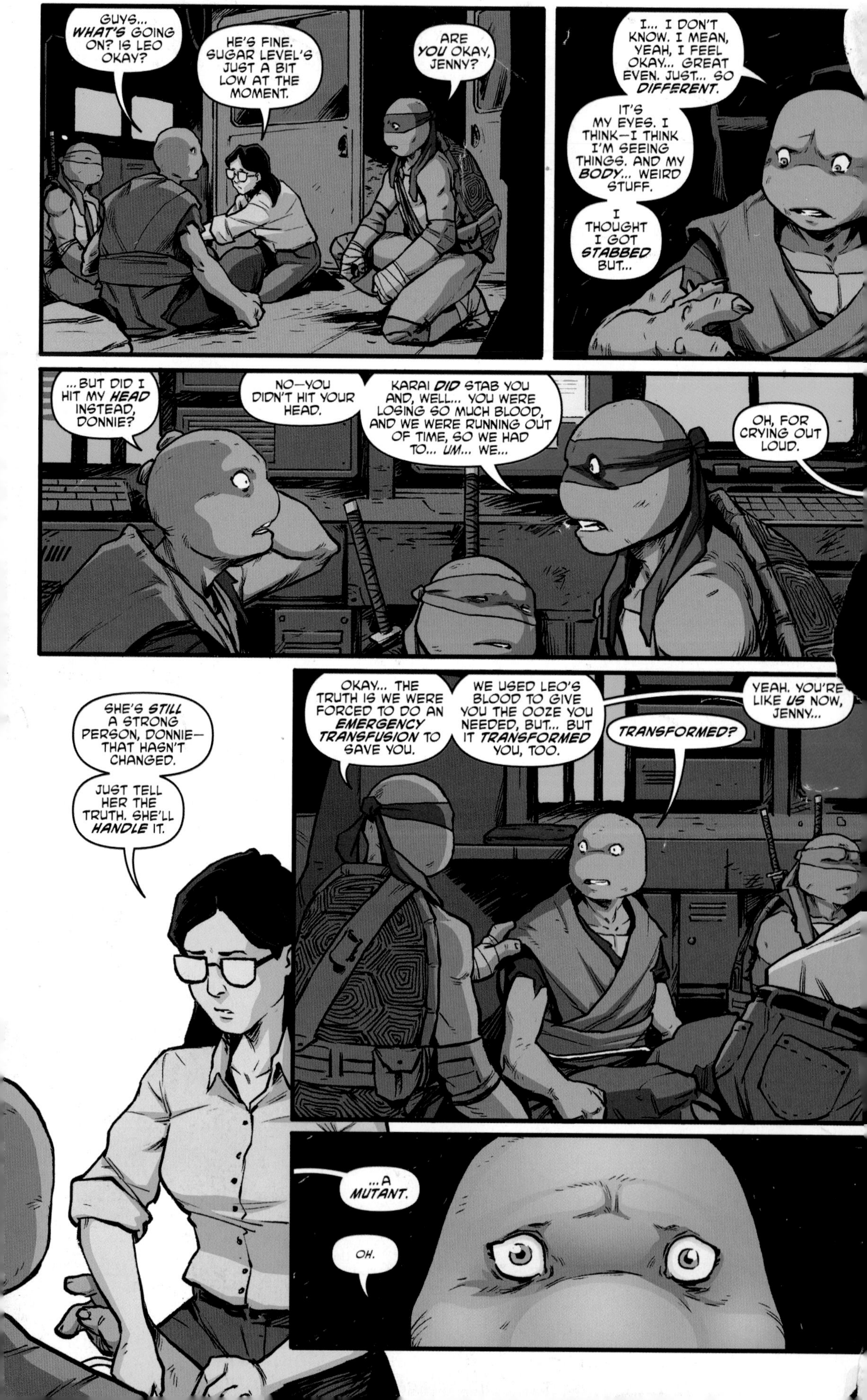

GUYS... WHAT'S GOING ON? IS LEO OKAY?
HE'S FINE. SUGAR LEVEL'S JUST A BIT LOW AT THE MOMENT.
ARE YOU OKAY, JENNY?
I... I DON'T KNOW. I MEAN, YEAH, I FEEL OKAY... GREAT EVEN. JUST... SO DIFFERENT.
IT'S MY EYES. I THINK—I THINK I'M SEEING THINGS. AND MY BODY... WEIRD STUFF.
I THOUGHT I GOT STABBED BUT...
...BUT DID I HIT MY HEAD INSTEAD, DONNIE?
NO—YOU DIDN'T HIT YOUR HEAD.
KARAI DID STAB YOU AND, WELL... YOU WERE LOSING SO MUCH BLOOD, AND WE WERE RUNNING OUT OF TIME, SO WE HAD TO... UM... WE...
OH, FOR CRYING OUT LOUD.
SHE'S STILL A STRONG PERSON, DONNIE— THAT HASN'T CHANGED.
JUST TELL HER THE TRUTH. SHE'LL HANDLE IT.
OKAY... THE TRUTH IS WE WERE FORCED TO DO AN EMERGENCY TRANSFUSION TO SAVE YOU.
WE USED LEO'S BLOOD TO GIVE YOU THE OOZE YOU NEEDED, BUT... BUT IT TRANSFORMED YOU, TOO.
TRANSFORMED?
YEAH. YOU'RE LIKE US NOW, JENNY...
...A MUTANT.
OH.

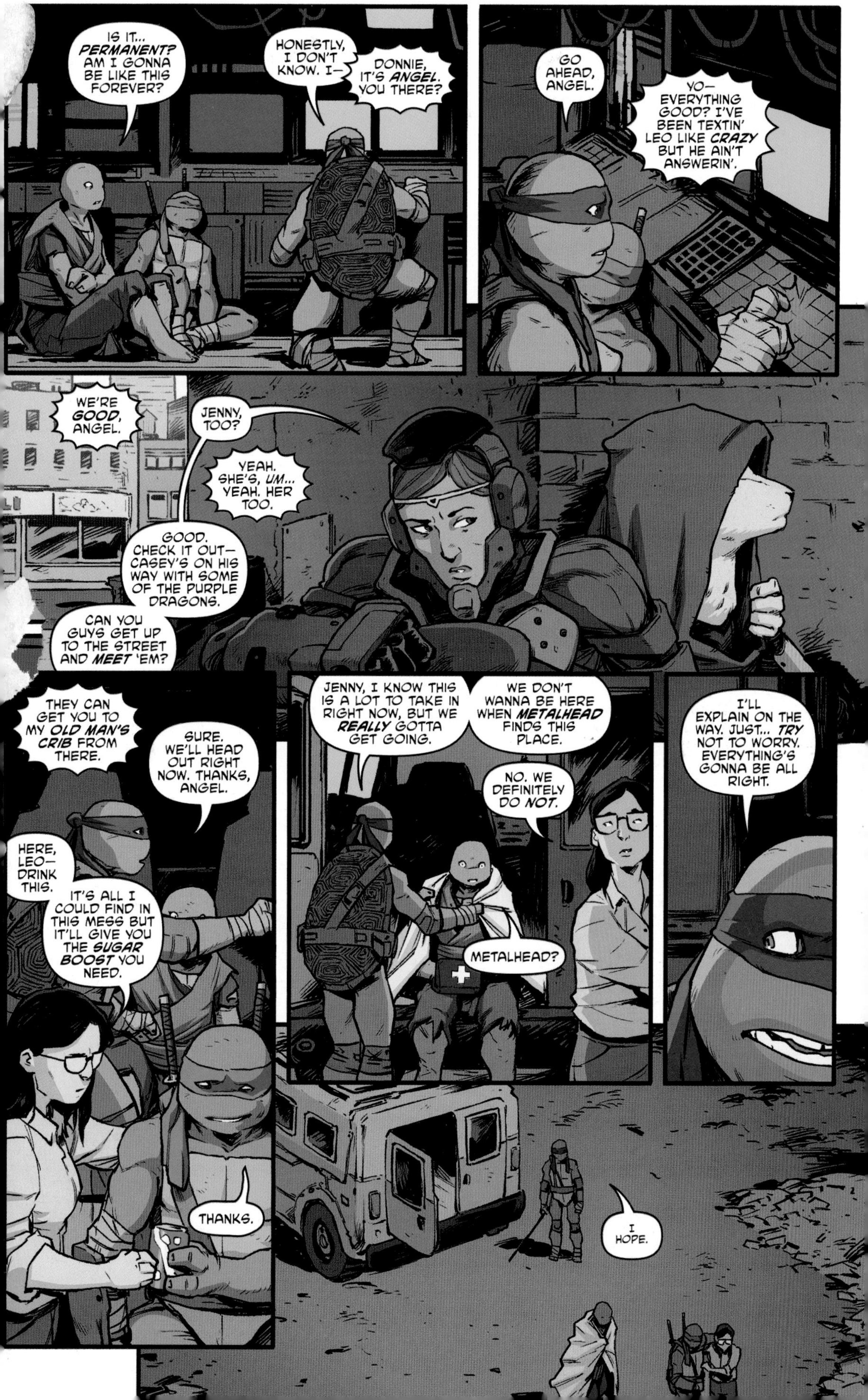
IS IT... PERMANENT? AM I GONNA BE LIKE THIS FOREVER?
HONESTLY, I DON'T KNOW. I—
DONNIE, IT'S ANGEL. YOU THERE?
GO AHEAD, ANGEL.
YO— EVERYTHING GOOD? I'VE BEEN TEXTIN' LEO LIKE CRAZY BUT HE AIN'T ANSWERIN'.
WE'RE GOOD, ANGEL.
JENNY, TOO?
YEAH. SHE'S, UM... YEAH. HER TOO.
GOOD. CHECK IT OUT— CASEY'S ON HIS WAY WITH SOME OF THE PURPLE DRAGONS.
CAN YOU GUYS GET UP TO THE STREET AND MEET 'EM?
THEY CAN GET YOU TO MY OLD MAN'S CRIB FROM THERE.
SURE. WE'LL HEAD OUT RIGHT NOW. THANKS, ANGEL.
HERE, LEO— DRINK THIS.
IT'S ALL I COULD FIND IN THIS MESS BUT IT'LL GIVE YOU THE SUGAR BOOST YOU NEED.
THANKS.
JENNY, I KNOW THIS IS A LOT TO TAKE IN RIGHT NOW, BUT WE REALLY GOTTA GET GOING.
WE DON'T WANNA BE HERE WHEN METALHEAD FINDS THIS PLACE.
NO. WE DEFINITELY DO NOT.
METALHEAD?
I'LL EXPLAIN ON THE WAY. JUST... TRY NOT TO WORRY. EVERYTHING'S GONNA BE ALL RIGHT.
I HOPE.

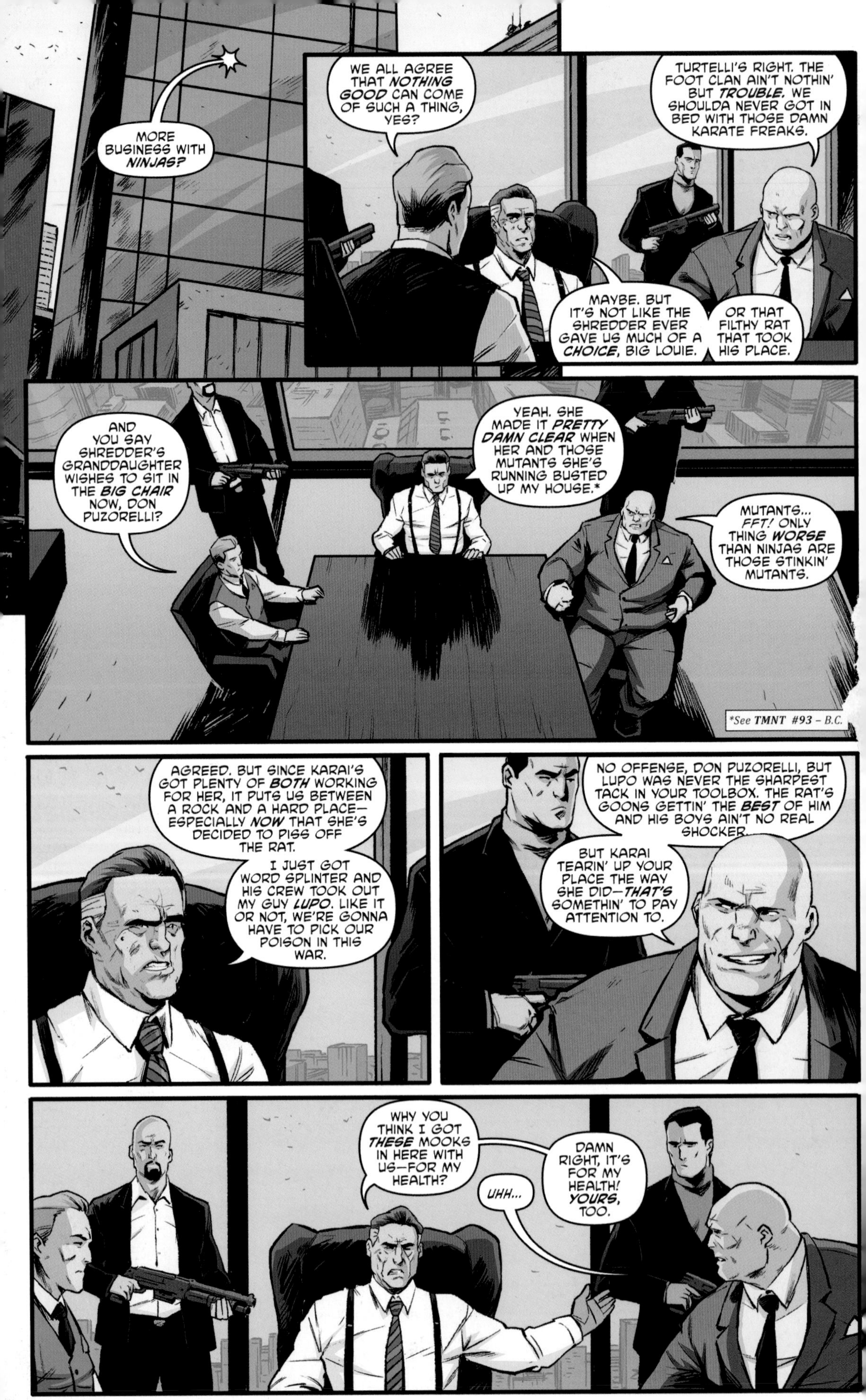
MORE BUSINESS WITH NINJAS?
WE ALL AGREE THAT NOTHING GOOD CAN COME OF SUCH A THING, YES?
TURTELLI'S RIGHT. THE FOOT CLAN AIN'T NOTHIN' BUT TROUBLE. WE SHOULDA NEVER GOT IN BED WITH THOSE DAMN KARATE FREAKS.
MAYBE. BUT IT'S NOT LIKE THE SHREDDER EVER GAVE US MUCH OF A CHOICE, BIG LOUIE.
OR THAT FILTHY RAT THAT TOOK HIS PLACE.
AND YOU SAY SHREDDER'S GRANDDAUGHTER WISHES TO SIT IN THE BIG CHAIR NOW, DON PUZORELLI?
YEAH. SHE MADE IT PRETTY DAMN CLEAR WHEN HER AND THOSE MUTANTS SHE'S RUNNING BUSTED UP MY HOUSE.*
MUTANTS... FFT! ONLY THING WORSE THAN NINJAS ARE THOSE STINKIN' MUTANTS.
*See TMNT #93 – B.C.
AGREED. BUT SINCE KARAI'S GOT PLENTY OF BOTH WORKING FOR HER, IT PUTS US BETWEEN A ROCK AND A HARD PLACE— ESPECIALLY NOW THAT SHE'S DECIDED TO PISS OFF THE RAT.
I JUST GOT WORD SPLINTER AND HIS CREW TOOK OUT MY GUY LUPO. LIKE IT OR NOT, WE'RE GONNA HAVE TO PICK OUR POISON IN THIS WAR.
NO OFFENSE, DON PUZORELLI, BUT LUPO WAS NEVER THE SHARPEST TACK IN YOUR TOOLBOX. THE RAT'S GOONS GETTIN' THE BEST OF HIM AND HIS BOYS AIN'T NO REAL SHOCKER.
BUT KARAI TEARIN' UP YOUR PLACE THE WAY SHE DID—THAT'S SOMETHIN' TO PAY ATTENTION TO.
WHY YOU THINK I GOT THESE MOOKS IN HERE WITH US—FOR MY HEALTH?
UHH...
DAMN RIGHT, IT'S FOR MY HEALTH! YOURS, TOO.

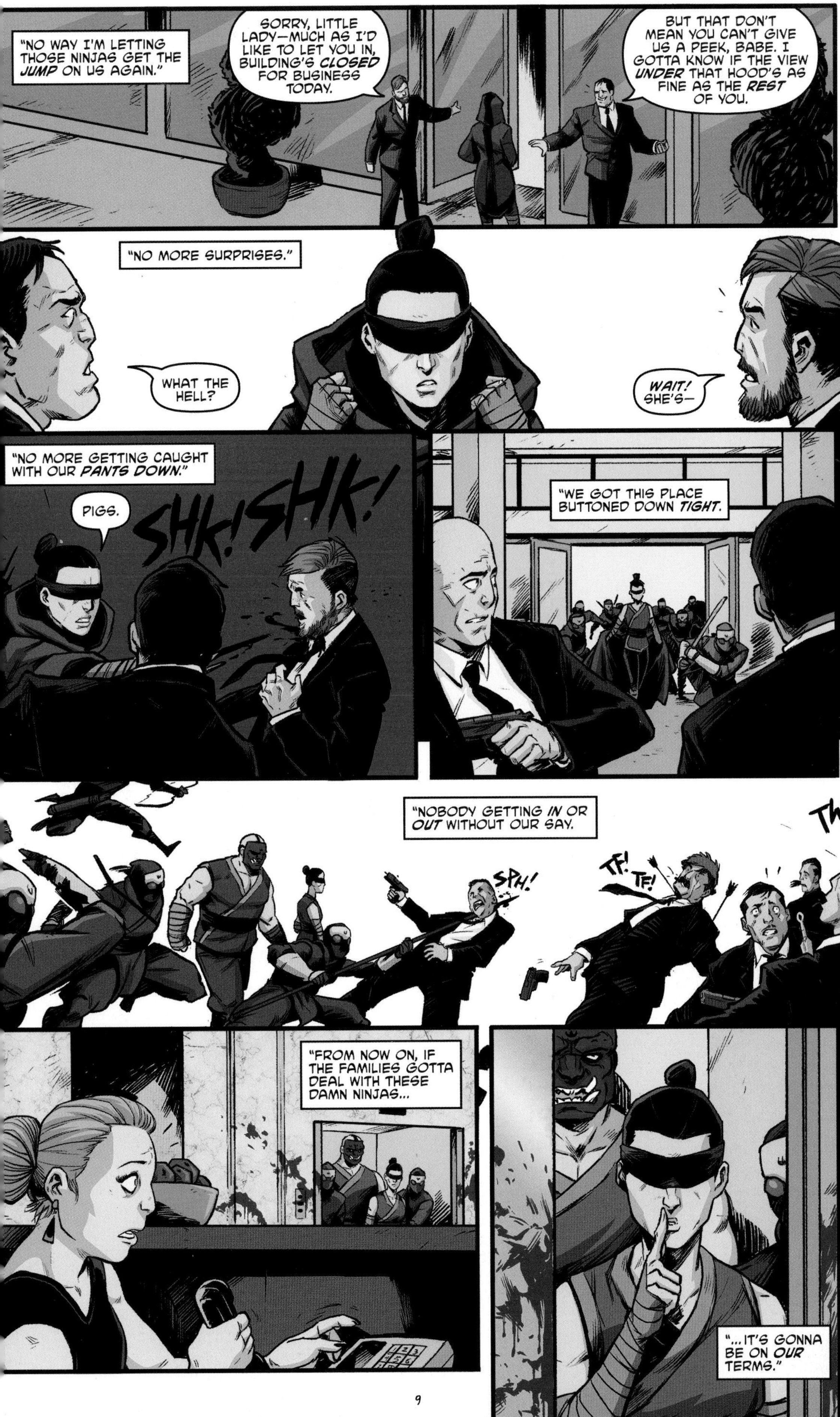
"NO WAY I'M LETTING THOSE NINJAS GET THE *JUMP* ON US AGAIN."
SORRY, LITTLE LADY—MUCH AS I'D LIKE TO LET YOU IN, BUILDING'S *CLOSED* FOR BUSINESS TODAY.
BUT THAT DON'T MEAN YOU CAN'T GIVE US A PEEK, BABE. I GOTTA KNOW IF THE VIEW *UNDER* THAT HOOD'S AS FINE AS THE *REST* OF YOU.
"NO MORE SURPRISES."
WHAT THE HELL?
WAIT! SHE'S—
"NO MORE GETTING CAUGHT WITH OUR *PANTS DOWN*."
PIGS.
SHK! SHK!
"WE GOT THIS PLACE BUTTONED DOWN *TIGHT*.
"NOBODY GETTING *IN* OR *OUT* WITHOUT OUR SAY.
SPH!
TF! TF!
TWK!
"FROM NOW ON, IF THE FAMILIES GOTTA DEAL WITH THESE DAMN NINJAS...
"...IT'S GONNA BE ON *OUR* TERMS."

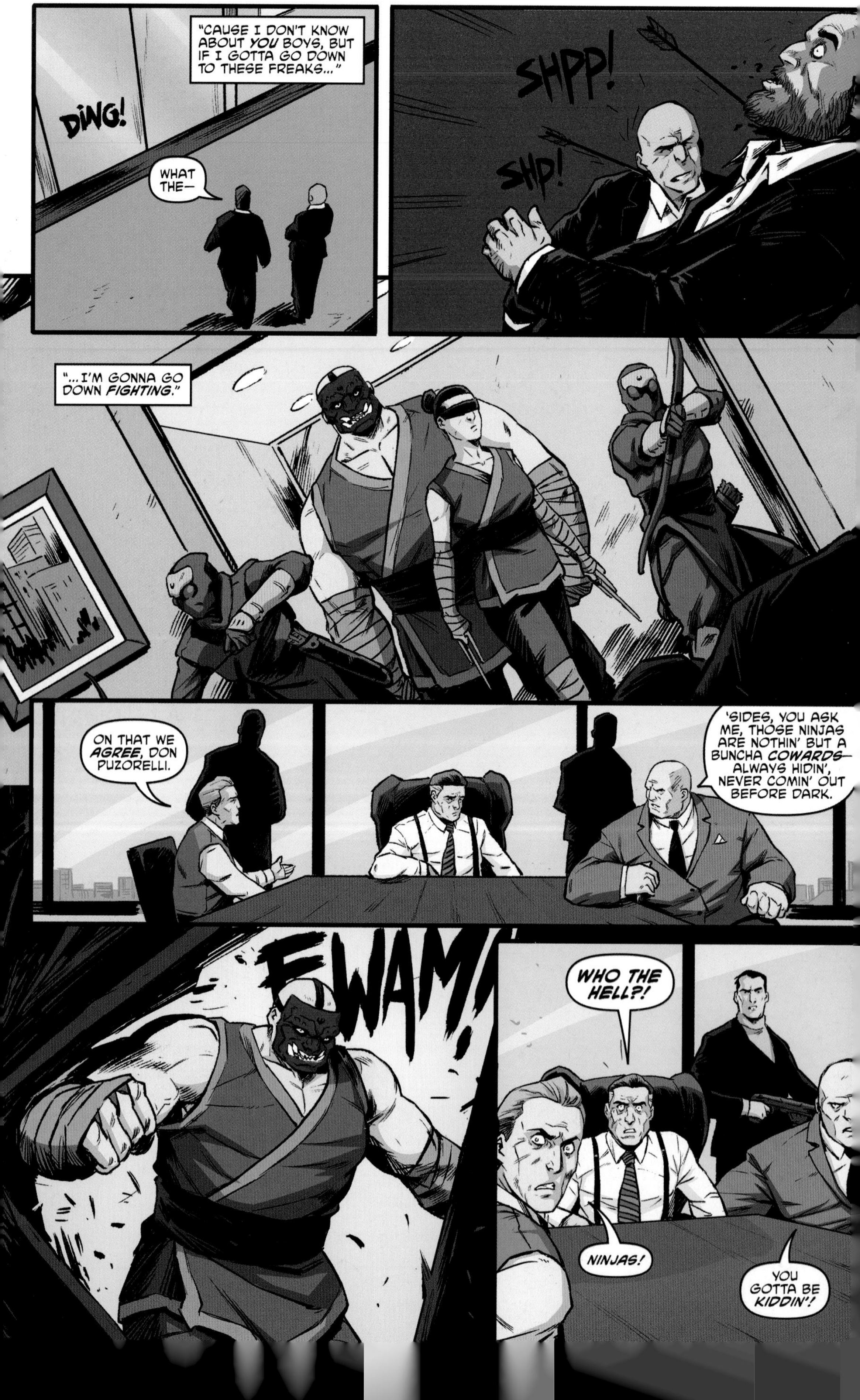
"CAUSE I DON'T KNOW ABOUT *YOU* BOYS, BUT IF I GOTTA GO DOWN TO THESE FREAKS..."
DING!
WHAT THE—
SHPP!
SHP!
"...I'M GONNA GO DOWN *FIGHTING*."
ON THAT WE *AGREE*, DON PUZORELLI.
'SIDES, YOU ASK ME, THOSE NINJAS ARE NOTHIN' BUT A BUNCHA *COWARDS*— ALWAYS HIDIN', NEVER COMIN' OUT BEFORE DARK.
FWAM!
WHO THE HELL?!
NINJAS!
YOU GOTTA BE *KIDDIN'*!

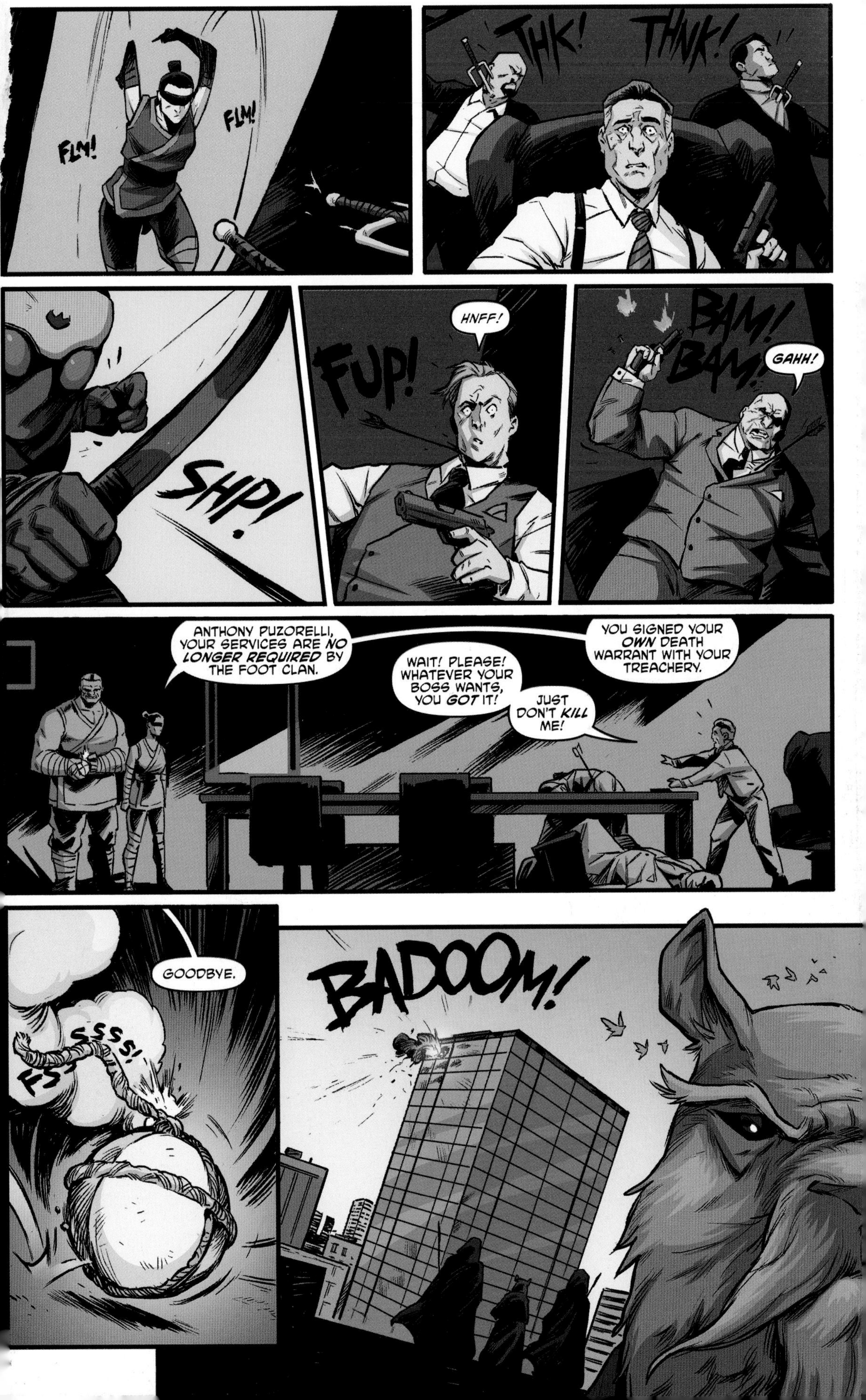
FLM!
FLM!
THK!
THNK!
SHP!
HNFF!
FUP!
BAM!
BAM!
GAHH!
ANTHONY PUZORELLI, YOUR SERVICES ARE *NO LONGER REQUIRED* BY THE FOOT CLAN.
WAIT! PLEASE! WHATEVER YOUR BOSS WANTS, YOU *GOT* IT!
JUST DON'T *KILL* ME!
YOU SIGNED YOUR *OWN* DEATH WARRANT WITH YOUR TREACHERY.
GOODBYE.
FSSSSS!
BADOOOM!

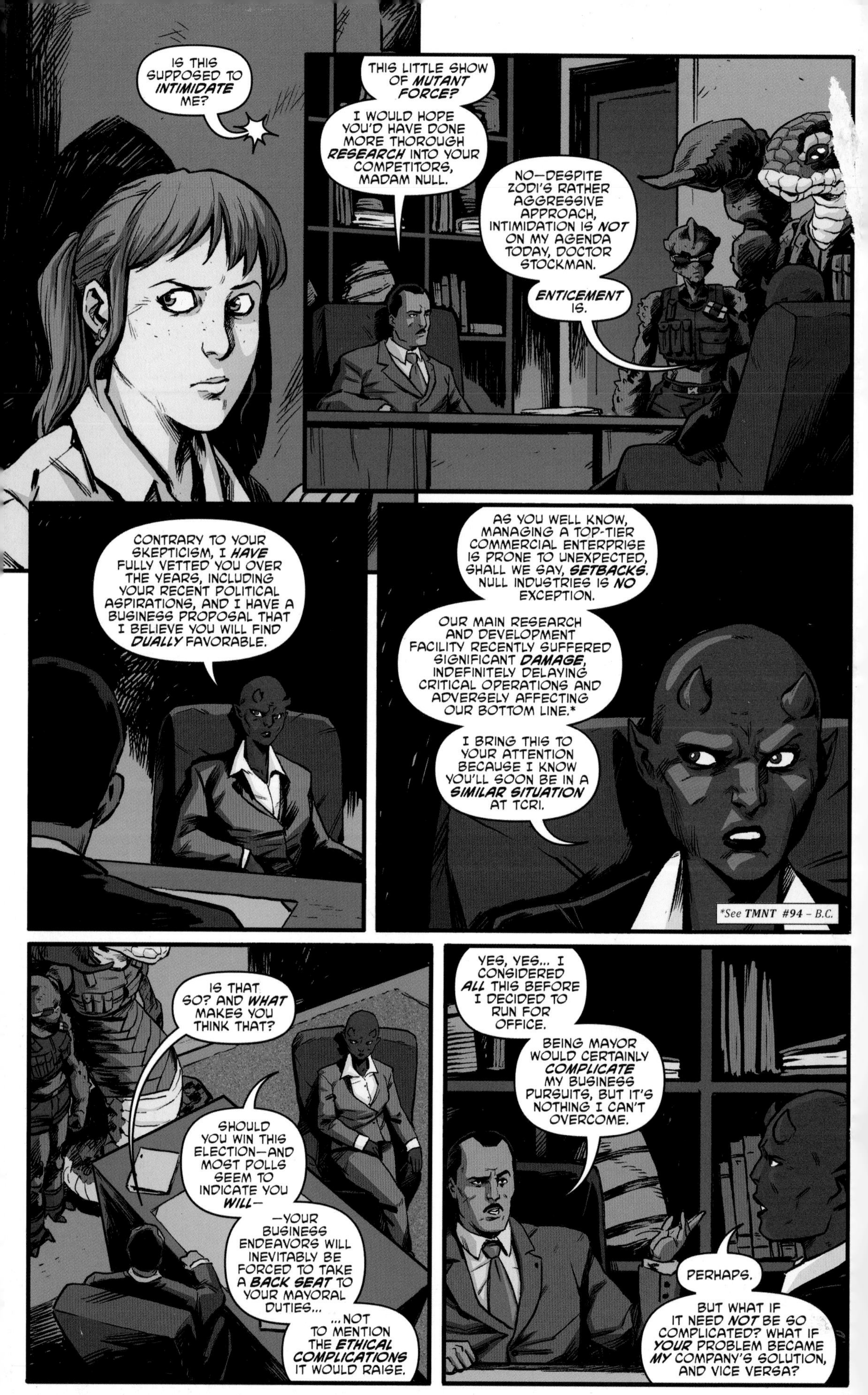
IS THIS SUPPOSED TO INTIMIDATE ME?
THIS LITTLE SHOW OF MUTANT FORCE?
I WOULD HOPE YOU'D HAVE DONE MORE THOROUGH RESEARCH INTO YOUR COMPETITORS, MADAM NULL.
NO—DESPITE ZODI'S RATHER AGGRESSIVE APPROACH, INTIMIDATION IS NOT ON MY AGENDA TODAY, DOCTOR STOCKMAN.
ENTICEMENT IS.
CONTRARY TO YOUR SKEPTICISM, I HAVE FULLY VETTED YOU OVER THE YEARS, INCLUDING YOUR RECENT POLITICAL ASPIRATIONS, AND I HAVE A BUSINESS PROPOSAL THAT I BELIEVE YOU WILL FIND DUALLY FAVORABLE.
AS YOU WELL KNOW, MANAGING A TOP-TIER COMMERCIAL ENTERPRISE IS PRONE TO UNEXPECTED, SHALL WE SAY, SETBACKS. NULL INDUSTRIES IS NO EXCEPTION.
OUR MAIN RESEARCH AND DEVELOPMENT FACILITY RECENTLY SUFFERED SIGNIFICANT DAMAGE, INDEFINITELY DELAYING CRITICAL OPERATIONS AND ADVERSELY AFFECTING OUR BOTTOM LINE.*
I BRING THIS TO YOUR ATTENTION BECAUSE I KNOW YOU'LL SOON BE IN A SIMILAR SITUATION AT TCRI.
*See TMNT #94 – B.C.
IS THAT SO? AND WHAT MAKES YOU THINK THAT?
SHOULD YOU WIN THIS ELECTION—AND MOST POLLS SEEM TO INDICATE YOU WILL—
—YOUR BUSINESS ENDEAVORS WILL INEVITABLY BE FORCED TO TAKE A BACK SEAT TO YOUR MAYORAL DUTIES...
...NOT TO MENTION THE ETHICAL COMPLICATIONS IT WOULD RAISE.
YES, YES... I CONSIDERED ALL THIS BEFORE I DECIDED TO RUN FOR OFFICE.
BEING MAYOR WOULD CERTAINLY COMPLICATE MY BUSINESS PURSUITS, BUT IT'S NOTHING I CAN'T OVERCOME.
PERHAPS.
BUT WHAT IF IT NEED NOT BE SO COMPLICATED? WHAT IF YOUR PROBLEM BECAME MY COMPANY'S SOLUTION, AND VICE VERSA?

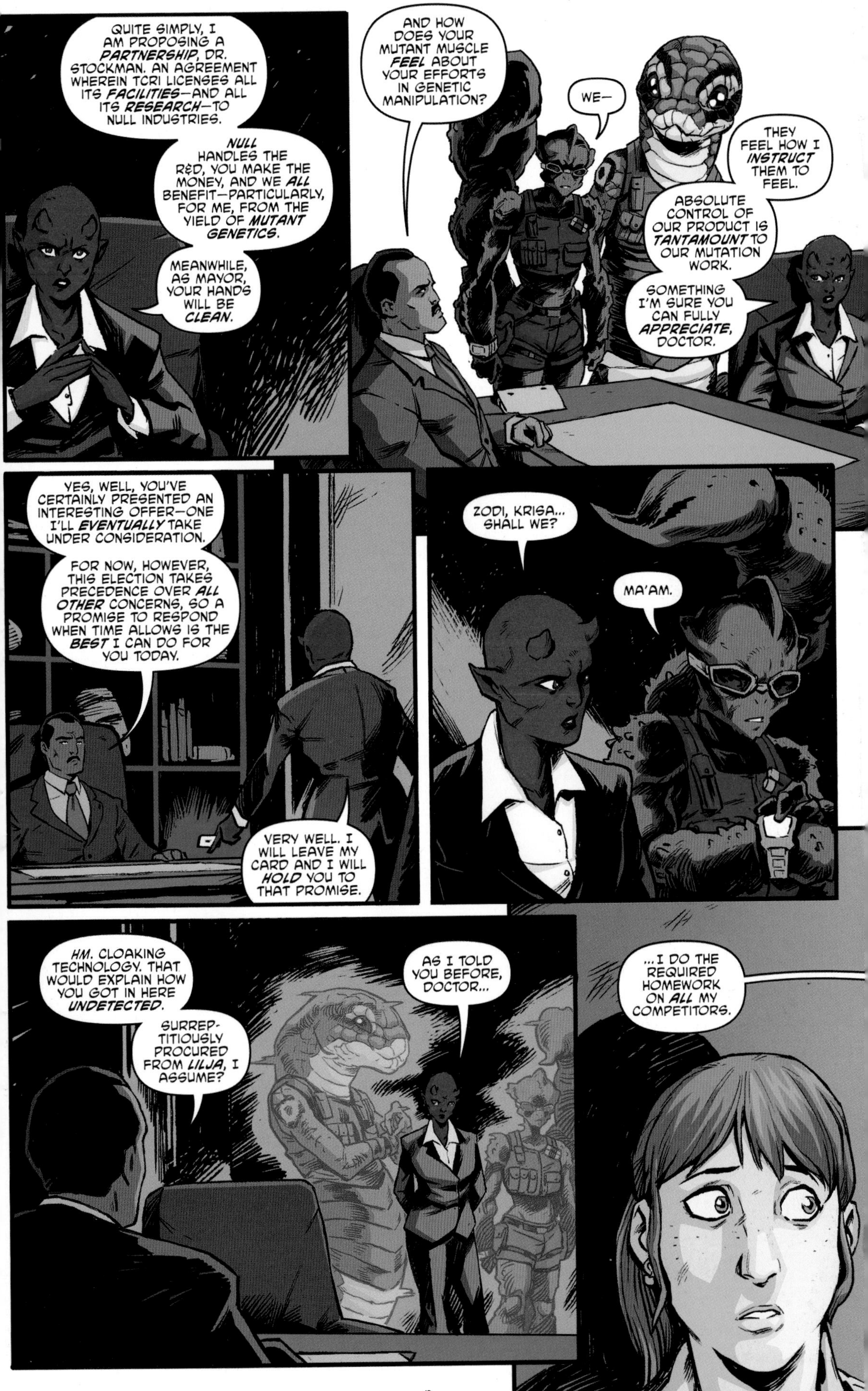
QUITE SIMPLY, I AM PROPOSING A PARTNERSHIP, DR. STOCKMAN. AN AGREEMENT WHEREIN TCRI LICENSES ALL ITS FACILITIES—AND ALL ITS RESEARCH—TO NULL INDUSTRIES.
NULL HANDLES THE R&D, YOU MAKE THE MONEY, AND WE ALL BENEFIT—PARTICULARLY, FOR ME, FROM THE YIELD OF MUTANT GENETICS.
MEANWHILE, AS MAYOR, YOUR HANDS WILL BE CLEAN.
AND HOW DOES YOUR MUTANT MUSCLE FEEL ABOUT YOUR EFFORTS IN GENETIC MANIPULATION?
WE—
THEY FEEL HOW I INSTRUCT THEM TO FEEL.
ABSOLUTE CONTROL OF OUR PRODUCT IS TANTAMOUNT TO OUR MUTATION WORK.
SOMETHING I'M SURE YOU CAN FULLY APPRECIATE, DOCTOR.
YES, WELL, YOU'VE CERTAINLY PRESENTED AN INTERESTING OFFER—ONE I'LL EVENTUALLY TAKE UNDER CONSIDERATION.
FOR NOW, HOWEVER, THIS ELECTION TAKES PRECEDENCE OVER ALL OTHER CONCERNS, SO A PROMISE TO RESPOND WHEN TIME ALLOWS IS THE BEST I CAN DO FOR YOU TODAY.
VERY WELL. I WILL LEAVE MY CARD AND I WILL HOLD YOU TO THAT PROMISE.
ZODI, KRISA... SHALL WE?
MA'AM.
HM. CLOAKING TECHNOLOGY. THAT WOULD EXPLAIN HOW YOU GOT IN HERE UNDETECTED.
SURREP-TITIOUSLY PROCURED FROM LILJA, I ASSUME?
AS I TOLD YOU BEFORE, DOCTOR...
...I DO THE REQUIRED HOMEWORK ON ALL MY COMPETITORS.

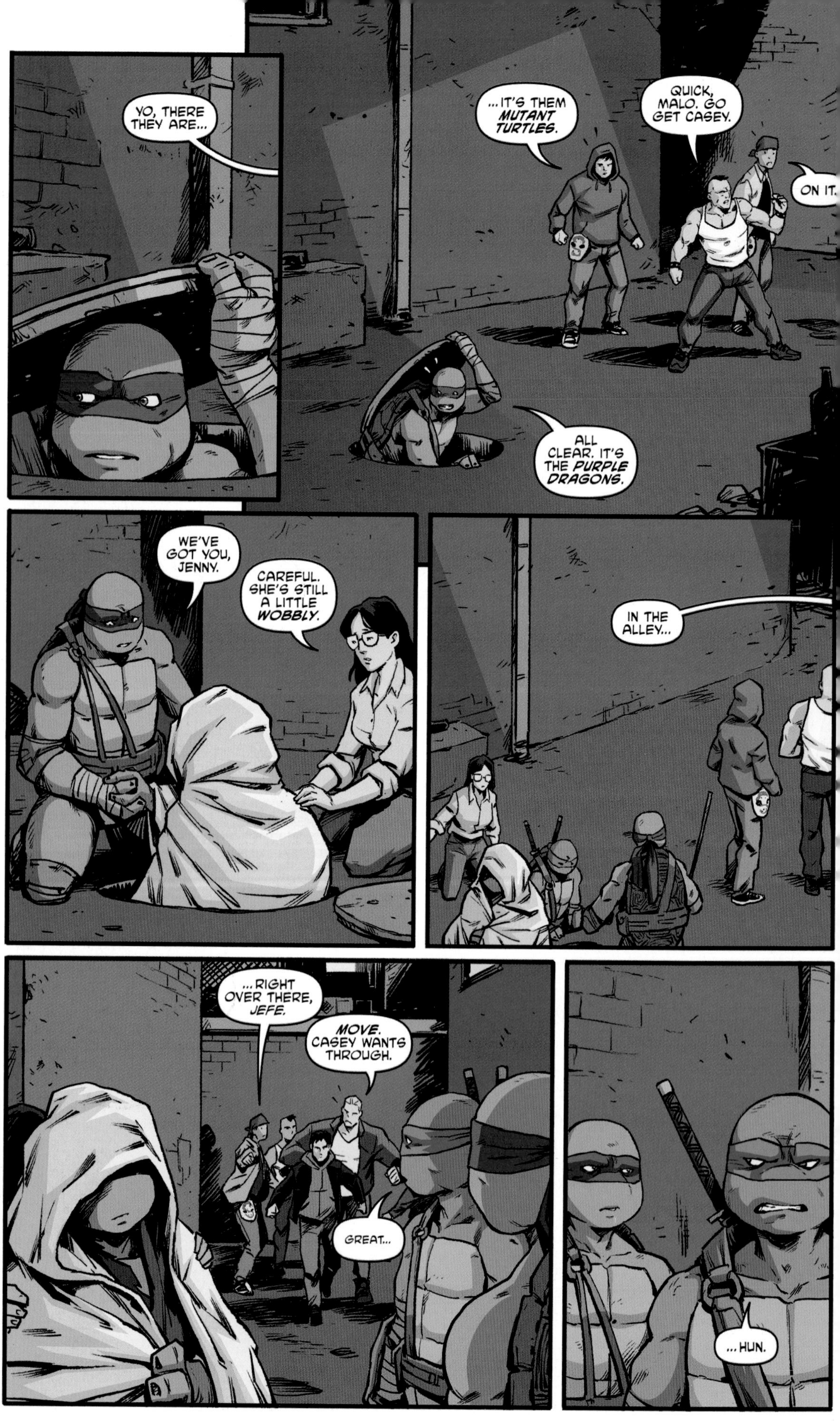
YO, THERE THEY ARE...
...IT'S THEM *MUTANT TURTLES*.
QUICK, MALO. GO GET CASEY.
ON IT.
ALL CLEAR. IT'S THE *PURPLE DRAGONS*.
WE'VE GOT YOU, JENNY.
CAREFUL. SHE'S STILL A LITTLE *WOBBLY*.
IN THE ALLEY...
...RIGHT OVER THERE, *JEFE*.
MOVE. CASEY WANTS THROUGH.
GREAT...
...HUN.

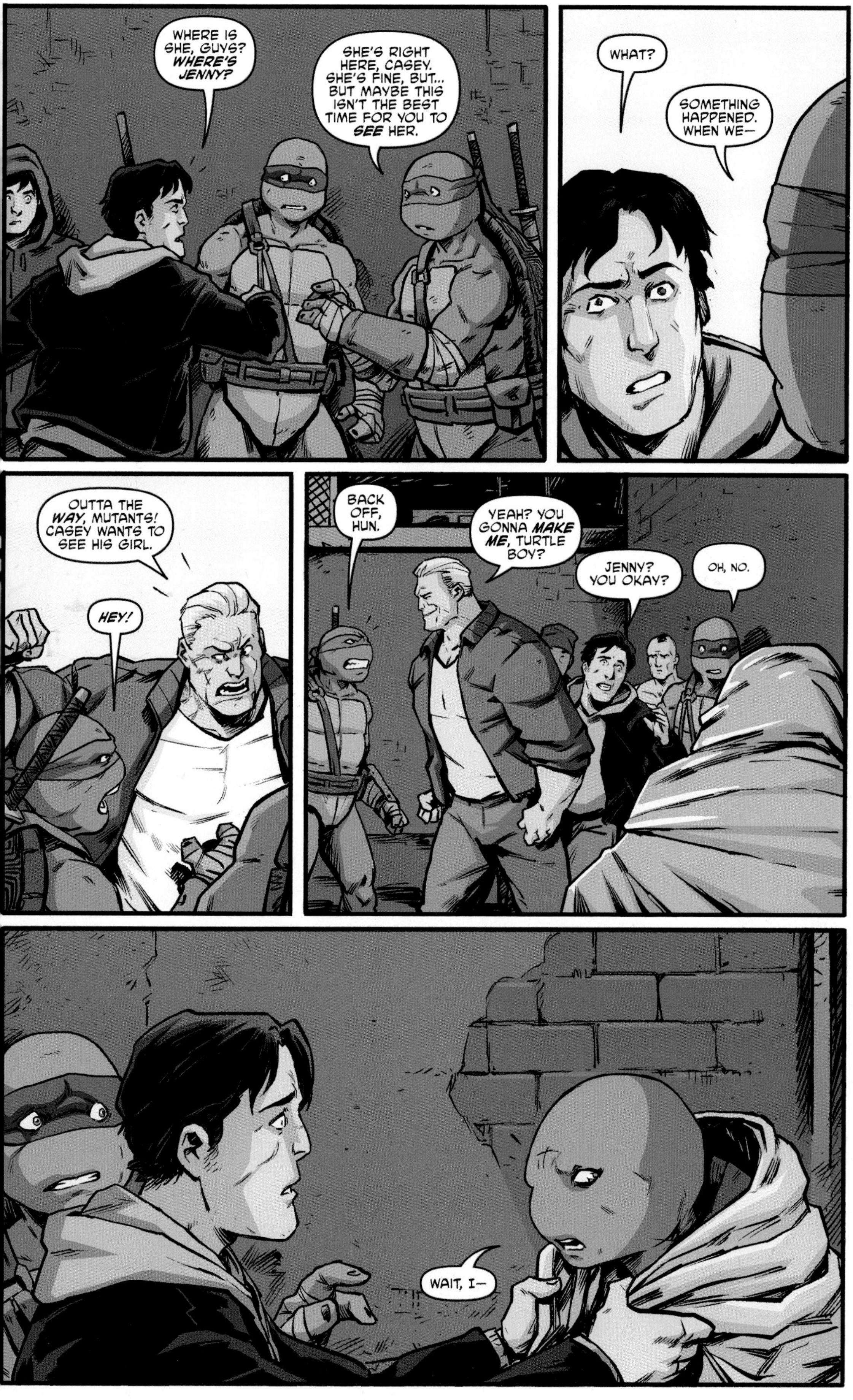
WHERE IS SHE, GUYS? WHERE'S JENNY?
SHE'S RIGHT HERE, CASEY. SHE'S FINE, BUT... BUT MAYBE THIS ISN'T THE BEST TIME FOR YOU TO SEE HER.
WHAT?
SOMETHING HAPPENED. WHEN WE—
OUTTA THE WAY, MUTANTS! CASEY WANTS TO SEE HIS GIRL.
HEY!
BACK OFF, HUN.
YEAH? YOU GONNA MAKE ME, TURTLE BOY?
JENNY? YOU OKAY?
OH, NO.
WAIT, I—

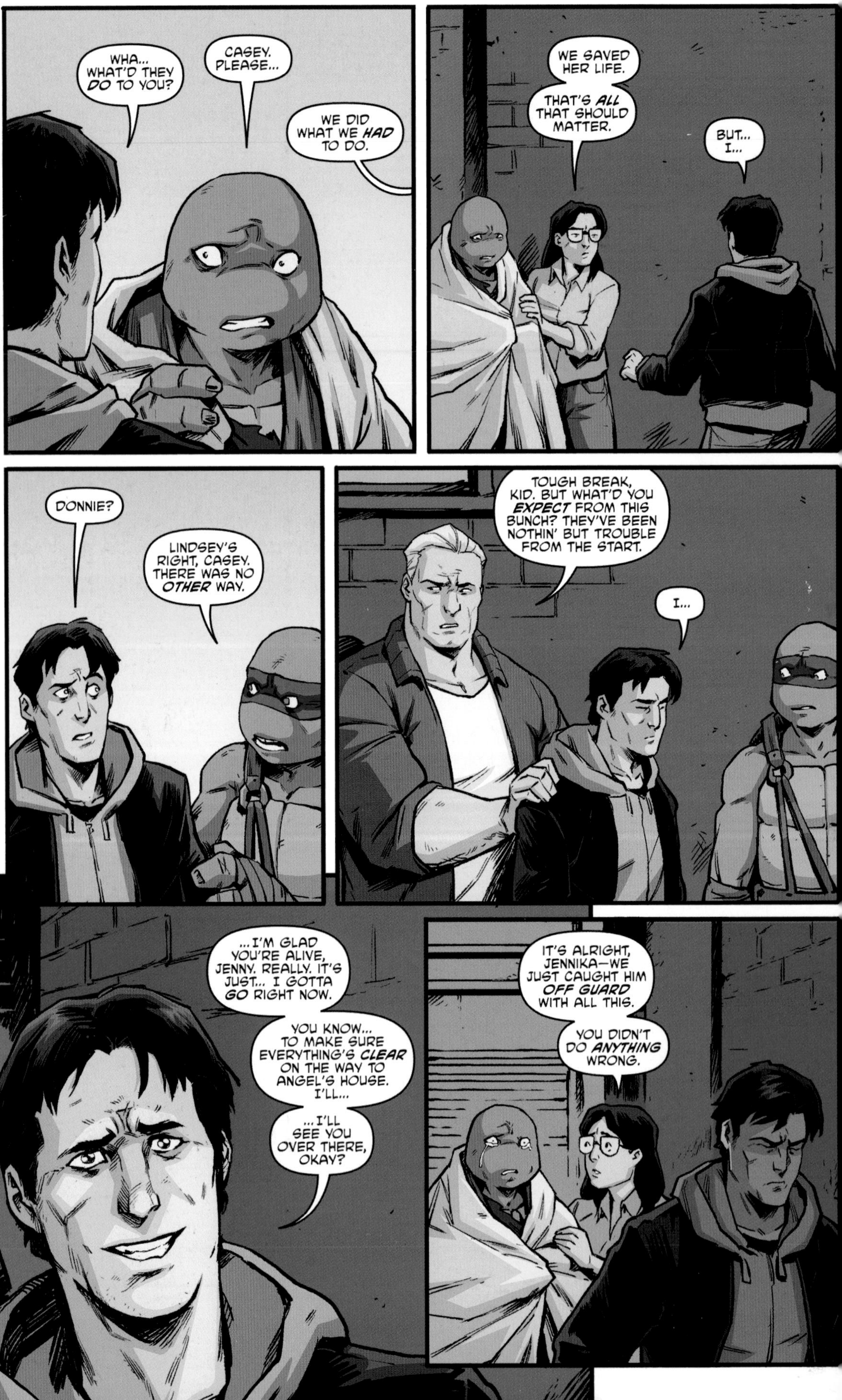
WHA... WHAT'D THEY DO TO YOU?
CASEY. PLEASE...
WE DID WHAT WE HAD TO DO.
WE SAVED HER LIFE.
THAT'S ALL THAT SHOULD MATTER.
BUT... I...
DONNIE?
LINDSEY'S RIGHT, CASEY. THERE WAS NO OTHER WAY.
TOUGH BREAK, KID. BUT WHAT'D YOU EXPECT FROM THIS BUNCH? THEY'VE BEEN NOTHIN' BUT TROUBLE FROM THE START.
I...
...I'M GLAD YOU'RE ALIVE, JENNY. REALLY. IT'S JUST... I GOTTA GO RIGHT NOW.
YOU KNOW... TO MAKE SURE EVERYTHING'S CLEAR ON THE WAY TO ANGEL'S HOUSE. I'LL...
...I'LL SEE YOU OVER THERE, OKAY?
IT'S ALRIGHT, JENNIKA—WE JUST CAUGHT HIM OFF GUARD WITH ALL THIS.
YOU DIDN'T DO ANYTHING WRONG.

THE HELL SHE *DIDN'T!* IT'S HER AND THE *REST* OF THE FREAKS LIKE HER! MAKIN' MY FAMILY MISERABLE AT *EVERY STINKIN'* TURN.

YEAH, YOU *SHOULD* BE CRYIN', GIRLIE.

I SAID *BACK OFF,* HUN.

OR WHAT? YOU GONNA TURN ME INTO A *SLIMY LIZARD* IF I DON'T?

NO. NO LIZARDS.

SHK!

YEAH, YEAH... WHATEVER. YOU AIN'T EVEN *WORTH* MY TIME.

LINK, GET THAT... *THING* OVER TO BROOKLYN'S PLACE. I'M GONNA GO HELP MY BOY.

YEAH... SURE, HUN.

UM... YOU READY?

COME ON. LET'S GET YOU OFF THE STREET.

GOOD IDEA, LINDSEY. I WISH WE COULD COME, BUT WE HAVE TO GET TO *FOOT HEADQUARTERS.* FATHER WILL WANNA KNOW YOU'RE OKAY.

AND WITH HAROLD AND LIBBY IN TROUBLE, WE'VE GOT *A LOT* TO DO. BUT ANGEL AND ALOPEX WILL TAKE *GOOD CARE* OF YOU, JENNY, NO WORRIES.

OKAY, DONNIE.

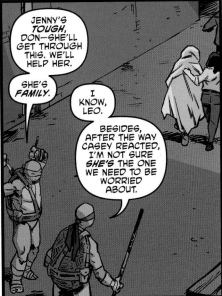

JENNY'S *TOUGH,* DON—SHE'LL GET THROUGH THIS. WE'LL HELP HER.

SHE'S *FAMILY.*

I KNOW, LEO.

BESIDES, AFTER THE WAY CASEY REACTED, I'M NOT SURE *SHE'S* THE ONE WE NEED TO BE WORRIED ABOUT.

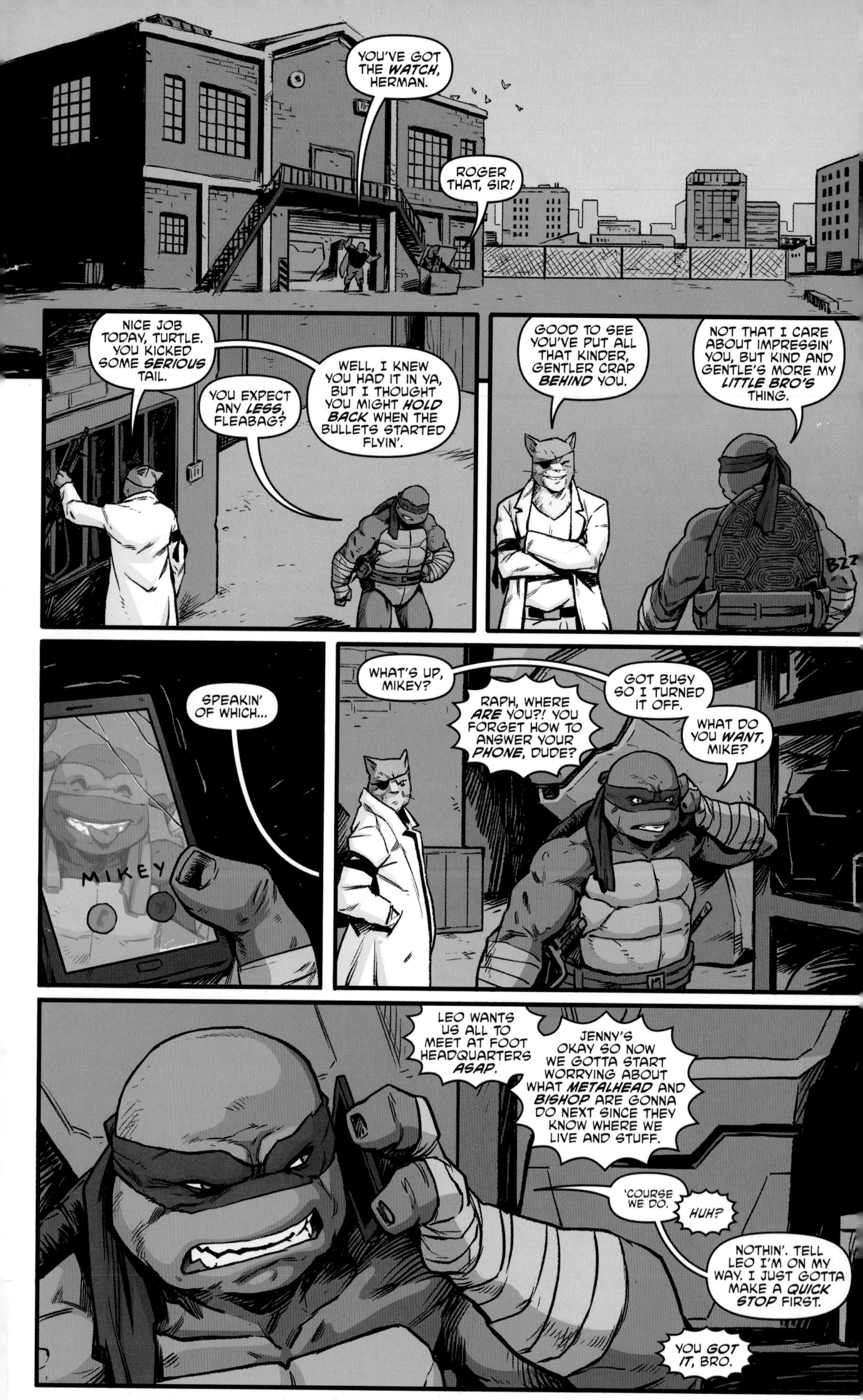
YOU'VE GOT THE WATCH, HERMAN.
ROGER THAT, SIR!
NICE JOB TODAY, TURTLE. YOU KICKED SOME SERIOUS TAIL.
YOU EXPECT ANY LESS, FLEABAG?
WELL, I KNEW YOU HAD IT IN YA, BUT I THOUGHT YOU MIGHT HOLD BACK WHEN THE BULLETS STARTED FLYIN'.
GOOD TO SEE YOU'VE PUT ALL THAT KINDER, GENTLER CRAP BEHIND YOU.
NOT THAT I CARE ABOUT IMPRESSIN' YOU, BUT KIND AND GENTLE'S MORE MY LITTLE BRO'S THING.
BZZ
SPEAKIN' OF WHICH...
MIKEY
WHAT'S UP, MIKEY?
RAPH, WHERE ARE YOU?! YOU FORGET HOW TO ANSWER YOUR PHONE, DUDE?
GOT BUSY SO I TURNED IT OFF.
WHAT DO YOU WANT, MIKE?
LEO WANTS US ALL TO MEET AT FOOT HEADQUARTERS ASAP.
JENNY'S OKAY SO NOW WE GOTTA START WORRYING ABOUT WHAT METALHEAD AND BISHOP ARE GONNA DO NEXT SINCE THEY KNOW WHERE WE LIVE AND STUFF.
'COURSE WE DO.
HUH?
NOTHIN'. TELL LEO I'M ON MY WAY. I JUST GOTTA MAKE A QUICK STOP FIRST.
YOU GOT IT, BRO.

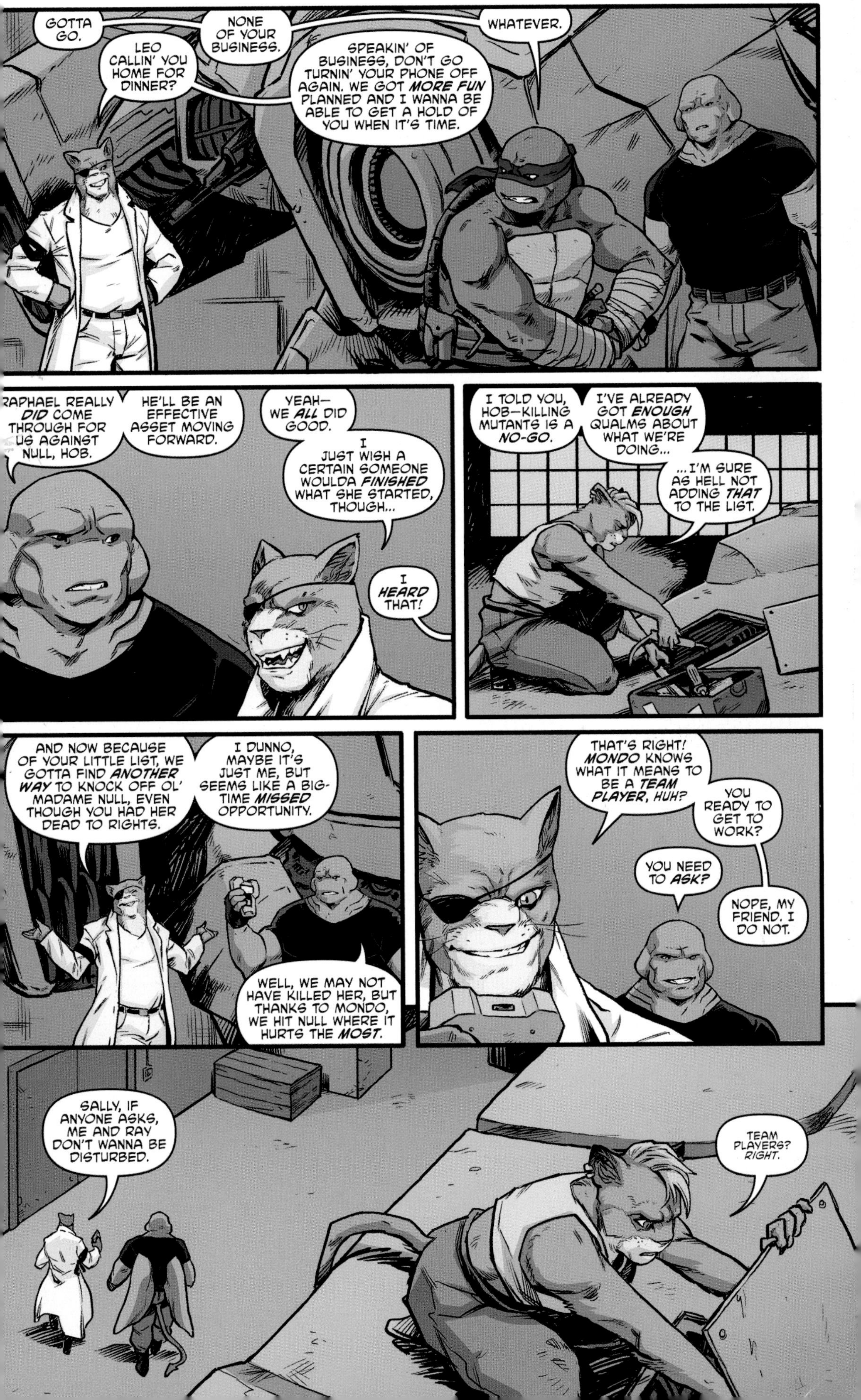
GOTTA GO.
LEO CALLIN' YOU HOME FOR DINNER?
NONE OF YOUR BUSINESS.
SPEAKIN' OF BUSINESS, DON'T GO TURNIN' YOUR PHONE OFF AGAIN. WE GOT MORE FUN PLANNED AND I WANNA BE ABLE TO GET A HOLD OF YOU WHEN IT'S TIME.
WHATEVER.
RAPHAEL REALLY DID COME THROUGH FOR US AGAINST NULL, HOB.
HE'LL BE AN EFFECTIVE ASSET MOVING FORWARD.
YEAH— WE ALL DID GOOD.
I JUST WISH A CERTAIN SOMEONE WOULDA FINISHED WHAT SHE STARTED, THOUGH...
I HEARD THAT!
I TOLD YOU, HOB—KILLING MUTANTS IS A NO-GO.
I'VE ALREADY GOT ENOUGH QUALMS ABOUT WHAT WE'RE DOING...
...I'M SURE AS HELL NOT ADDING THAT TO THE LIST.
AND NOW BECAUSE OF YOUR LITTLE LIST, WE GOTTA FIND ANOTHER WAY TO KNOCK OFF OL' MADAME NULL, EVEN THOUGH YOU HAD HER DEAD TO RIGHTS.
I DUNNO, MAYBE IT'S JUST ME, BUT SEEMS LIKE A BIG-TIME MISSED OPPORTUNITY.
WELL, WE MAY NOT HAVE KILLED HER, BUT THANKS TO MONDO, WE HIT NULL WHERE IT HURTS THE MOST.
THAT'S RIGHT! MONDO KNOWS WHAT IT MEANS TO BE A TEAM PLAYER, HUH?
YOU READY TO GET TO WORK?
YOU NEED TO ASK?
NOPE, MY FRIEND. I DO NOT.
SALLY, IF ANYONE ASKS, ME AND RAY DON'T WANNA BE DISTURBED.
TEAM PLAYERS? RIGHT.

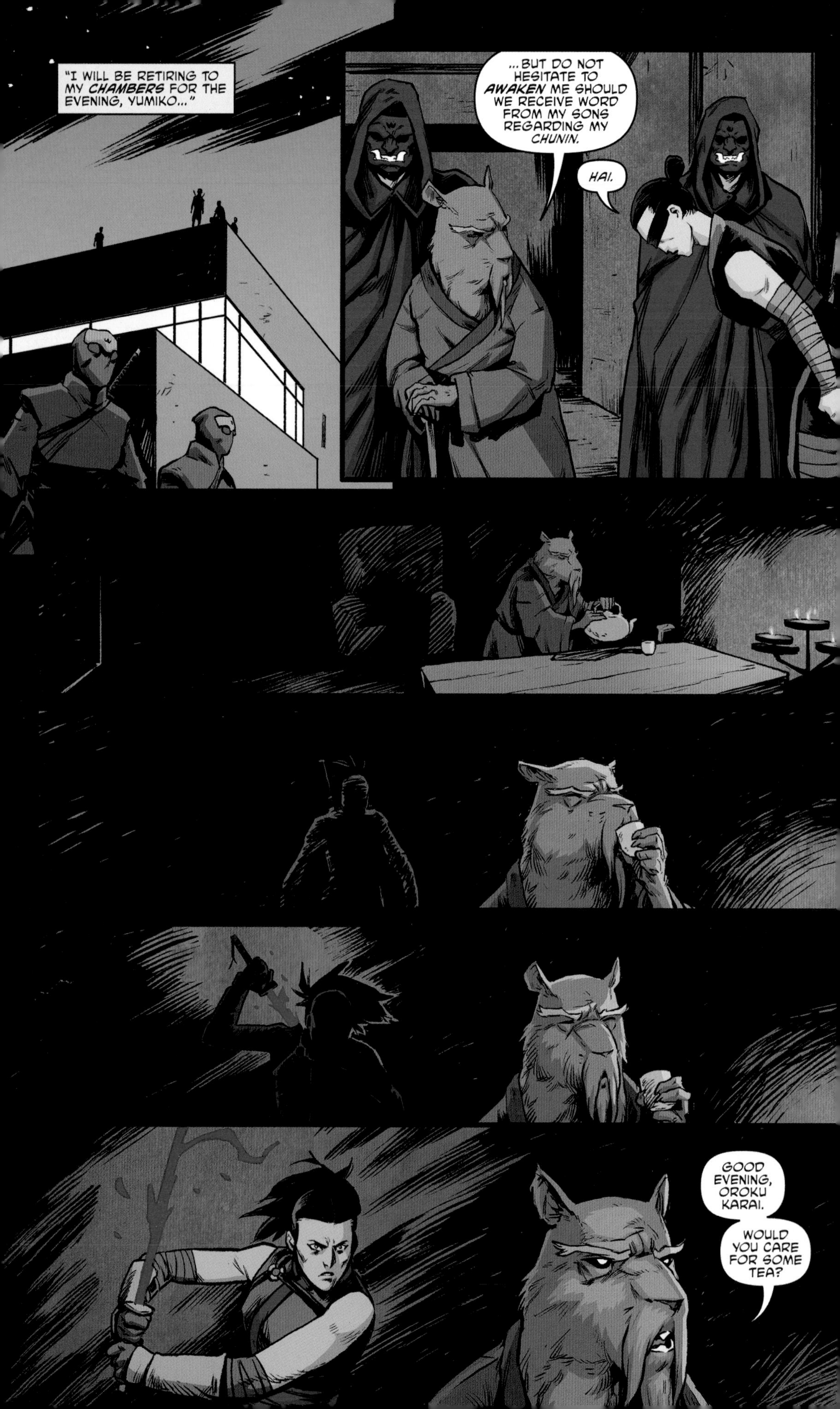
"I WILL BE RETIRING TO MY *CHAMBERS* FOR THE EVENING, YUMIKO..."
...BUT DO NOT HESITATE TO *AWAKEN* ME SHOULD WE RECEIVE WORD FROM MY SONS REGARDING MY *CHUNIN.*
HAI.
GOOD EVENING, OROKU KARAI.
WOULD YOU CARE FOR SOME TEA?

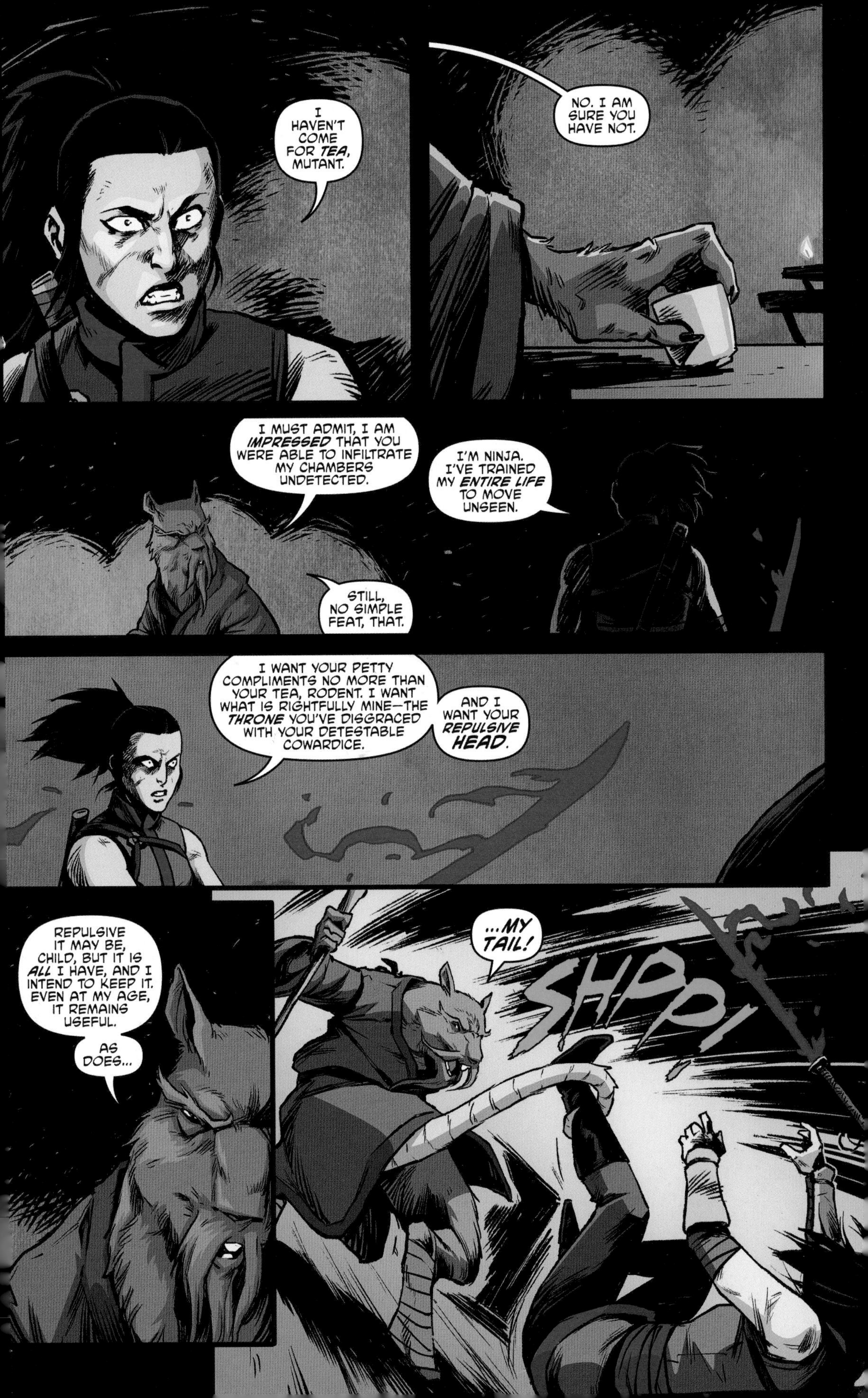

I HAVEN'T COME FOR TEA, MUTANT.
NO. I AM SURE YOU HAVE NOT.
I MUST ADMIT, I AM IMPRESSED THAT YOU WERE ABLE TO INFILTRATE MY CHAMBERS UNDETECTED.
I'M NINJA. I'VE TRAINED MY ENTIRE LIFE TO MOVE UNSEEN.
STILL, NO SIMPLE FEAT, THAT.
I WANT YOUR PETTY COMPLIMENTS NO MORE THAN YOUR TEA, RODENT. I WANT WHAT IS RIGHTFULLY MINE—THE THRONE YOU'VE DISGRACED WITH YOUR DETESTABLE COWARDICE.
AND I WANT YOUR REPULSIVE HEAD.
REPULSIVE IT MAY BE, CHILD, BUT IT IS ALL I HAVE, AND I INTEND TO KEEP IT. EVEN AT MY AGE, IT REMAINS USEFUL.
AS DOES...
...MY TAIL!
SHPP!

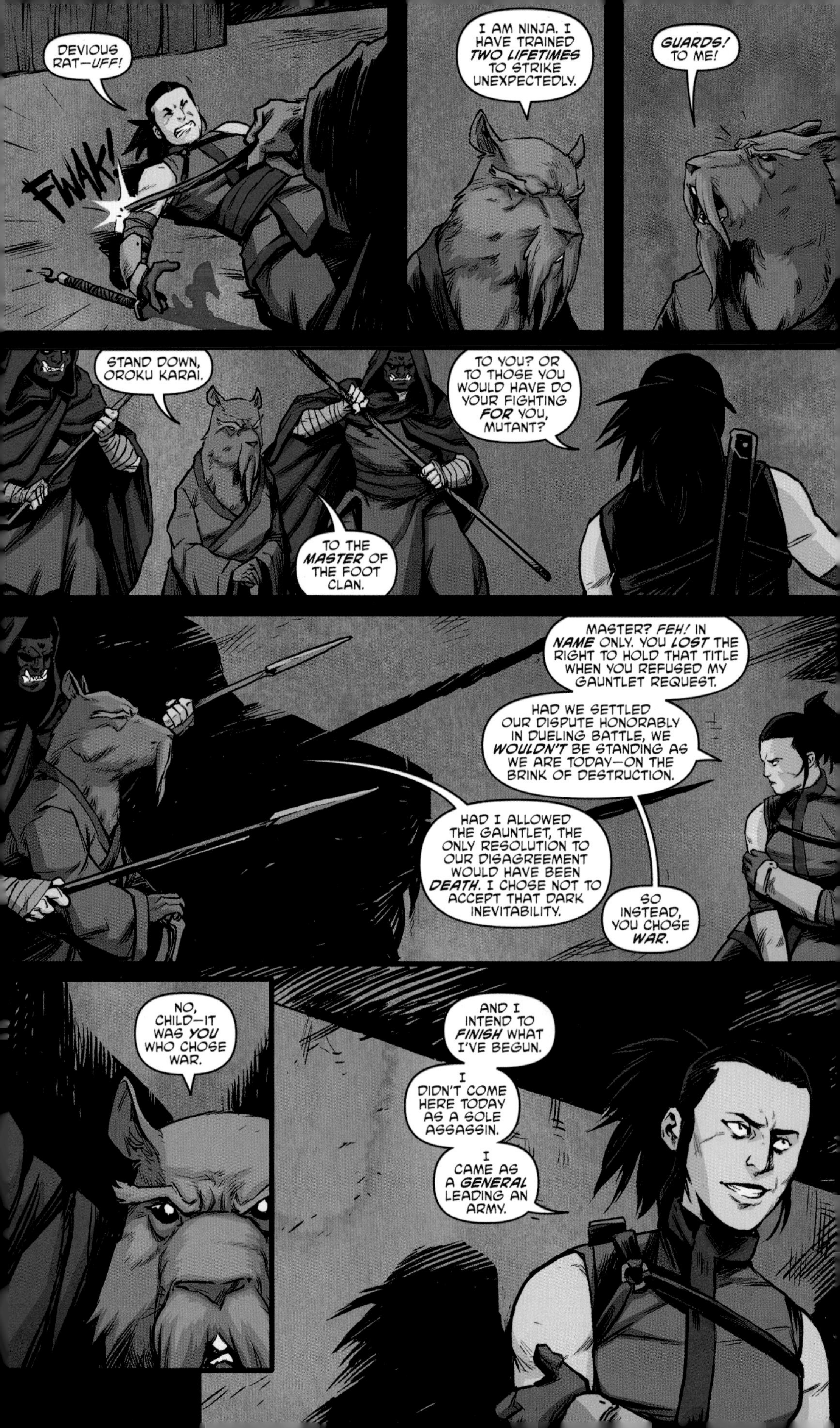
DEVIOUS RAT—UFF!
FWAK!
I AM NINJA. I HAVE TRAINED TWO LIFETIMES TO STRIKE UNEXPECTEDLY.
GUARDS! TO ME!
STAND DOWN, OROKU KARAI.
TO YOU? OR TO THOSE YOU WOULD HAVE DO YOUR FIGHTING FOR YOU, MUTANT?
TO THE MASTER OF THE FOOT CLAN.
MASTER? FEH! IN NAME ONLY. YOU LOST THE RIGHT TO HOLD THAT TITLE WHEN YOU REFUSED MY GAUNTLET REQUEST.
HAD WE SETTLED OUR DISPUTE HONORABLY IN DUELING BATTLE, WE WOULDN'T BE STANDING AS WE ARE TODAY—ON THE BRINK OF DESTRUCTION.
HAD I ALLOWED THE GAUNTLET, THE ONLY RESOLUTION TO OUR DISAGREEMENT WOULD HAVE BEEN DEATH. I CHOSE NOT TO ACCEPT THAT DARK INEVITABILITY.
SO INSTEAD, YOU CHOSE WAR.
NO, CHILD—IT WAS YOU WHO CHOSE WAR.
AND I INTEND TO FINISH WHAT I'VE BEGUN.
I DIDN'T COME HERE TODAY AS A SOLE ASSASSIN.
I CAME AS A GENERAL LEADING AN ARMY.

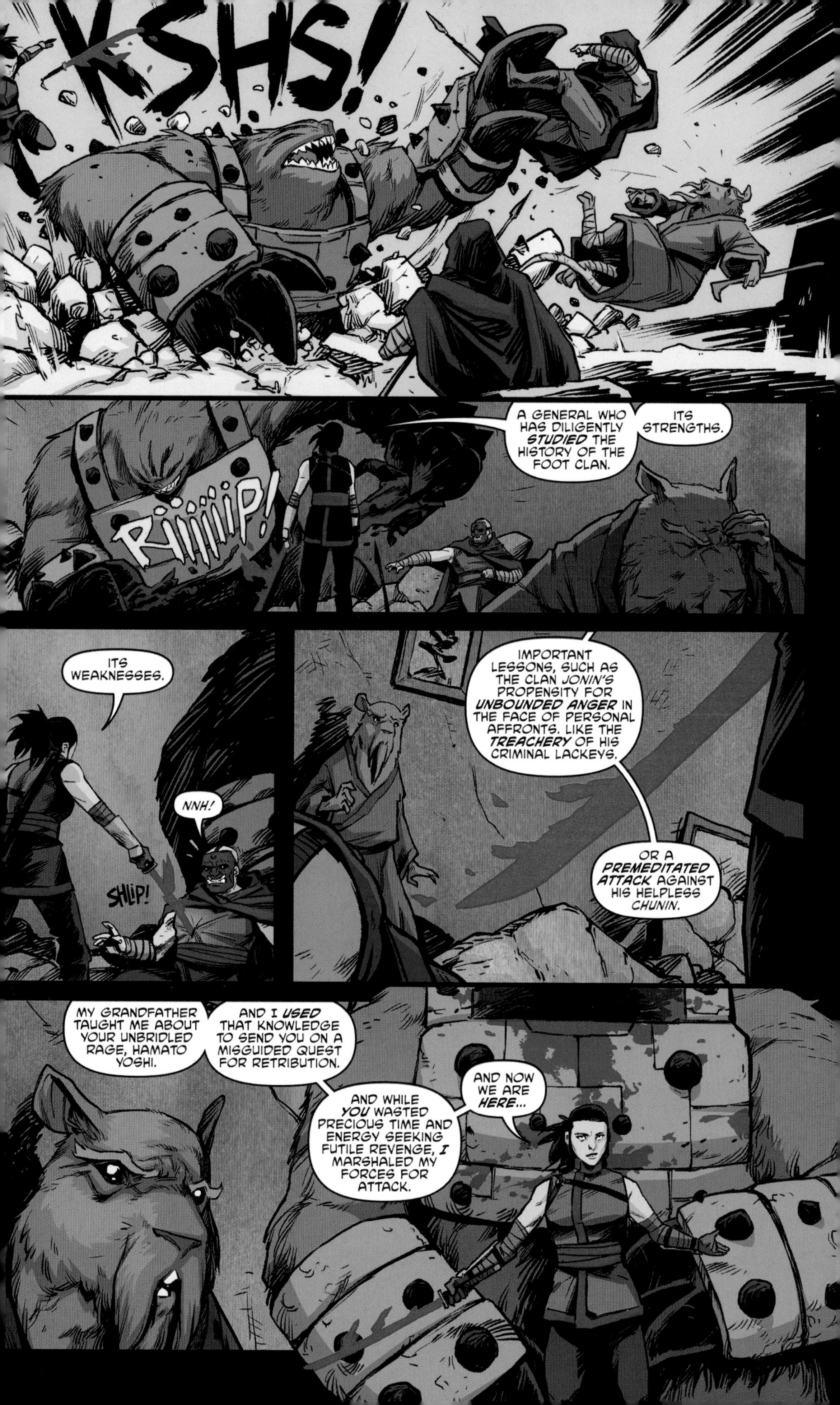
KSHS!
A GENERAL WHO HAS DILIGENTLY STUDIED THE HISTORY OF THE FOOT CLAN.
ITS STRENGTHS.
RIIIIIP!
ITS WEAKNESSES.
NNH!
SHLIP!
IMPORTANT LESSONS, SUCH AS THE CLAN JONIN'S PROPENSITY FOR UNBOUNDED ANGER IN THE FACE OF PERSONAL AFFRONTS. LIKE THE TREACHERY OF HIS CRIMINAL LACKEYS.
OR A PREMEDITATED ATTACK AGAINST HIS HELPLESS CHUNIN.
MY GRANDFATHER TAUGHT ME ABOUT YOUR UNBRIDLED RAGE, HAMATO YOSHI.
AND I USED THAT KNOWLEDGE TO SEND YOU ON A MISGUIDED QUEST FOR RETRIBUTION.
AND WHILE YOU WASTED PRECIOUS TIME AND ENERGY SEEKING FUTILE REVENGE, I MARSHALED MY FORCES FOR ATTACK.
AND NOW WE ARE HERE...

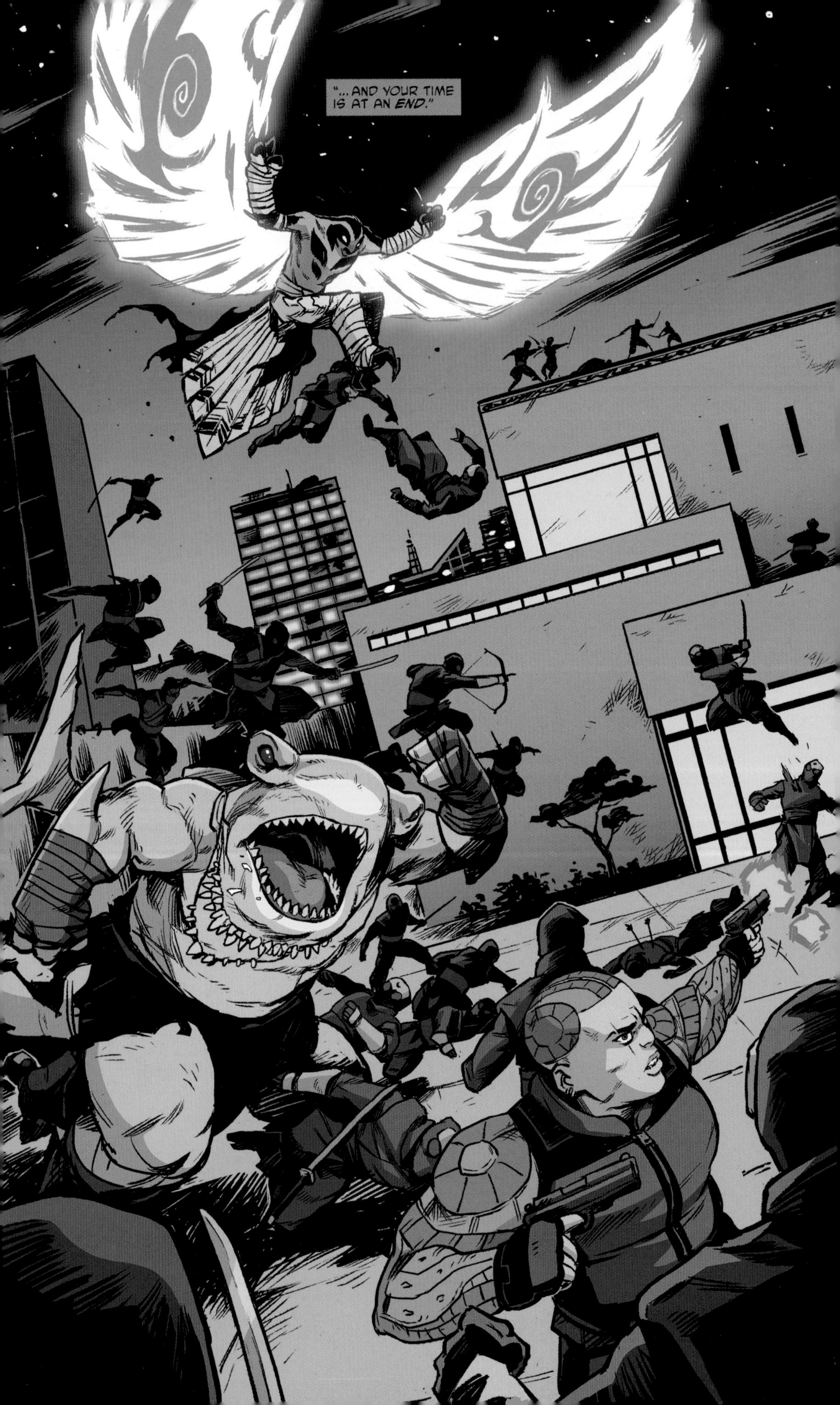
"...AND YOUR TIME IS AT AN *END*."

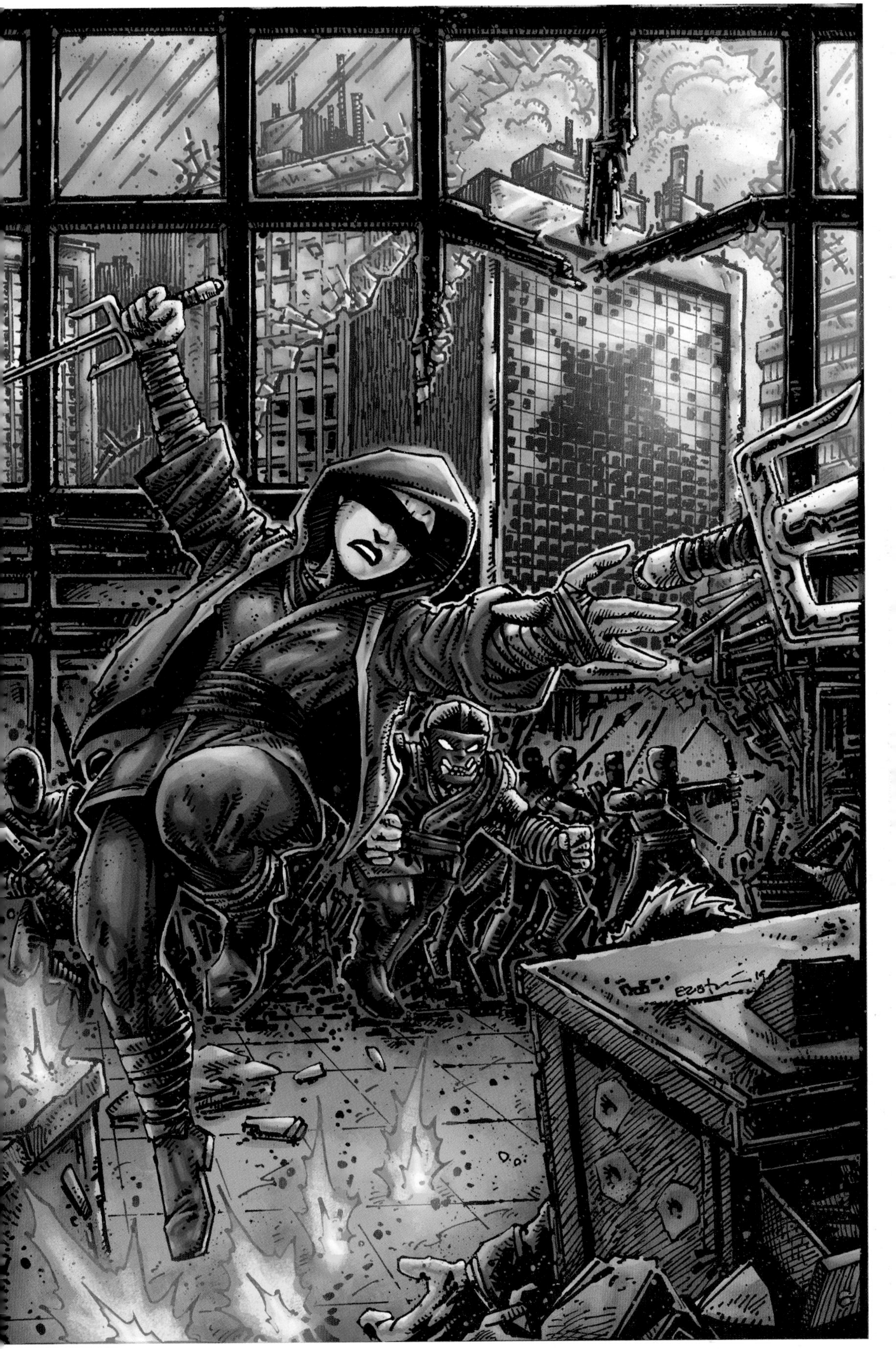

ART BY KEVIN EASTMAN · COLORS BY TOMI VARGA

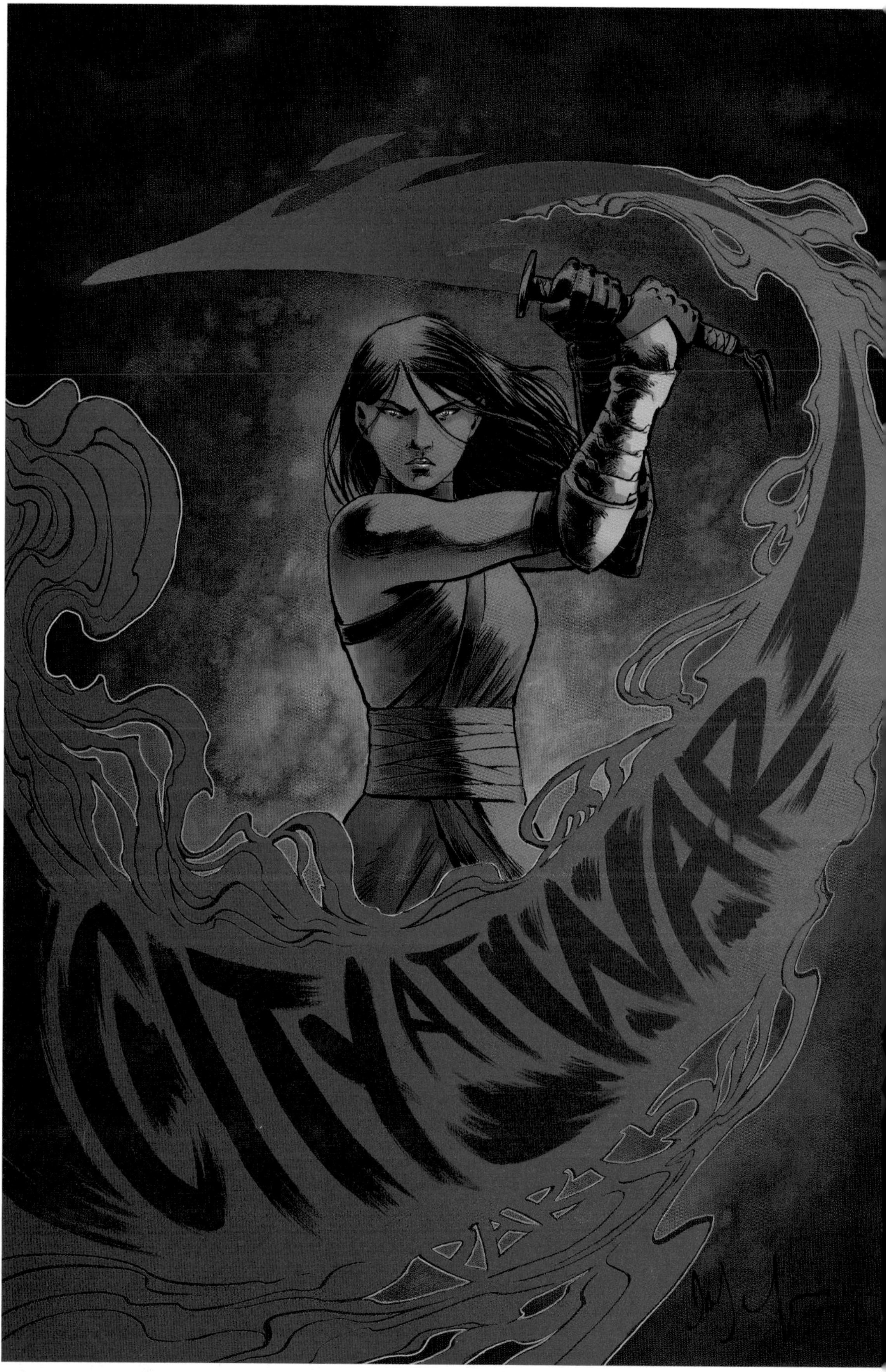
CITY AT WAR

ART BY DAVE WACHTER

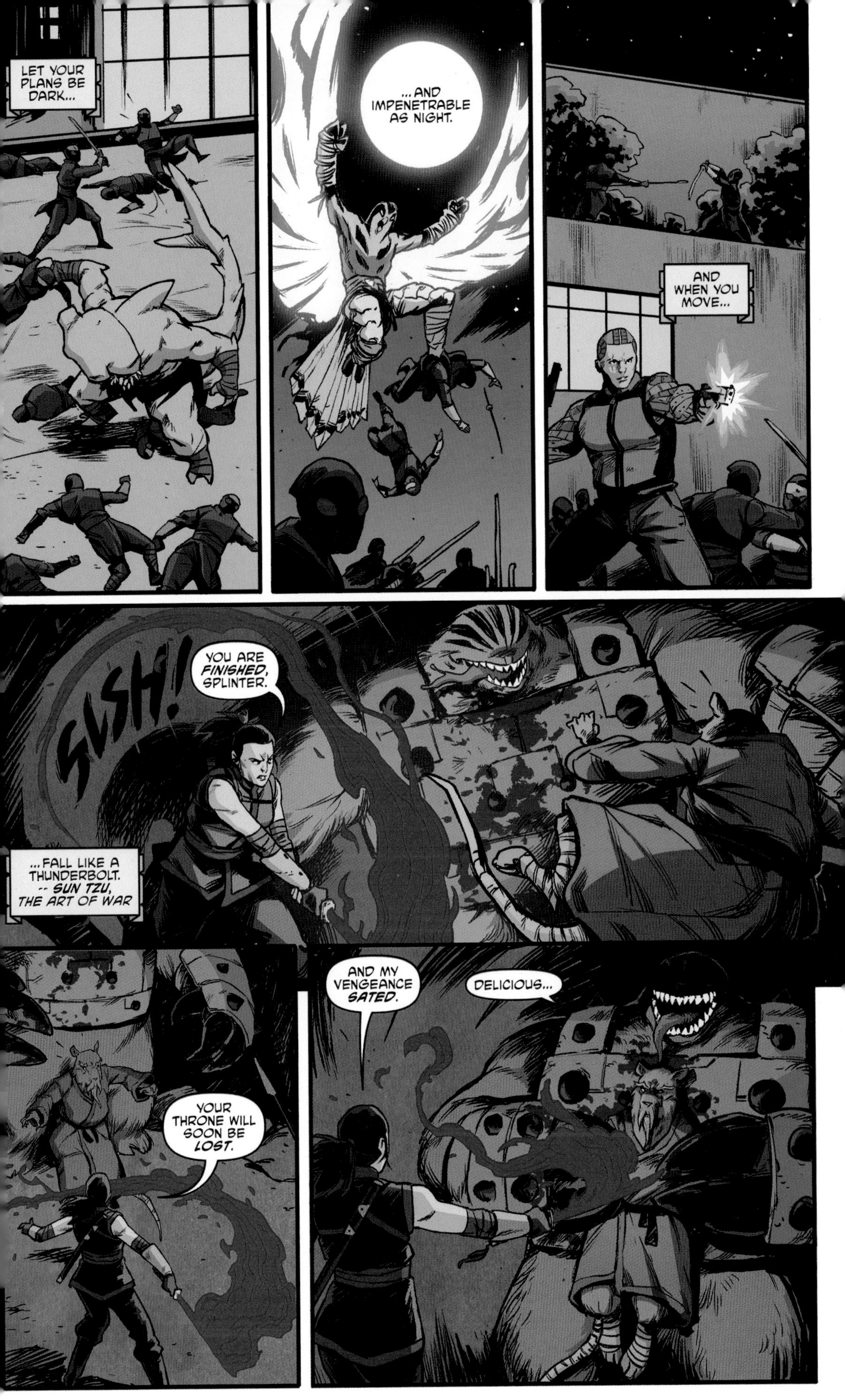

LET YOUR PLANS BE DARK...
...AND IMPENETRABLE AS NIGHT.
AND WHEN YOU MOVE...
SLSH!!
YOU ARE *FINISHED*, SPLINTER.
...FALL LIKE A THUNDERBOLT. -- *SUN TZU, THE ART OF WAR*
YOUR THRONE WILL SOON BE *LOST*.
AND MY VENGEANCE *SATED*.
DELICIOUS...

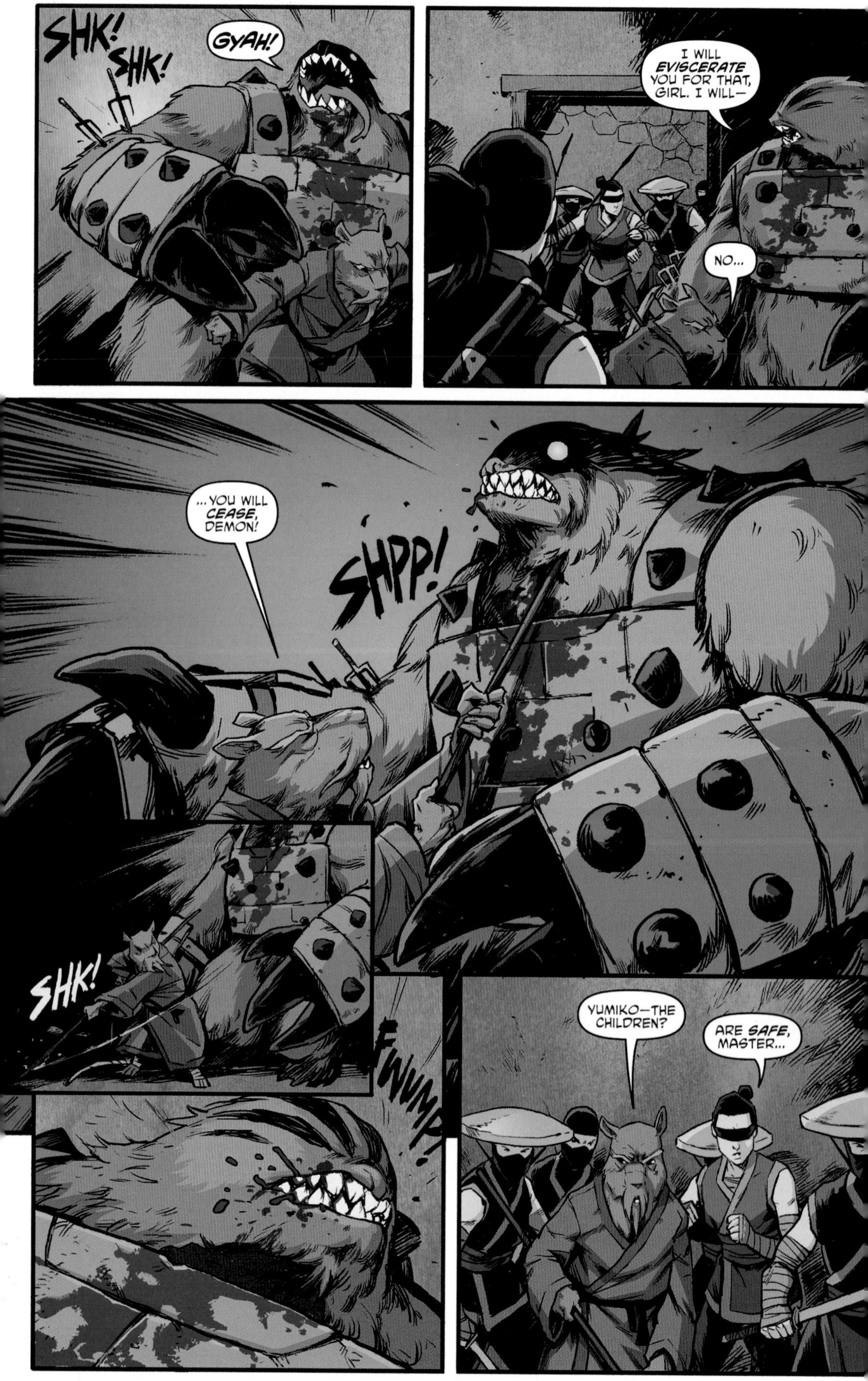
SHK!
SHK!
GYAH!
I WILL EVISCERATE YOU FOR THAT, GIRL. I WILL—
NO...
...YOU WILL CEASE, DEMON!
SHPP!
SHK!
FWUMP!
YUMIKO—THE CHILDREN?
ARE SAFE, MASTER...

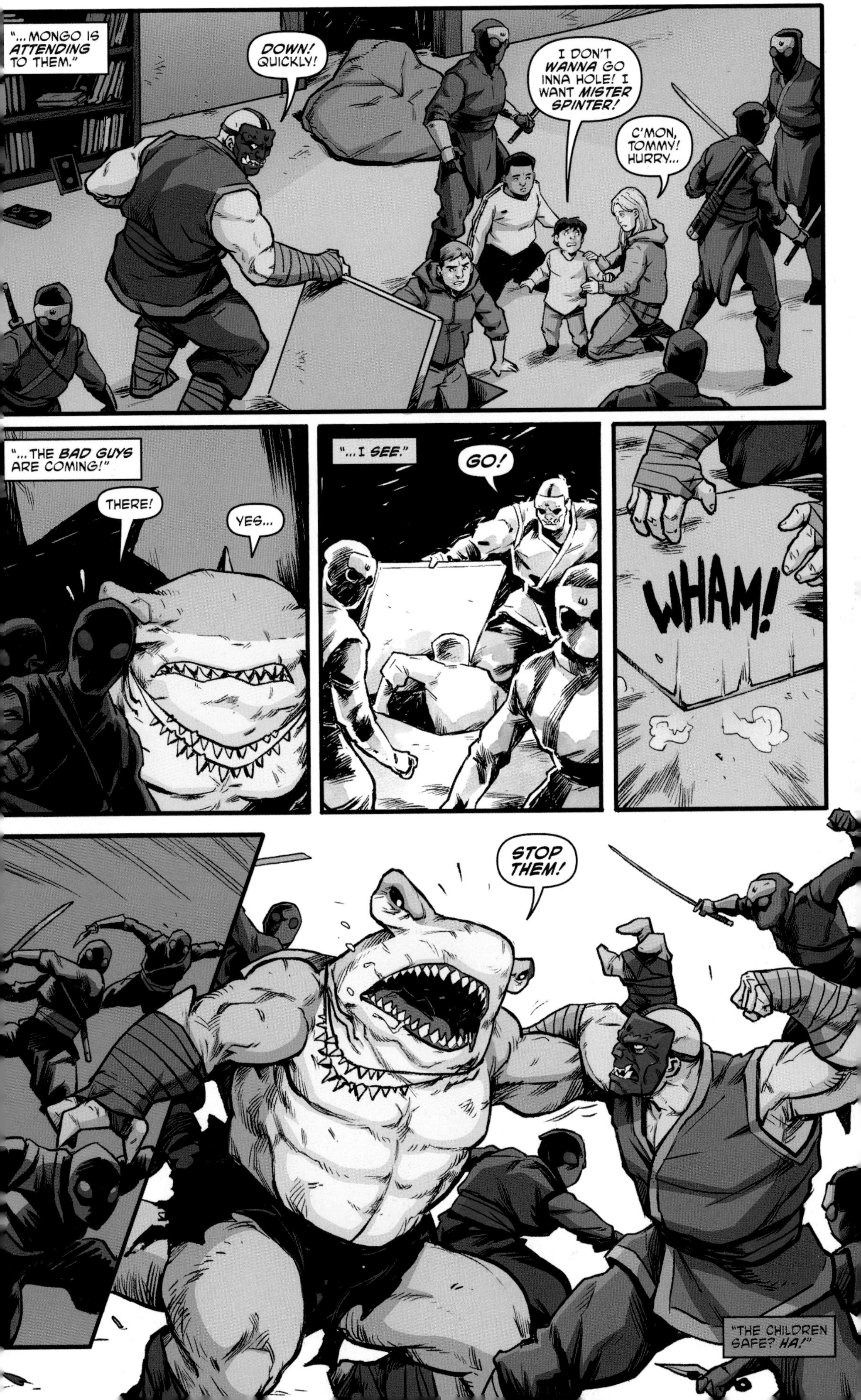
"...MONGO IS ATTENDING TO THEM."
DOWN! QUICKLY!
I DON'T WANNA GO INNA HOLE! I WANT MISTER SPINTER!
C'MON, TOMMY! HURRY...
"...THE BAD GUYS ARE COMING!"
THERE!
YES...
"...I SEE."
GO!
WHAM!
STOP THEM!
"THE CHILDREN SAFE? HA!"

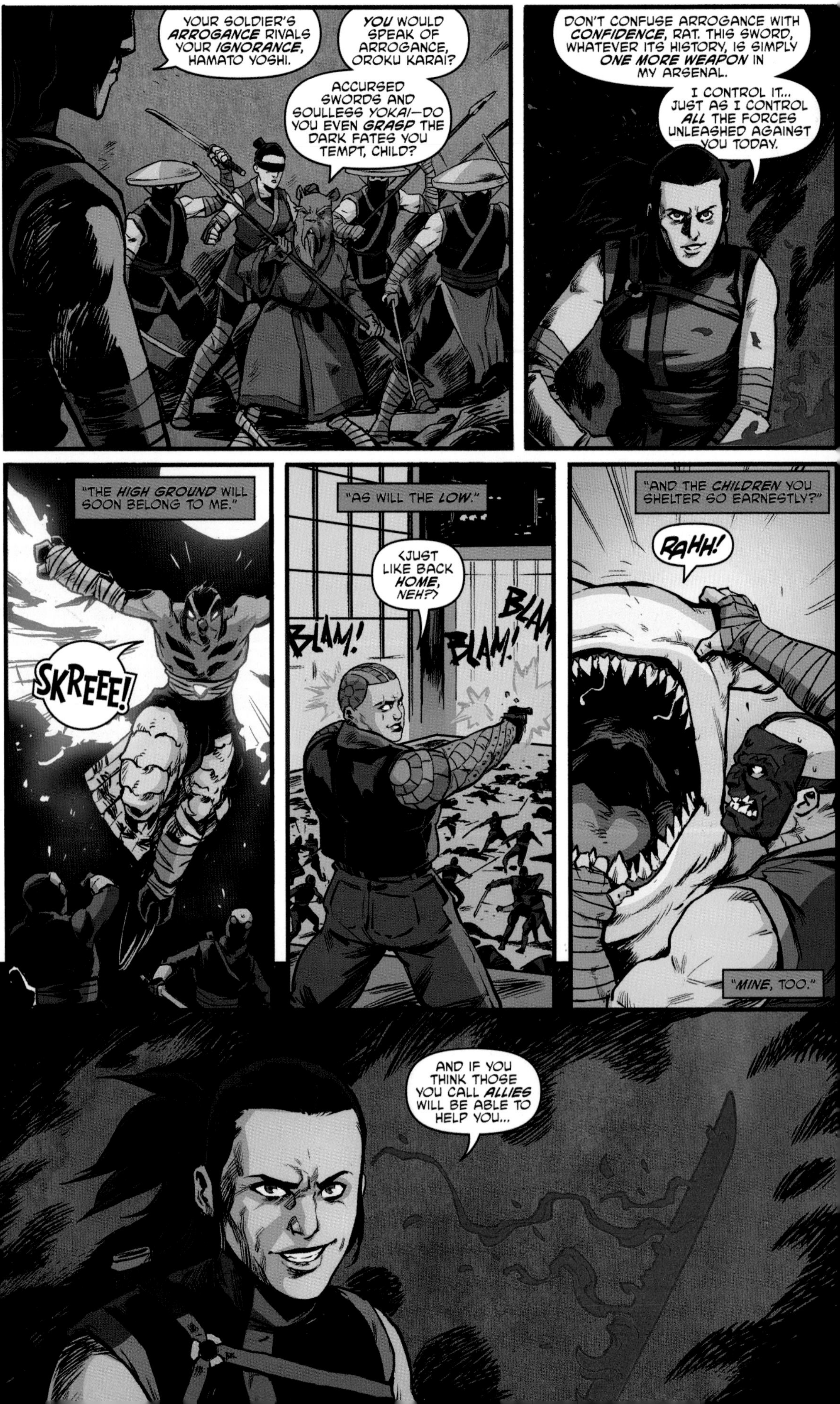

YOUR SOLDIER'S *ARROGANCE* RIVALS YOUR *IGNORANCE*, HAMATO YOSHI.
YOU WOULD SPEAK OF ARROGANCE, OROKU KARAI?
ACCURSED SWORDS AND SOULLESS *YOKAI*—DO YOU EVEN *GRASP* THE DARK FATES YOU TEMPT, CHILD?
DON'T CONFUSE ARROGANCE WITH *CONFIDENCE*, RAT. THIS SWORD, WHATEVER ITS HISTORY, IS SIMPLY *ONE MORE WEAPON* IN MY ARSENAL.
I CONTROL IT... JUST AS I CONTROL *ALL* THE FORCES UNLEASHED AGAINST YOU TODAY.
"THE *HIGH GROUND* WILL SOON BELONG TO ME."
SKREEE!
"AS WILL THE *LOW*."
<JUST LIKE BACK *HOME*, NEH?>
BLAM!
BLAM!
BLAM!
"AND THE *CHILDREN* YOU SHELTER SO EARNESTLY?"
RAHH!
"*MINE*, TOO."
AND IF YOU THINK THOSE YOU CALL *ALLIES* WILL BE ABLE TO HELP YOU...

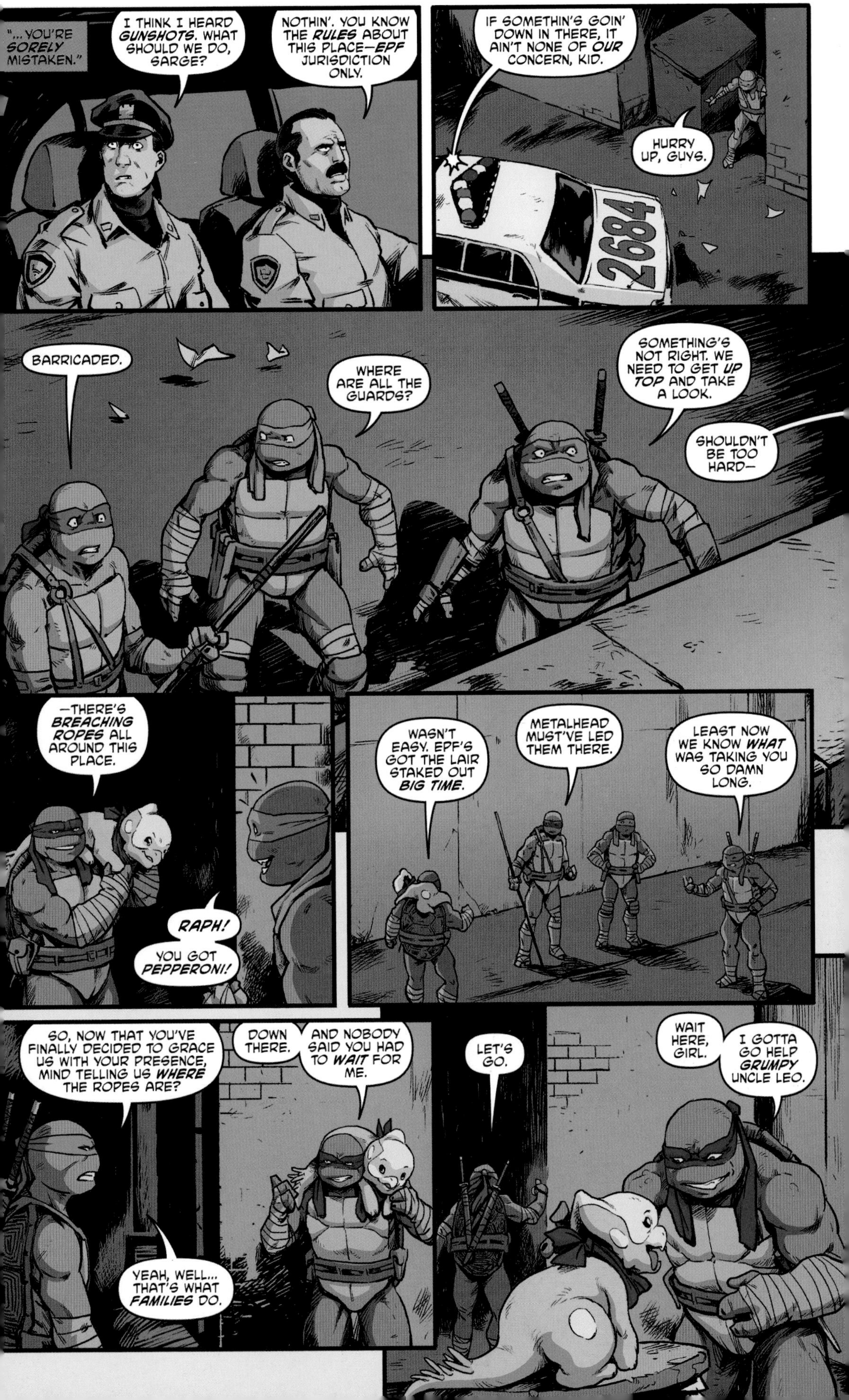
"...YOU'RE SORELY MISTAKEN."
I THINK I HEARD GUNSHOTS. WHAT SHOULD WE DO, SARGE?
NOTHIN'. YOU KNOW THE RULES ABOUT THIS PLACE—EPF JURISDICTION ONLY.
IF SOMETHIN'S GOIN' DOWN IN THERE, IT AIN'T NONE OF OUR CONCERN, KID.
HURRY UP, GUYS.
2684
BARRICADED.
WHERE ARE ALL THE GUARDS?
SOMETHING'S NOT RIGHT. WE NEED TO GET UP TOP AND TAKE A LOOK.
SHOULDN'T BE TOO HARD—
—THERE'S BREACHING ROPES ALL AROUND THIS PLACE.
RAPH!
YOU GOT PEPPERONI!
WASN'T EASY. EPF'S GOT THE LAIR STAKED OUT BIG TIME.
METALHEAD MUST'VE LED THEM THERE.
LEAST NOW WE KNOW WHAT WAS TAKING YOU SO DAMN LONG.
SO, NOW THAT YOU'VE FINALLY DECIDED TO GRACE US WITH YOUR PRESENCE, MIND TELLING US WHERE THE ROPES ARE?
YEAH, WELL... THAT'S WHAT FAMILIES DO.
DOWN THERE.
AND NOBODY SAID YOU HAD TO WAIT FOR ME.
LET'S GO.
WAIT HERE, GIRL.
I GOTTA GO HELP GRUMPY UNCLE LEO.

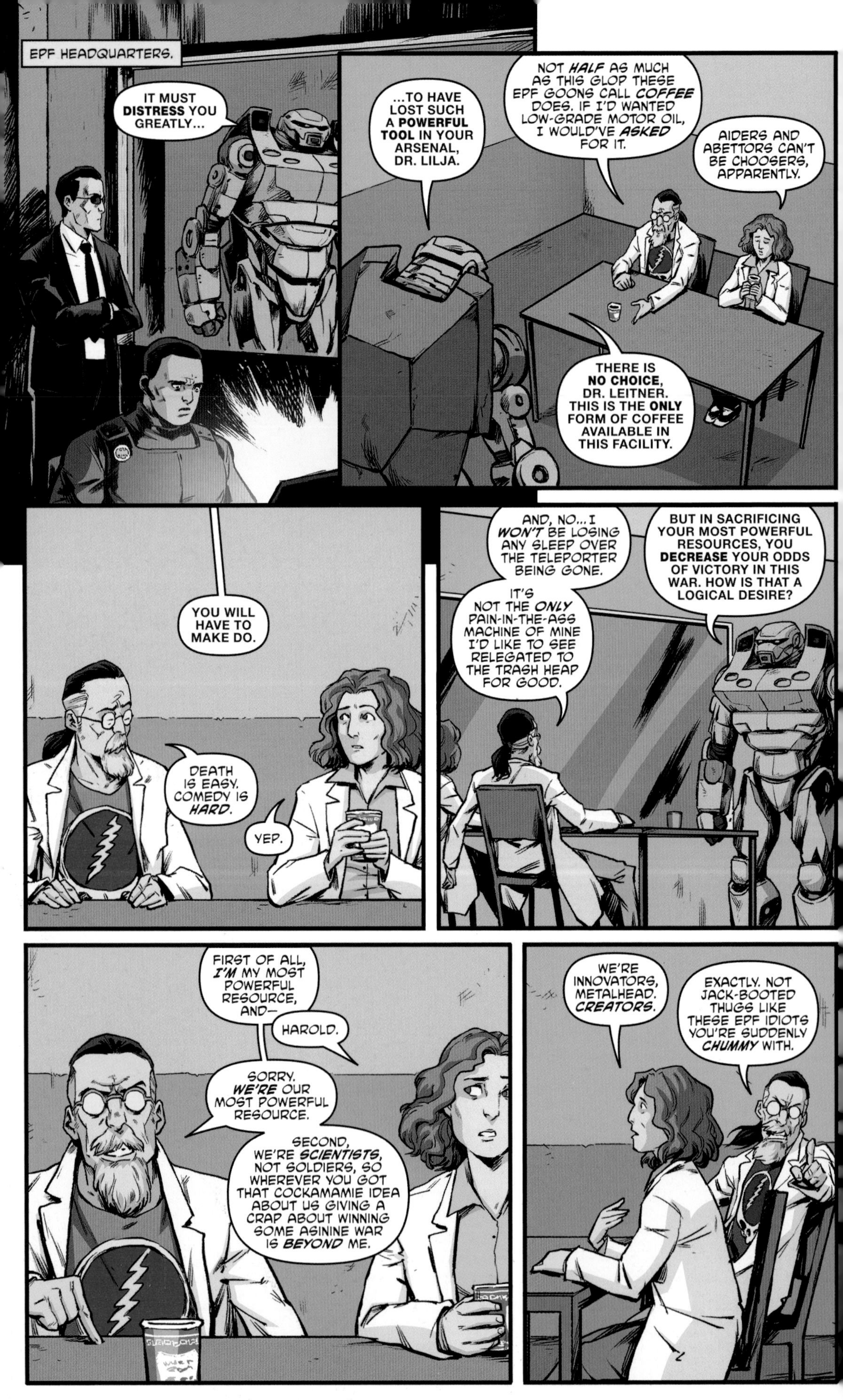
EPF HEADQUARTERS.
IT MUST DISTRESS YOU GREATLY...
...TO HAVE LOST SUCH A POWERFUL TOOL IN YOUR ARSENAL, DR. LILJA.
NOT HALF AS MUCH AS THIS GLOP THESE EPF GOONS CALL COFFEE DOES. IF I'D WANTED LOW-GRADE MOTOR OIL, I WOULD'VE ASKED FOR IT.
AIDERS AND ABETTORS CAN'T BE CHOOSERS, APPARENTLY.
THERE IS NO CHOICE, DR. LEITNER. THIS IS THE ONLY FORM OF COFFEE AVAILABLE IN THIS FACILITY.
YOU WILL HAVE TO MAKE DO.
DEATH IS EASY. COMEDY IS HARD.
YEP.
AND, NO... I WON'T BE LOSING ANY SLEEP OVER THE TELEPORTER BEING GONE.
IT'S NOT THE ONLY PAIN-IN-THE-ASS MACHINE OF MINE I'D LIKE TO SEE RELEGATED TO THE TRASH HEAP FOR GOOD.
BUT IN SACRIFICING YOUR MOST POWERFUL RESOURCES, YOU DECREASE YOUR ODDS OF VICTORY IN THIS WAR. HOW IS THAT A LOGICAL DESIRE?
FIRST OF ALL, I'M MY MOST POWERFUL RESOURCE, AND—
HAROLD.
SORRY. WE'RE OUR MOST POWERFUL RESOURCE.
SECOND, WE'RE SCIENTISTS, NOT SOLDIERS, SO WHEREVER YOU GOT THAT COCKAMAMIE IDEA ABOUT US GIVING A CRAP ABOUT WINNING SOME ASININE WAR IS BEYOND ME.
WE'RE INNOVATORS, METALHEAD. CREATORS.
EXACTLY. NOT JACK-BOOTED THUGS LIKE THESE EPF IDIOTS YOU'RE SUDDENLY CHUMMY WITH.

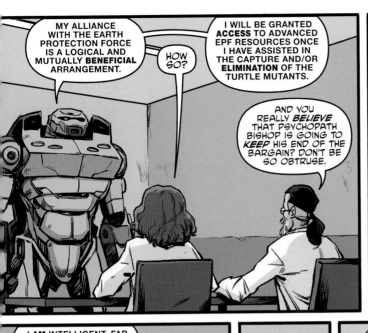

MY ALLIANCE WITH THE EARTH PROTECTION FORCE IS A LOGICAL AND MUTUALLY **BENEFICIAL** ARRANGEMENT.

HOW SO?

I WILL BE GRANTED **ACCESS** TO ADVANCED EPF RESOURCES ONCE I HAVE ASSISTED IN THE CAPTURE AND/OR **ELIMINATION** OF THE TURTLE MUTANTS.

AND YOU REALLY **BELIEVE** THAT PSYCHOPATH BISHOP IS GOING TO **KEEP** HIS END OF THE BARGAIN? DON'T BE SO OBTRUSE.

I THOUGHT I MADE YOU **SMARTER** THAN THAT.

I **AM** INTELLIGENT. FAR MORE INTELLIGENT THAN WHEN YOU **CREATED** ME. MORE INTELLIGENT THAN **YOU**.

BUT I REQUIRE **MORE**.

MEH. INPUT, OUTPUT— THAT'S **ALL** IT IS.

THERE'S A REASON IT'S CALLED **ARTIFICIAL** INTELLIGENCE, YOU KNOW.

EXPLAIN.

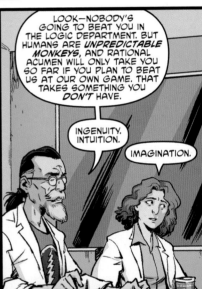

LOOK—NOBODY'S GOING TO BEAT YOU IN THE LOGIC DEPARTMENT. BUT HUMANS ARE **UNPREDICTABLE MONKEYS**, AND RATIONAL ACUMEN WILL ONLY TAKE YOU SO FAR IF YOU PLAN TO BEAT US AT OUR OWN GAME. THAT TAKES SOMETHING YOU **DON'T** HAVE.

INGENUITY. INTUITION.

IMAGINATION.

YOU'RE ONLY AS SMART AS THE DATA YOU **DOWNLOAD**. AND NO MATTER HOW MANY LOGIC BYTES YOU FILL THAT TIN CAN BRAIN OF YOURS WITH, SIMPLE HUMAN NUANCE WILL TRIP YOU UP **EVERY SINGLE TIME**.

HELL, YOU DIDN'T EVEN GET LIBBY'S LITTLE COFFEE PUN EARLIER, WHICH TELLS ME **ALL** I NEED TO KNOW.

AND WHAT IS THAT?

THAT YOU'RE GONNA BE **SCREWED** WHEN YOU FIND OUT THE BIG JOKE'S ON **YOU**.

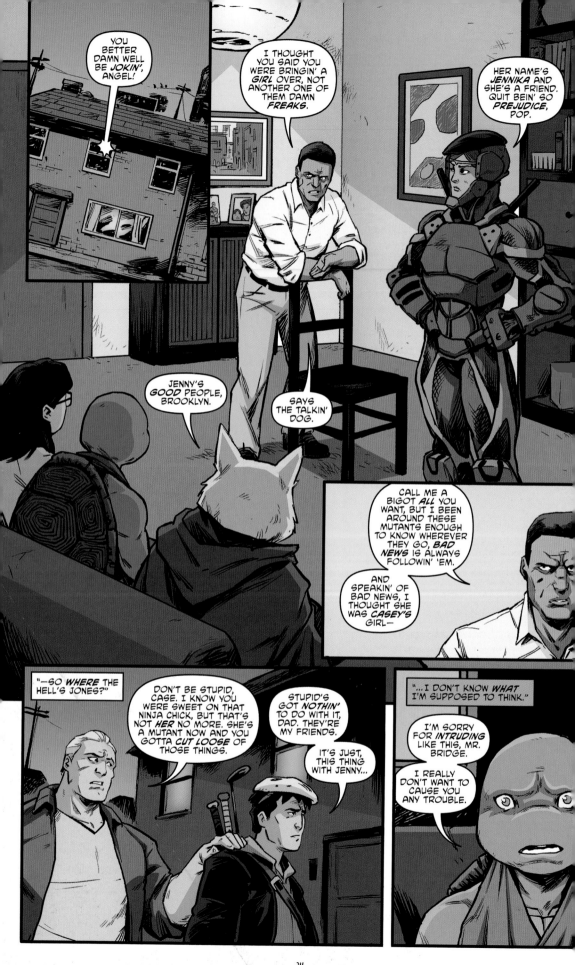

YOU BETTER DAMN WELL BE *JOKIN'*, ANGEL!

I THOUGHT YOU SAID YOU WERE BRINGIN' A *GIRL* OVER, NOT ANOTHER ONE OF THEM DAMN *FREAKS*.

HER NAME'S *JENNIKA* AND SHE'S A FRIEND. QUIT BEIN' SO *PREJUDICE*, POP.

JENNY'S *GOOD* PEOPLE, BROOKLYN.

SAYS THE TALKIN' DOG.

CALL ME A BIGOT *ALL* YOU WANT, BUT I BEEN AROUND THESE MUTANTS ENOUGH TO KNOW WHEREVER THEY GO, *BAD NEWS* IS ALWAYS FOLLOWIN' 'EM.

AND SPEAKIN' OF BAD NEWS, I THOUGHT SHE WAS *CASEY'S* GIRL—

"—SO *WHERE* THE HELL'S JONES?"

DON'T BE STUPID, CASE. I KNOW YOU WERE SWEET ON THAT NINJA CHICK, BUT THAT'S NOT *HER* NO MORE. SHE'S A MUTANT NOW AND YOU GOTTA *CUT LOOSE* OF THOSE THINGS.

STUPID'S GOT *NOTHIN'* TO DO WITH IT, DAD. THEY'RE MY FRIENDS.

IT'S JUST, THIS THING WITH JENNY...

"...I DON'T KNOW *WHAT* I'M SUPPOSED TO THINK."

I'M SORRY FOR *INTRUDING* LIKE THIS, MR. BRIDGE.

I REALLY DON'T WANT TO CAUSE YOU ANY TROUBLE.

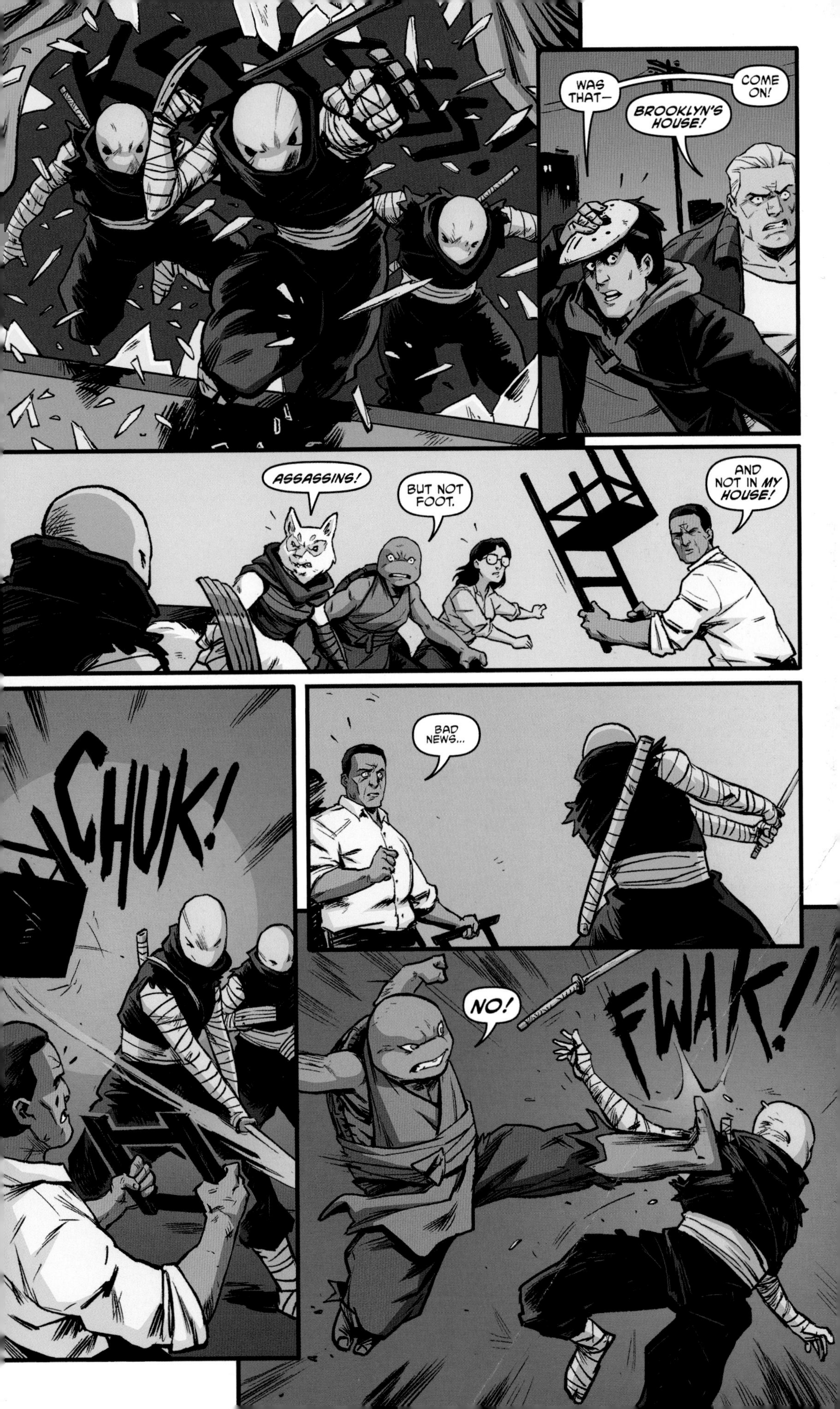
WAS THAT—
BROOKLYN'S HOUSE!
COME ON!
ASSASSINS!
BUT NOT FOOT.
AND NOT IN MY HOUSE!
CHUK!
BAD NEWS...
NO!
FWAK!

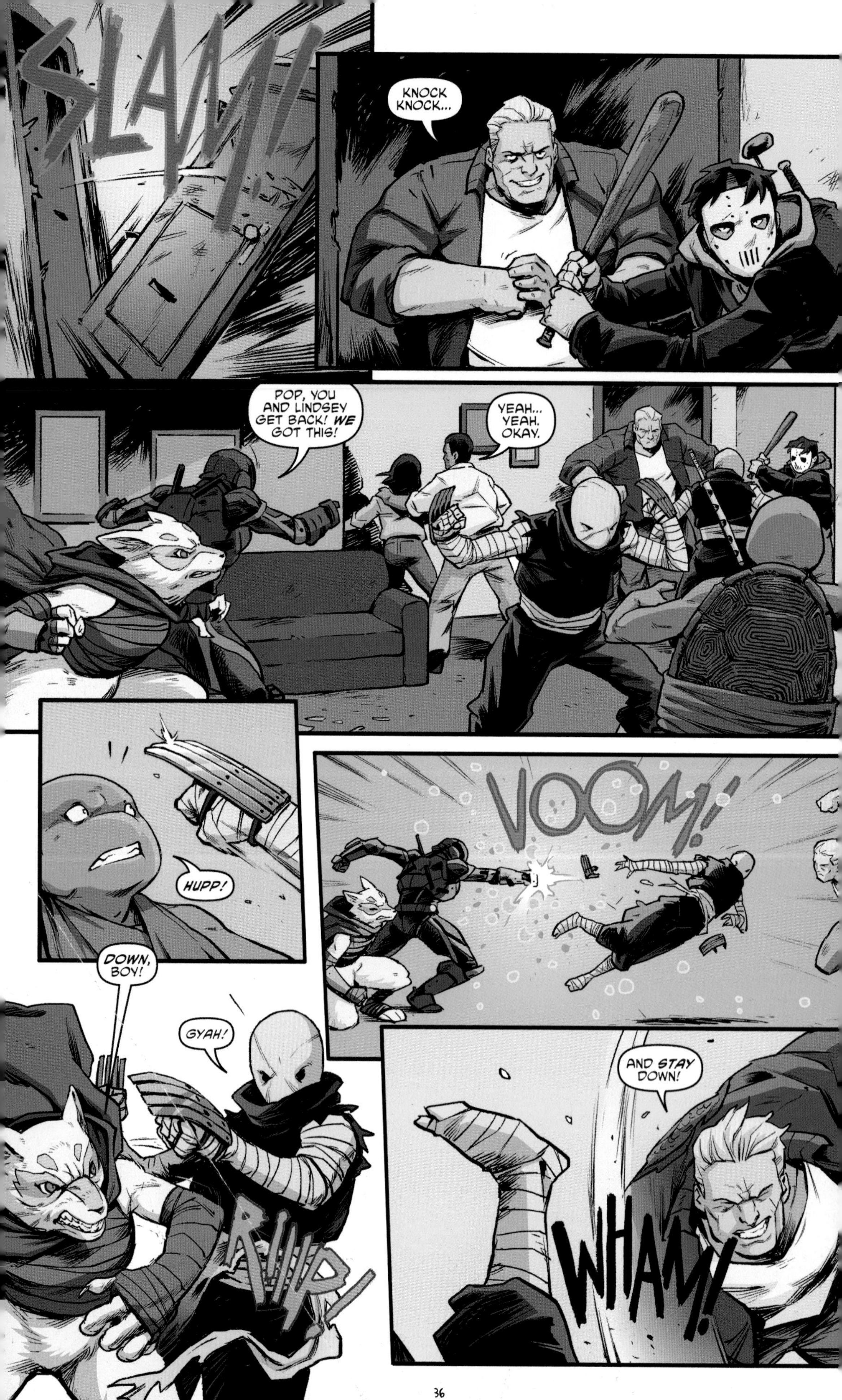
SLAM!
KNOCK KNOCK...
POP, YOU AND LINDSEY GET BACK! WE GOT THIS!
YEAH... YEAH. OKAY.
HUPP!
VOOM!
DOWN, BOY!
GYAH!
RIIIP!
AND STAY DOWN!
WHAM!

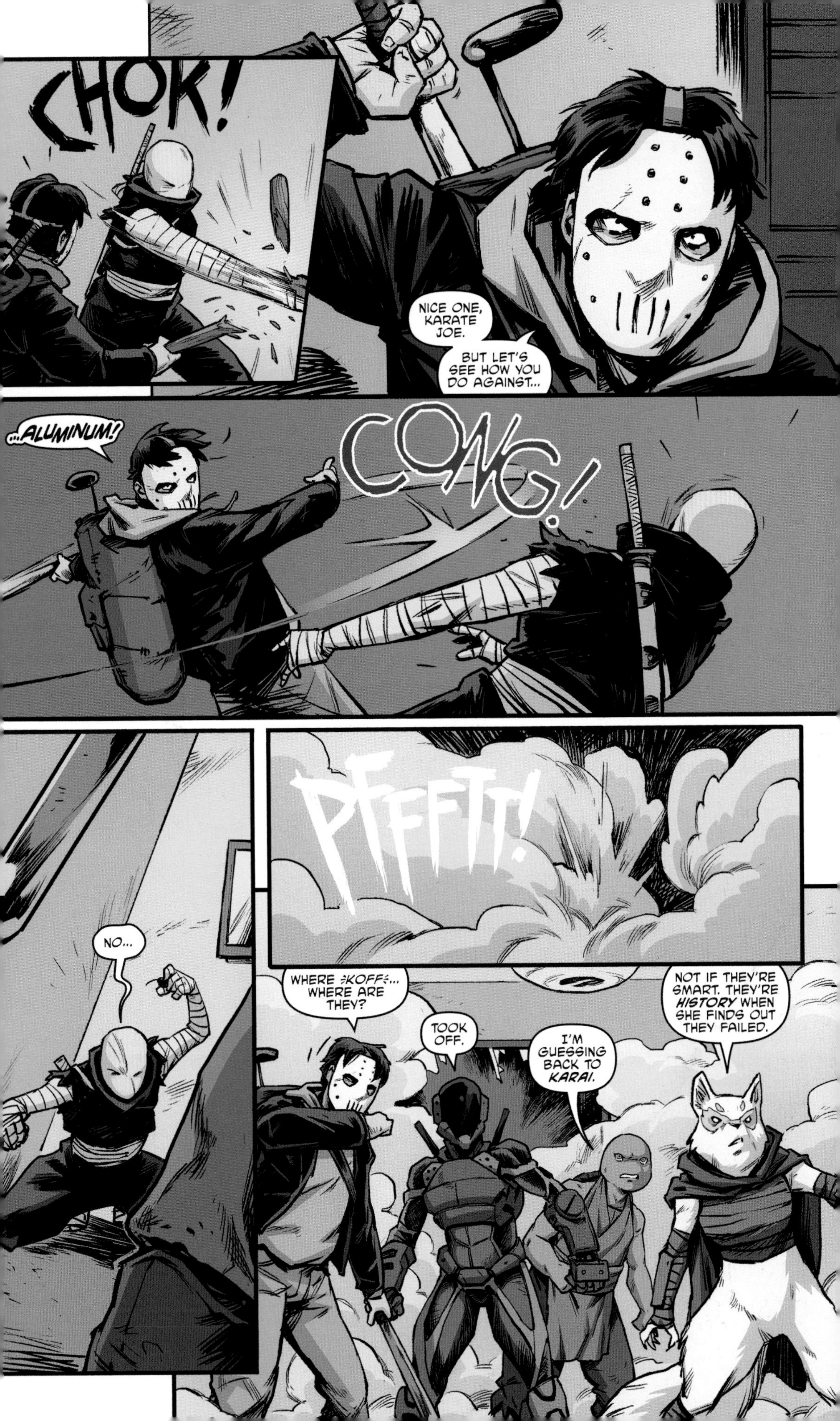
CHOK!
NICE ONE, KARATE JOE.
BUT LET'S SEE HOW YOU DO AGAINST...
...ALUMINUM!
CONG!
PFFFTT!
NO...
WHERE ≠KOFF≠... WHERE ARE THEY?
TOOK OFF.
I'M GUESSING BACK TO KARAI.
NOT IF THEY'RE SMART. THEY'RE HISTORY WHEN SHE FINDS OUT THEY FAILED.

DAMN.

SORRY 'BOUT YOUR *DOOR*, BROOKLYN.

BETTER A BROKEN DOOR THAN A *MISSIN' HEAD*, I GUESS.

EVEN THOUGH YOU BEIN' HERE'S PROBABLY WHAT *CAUSED* THIS MESS, I WANNA SAY THANKS.

YOU *SAVED* MY SKIN BACK THERE, TURTLE.

NINJA TURTLE.

GO AHEAD. TRY IT ON. YOU MIGHT BE SURPRISED HOW GOOD A *NEW MASK* FEELS.

I KNOW I WAS.*

*See TMNT #66 – B.C.

SO? HOW DO I LOOK?

LIKE THE *BADASS* YOU ARE, GIRL.

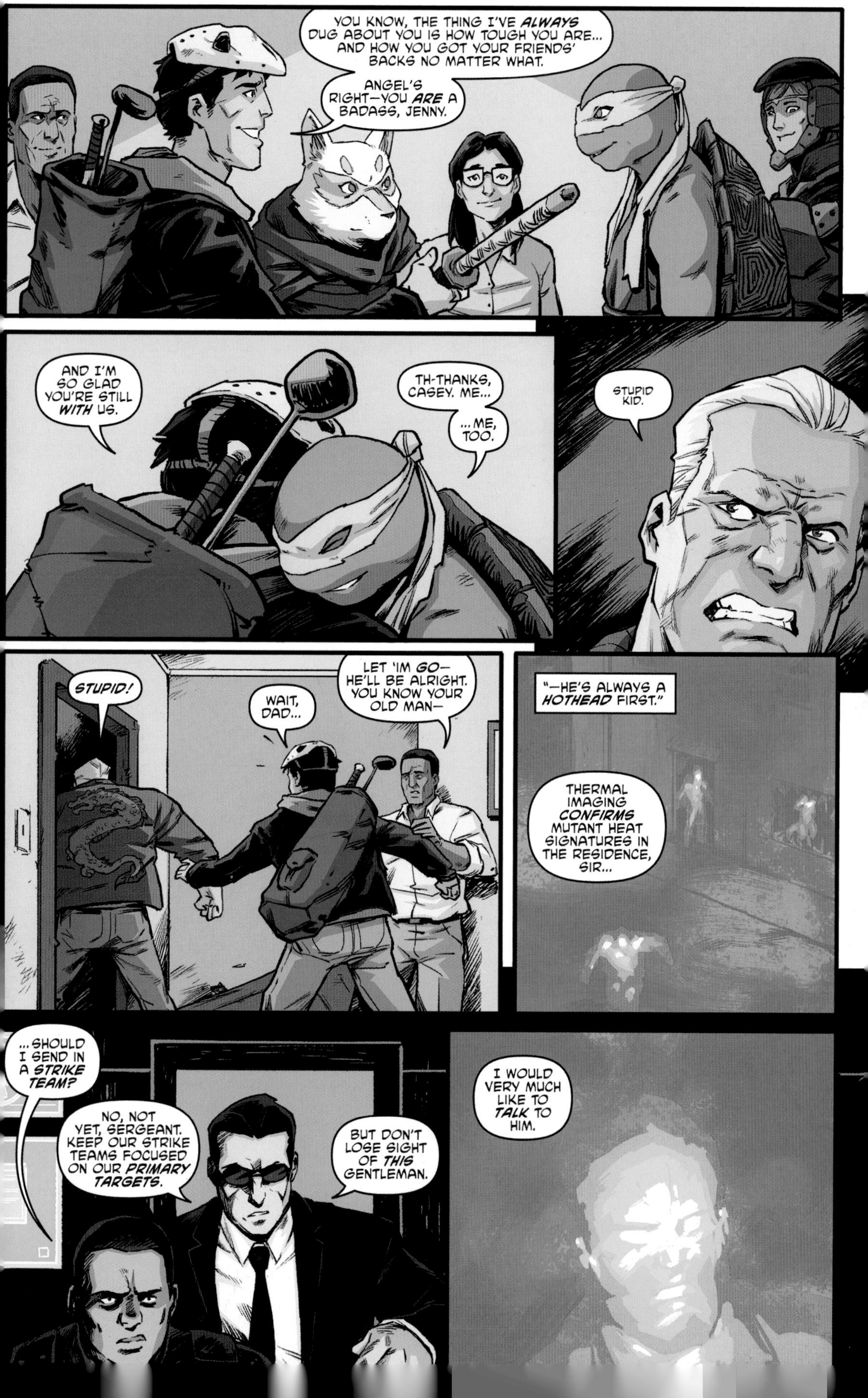

YOU KNOW, THE THING I'VE ALWAYS DUG ABOUT YOU IS HOW TOUGH YOU ARE... AND HOW YOU GOT YOUR FRIENDS' BACKS NO MATTER WHAT.
ANGEL'S RIGHT—YOU ARE A BADASS, JENNY.
AND I'M SO GLAD YOU'RE STILL WITH US.
TH-THANKS, CASEY. ME...
...ME, TOO.
STUPID KID.
STUPID!
WAIT, DAD...
LET 'IM GO—HE'LL BE ALRIGHT. YOU KNOW YOUR OLD MAN—
"—HE'S ALWAYS A HOTHEAD FIRST."
THERMAL IMAGING CONFIRMS MUTANT HEAT SIGNATURES IN THE RESIDENCE, SIR...
...SHOULD I SEND IN A STRIKE TEAM?
NO, NOT YET, SERGEANT. KEEP OUR STRIKE TEAMS FOCUSED ON OUR PRIMARY TARGETS.
BUT DON'T LOSE SIGHT OF THIS GENTLEMAN.
I WOULD VERY MUCH LIKE TO TALK TO HIM.

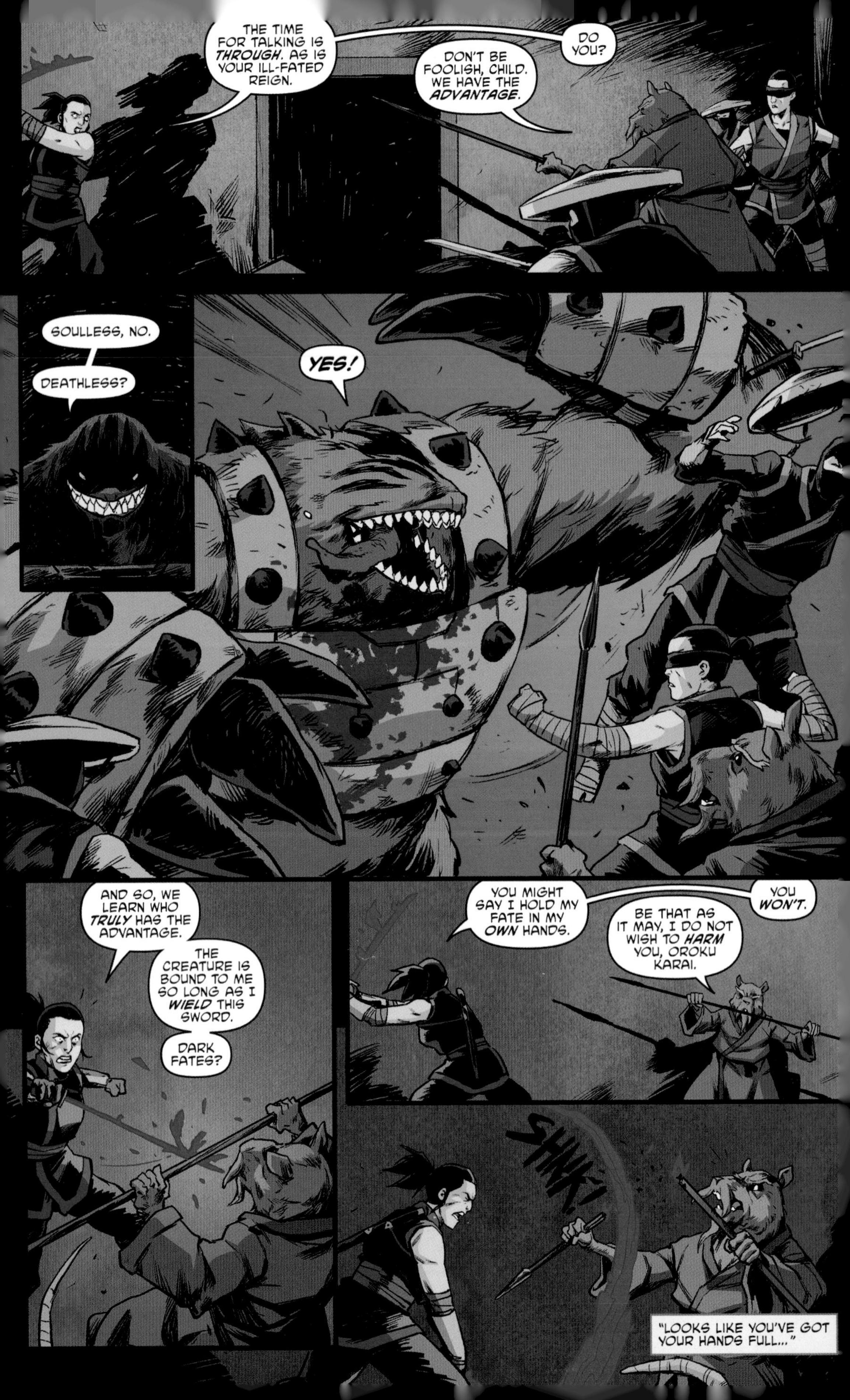
THE TIME FOR TALKING IS *THROUGH*. AS IS YOUR ILL-FATED REIGN.
DON'T BE FOOLISH, CHILD. WE HAVE THE *ADVANTAGE*.
DO YOU?
SOULLESS, NO.
DEATHLESS?
YES!
AND SO, WE LEARN WHO *TRULY* HAS THE ADVANTAGE.
THE CREATURE IS BOUND TO ME SO LONG AS I *WIELD* THIS SWORD.
DARK FATES?
YOU MIGHT SAY I HOLD MY FATE IN MY *OWN* HANDS.
YOU *WON'T*.
BE THAT AS IT MAY, I DO NOT WISH TO *HARM* YOU, OROKU KARAI.
SHNK!
"LOOKS LIKE YOU'VE GOT YOUR HANDS FULL..."

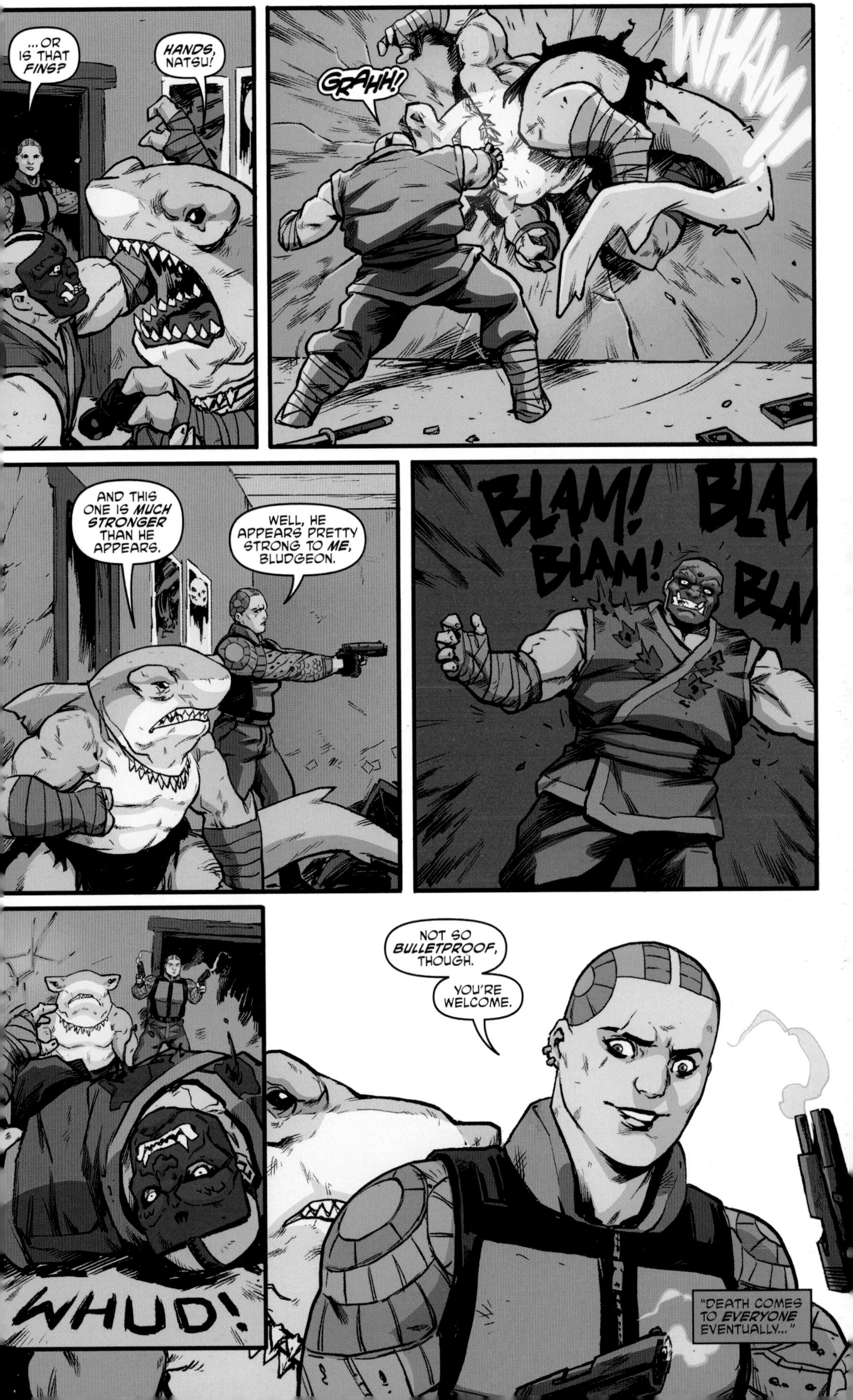
...OR IS THAT *FINS?*
HANDS, NATSU!
GRAHH!
WHAM!
AND THIS ONE IS *MUCH STRONGER* THAN HE APPEARS.
WELL, HE APPEARS PRETTY STRONG TO *ME,* BLUDGEON.
BLAM! BLAM!
BLAM!
NOT SO *BULLETPROOF,* THOUGH.
YOU'RE WELCOME.
WHUD!
"DEATH COMES TO *EVERYONE* EVENTUALLY..."

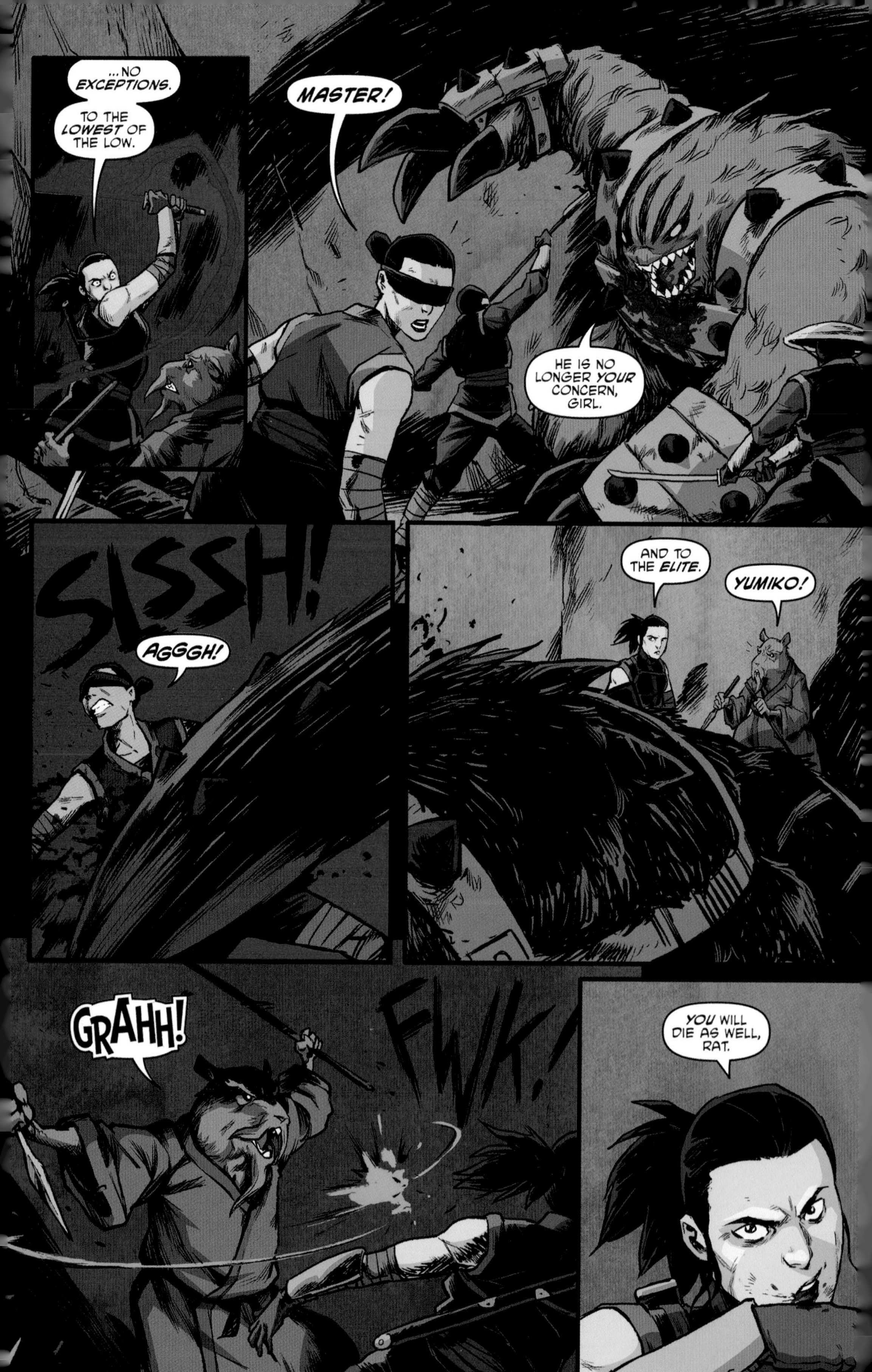

...NO EXCEPTIONS.
TO THE LOWEST OF THE LOW.
MASTER!
HE IS NO LONGER YOUR CONCERN, GIRL.
SISSH!
AGGGH!
AND TO THE ELITE.
YUMIKO!
GRAHH!
FWK!
YOU WILL DIE AS WELL, RAT.
"ALMOST THERE..."

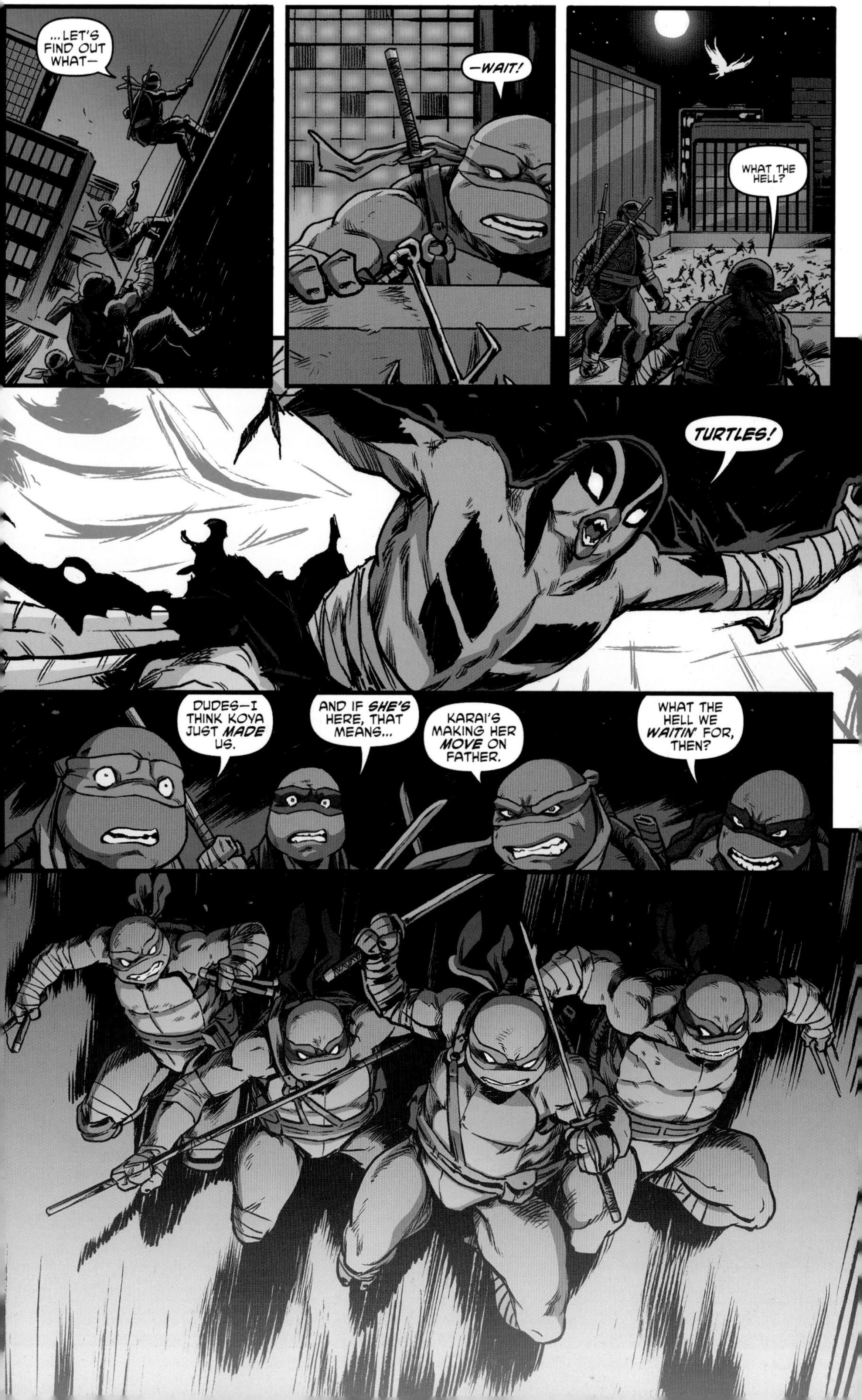
...LET'S FIND OUT WHAT—
—WAIT!
WHAT THE HELL?
TURTLES!
DUDES—I THINK KOYA JUST MADE US.
AND IF SHE'S HERE, THAT MEANS...
KARAI'S MAKING HER MOVE ON FATHER.
WHAT THE HELL WE WAITIN' FOR, THEN?

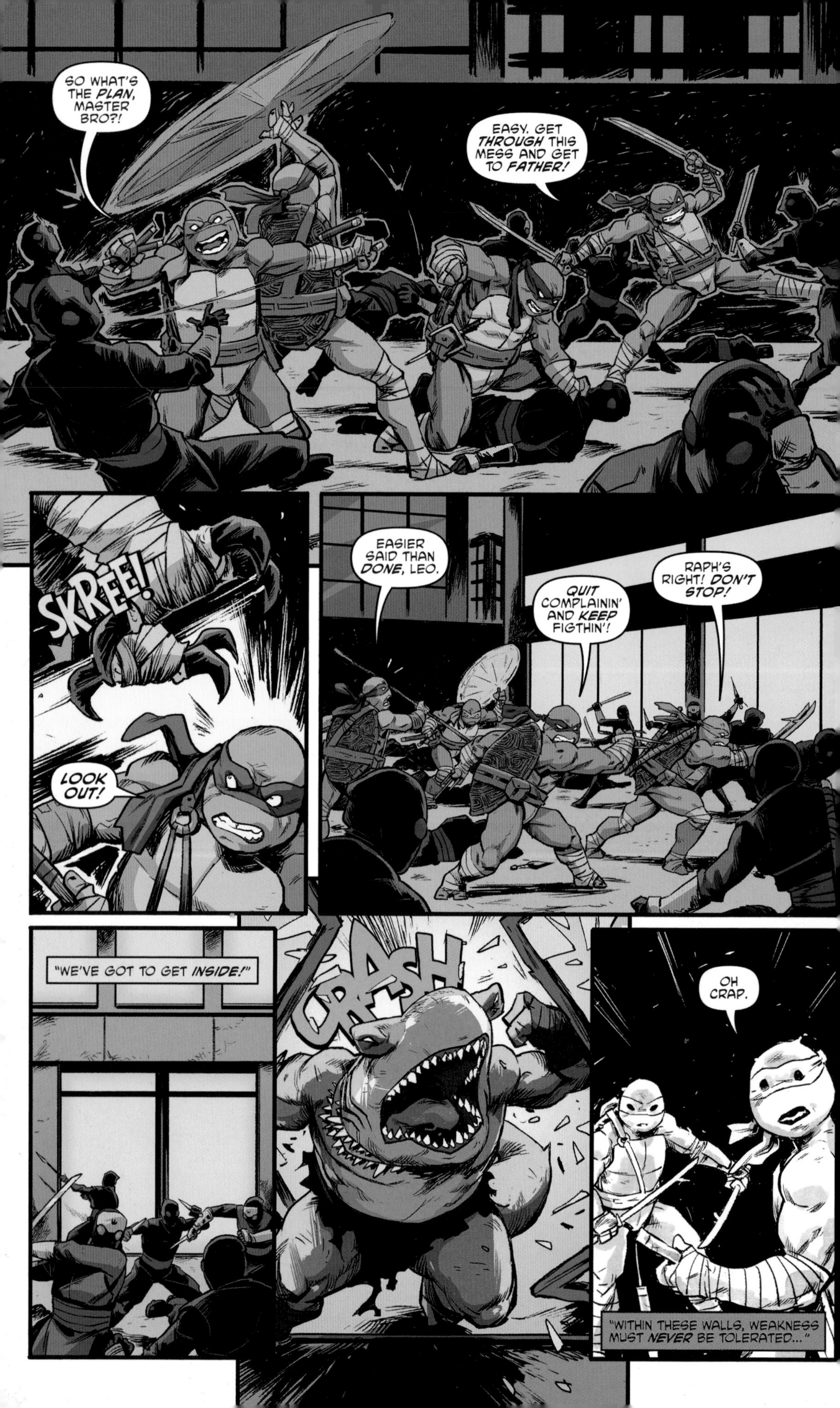
SO WHAT'S THE *PLAN*, MASTER BRO?!
EASY. GET *THROUGH* THIS MESS AND GET TO *FATHER!*
SKREE!
LOOK OUT!
EASIER SAID THAN *DONE*, LEO.
QUIT COMPLAININ' AND *KEEP* FIGTHIN'!
RAPH'S RIGHT! *DON'T STOP!*
"WE'VE GOT TO GET *INSIDE!*"
CRASH!
OH CRAP.
"WITHIN THESE WALLS, WEAKNESS MUST *NEVER* BE TOLERATED..."

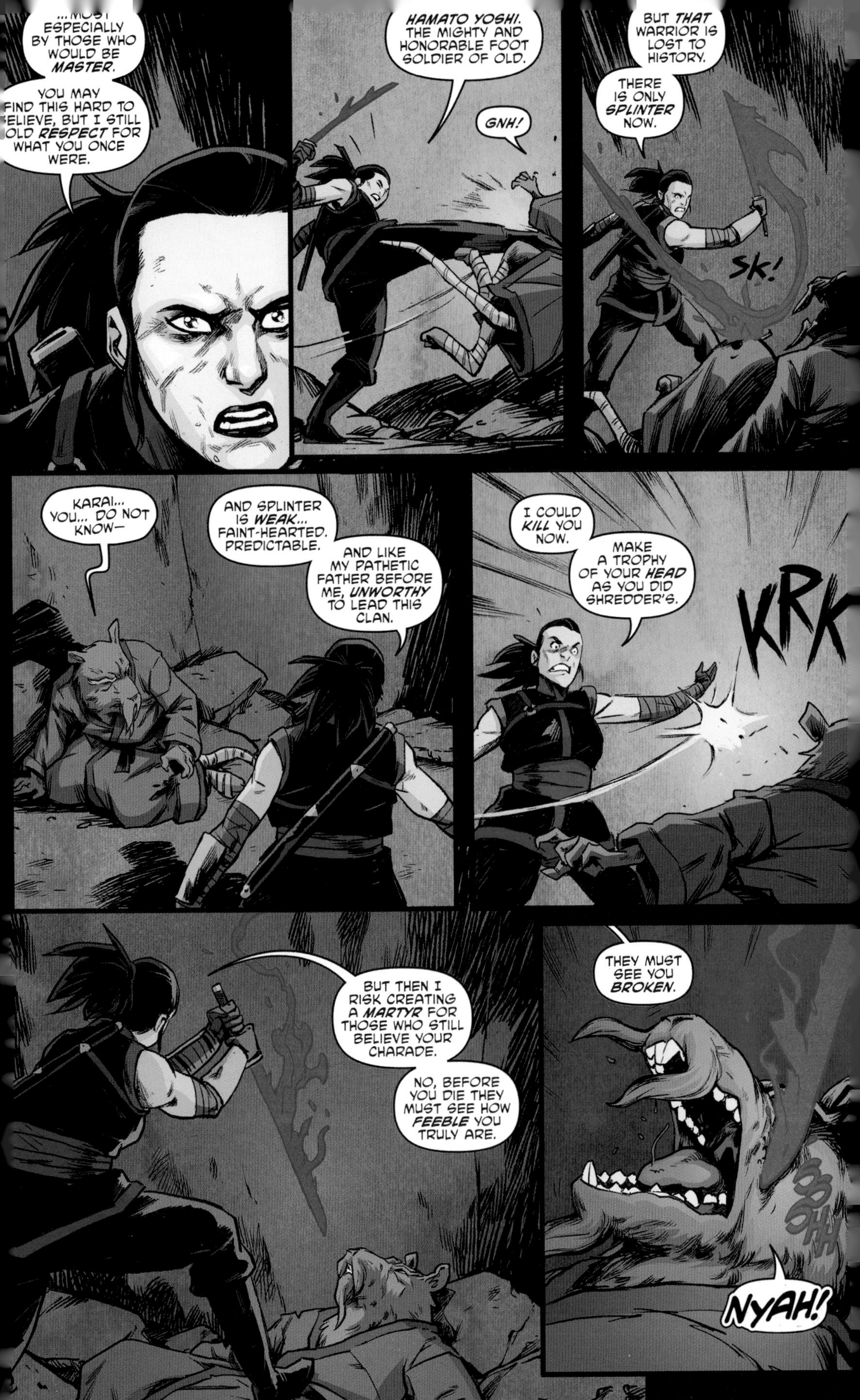
...MOST ESPECIALLY BY THOSE WHO WOULD BE MASTER.
YOU MAY FIND THIS HARD TO BELIEVE, BUT I STILL HOLD RESPECT FOR WHAT YOU ONCE WERE.
HAMATO YOSHI. THE MIGHTY AND HONORABLE FOOT SOLDIER OF OLD.
GNH!
BUT THAT WARRIOR IS LOST TO HISTORY.
THERE IS ONLY SPLINTER NOW.
SK!
KARAI... YOU... DO NOT KNOW—
AND SPLINTER IS WEAK... FAINT-HEARTED. PREDICTABLE.
AND LIKE MY PATHETIC FATHER BEFORE ME, UNWORTHY TO LEAD THIS CLAN.
I COULD KILL YOU NOW.
MAKE A TROPHY OF YOUR HEAD AS YOU DID SHREDDER'S.
KRK
BUT THEN I RISK CREATING A MARTYR FOR THOSE WHO STILL BELIEVE YOUR CHARADE.
NO, BEFORE YOU DIE THEY MUST SEE HOW FEEBLE YOU TRULY ARE.
THEY MUST SEE YOU BROKEN.
NYAH!

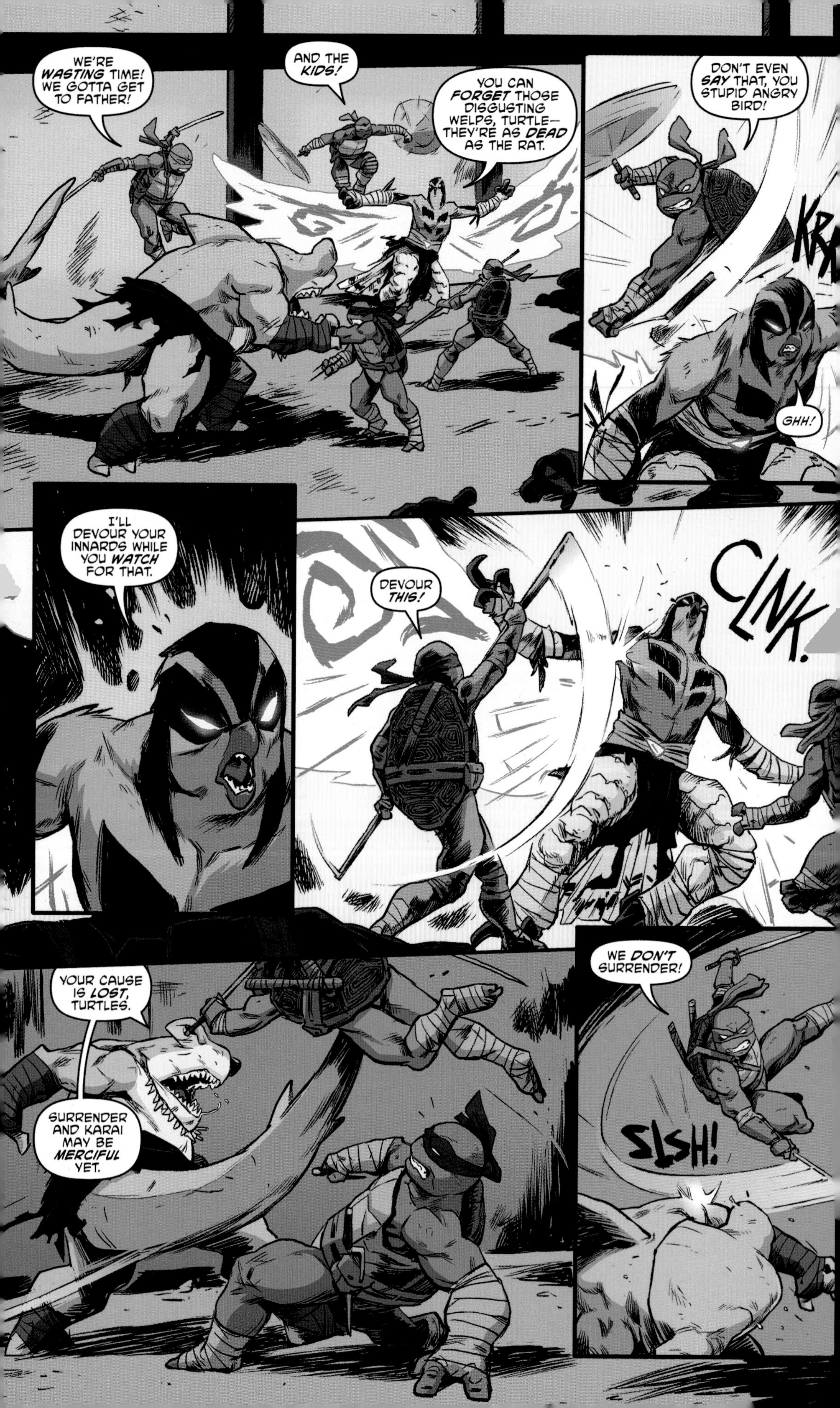
WE'RE WASTING TIME! WE GOTTA GET TO FATHER!
AND THE KIDS!
YOU CAN FORGET THOSE DISGUSTING WELPS, TURTLE— THEY'RE AS DEAD AS THE RAT.
DON'T EVEN SAY THAT, YOU STUPID ANGRY BIRD!
GHH!
I'LL DEVOUR YOUR INNARDS WHILE YOU WATCH FOR THAT.
DEVOUR THIS!
CLINK.
YOUR CAUSE IS LOST, TURTLES.
SURRENDER AND KARAI MAY BE MERCIFUL YET.
WE DON'T SURRENDER!
SLISH!

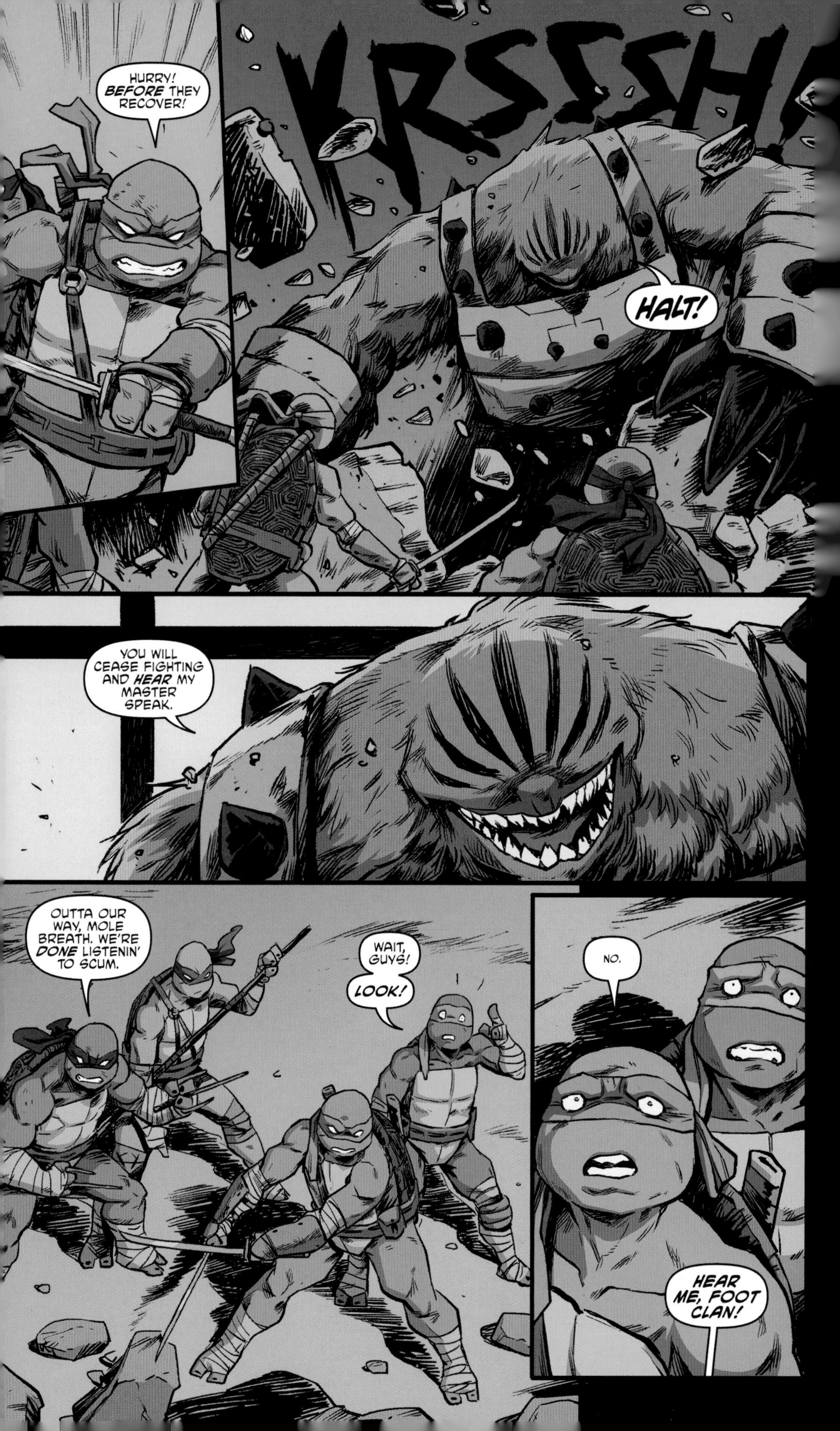
HURRY! BEFORE THEY RECOVER!
KRSSH!
HALT!
YOU WILL CEASE FIGHTING AND HEAR MY MASTER SPEAK.
OUTTA OUR WAY, MOLE BREATH. WE'RE DONE LISTENIN' TO SCUM.
WAIT, GUYS!
LOOK!
NO.
HEAR ME, FOOT CLAN!

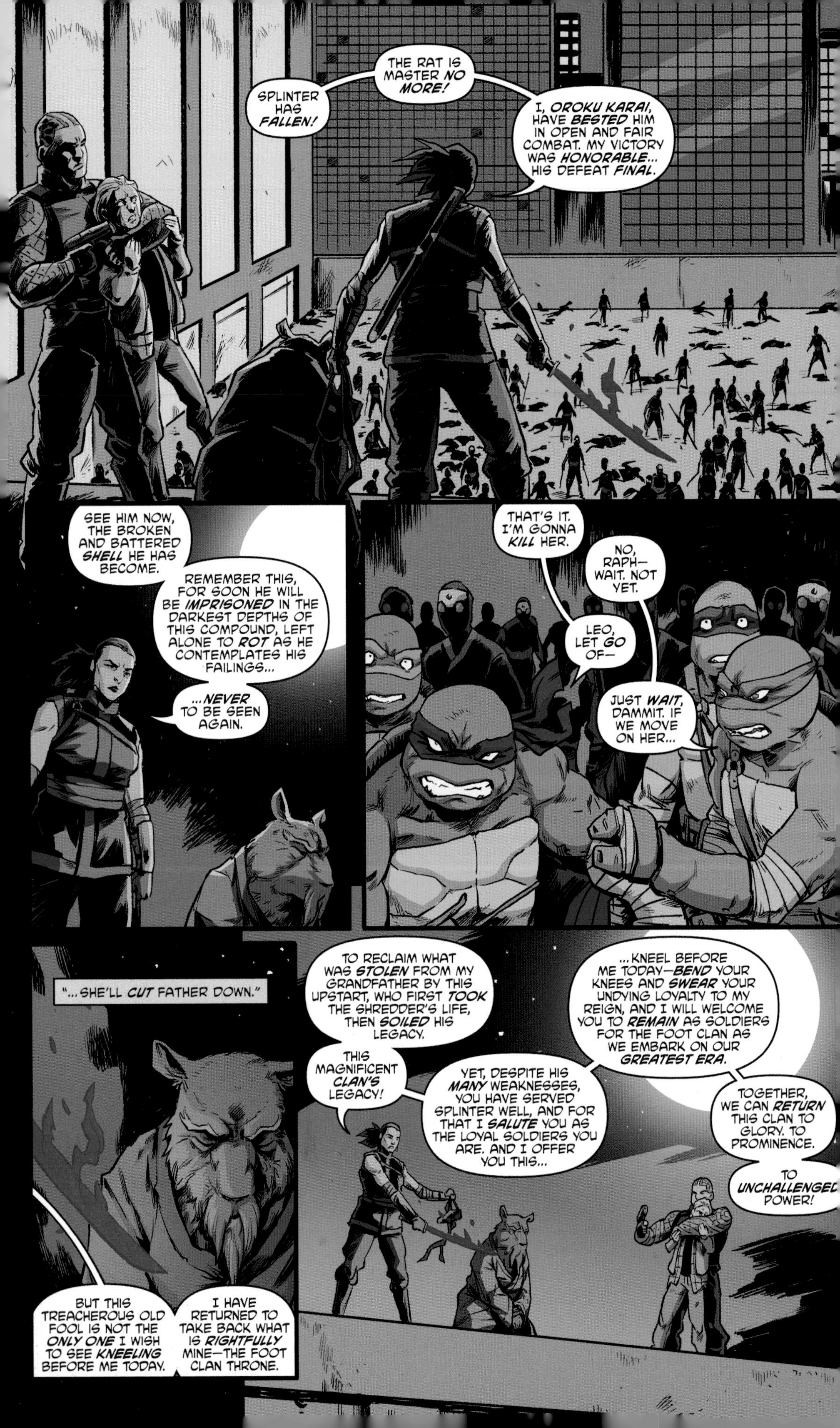
SPLINTER HAS FALLEN!
THE RAT IS MASTER NO MORE!
I, OROKU KARAI, HAVE BESTED HIM IN OPEN AND FAIR COMBAT. MY VICTORY WAS HONORABLE... HIS DEFEAT FINAL.
SEE HIM NOW, THE BROKEN AND BATTERED SHELL HE HAS BECOME.
REMEMBER THIS, FOR SOON HE WILL BE IMPRISONED IN THE DARKEST DEPTHS OF THIS COMPOUND, LEFT ALONE TO ROT AS HE CONTEMPLATES HIS FAILINGS...
...NEVER TO BE SEEN AGAIN.
THAT'S IT. I'M GONNA KILL HER.
NO, RAPH— WAIT. NOT YET.
LEO, LET GO OF—
JUST WAIT, DAMMIT. IF WE MOVE ON HER...
"...SHE'LL CUT FATHER DOWN."
BUT THIS TREACHEROUS OLD FOOL IS NOT THE ONLY ONE I WISH TO SEE KNEELING BEFORE ME TODAY.
I HAVE RETURNED TO TAKE BACK WHAT IS RIGHTFULLY MINE—THE FOOT CLAN THRONE.
TO RECLAIM WHAT WAS STOLEN FROM MY GRANDFATHER BY THIS UPSTART, WHO FIRST TOOK THE SHREDDER'S LIFE, THEN SOILED HIS LEGACY.
THIS MAGNIFICENT CLAN'S LEGACY!
YET, DESPITE HIS MANY WEAKNESSES, YOU HAVE SERVED SPLINTER WELL, AND FOR THAT I SALUTE YOU AS THE LOYAL SOLDIERS YOU ARE. AND I OFFER YOU THIS...
...KNEEL BEFORE ME TODAY—BEND YOUR KNEES AND SWEAR YOUR UNDYING LOYALTY TO MY REIGN, AND I WILL WELCOME YOU TO REMAIN AS SOLDIERS FOR THE FOOT CLAN AS WE EMBARK ON OUR GREATEST ERA.
TOGETHER, WE CAN RETURN THIS CLAN TO GLORY. TO PROMINENCE.
TO UNCHALLENGED POWER!

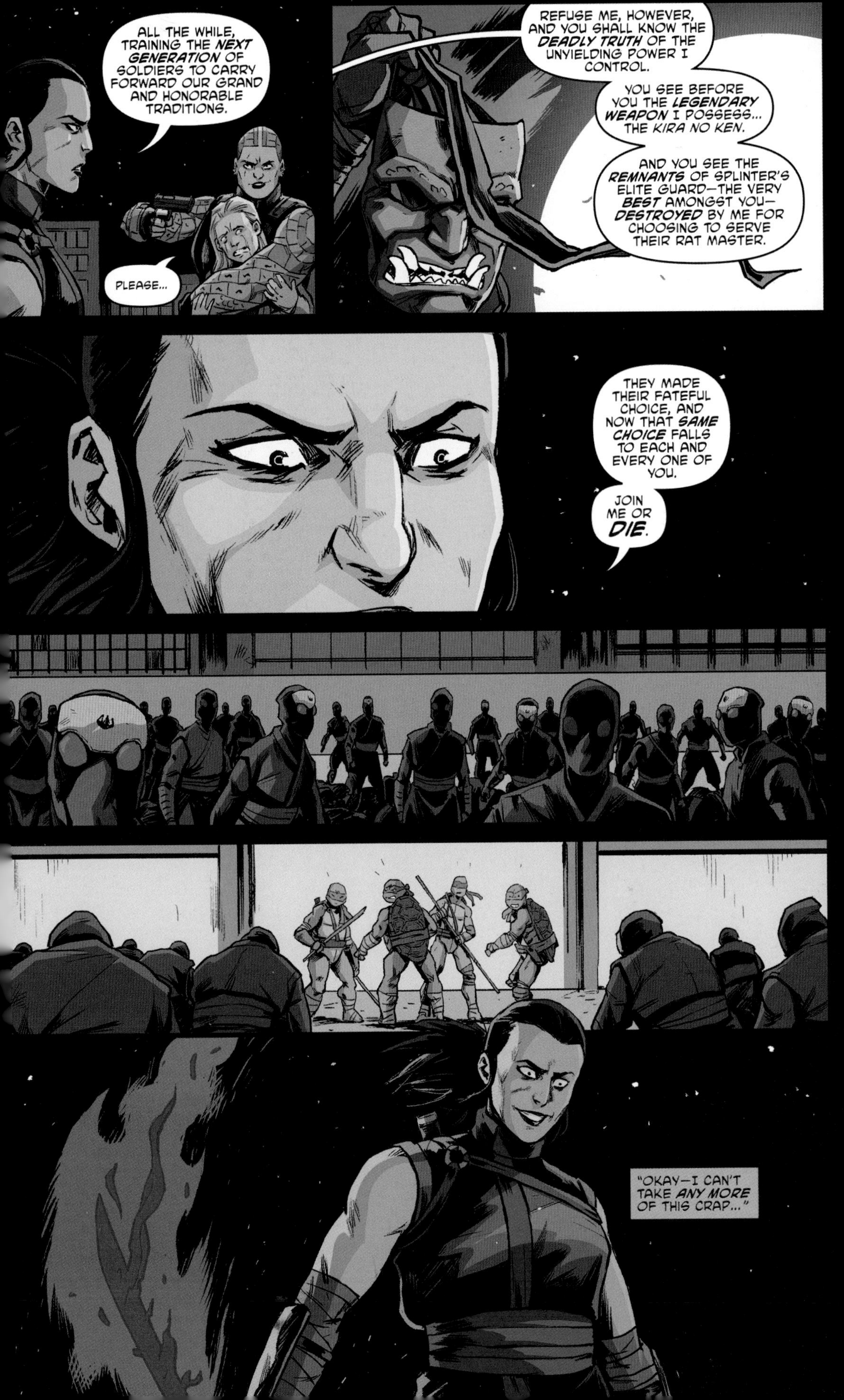
ALL THE WHILE, TRAINING THE NEXT GENERATION OF SOLDIERS TO CARRY FORWARD OUR GRAND AND HONORABLE TRADITIONS.
PLEASE...
REFUSE ME, HOWEVER, AND YOU SHALL KNOW THE DEADLY TRUTH OF THE UNYIELDING POWER I CONTROL.
YOU SEE BEFORE YOU THE LEGENDARY WEAPON I POSSESS... THE KIRA NO KEN.
AND YOU SEE THE REMNANTS OF SPLINTER'S ELITE GUARD—THE VERY BEST AMONGST YOU—DESTROYED BY ME FOR CHOOSING TO SERVE THEIR RAT MASTER.
THEY MADE THEIR FATEFUL CHOICE, AND NOW THAT SAME CHOICE FALLS TO EACH AND EVERY ONE OF YOU.
JOIN ME OR DIE.
"OKAY—I CAN'T TAKE ANY MORE OF THIS CRAP..."

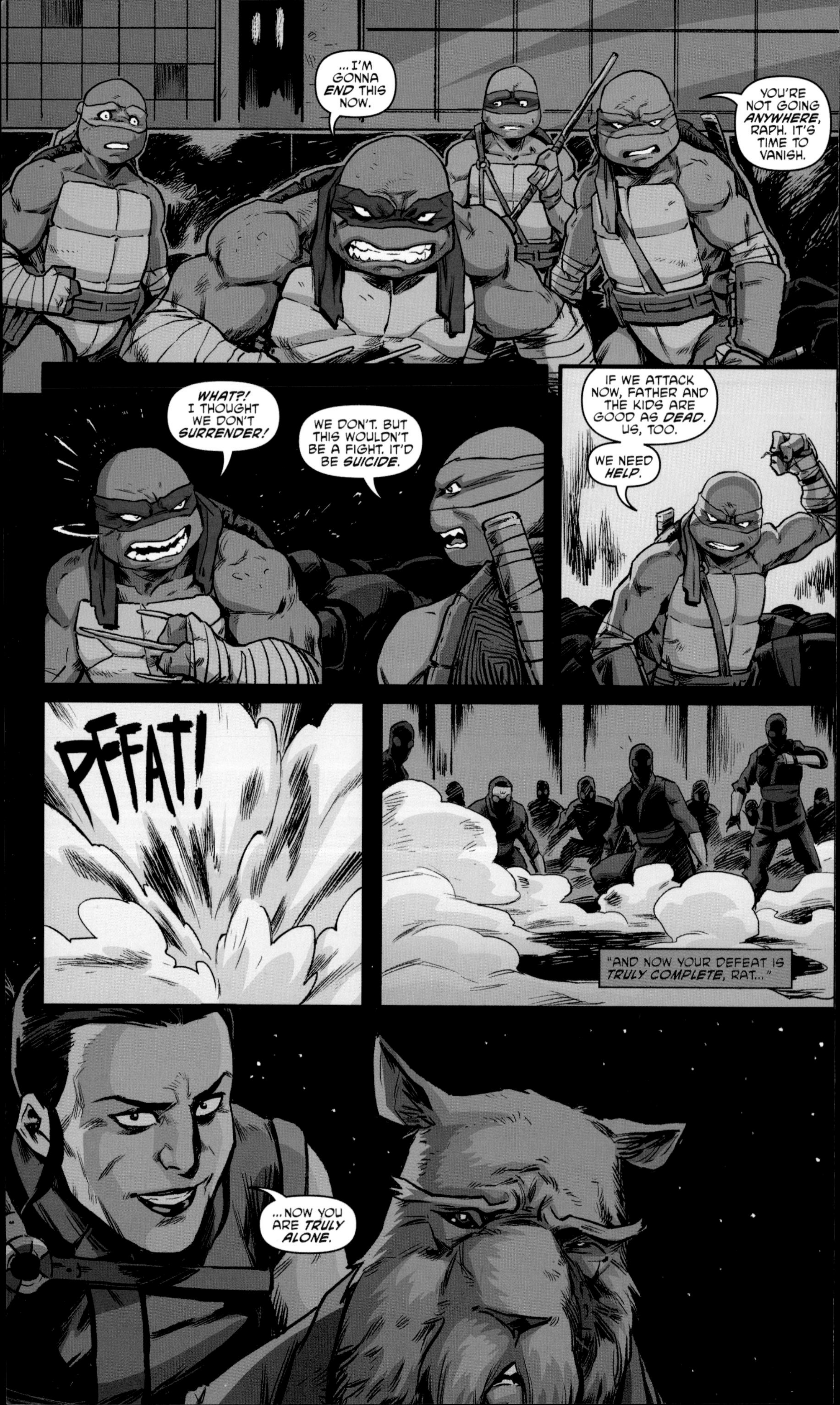

...I'M GONNA END THIS NOW.
YOU'RE NOT GOING ANYWHERE, RAPH. IT'S TIME TO VANISH.
WHAT?! I THOUGHT WE DON'T SURRENDER!
WE DON'T. BUT THIS WOULDN'T BE A FIGHT. IT'D BE SUICIDE.
IF WE ATTACK NOW, FATHER AND THE KIDS ARE GOOD AS DEAD. US, TOO.
WE NEED HELP.
PFFAT!
"AND NOW YOUR DEFEAT IS TRULY COMPLETE, RAT..."
...NOW YOU ARE TRULY ALONE.

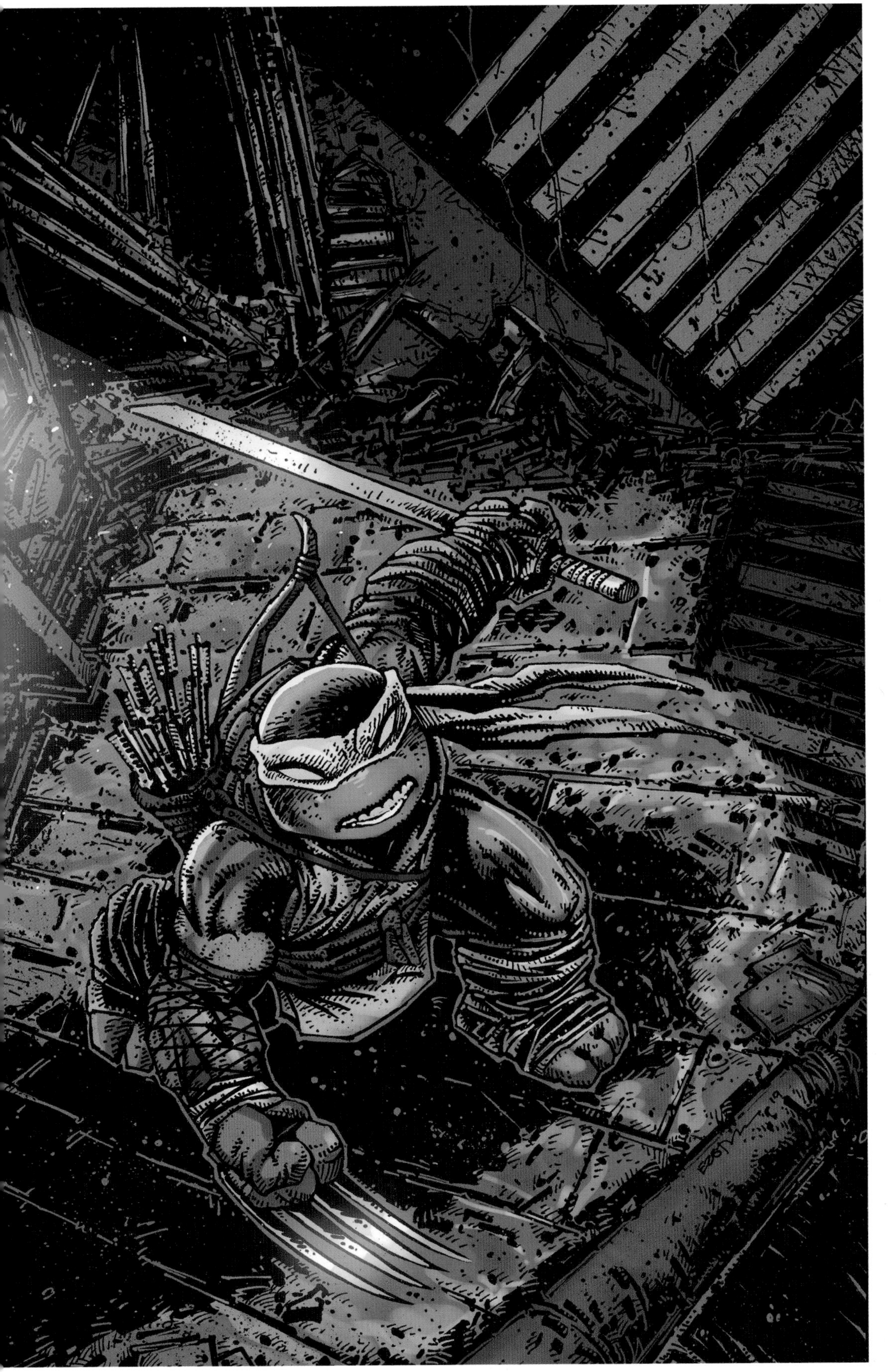

ART BY KEVIN EASTMAN · COLORS BY FAHRIZA KAMAPUTRA

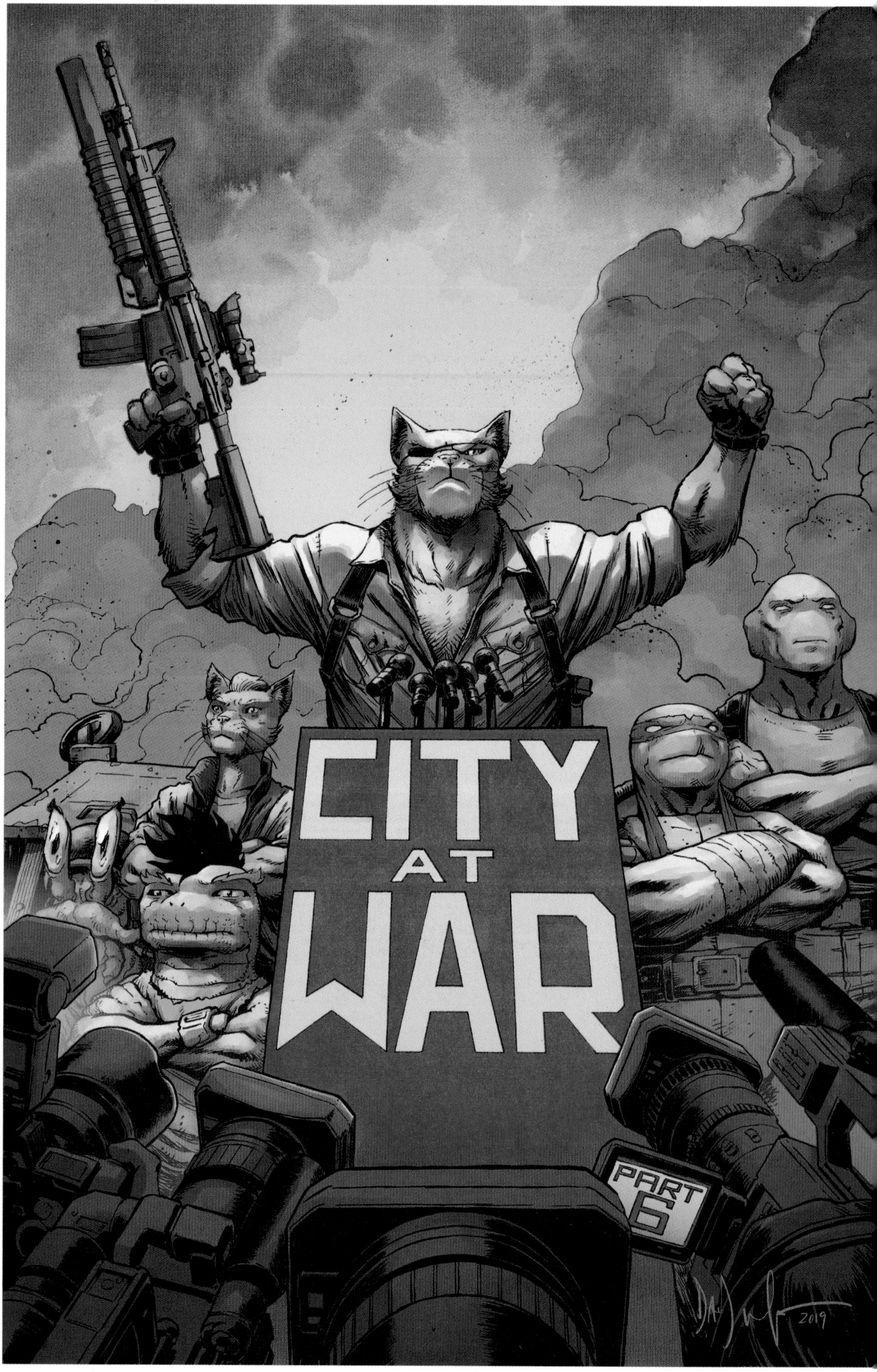
CITY
AT
WAR
PART
6
2019

ART BY DAVE WACHTER

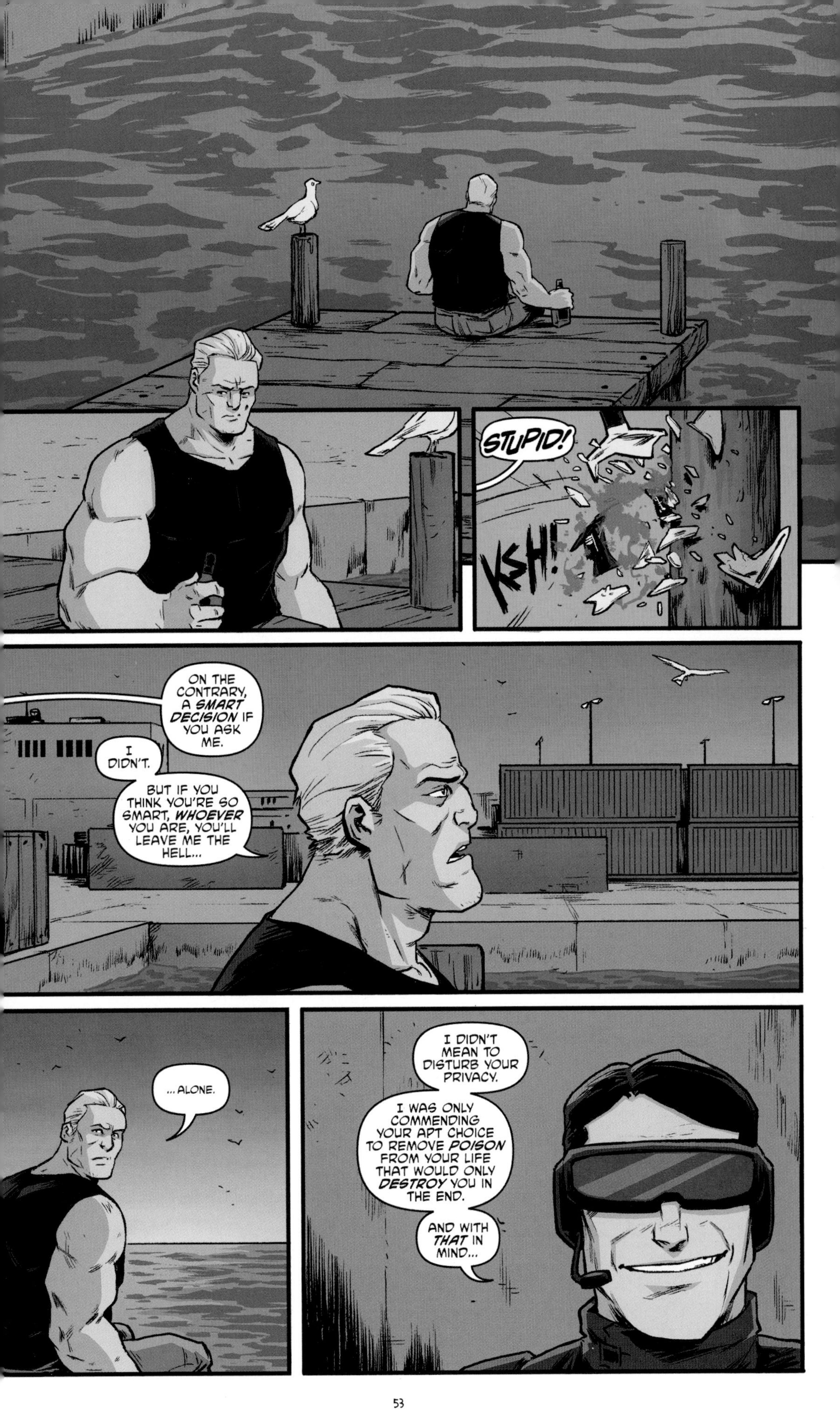
STUPID!
KSH!
ON THE CONTRARY, A SMART DECISION IF YOU ASK ME.
I DIDN'T.
BUT IF YOU THINK YOU'RE SO SMART, WHOEVER YOU ARE, YOU'LL LEAVE ME THE HELL...
...ALONE.
I DIDN'T MEAN TO DISTURB YOUR PRIVACY.
I WAS ONLY COMMENDING YOUR APT CHOICE TO REMOVE POISON FROM YOUR LIFE THAT WOULD ONLY DESTROY YOU IN THE END.
AND WITH THAT IN MIND...

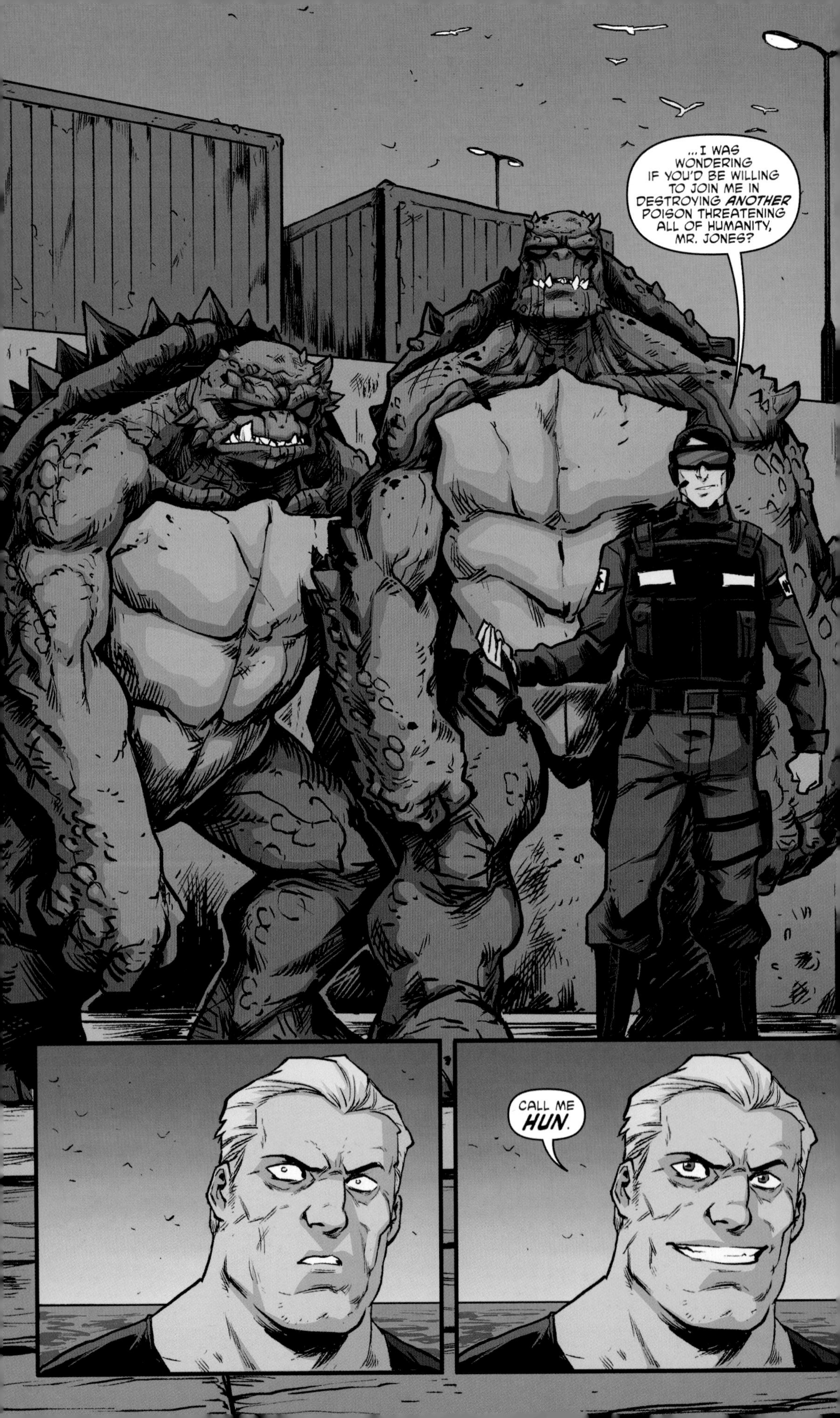
...I WAS WONDERING IF YOU'D BE WILLING TO JOIN ME IN DESTROYING *ANOTHER* POISON THREATENING ALL OF HUMANITY, MR. JONES?
CALL ME *HUN*.

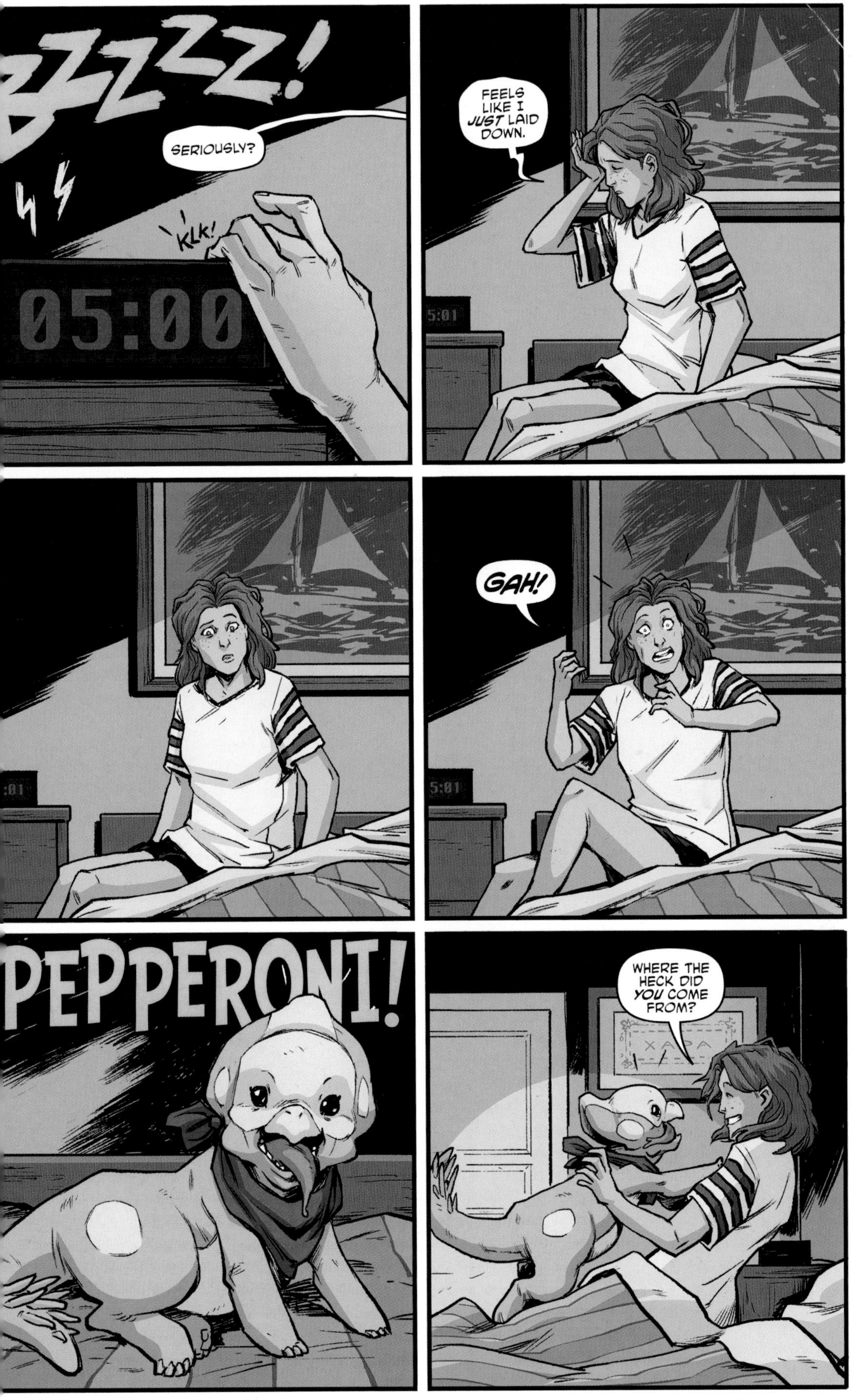
BZZZZ!
SERIOUSLY?
KLK!
05:00
FEELS LIKE I JUST LAID DOWN.
5:01
:01
GAH!
5:01
PEPPERONI!
WHERE THE HECK DID YOU COME FROM?

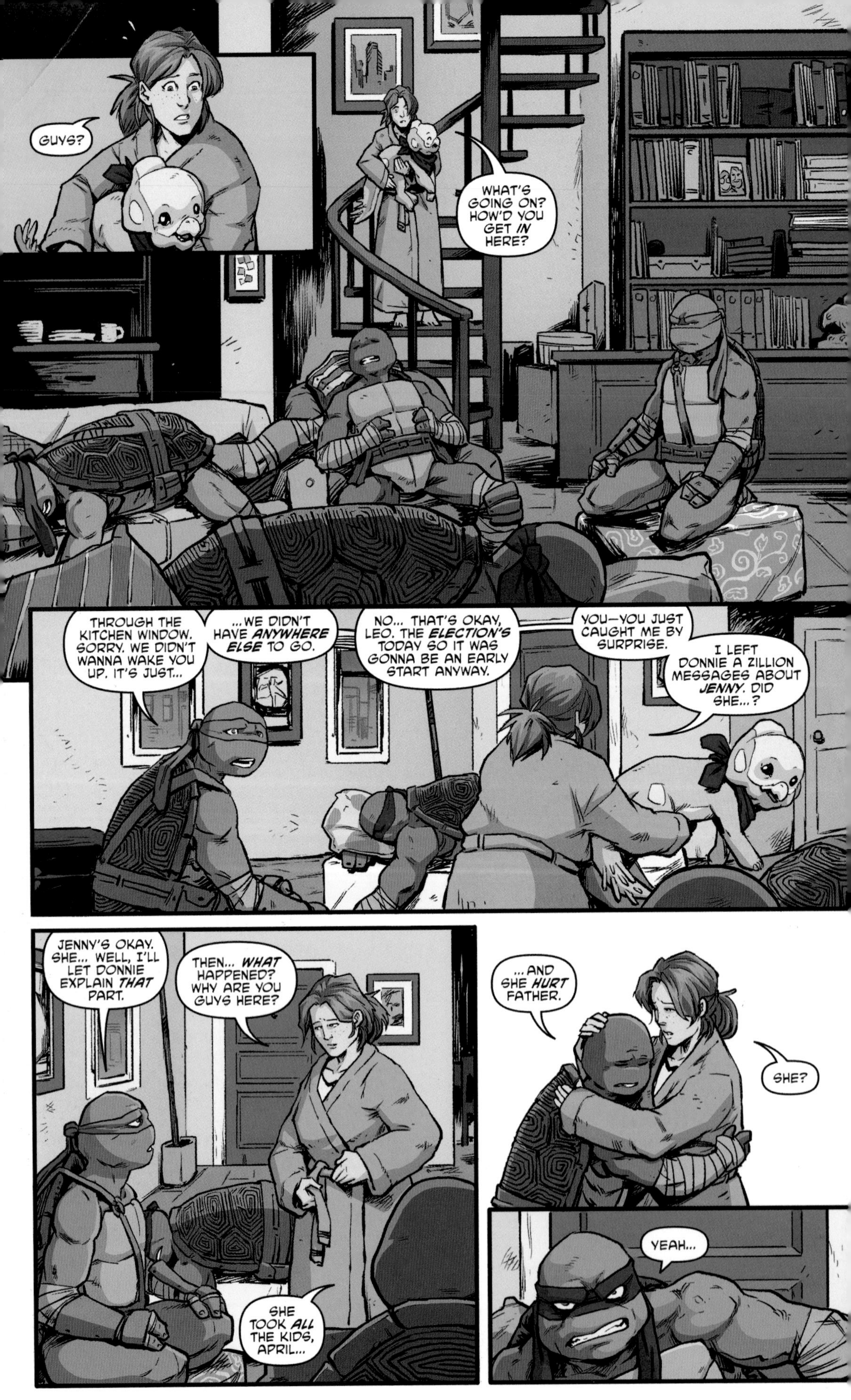
GUYS?
WHAT'S GOING ON? HOW'D YOU GET *IN* HERE?
THROUGH THE KITCHEN WINDOW. SORRY. WE DIDN'T WANNA WAKE YOU UP. IT'S JUST...
...WE DIDN'T HAVE *ANYWHERE ELSE* TO GO.
NO... THAT'S OKAY, LEO. THE *ELECTION'S* TODAY SO IT WAS GONNA BE AN EARLY START ANYWAY.
YOU—YOU JUST CAUGHT ME BY SURPRISE.
I LEFT DONNIE A ZILLION MESSAGES ABOUT *JENNY*. DID SHE...?
JENNY'S OKAY. SHE... WELL, I'LL LET DONNIE EXPLAIN *THAT* PART.
THEN... *WHAT* HAPPENED? WHY ARE YOU GUYS HERE?
SHE TOOK *ALL* THE KIDS, APRIL...
...AND SHE *HURT* FATHER.
SHE?
YEAH...

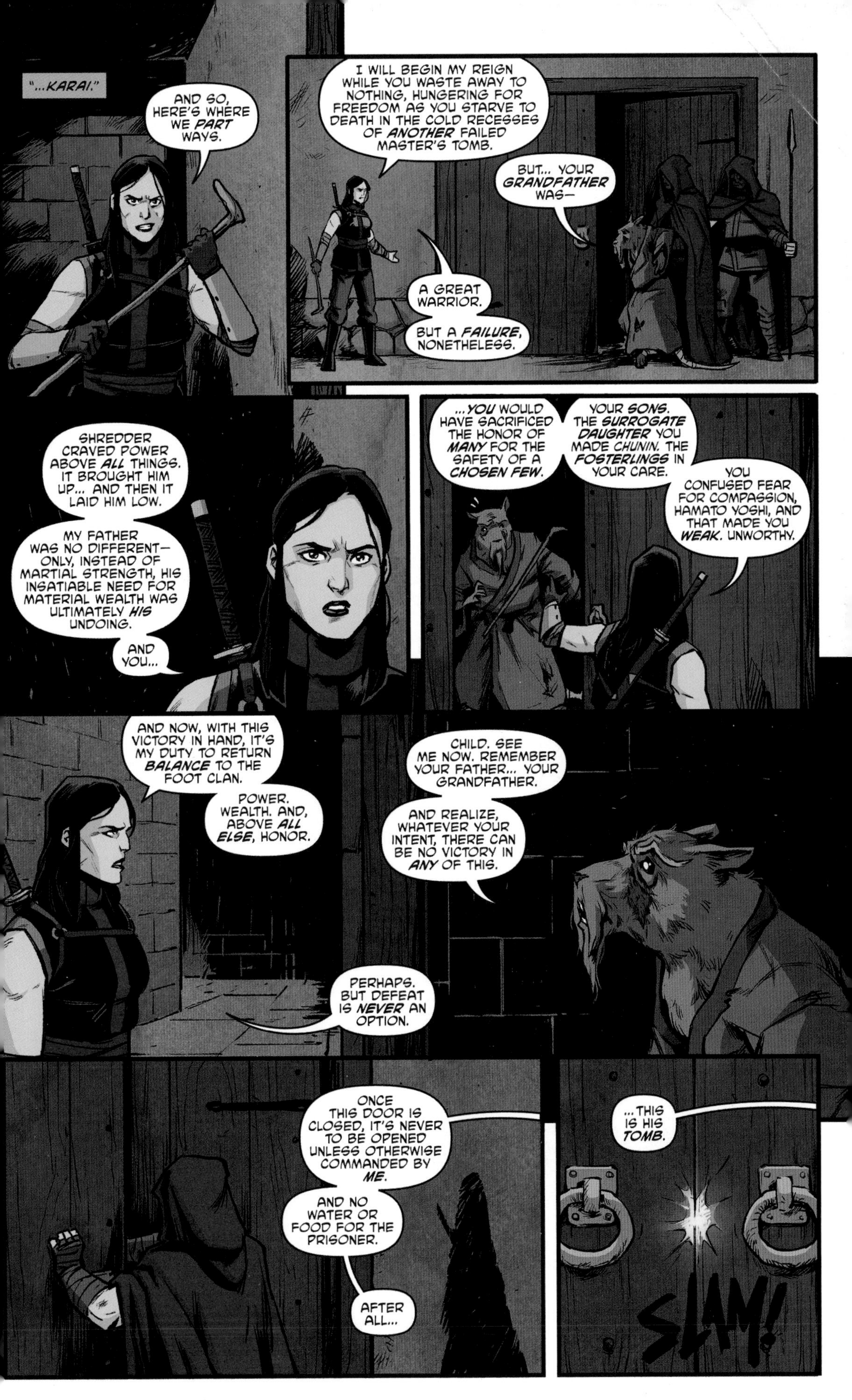
"...KARAI."
AND SO, HERE'S WHERE WE PART WAYS.
I WILL BEGIN MY REIGN WHILE YOU WASTE AWAY TO NOTHING, HUNGERING FOR FREEDOM AS YOU STARVE TO DEATH IN THE COLD RECESSES OF ANOTHER FAILED MASTER'S TOMB.
BUT... YOUR GRANDFATHER WAS—
A GREAT WARRIOR.
BUT A FAILURE, NONETHELESS.
SHREDDER CRAVED POWER ABOVE ALL THINGS. IT BROUGHT HIM UP... AND THEN IT LAID HIM LOW.
MY FATHER WAS NO DIFFERENT— ONLY, INSTEAD OF MARTIAL STRENGTH, HIS INSATIABLE NEED FOR MATERIAL WEALTH WAS ULTIMATELY HIS UNDOING.
AND YOU...
...YOU WOULD HAVE SACRIFICED THE HONOR OF MANY FOR THE SAFETY OF A CHOSEN FEW.
YOUR SONS. THE SURROGATE DAUGHTER YOU MADE CHUNIN. THE FOSTERLINGS IN YOUR CARE.
YOU CONFUSED FEAR FOR COMPASSION, HAMATO YOSHI, AND THAT MADE YOU WEAK. UNWORTHY.
AND NOW, WITH THIS VICTORY IN HAND, IT'S MY DUTY TO RETURN BALANCE TO THE FOOT CLAN.
POWER. WEALTH. AND, ABOVE ALL ELSE, HONOR.
CHILD. SEE ME NOW. REMEMBER YOUR FATHER... YOUR GRANDFATHER.
AND REALIZE, WHATEVER YOUR INTENT, THERE CAN BE NO VICTORY IN ANY OF THIS.
PERHAPS. BUT DEFEAT IS NEVER AN OPTION.
ONCE THIS DOOR IS CLOSED, IT'S NEVER TO BE OPENED UNLESS OTHERWISE COMMANDED BY ME.
AND NO WATER OR FOOD FOR THE PRISONER.
AFTER ALL...
...THIS IS HIS TOMB.
SLAM!

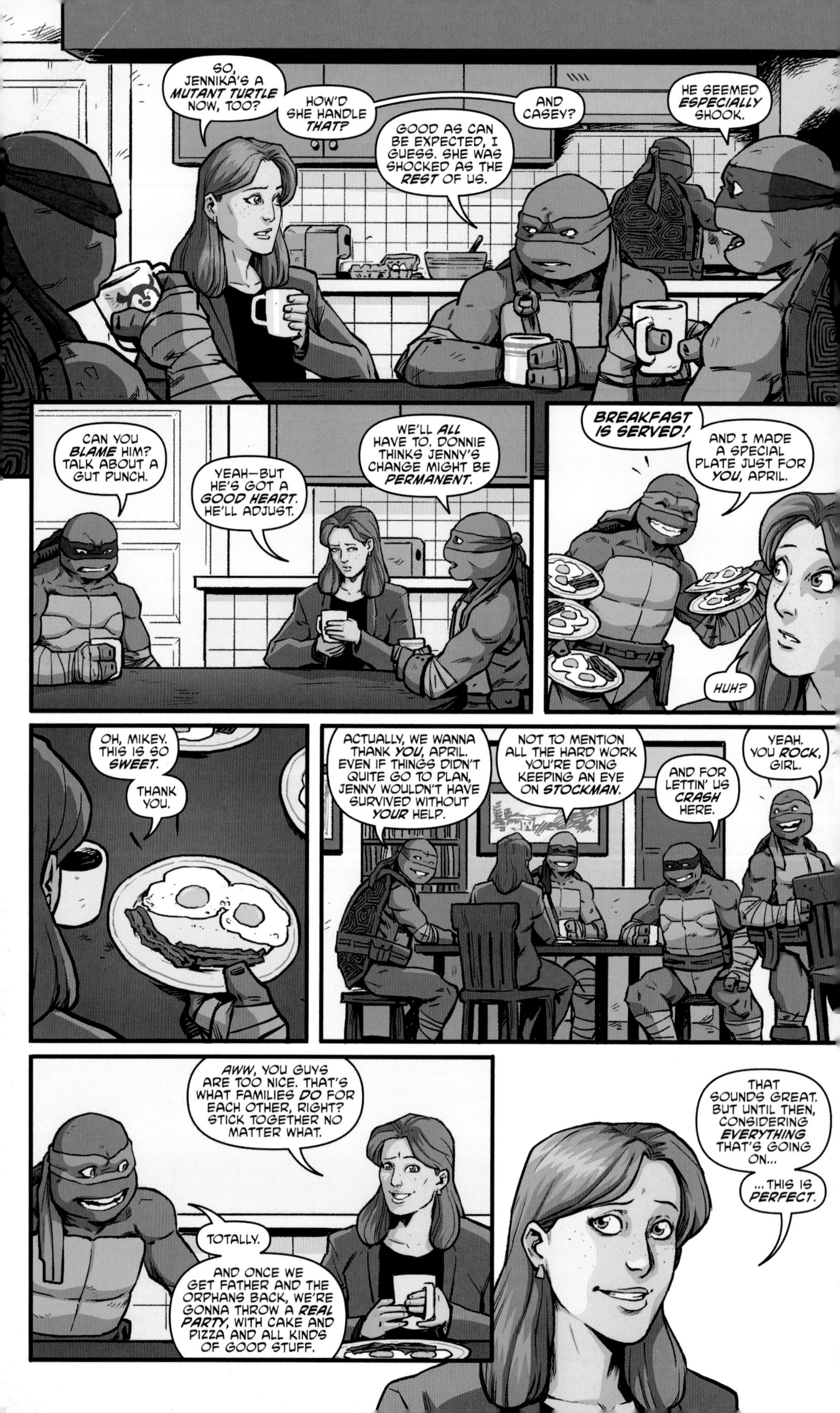

SO, JENNIKA'S A MUTANT TURTLE NOW, TOO?
HOW'D SHE HANDLE THAT?
GOOD AS CAN BE EXPECTED, I GUESS. SHE WAS SHOCKED AS THE REST OF US.
AND CASEY?
HE SEEMED ESPECIALLY SHOOK.
CAN YOU BLAME HIM? TALK ABOUT A GUT PUNCH.
YEAH—BUT HE'S GOT A GOOD HEART. HE'LL ADJUST.
WE'LL ALL HAVE TO. DONNIE THINKS JENNY'S CHANGE MIGHT BE PERMANENT.
BREAKFAST IS SERVED!
AND I MADE A SPECIAL PLATE JUST FOR YOU, APRIL.
HUH?
OH, MIKEY. THIS IS SO SWEET.
THANK YOU.
ACTUALLY, WE WANNA THANK YOU, APRIL. EVEN IF THINGS DIDN'T QUITE GO TO PLAN, JENNY WOULDN'T HAVE SURVIVED WITHOUT YOUR HELP.
NOT TO MENTION ALL THE HARD WORK YOU'RE DOING KEEPING AN EYE ON STOCKMAN.
AND FOR LETTIN' US CRASH HERE.
YEAH. YOU ROCK, GIRL.
AWW, YOU GUYS ARE TOO NICE. THAT'S WHAT FAMILIES DO FOR EACH OTHER, RIGHT? STICK TOGETHER NO MATTER WHAT.
TOTALLY.
AND ONCE WE GET FATHER AND THE ORPHANS BACK, WE'RE GONNA THROW A REAL PARTY, WITH CAKE AND PIZZA AND ALL KINDS OF GOOD STUFF.
THAT SOUNDS GREAT. BUT UNTIL THEN, CONSIDERING EVERYTHING THAT'S GOING ON...
...THIS IS PERFECT.

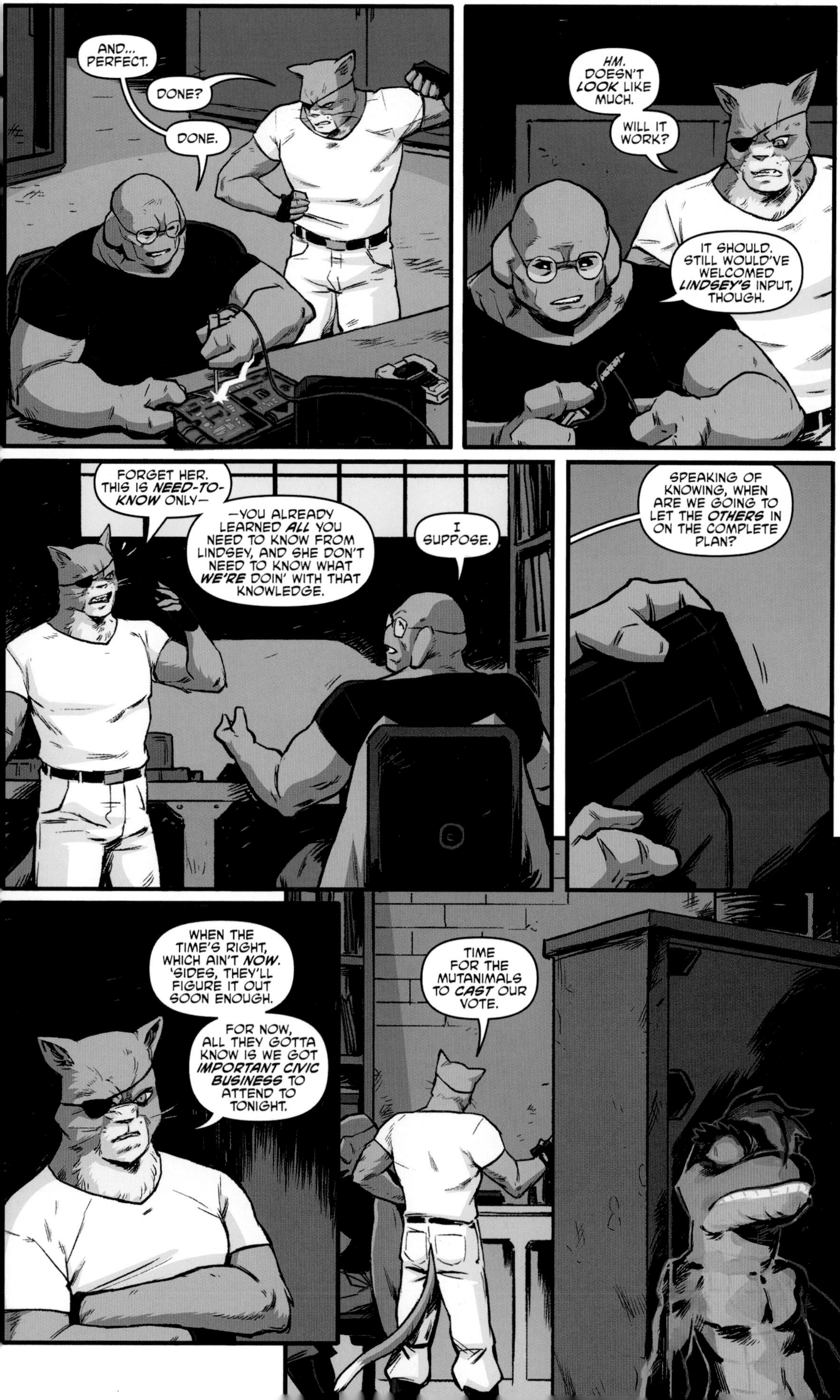
AND... PERFECT.
DONE?
DONE.
HM. DOESN'T LOOK LIKE MUCH.
WILL IT WORK?
IT SHOULD. STILL WOULD'VE WELCOMED LINDSEY'S INPUT, THOUGH.
FORGET HER. THIS IS NEED-TO-KNOW ONLY—
—YOU ALREADY LEARNED ALL YOU NEED TO KNOW FROM LINDSEY, AND SHE DON'T NEED TO KNOW WHAT WE'RE DOIN' WITH THAT KNOWLEDGE.
I SUPPOSE.
SPEAKING OF KNOWING, WHEN ARE WE GOING TO LET THE OTHERS IN ON THE COMPLETE PLAN?
WHEN THE TIME'S RIGHT, WHICH AIN'T NOW. 'SIDES, THEY'LL FIGURE IT OUT SOON ENOUGH.
FOR NOW, ALL THEY GOTTA KNOW IS WE GOT IMPORTANT CIVIC BUSINESS TO ATTEND TO TONIGHT.
TIME FOR THE MUTANIMALS TO CAST OUR VOTE.

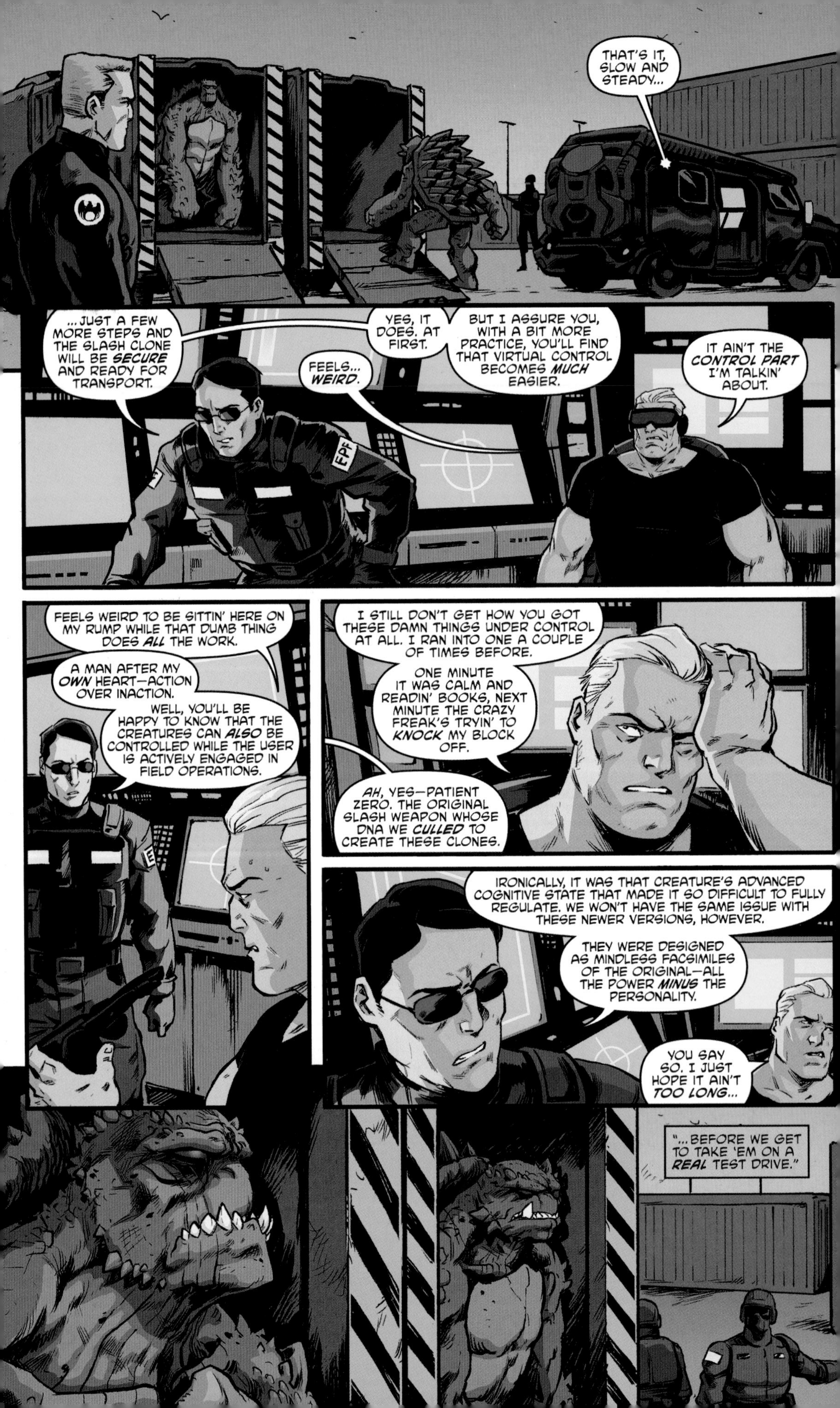
THAT'S IT, SLOW AND STEADY...
...JUST A FEW MORE STEPS AND THE SLASH CLONE WILL BE *SECURE* AND READY FOR TRANSPORT.
FEELS... *WEIRD*.
YES, IT DOES. AT FIRST.
BUT I ASSURE YOU, WITH A BIT MORE PRACTICE, YOU'LL FIND THAT VIRTUAL CONTROL BECOMES *MUCH* EASIER.
IT AIN'T THE *CONTROL PART* I'M TALKIN' ABOUT.
FEELS WEIRD TO BE SITTIN' HERE ON MY RUMP WHILE THAT DUMB THING DOES *ALL* THE WORK.
A MAN AFTER MY *OWN* HEART—ACTION OVER INACTION.
WELL, YOU'LL BE HAPPY TO KNOW THAT THE CREATURES CAN *ALSO* BE CONTROLLED WHILE THE USER IS ACTIVELY ENGAGED IN FIELD OPERATIONS.
I STILL DON'T GET HOW YOU GOT THESE DAMN THINGS UNDER CONTROL AT ALL. I RAN INTO ONE A COUPLE OF TIMES BEFORE.
ONE MINUTE IT WAS CALM AND READIN' BOOKS, NEXT MINUTE THE CRAZY FREAK'S TRYIN' TO *KNOCK* MY BLOCK OFF.
AH, YES—PATIENT ZERO. THE ORIGINAL SLASH WEAPON WHOSE DNA WE *CULLED* TO CREATE THESE CLONES.
IRONICALLY, IT WAS THAT CREATURE'S ADVANCED COGNITIVE STATE THAT MADE IT SO DIFFICULT TO FULLY REGULATE. WE WON'T HAVE THE SAME ISSUE WITH THESE NEWER VERSIONS, HOWEVER.
THEY WERE DESIGNED AS MINDLESS FACSIMILES OF THE ORIGINAL—ALL THE POWER *MINUS* THE PERSONALITY.
YOU SAY SO. I JUST HOPE IT AIN'T *TOO LONG*...
"...BEFORE WE GET TO TAKE 'EM ON A *REAL* TEST DRIVE."

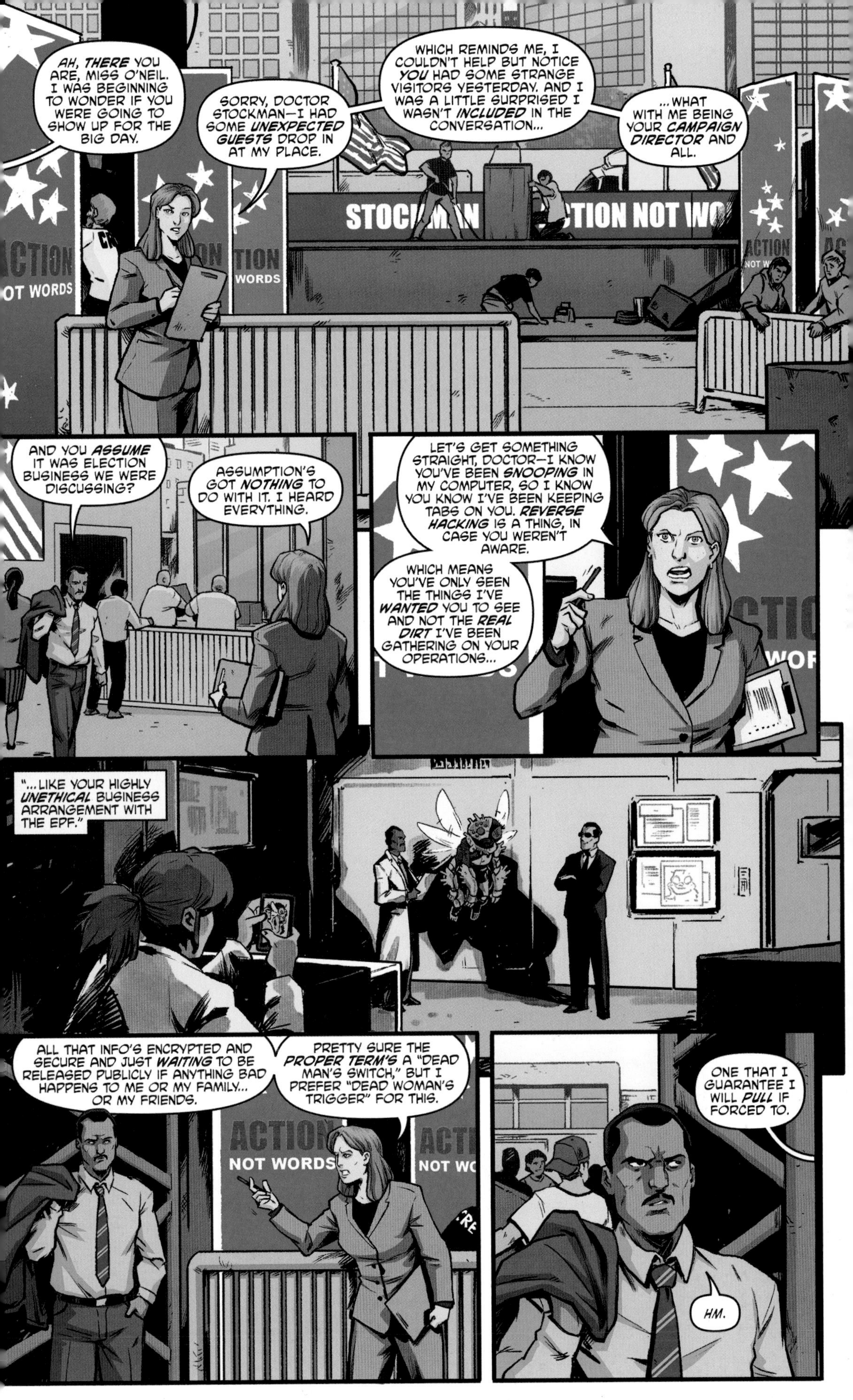
AH, THERE YOU ARE, MISS O'NEIL. I WAS BEGINNING TO WONDER IF YOU WERE GOING TO SHOW UP FOR THE BIG DAY.
SORRY, DOCTOR STOCKMAN—I HAD SOME UNEXPECTED GUESTS DROP IN AT MY PLACE.
WHICH REMINDS ME, I COULDN'T HELP BUT NOTICE YOU HAD SOME STRANGE VISITORS YESTERDAY. AND I WAS A LITTLE SURPRISED I WASN'T INCLUDED IN THE CONVERSATION...
...WHAT WITH ME BEING YOUR CAMPAIGN DIRECTOR AND ALL.
AND YOU ASSUME IT WAS ELECTION BUSINESS WE WERE DISCUSSING?
ASSUMPTION'S GOT NOTHING TO DO WITH IT. I HEARD EVERYTHING.
LET'S GET SOMETHING STRAIGHT, DOCTOR—I KNOW YOU'VE BEEN SNOOPING IN MY COMPUTER, SO I KNOW YOU KNOW I'VE BEEN KEEPING TABS ON YOU. REVERSE HACKING IS A THING, IN CASE YOU WEREN'T AWARE.
WHICH MEANS YOU'VE ONLY SEEN THE THINGS I'VE WANTED YOU TO SEE AND NOT THE REAL DIRT I'VE BEEN GATHERING ON YOUR OPERATIONS...
"...LIKE YOUR HIGHLY UNETHICAL BUSINESS ARRANGEMENT WITH THE EPF."
ALL THAT INFO'S ENCRYPTED AND SECURE AND JUST WAITING TO BE RELEASED PUBLICLY IF ANYTHING BAD HAPPENS TO ME OR MY FAMILY... OR MY FRIENDS.
PRETTY SURE THE PROPER TERM'S A "DEAD MAN'S SWITCH," BUT I PREFER "DEAD WOMAN'S TRIGGER" FOR THIS.
ONE THAT I GUARANTEE I WILL PULL IF FORCED TO.
HM.

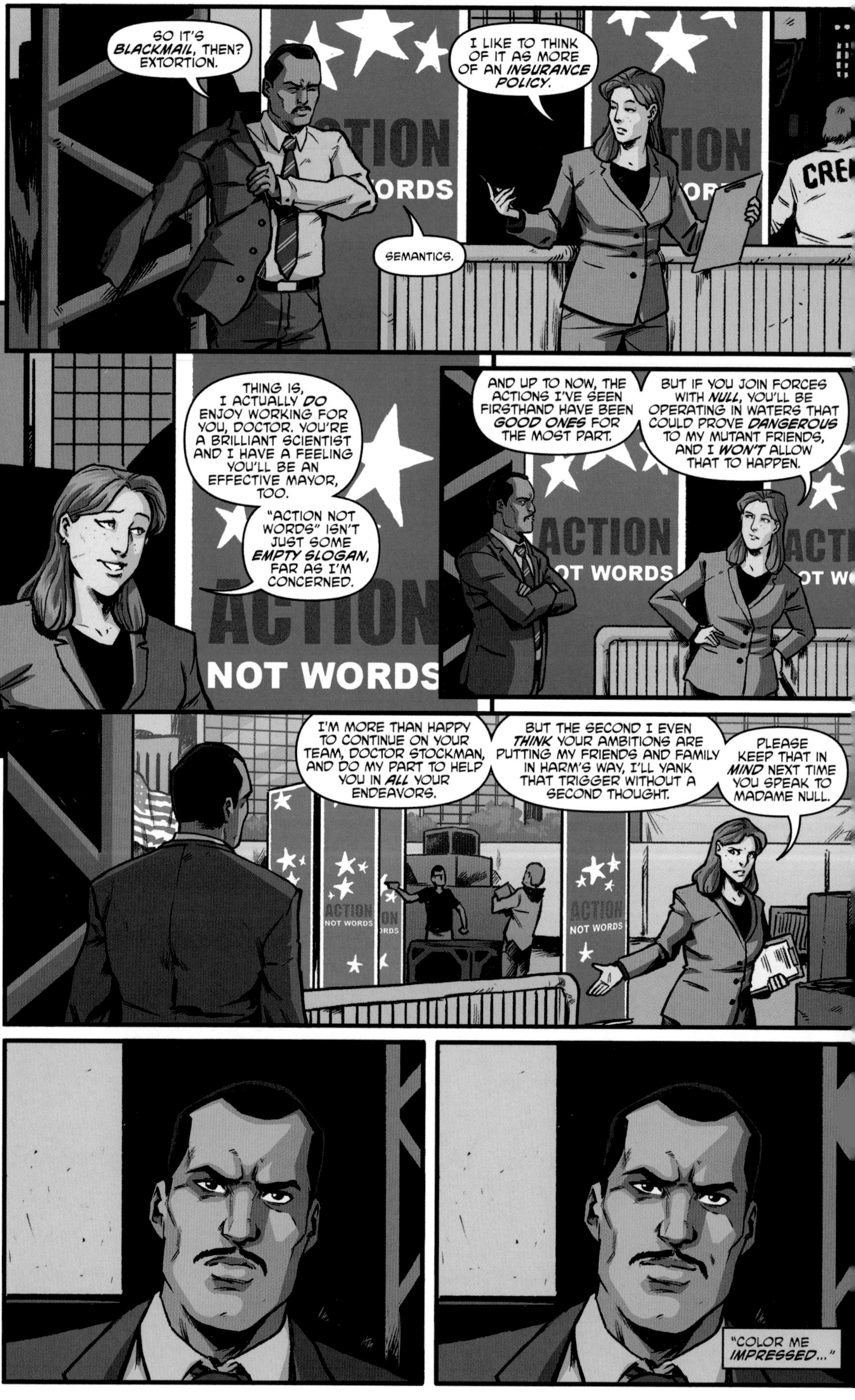

SO IT'S BLACKMAIL, THEN? EXTORTION.
I LIKE TO THINK OF IT AS MORE OF AN INSURANCE POLICY.
SEMANTICS.
ACTION NOT WORDS
THING IS, I ACTUALLY DO ENJOY WORKING FOR YOU, DOCTOR. YOU'RE A BRILLIANT SCIENTIST AND I HAVE A FEELING YOU'LL BE AN EFFECTIVE MAYOR, TOO.
"ACTION NOT WORDS" ISN'T JUST SOME EMPTY SLOGAN, FAR AS I'M CONCERNED.
AND UP TO NOW, THE ACTIONS I'VE SEEN FIRSTHAND HAVE BEEN GOOD ONES FOR THE MOST PART.
BUT IF YOU JOIN FORCES WITH NULL, YOU'LL BE OPERATING IN WATERS THAT COULD PROVE DANGEROUS TO MY MUTANT FRIENDS, AND I WON'T ALLOW THAT TO HAPPEN.
I'M MORE THAN HAPPY TO CONTINUE ON YOUR TEAM, DOCTOR STOCKMAN, AND DO MY PART TO HELP YOU IN ALL YOUR ENDEAVORS.
BUT THE SECOND I EVEN THINK YOUR AMBITIONS ARE PUTTING MY FRIENDS AND FAMILY IN HARM'S WAY, I'LL YANK THAT TRIGGER WITHOUT A SECOND THOUGHT.
PLEASE KEEP THAT IN MIND NEXT TIME YOU SPEAK TO MADAME NULL.
"COLOR ME IMPRESSED..."

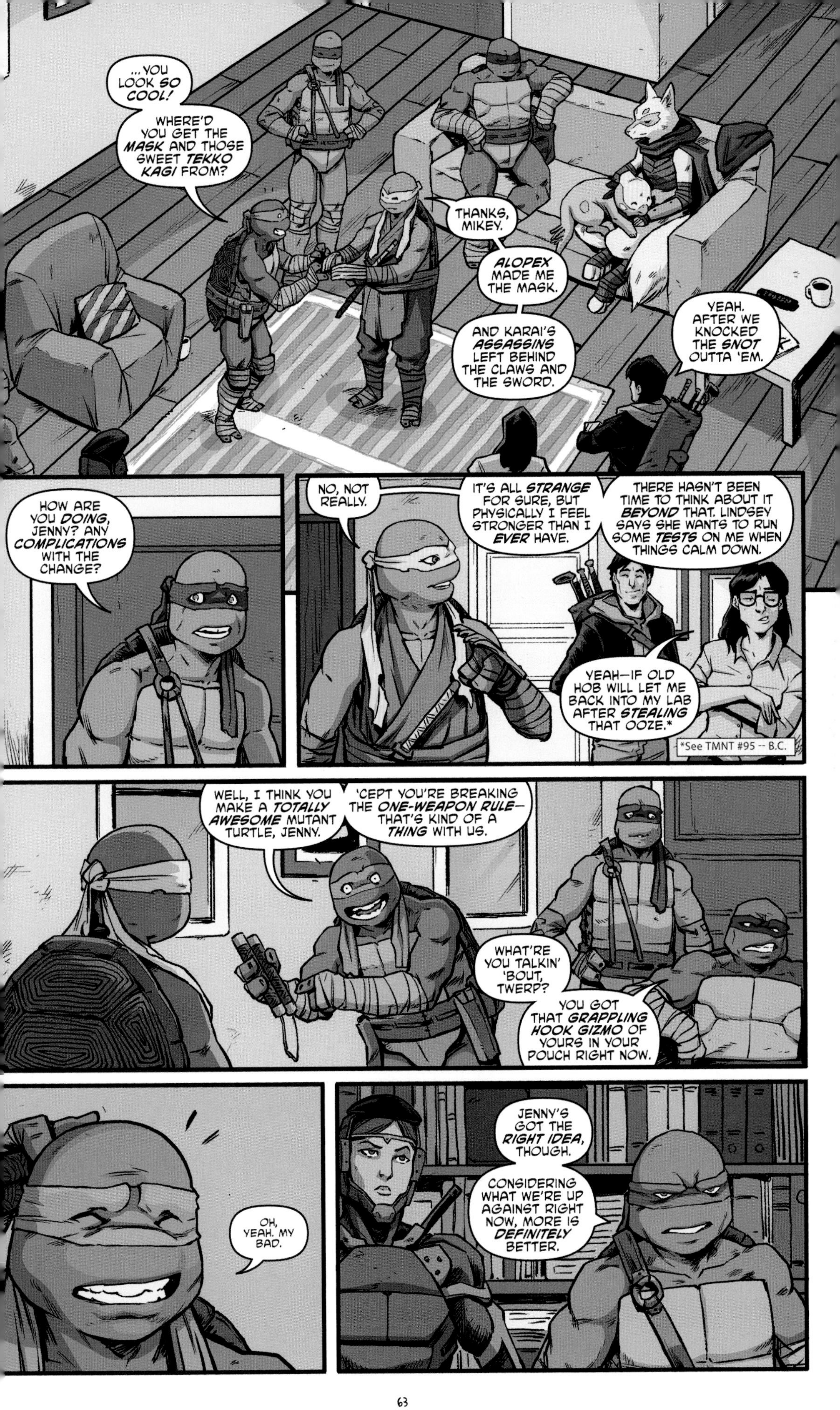

...YOU LOOK SO COOL!
WHERE'D YOU GET THE MASK AND THOSE SWEET TEKKO KAGI FROM?
THANKS, MIKEY.
ALOPEX MADE ME THE MASK.
AND KARAI'S ASSASSINS LEFT BEHIND THE CLAWS AND THE SWORD.
YEAH. AFTER WE KNOCKED THE SNOT OUTTA 'EM.
HOW ARE YOU DOING, JENNY? ANY COMPLICATIONS WITH THE CHANGE?
NO, NOT REALLY.
IT'S ALL STRANGE FOR SURE, BUT PHYSICALLY I FEEL STRONGER THAN I EVER HAVE.
THERE HASN'T BEEN TIME TO THINK ABOUT IT BEYOND THAT. LINDSEY SAYS SHE WANTS TO RUN SOME TESTS ON ME WHEN THINGS CALM DOWN.
YEAH—IF OLD HOB WILL LET ME BACK INTO MY LAB AFTER STEALING THAT OOZE.*
*See TMNT #95 -- B.C.
WELL, I THINK YOU MAKE A TOTALLY AWESOME MUTANT TURTLE, JENNY.
'CEPT YOU'RE BREAKING THE ONE-WEAPON RULE—THAT'S KIND OF A THING WITH US.
WHAT'RE YOU TALKIN' 'BOUT, TWERP?
YOU GOT THAT GRAPPLING HOOK GIZMO OF YOURS IN YOUR POUCH RIGHT NOW.
OH, YEAH. MY BAD.
JENNY'S GOT THE RIGHT IDEA, THOUGH.
CONSIDERING WHAT WE'RE UP AGAINST RIGHT NOW, MORE IS DEFINITELY BETTER.

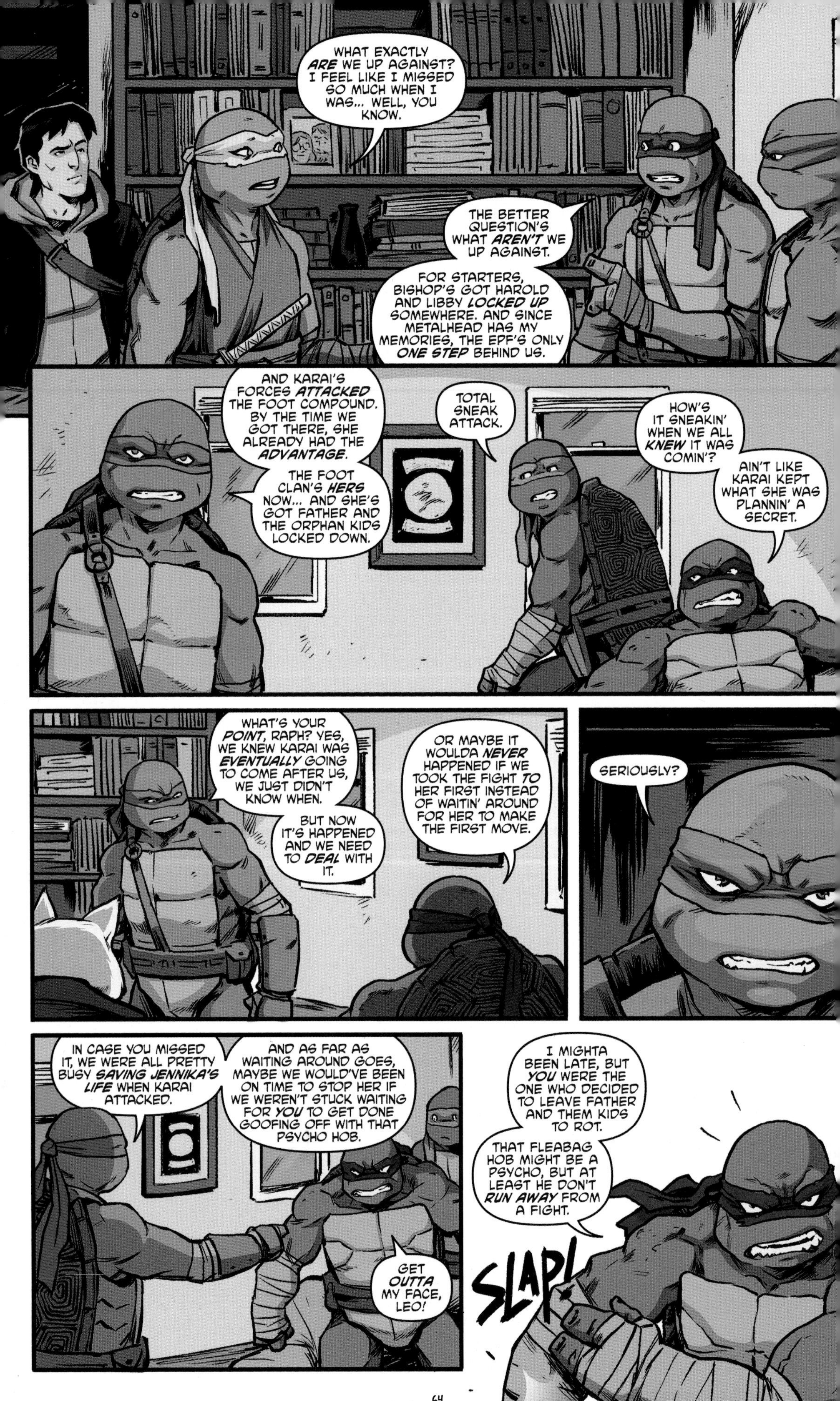
WHAT EXACTLY ARE WE UP AGAINST? I FEEL LIKE I MISSED SO MUCH WHEN I WAS... WELL, YOU KNOW.
THE BETTER QUESTION'S WHAT AREN'T WE UP AGAINST.
FOR STARTERS, BISHOP'S GOT HAROLD AND LIBBY LOCKED UP SOMEWHERE. AND SINCE METALHEAD HAS MY MEMORIES, THE EPF'S ONLY ONE STEP BEHIND US.
AND KARAI'S FORCES ATTACKED THE FOOT COMPOUND. BY THE TIME WE GOT THERE, SHE ALREADY HAD THE ADVANTAGE.
THE FOOT CLAN'S HERS NOW... AND SHE'S GOT FATHER AND THE ORPHAN KIDS LOCKED DOWN.
TOTAL SNEAK ATTACK.
HOW'S IT SNEAKIN' WHEN WE ALL KNEW IT WAS COMIN'?
AIN'T LIKE KARAI KEPT WHAT SHE WAS PLANNIN' A SECRET.
WHAT'S YOUR POINT, RAPH? YES, WE KNEW KARAI WAS EVENTUALLY GOING TO COME AFTER US, WE JUST DIDN'T KNOW WHEN.
BUT NOW IT'S HAPPENED AND WE NEED TO DEAL WITH IT.
OR MAYBE IT WOULDA NEVER HAPPENED IF WE TOOK THE FIGHT TO HER FIRST INSTEAD OF WAITIN' AROUND FOR HER TO MAKE THE FIRST MOVE.
SERIOUSLY?
IN CASE YOU MISSED IT, WE WERE ALL PRETTY BUSY SAVING JENNIKA'S LIFE WHEN KARAI ATTACKED.
AND AS FAR AS WAITING AROUND GOES, MAYBE WE WOULD'VE BEEN ON TIME TO STOP HER IF WE WEREN'T STUCK WAITING FOR YOU TO GET DONE GOOFING OFF WITH THAT PSYCHO HOB.
GET OUTTA MY FACE, LEO!
I MIGHTA BEEN LATE, BUT YOU WERE THE ONE WHO DECIDED TO LEAVE FATHER AND THEM KIDS TO ROT.
THAT FLEABAG HOB MIGHT BE A PSYCHO, BUT AT LEAST HE DON'T RUN AWAY FROM A FIGHT.
SLAP!

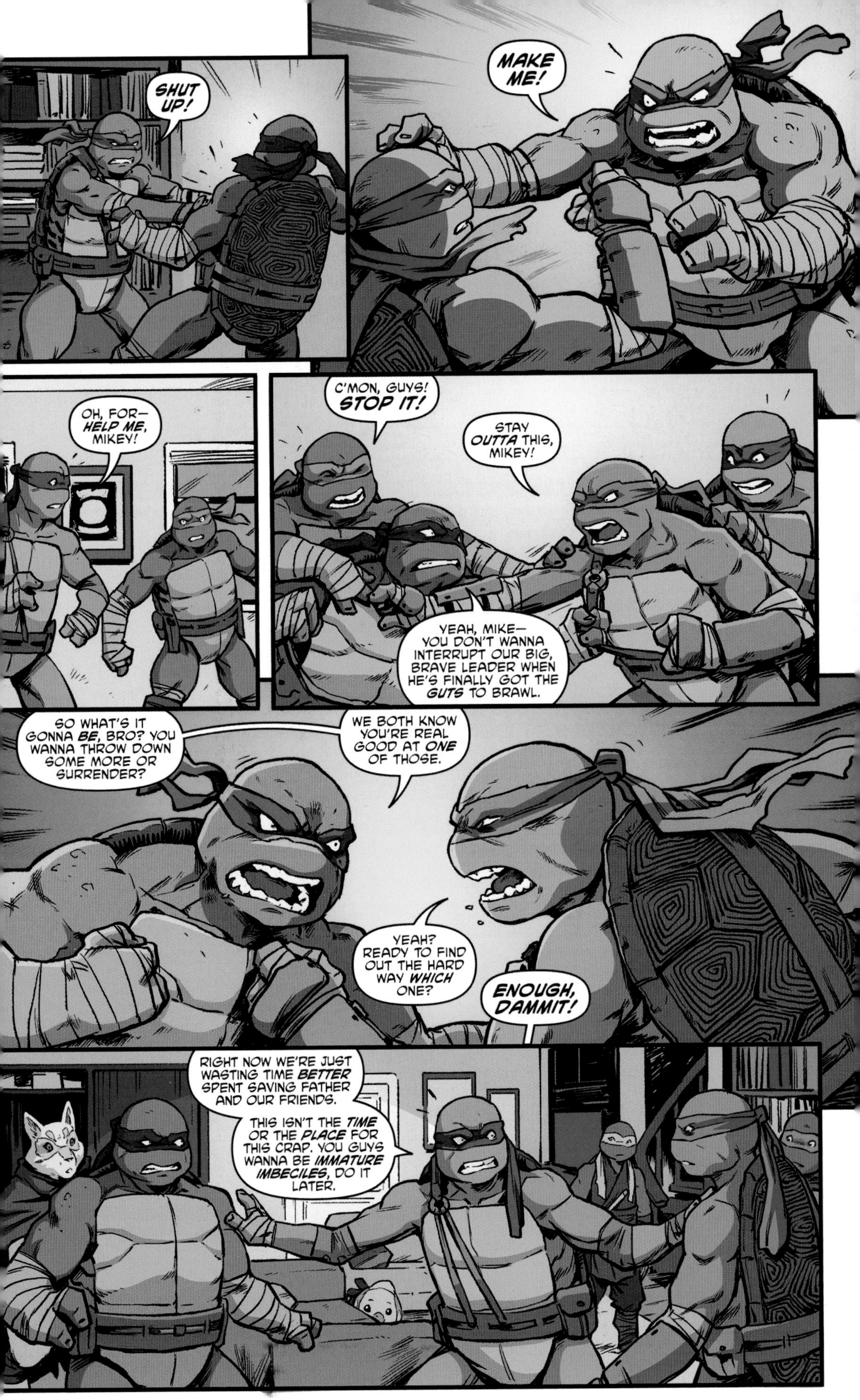

SHUT UP!
MAKE ME!
OH, FOR— HELP ME, MIKEY!
C'MON, GUYS! STOP IT!
STAY OUTTA THIS, MIKEY!
YEAH, MIKE— YOU DON'T WANNA INTERRUPT OUR BIG, BRAVE LEADER WHEN HE'S FINALLY GOT THE GUTS TO BRAWL.
SO WHAT'S IT GONNA BE, BRO? YOU WANNA THROW DOWN SOME MORE OR SURRENDER?
WE BOTH KNOW YOU'RE REAL GOOD AT ONE OF THOSE.
YEAH? READY TO FIND OUT THE HARD WAY WHICH ONE?
ENOUGH, DAMMIT!
RIGHT NOW WE'RE JUST WASTING TIME BETTER SPENT SAVING FATHER AND OUR FRIENDS.
THIS ISN'T THE TIME OR THE PLACE FOR THIS CRAP. YOU GUYS WANNA BE IMMATURE IMBECILES, DO IT LATER.

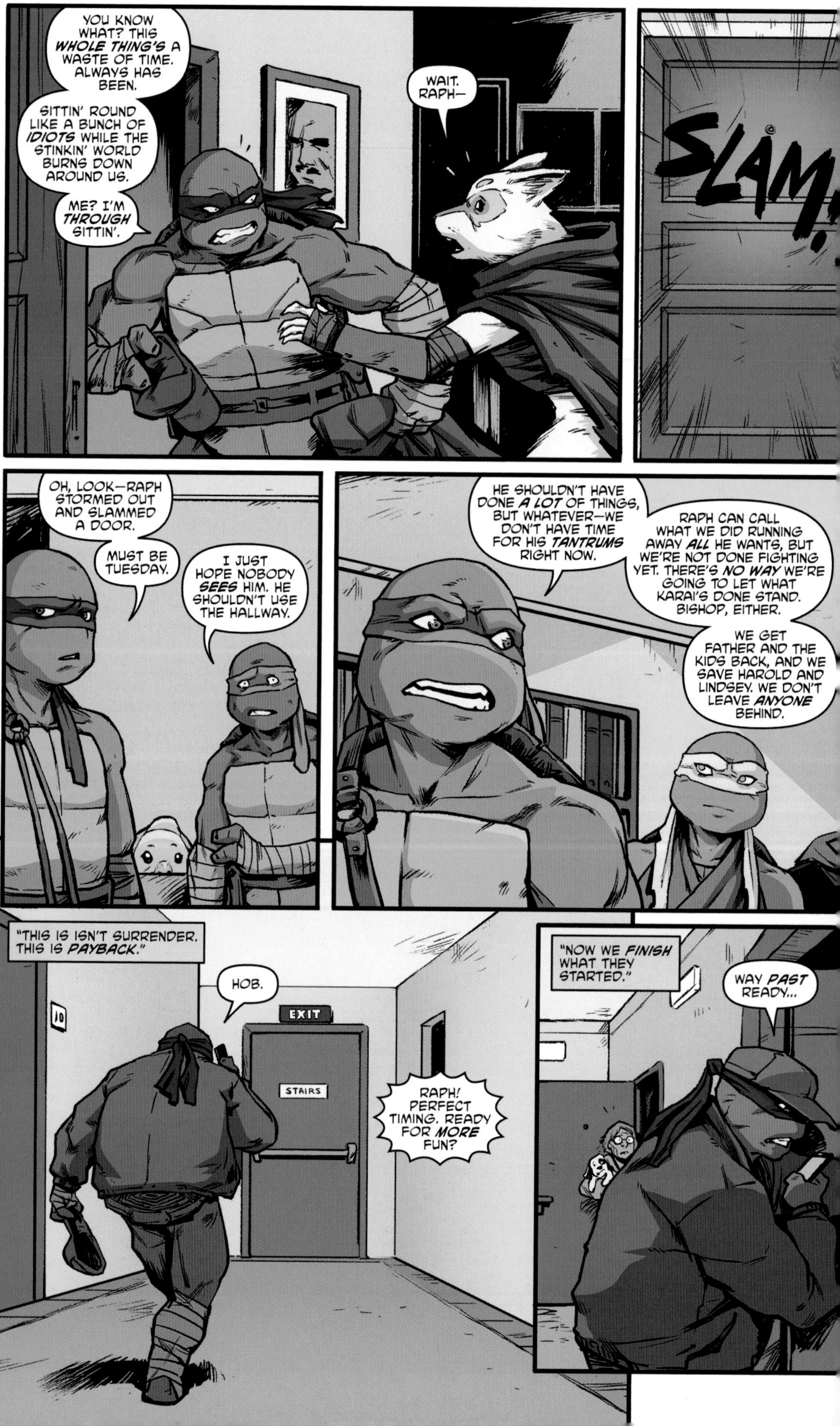
YOU KNOW WHAT? THIS WHOLE THING'S A WASTE OF TIME. ALWAYS HAS BEEN.
SITTIN' ROUND LIKE A BUNCH OF IDIOTS WHILE THE STINKIN' WORLD BURNS DOWN AROUND US.
ME? I'M THROUGH SITTIN'.
WAIT. RAPH—
SLAM!
OH, LOOK—RAPH STORMED OUT AND SLAMMED A DOOR.
MUST BE TUESDAY.
I JUST HOPE NOBODY SEES HIM. HE SHOULDN'T USE THE HALLWAY.
HE SHOULDN'T HAVE DONE A LOT OF THINGS, BUT WHATEVER—WE DON'T HAVE TIME FOR HIS TANTRUMS RIGHT NOW.
RAPH CAN CALL WHAT WE DID RUNNING AWAY ALL HE WANTS, BUT WE'RE NOT DONE FIGHTING YET. THERE'S NO WAY WE'RE GOING TO LET WHAT KARAI'S DONE STAND. BISHOP, EITHER.
WE GET FATHER AND THE KIDS BACK, AND WE SAVE HAROLD AND LINDSEY. WE DON'T LEAVE ANYONE BEHIND.
"THIS IS ISN'T SURRENDER. THIS IS PAYBACK."
HOB.
EXIT
10
STAIRS
RAPH! PERFECT TIMING. READY FOR MORE FUN?
"NOW WE FINISH WHAT THEY STARTED."
WAY PAST READY...

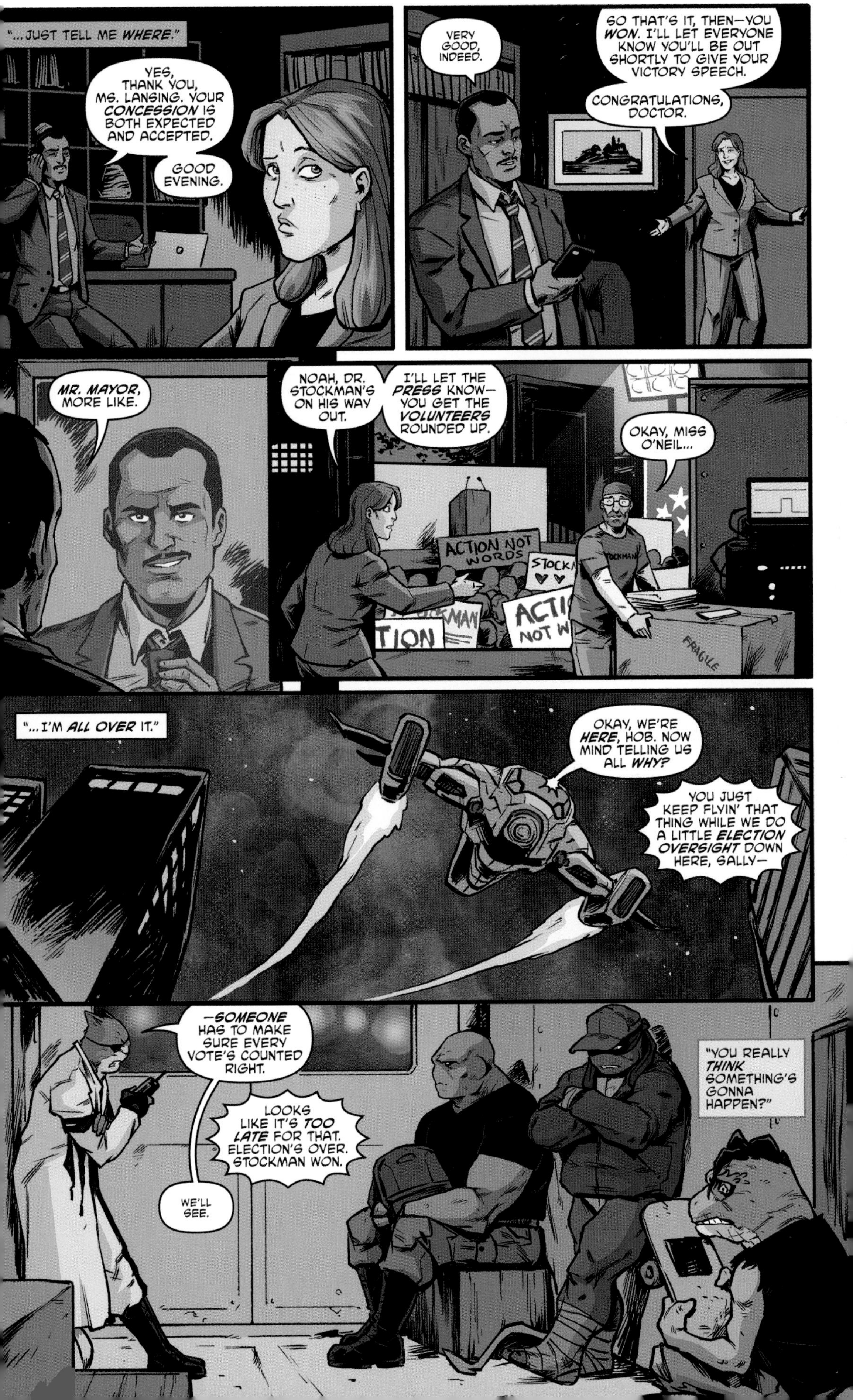
"...JUST TELL ME *WHERE.*"
YES, THANK YOU, MS. LANSING. YOUR *CONCESSION* IS BOTH EXPECTED AND ACCEPTED.
GOOD EVENING.
VERY GOOD, INDEED.
SO THAT'S IT, THEN—YOU *WON.* I'LL LET EVERYONE KNOW YOU'LL BE OUT SHORTLY TO GIVE YOUR VICTORY SPEECH.
CONGRATULATIONS, DOCTOR.
MR. MAYOR, MORE LIKE.
NOAH, DR. STOCKMAN'S ON HIS WAY OUT.
I'LL LET THE *PRESS* KNOW—YOU GET THE *VOLUNTEERS* ROUNDED UP.
OKAY, MISS O'NEIL...
ACTION NOT WORDS
STOCKMAN
FRAGILE
"...I'M *ALL OVER* IT."
OKAY, WE'RE *HERE,* HOB. NOW MIND TELLING US ALL *WHY?*
YOU JUST KEEP FLYIN' THAT THING WHILE WE DO A LITTLE *ELECTION OVERSIGHT* DOWN HERE, SALLY—
—*SOMEONE* HAS TO MAKE SURE EVERY VOTE'S COUNTED RIGHT.
LOOKS LIKE IT'S *TOO LATE* FOR THAT. ELECTION'S OVER. STOCKMAN WON.
WE'LL SEE.
"YOU REALLY *THINK* SOMETHING'S GONNA HAPPEN?"

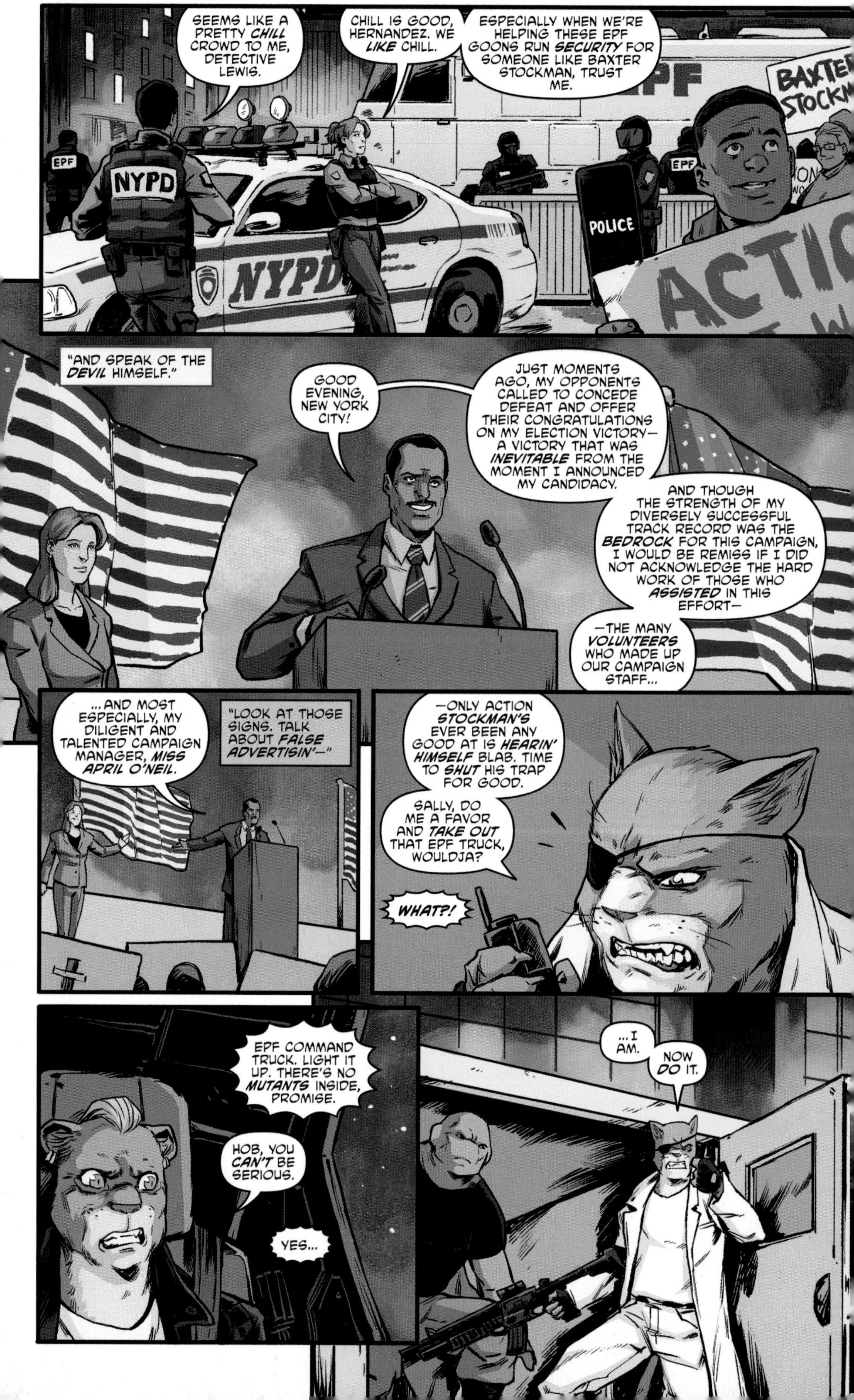
SEEMS LIKE A PRETTY CHILL CROWD TO ME, DETECTIVE LEWIS.
CHILL IS GOOD, HERNANDEZ. WE LIKE CHILL.
ESPECIALLY WHEN WE'RE HELPING THESE EPF GOONS RUN SECURITY FOR SOMEONE LIKE BAXTER STOCKMAN, TRUST ME.
EPF
NYPD
POLICE
"AND SPEAK OF THE DEVIL HIMSELF."
GOOD EVENING, NEW YORK CITY!
JUST MOMENTS AGO, MY OPPONENTS CALLED TO CONCEDE DEFEAT AND OFFER THEIR CONGRATULATIONS ON MY ELECTION VICTORY—A VICTORY THAT WAS INEVITABLE FROM THE MOMENT I ANNOUNCED MY CANDIDACY.
AND THOUGH THE STRENGTH OF MY DIVERSELY SUCCESSFUL TRACK RECORD WAS THE BEDROCK FOR THIS CAMPAIGN, I WOULD BE REMISS IF I DID NOT ACKNOWLEDGE THE HARD WORK OF THOSE WHO ASSISTED IN THIS EFFORT—
—THE MANY VOLUNTEERS WHO MADE UP OUR CAMPAIGN STAFF...
...AND MOST ESPECIALLY, MY DILIGENT AND TALENTED CAMPAIGN MANAGER, MISS APRIL O'NEIL.
"LOOK AT THOSE SIGNS. TALK ABOUT FALSE ADVERTISIN'—"
—ONLY ACTION STOCKMAN'S EVER BEEN ANY GOOD AT IS HEARIN' HIMSELF BLAB. TIME TO SHUT HIS TRAP FOR GOOD.
SALLY, DO ME A FAVOR AND TAKE OUT THAT EPF TRUCK, WOULDJA?
WHAT?!
EPF COMMAND TRUCK. LIGHT IT UP. THERE'S NO MUTANTS INSIDE, PROMISE.
HOB, YOU CAN'T BE SERIOUS.
YES...
...I AM.
NOW DO IT.

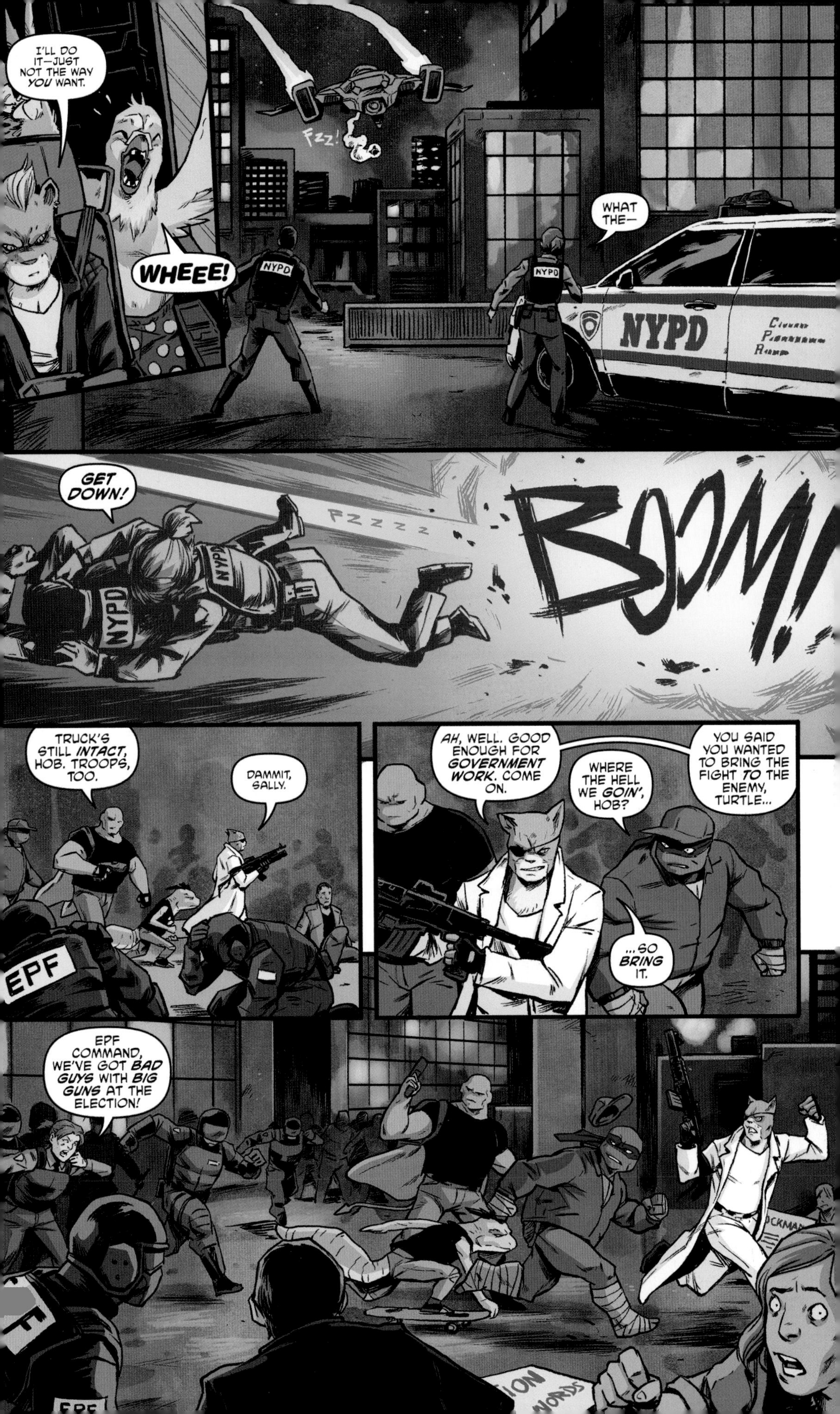
I'LL DO IT—JUST NOT THE WAY *YOU* WANT.
WHEEE!
FZZ!
WHAT THE—
NYPD
GET DOWN!
FZZZZZ
BOOM!!
TRUCK'S STILL *INTACT*, HOB. TROOPS, TOO.
DAMMIT, SALLY.
EPF
AH, WELL. GOOD ENOUGH FOR *GOVERNMENT WORK*. COME ON.
WHERE THE HELL WE *GOIN'*, HOB?
YOU SAID YOU WANTED TO BRING THE FIGHT *TO* THE ENEMY, TURTLE...
...SO *BRING* IT.
EPF COMMAND, WE'VE GOT *BAD GUYS* WITH *BIG GUNS* AT THE ELECTION!

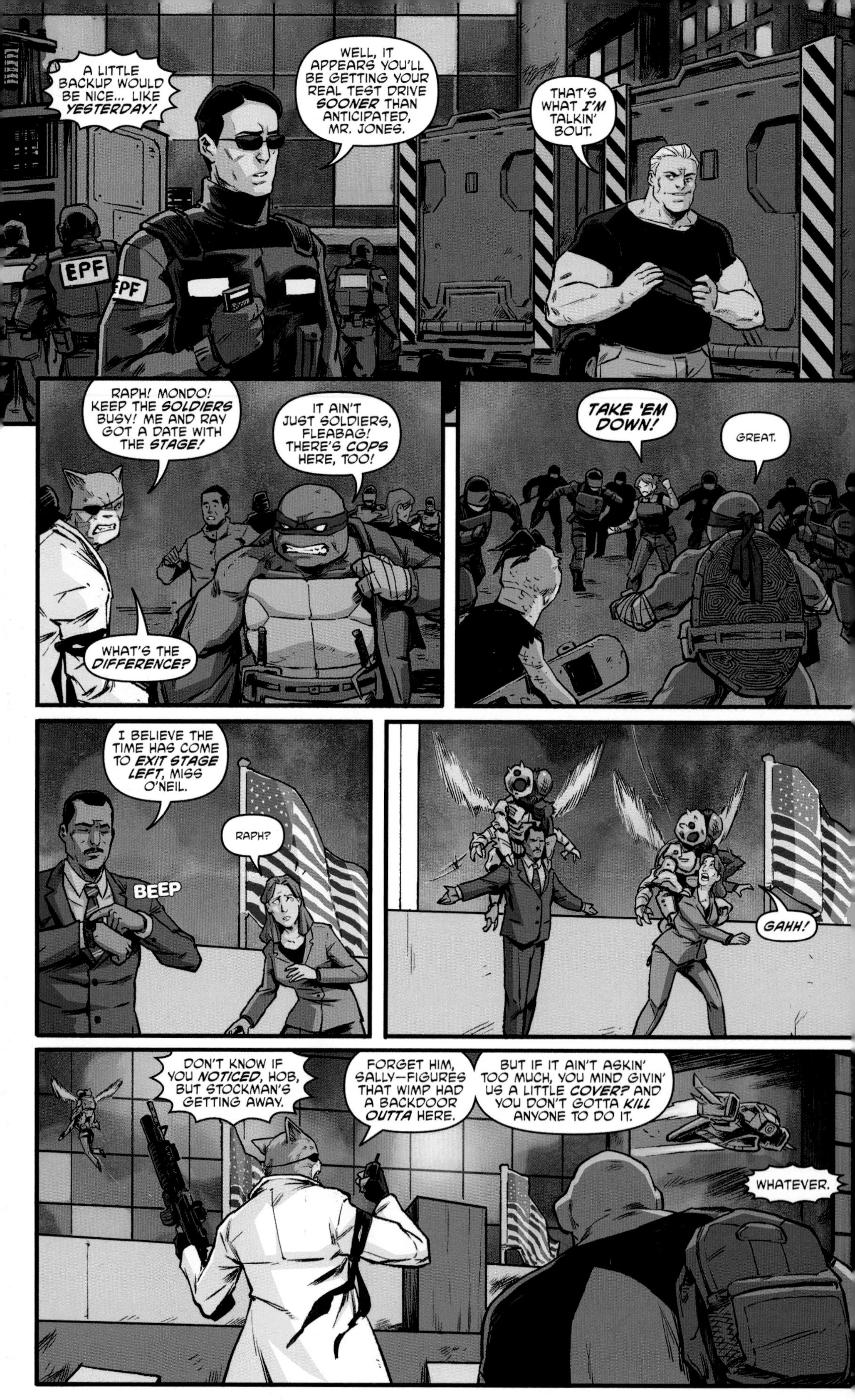

A LITTLE BACKUP WOULD BE NICE... LIKE YESTERDAY!
WELL, IT APPEARS YOU'LL BE GETTING YOUR REAL TEST DRIVE SOONER THAN ANTICIPATED, MR. JONES.
THAT'S WHAT I'M TALKIN' BOUT.
EPF
EPF
RAPH! MONDO! KEEP THE SOLDIERS BUSY! ME AND RAY GOT A DATE WITH THE STAGE!
IT AIN'T JUST SOLDIERS, FLEABAG! THERE'S COPS HERE, TOO!
WHAT'S THE DIFFERENCE?
TAKE 'EM DOWN!
GREAT.
I BELIEVE THE TIME HAS COME TO EXIT STAGE LEFT, MISS O'NEIL.
RAPH?
BEEP
GAHH!
DON'T KNOW IF YOU NOTICED, HOB, BUT STOCKMAN'S GETTING AWAY.
FORGET HIM, SALLY—FIGURES THAT WIMP HAD A BACKDOOR OUTTA HERE.
BUT IF IT AIN'T ASKIN' TOO MUCH, YOU MIND GIVIN' US A LITTLE COVER? AND YOU DON'T GOTTA KILL ANYONE TO DO IT.
WHATEVER.

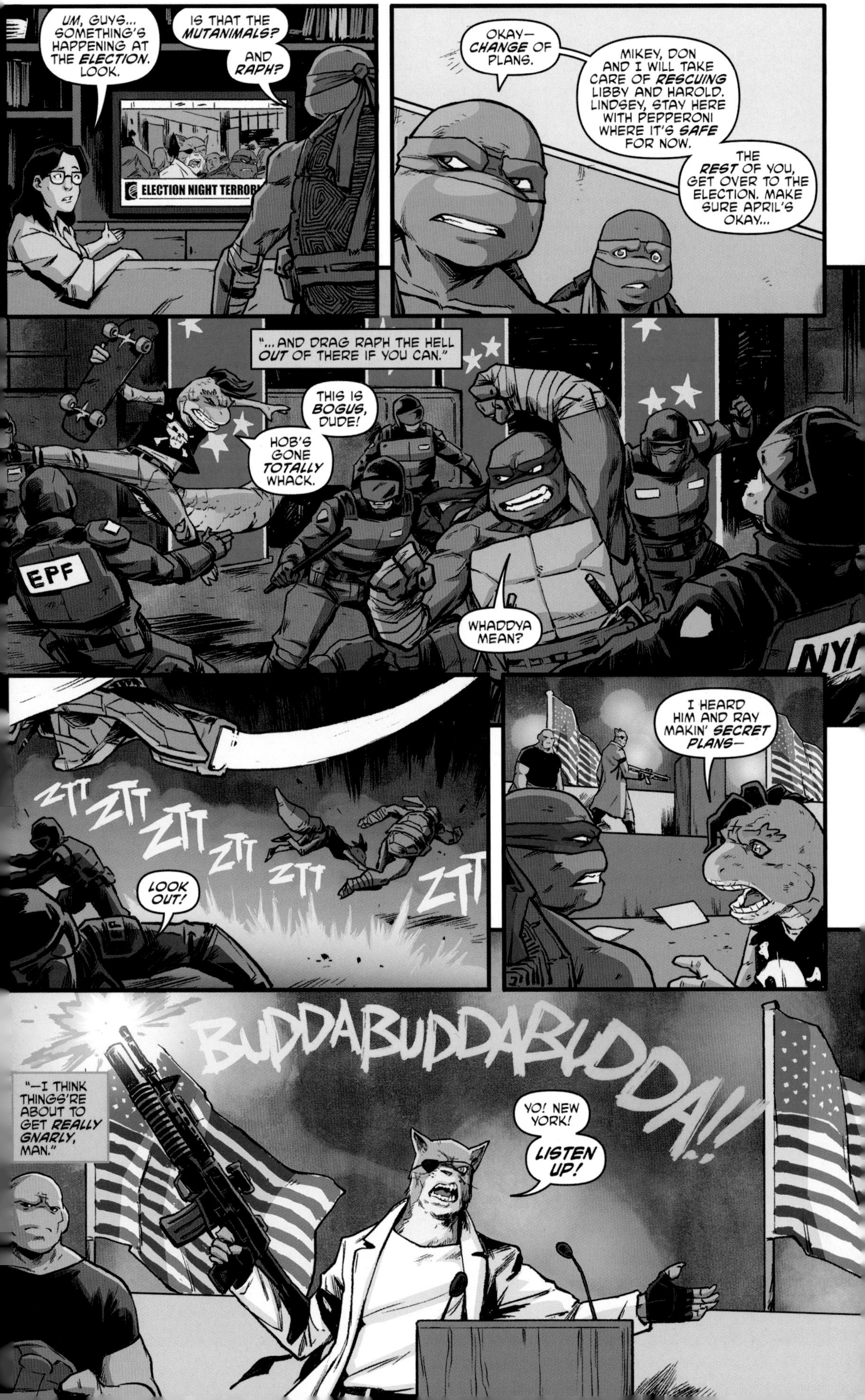

UM, GUYS... SOMETHING'S HAPPENING AT THE ELECTION. LOOK.
IS THAT THE MUTANIMALS?
AND RAPH?
ELECTION NIGHT TERROR
OKAY— CHANGE OF PLANS.
MIKEY, DON AND I WILL TAKE CARE OF RESCUING LIBBY AND HAROLD. LINDSEY, STAY HERE WITH PEPPERONI WHERE IT'S SAFE FOR NOW.
THE REST OF YOU, GET OVER TO THE ELECTION. MAKE SURE APRIL'S OKAY...
"...AND DRAG RAPH THE HELL OUT OF THERE IF YOU CAN."
THIS IS BOGUS, DUDE!
HOB'S GONE TOTALLY WHACK.
EPF
WHADDYA MEAN?
ZTT ZTT ZTT ZTT ZTT ZTT
LOOK OUT!
I HEARD HIM AND RAY MAKIN' SECRET PLANS—
BUDDABUDDABUDDA!!
"—I THINK THINGS'RE ABOUT TO GET REALLY GNARLY, MAN."
YO! NEW YORK!
LISTEN UP!

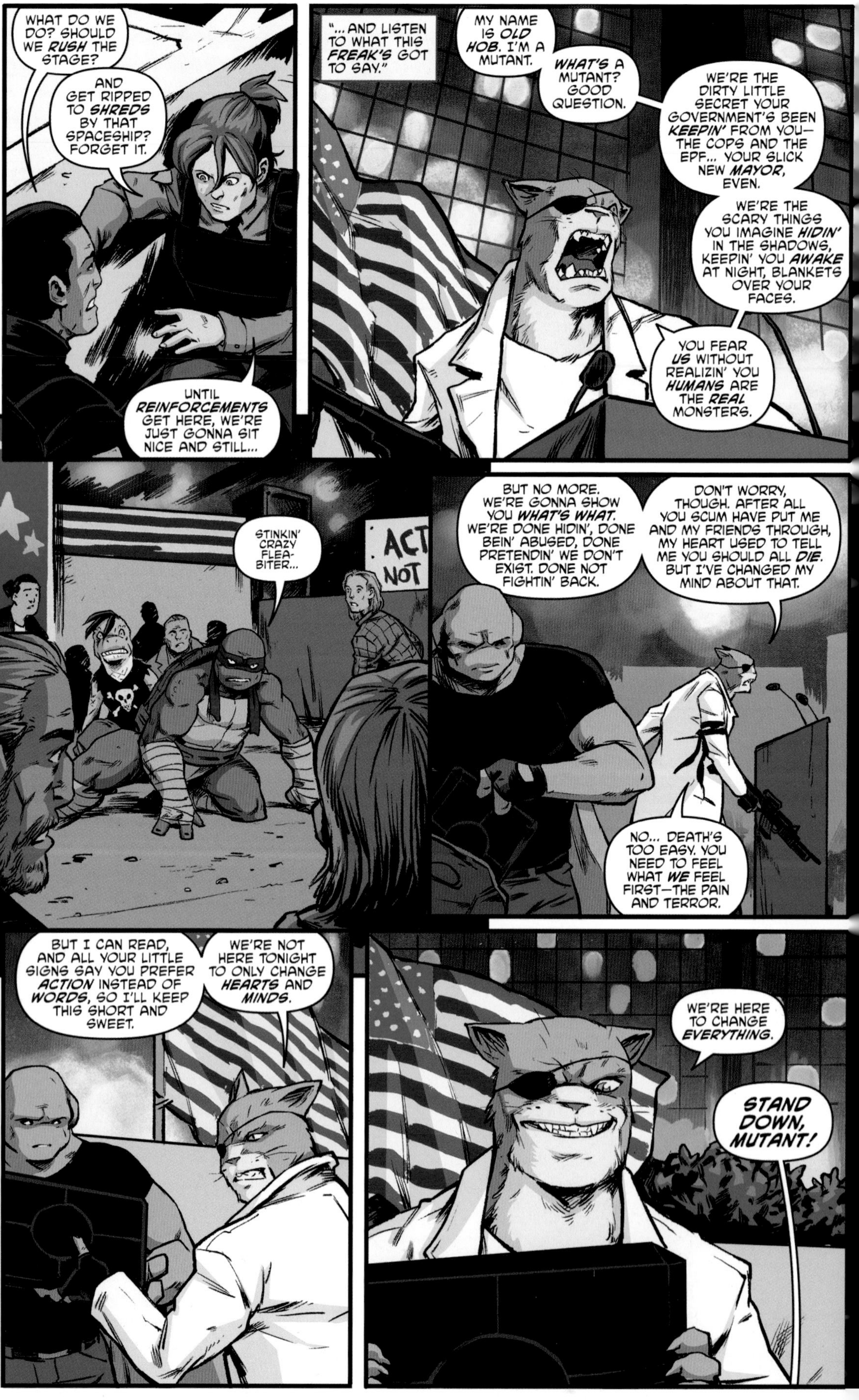
WHAT DO WE DO? SHOULD WE *RUSH* THE STAGE?
AND GET RIPPED TO *SHREDS* BY THAT SPACESHIP? FORGET IT.
UNTIL *REINFORCEMENTS* GET HERE, WE'RE JUST GONNA SIT NICE AND STILL...
"...AND LISTEN TO WHAT THIS *FREAK'S* GOT TO SAY."
MY NAME IS *OLD HOB*. I'M A MUTANT.
WHAT'S A MUTANT? GOOD QUESTION.
WE'RE THE DIRTY LITTLE SECRET YOUR GOVERNMENT'S BEEN *KEEPIN'* FROM YOU— THE COPS AND THE EPF... YOUR SLICK NEW *MAYOR*, EVEN.
WE'RE THE SCARY THINGS YOU IMAGINE *HIDIN'* IN THE SHADOWS, KEEPIN' YOU *AWAKE* AT NIGHT, BLANKETS OVER YOUR FACES.
YOU FEAR *US* WITHOUT REALIZIN' YOU *HUMANS* ARE THE *REAL* MONSTERS.
ACT NOT
STINKIN' CRAZY FLEA-BITER...
BUT NO MORE. WE'RE GONNA SHOW YOU *WHAT'S WHAT*. WE'RE DONE HIDIN', DONE BEIN' ABUSED, DONE PRETENDIN' WE DON'T EXIST. DONE NOT FIGHTIN' BACK.
DON'T WORRY, THOUGH. AFTER ALL YOU SCUM HAVE PUT ME AND MY FRIENDS THROUGH, MY HEART USED TO TELL ME YOU SHOULD ALL *DIE*. BUT I'VE CHANGED MY MIND ABOUT THAT.
NO... DEATH'S TOO EASY. YOU NEED TO FEEL WHAT *WE* FEEL FIRST—THE PAIN AND TERROR.
BUT I CAN READ, AND ALL YOUR LITTLE SIGNS SAY YOU PREFER *ACTION* INSTEAD OF *WORDS*, SO I'LL KEEP THIS SHORT AND SWEET.
WE'RE NOT HERE TONIGHT TO ONLY CHANGE *HEARTS* AND *MINDS*.
WE'RE HERE TO CHANGE *EVERYTHING*.
STAND DOWN, MUTANT!

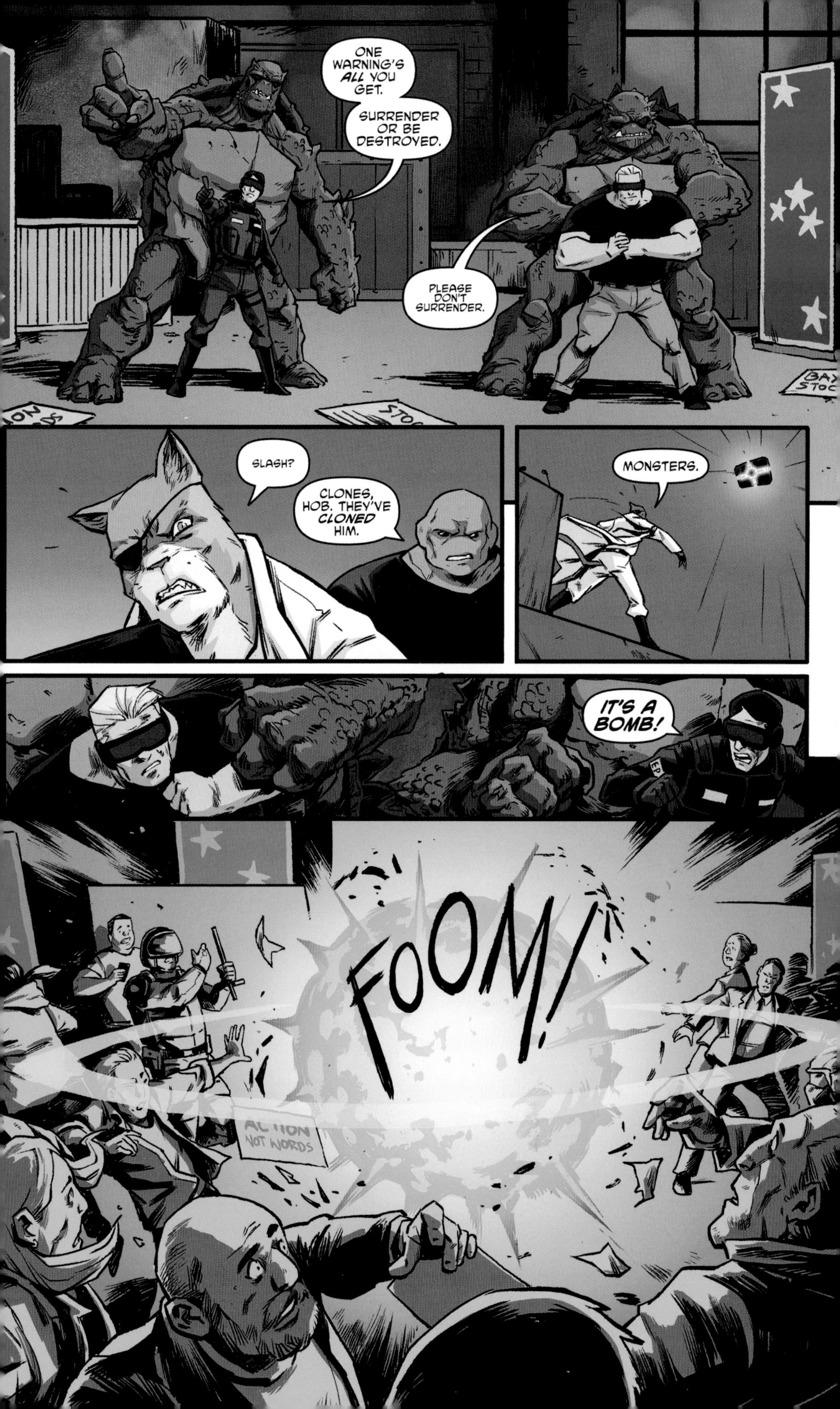
ONE WARNING'S ALL YOU GET.
SURRENDER OR BE DESTROYED.
PLEASE DON'T SURRENDER.
SLASH?
CLONES, HOB. THEY'VE CLONED HIM.
MONSTERS.
IT'S A BOMB!
FOOM!
ACTION NOT WORDS

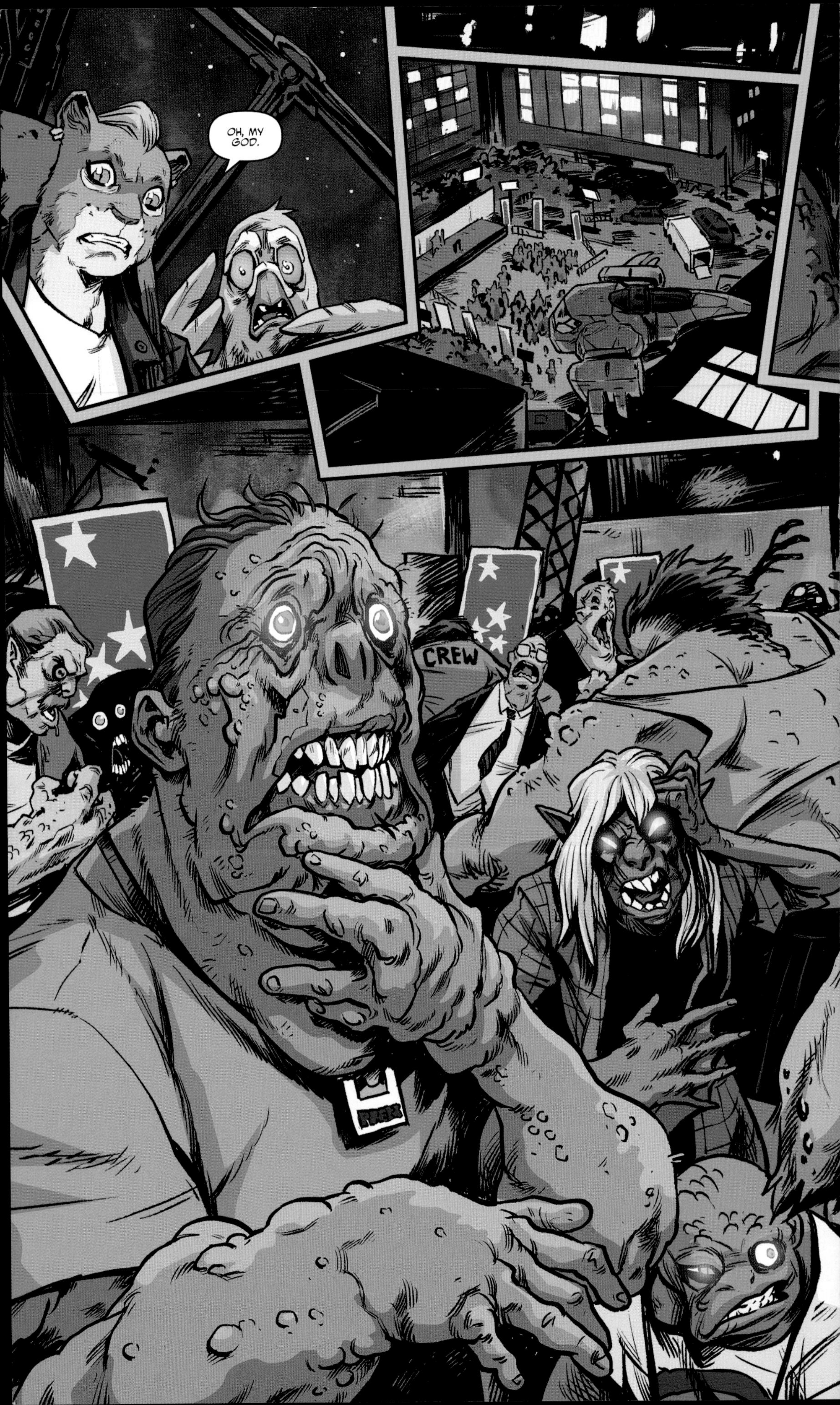

OH, MY GOD.
CREW

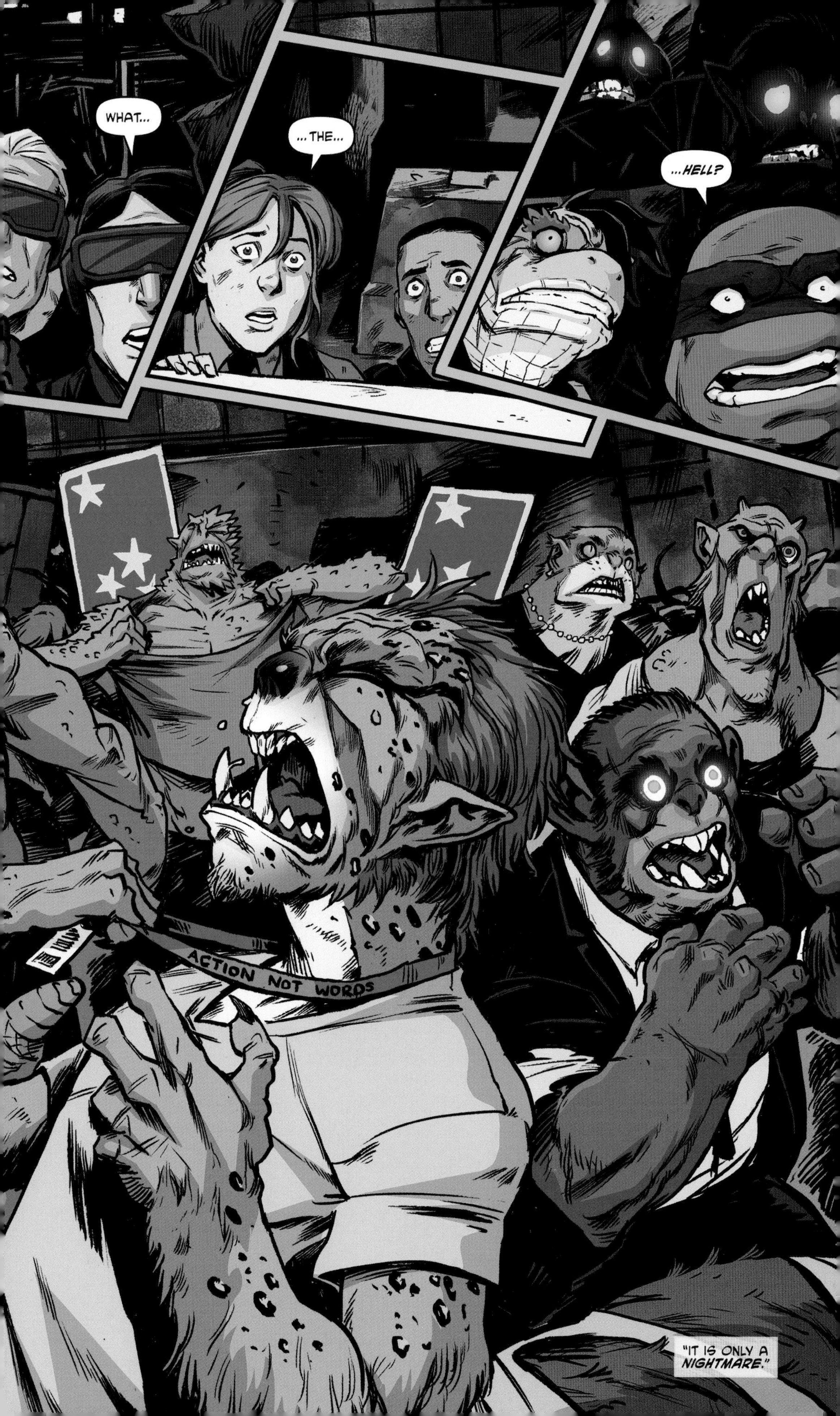
WHAT...
...THE...
...HELL?
ACTION NOT WORDS
"IT IS ONLY A NIGHTMARE."

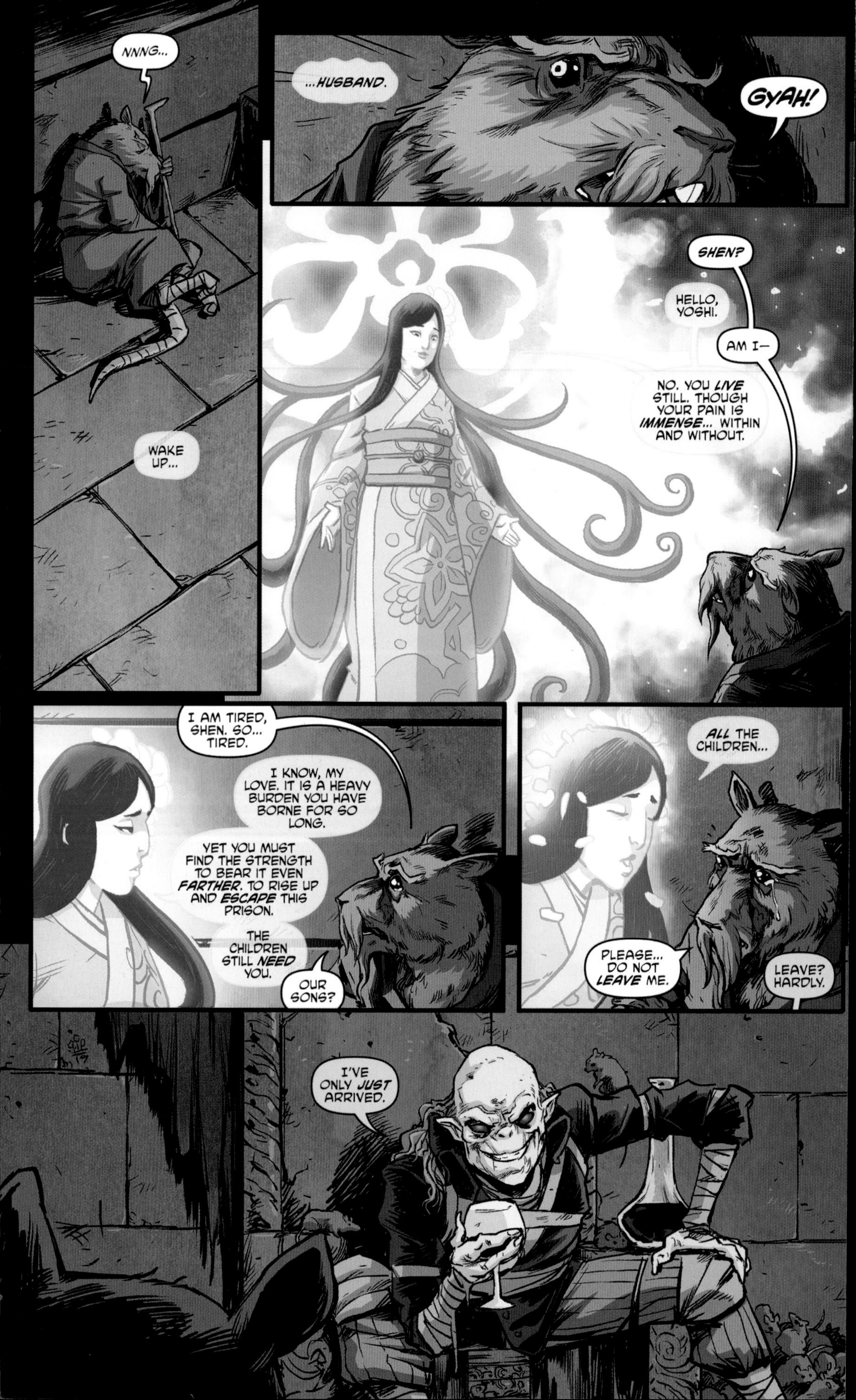
NNNG...
...HUSBAND.
GYAH!
WAKE UP...
SHEN?
HELLO, YOSHI.
AM I—
NO. YOU LIVE STILL. THOUGH YOUR PAIN IS IMMENSE... WITHIN AND WITHOUT.
I AM TIRED, SHEN. SO... TIRED.
I KNOW, MY LOVE. IT IS A HEAVY BURDEN YOU HAVE BORNE FOR SO LONG.
YET YOU MUST FIND THE STRENGTH TO BEAR IT EVEN FARTHER. TO RISE UP AND ESCAPE THIS PRISON.
THE CHILDREN STILL NEED YOU.
OUR SONS?
ALL THE CHILDREN...
PLEASE... DO NOT LEAVE ME.
LEAVE? HARDLY.
I'VE ONLY JUST ARRIVED.

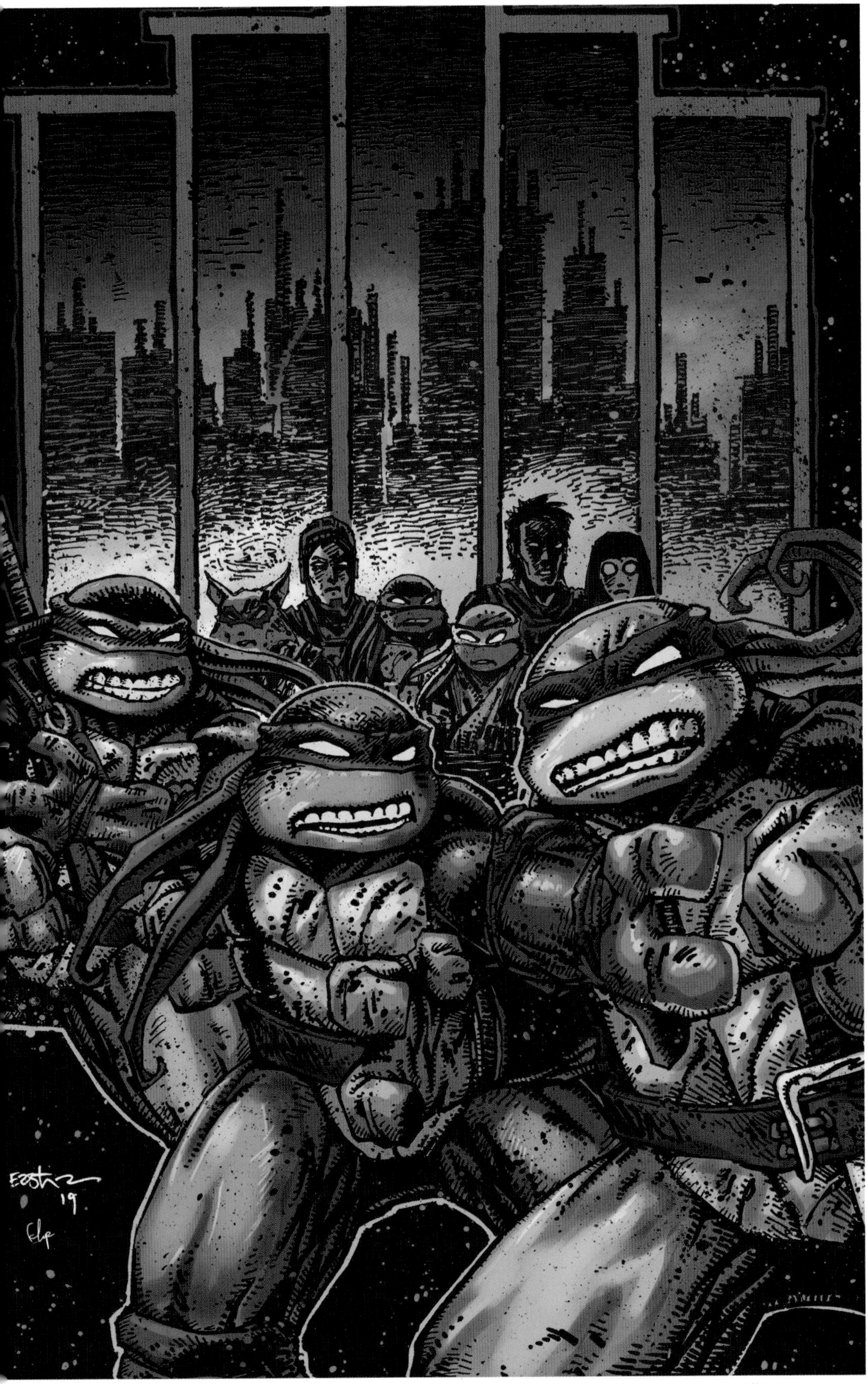
EASTMAN
19

ART BY KEVIN EASTMAN · COLORS BY FAHRIZA KAMAPUTRA

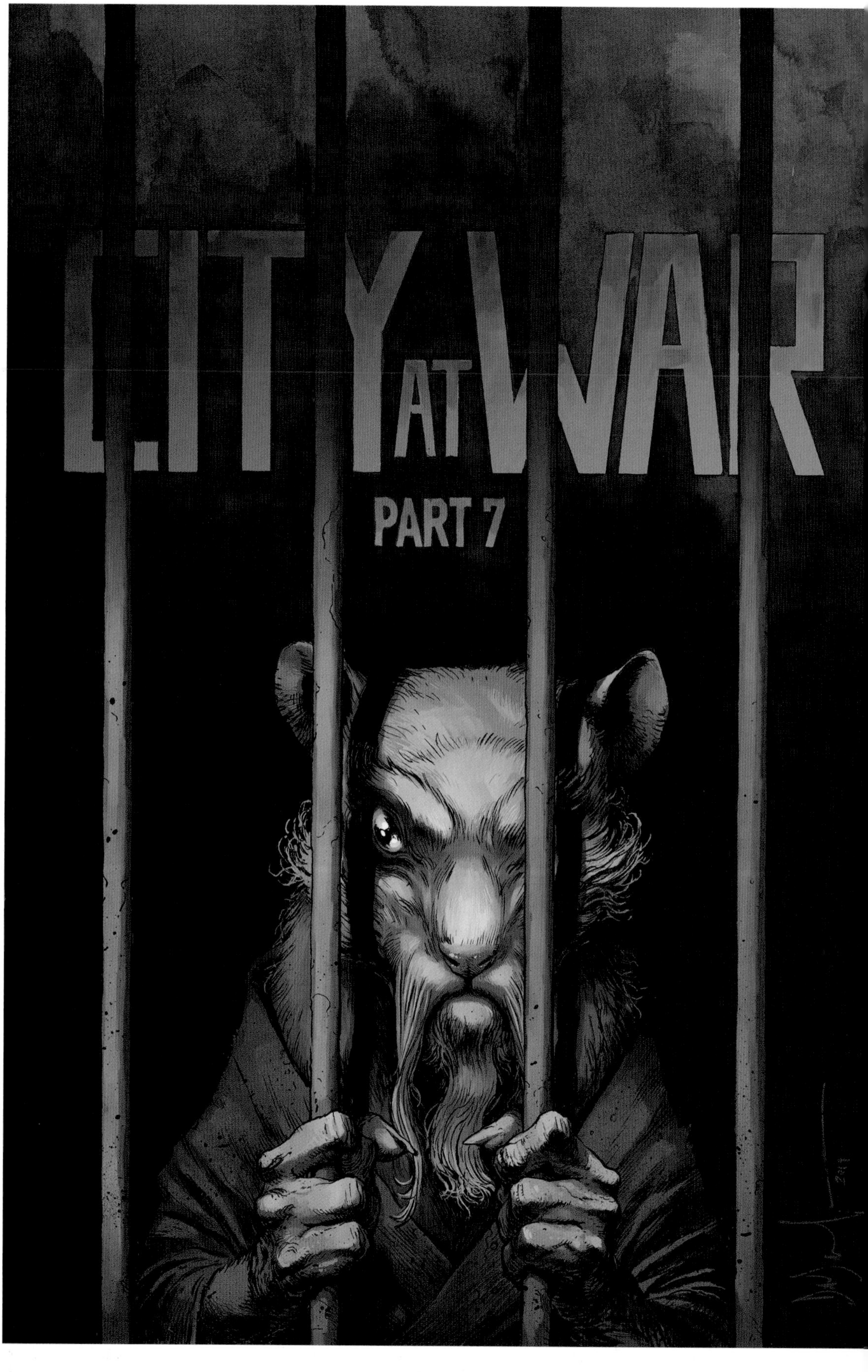
CITY AT WAR
PART 7

ART BY DAVE WACHTER

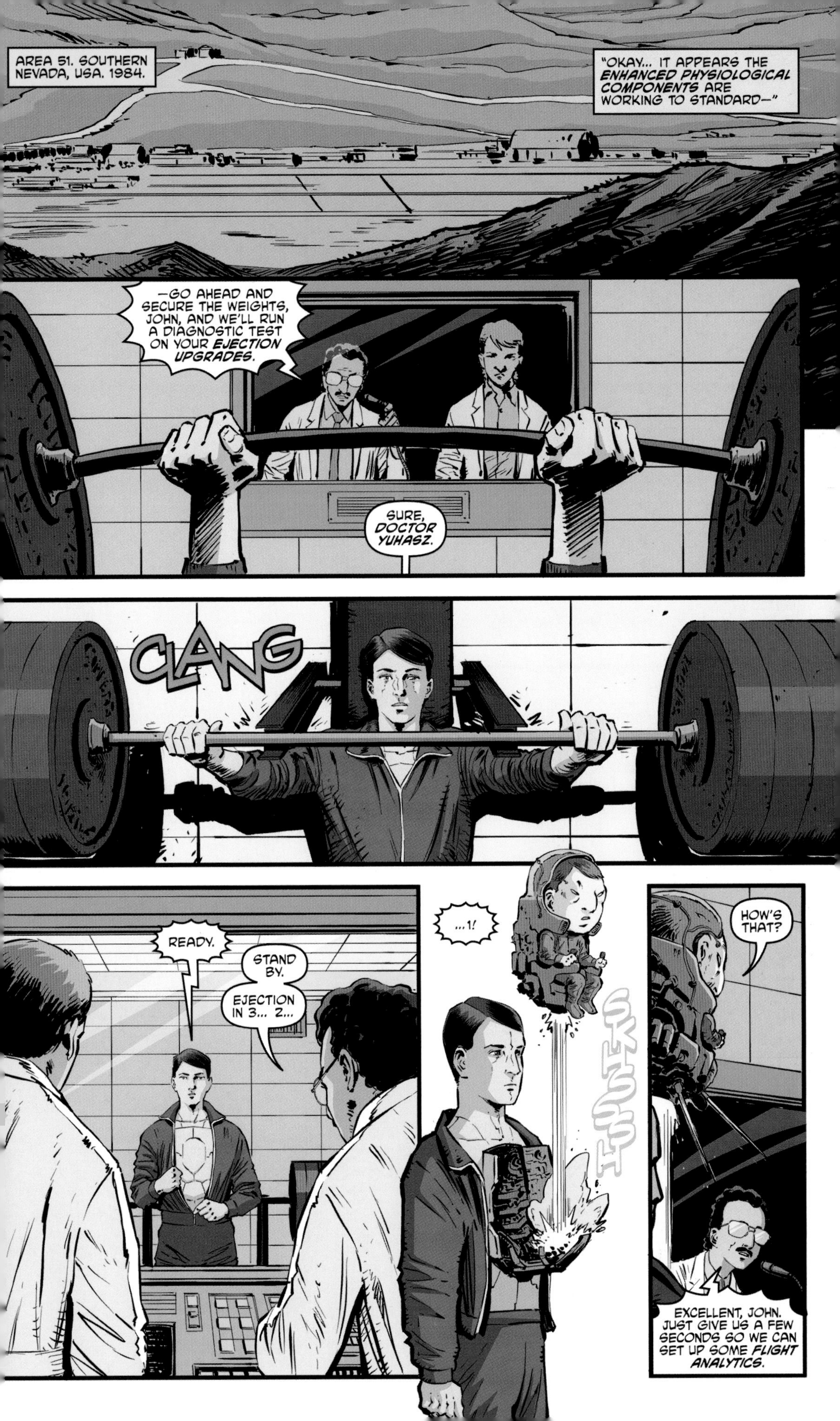
AREA 51. SOUTHERN NEVADA, USA. 1984.
"OKAY... IT APPEARS THE *ENHANCED PHYSIOLOGICAL COMPONENTS* ARE WORKING TO STANDARD—"
—GO AHEAD AND SECURE THE WEIGHTS, JOHN, AND WE'LL RUN A DIAGNOSTIC TEST ON YOUR *EJECTION UPGRADES*.
SURE, *DOCTOR YUHASZ*.
CLANG
READY.
STAND BY.
EJECTION IN 3... 2...
...1!
SKLSSH
HOW'S THAT?
EXCELLENT, JOHN. JUST GIVE US A FEW SECONDS SO WE CAN SET UP SOME *FLIGHT ANALYTICS*.

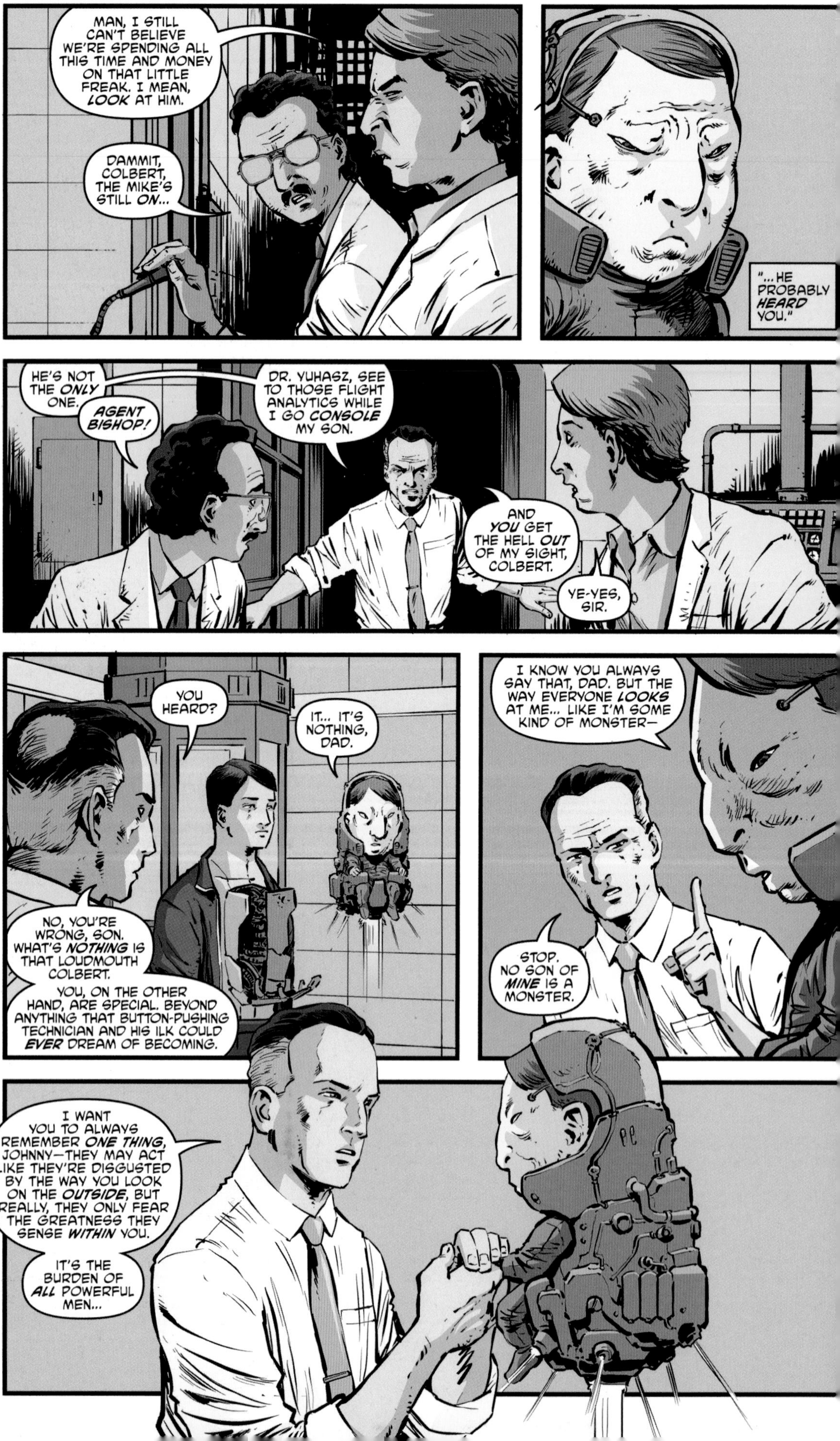
MAN, I STILL CAN'T BELIEVE WE'RE SPENDING ALL THIS TIME AND MONEY ON THAT LITTLE FREAK. I MEAN, *LOOK* AT HIM.
DAMMIT, COLBERT, THE MIKE'S STILL *ON*...
"...HE PROBABLY *HEARD* YOU."
HE'S NOT THE *ONLY* ONE.
AGENT BISHOP!
DR. YUHASZ, SEE TO THOSE FLIGHT ANALYTICS WHILE I GO *CONSOLE* MY SON.
AND *YOU* GET THE HELL *OUT* OF MY SIGHT, COLBERT.
YE-YES, SIR.
YOU HEARD?
IT... IT'S NOTHING, DAD.
NO, YOU'RE WRONG, SON. WHAT'S *NOTHING* IS THAT LOUDMOUTH COLBERT.
YOU, ON THE OTHER HAND, ARE SPECIAL. BEYOND ANYTHING THAT BUTTON-PUSHING TECHNICIAN AND HIS ILK COULD *EVER* DREAM OF BECOMING.
I KNOW YOU ALWAYS SAY THAT, DAD. BUT THE WAY EVERYONE *LOOKS* AT ME... LIKE I'M SOME KIND OF MONSTER—
STOP. NO SON OF *MINE* IS A MONSTER.
I WANT YOU TO ALWAYS REMEMBER *ONE THING*, JOHNNY—THEY MAY ACT LIKE THEY'RE DISGUSTED BY THE WAY YOU LOOK ON THE *OUTSIDE*, BUT REALLY, THEY ONLY FEAR THE GREATNESS THEY SENSE *WITHIN* YOU.
IT'S THE BURDEN OF *ALL* POWERFUL MEN...

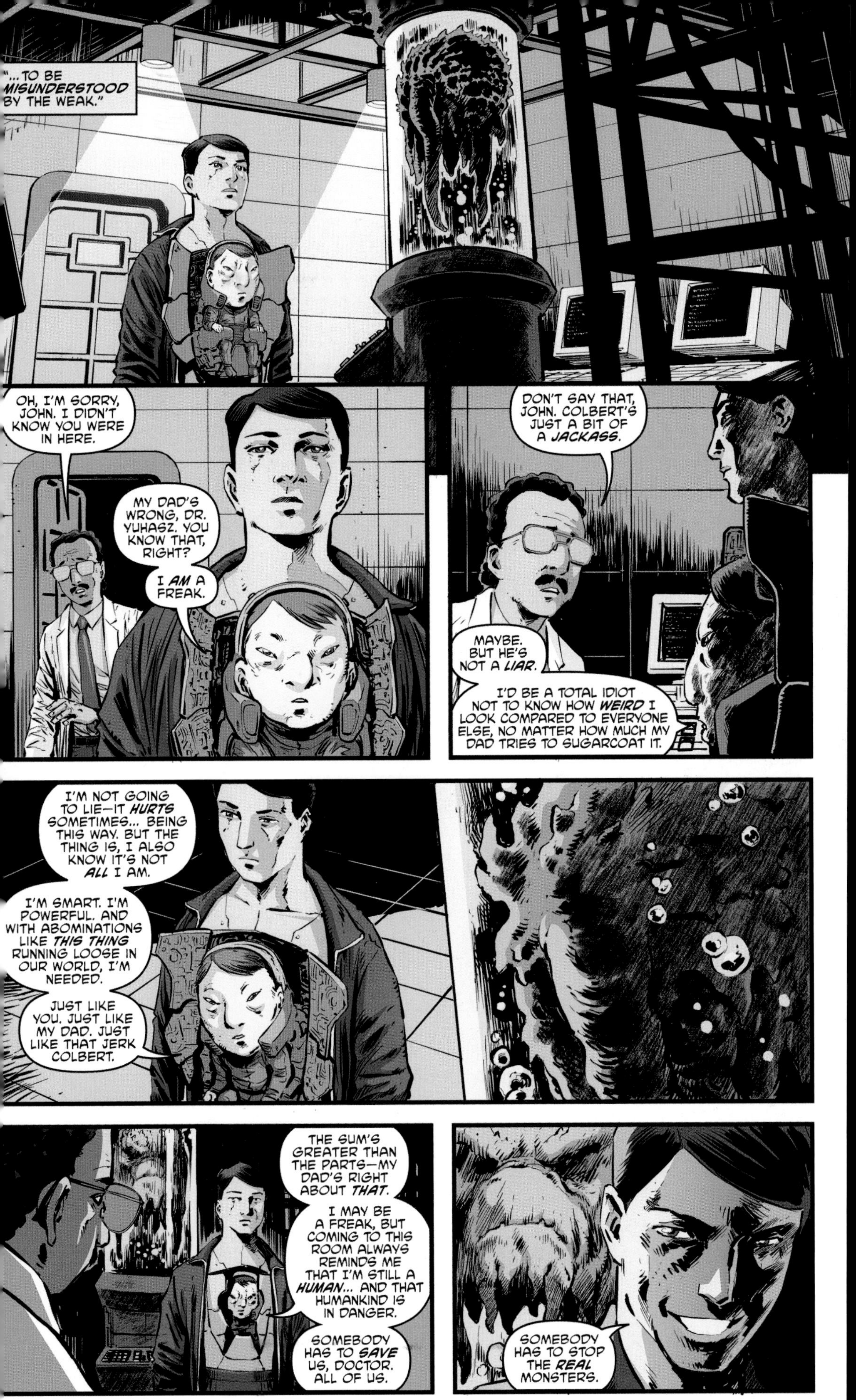
"...TO BE MISUNDERSTOOD BY THE WEAK."
OH, I'M SORRY, JOHN. I DIDN'T KNOW YOU WERE IN HERE.
MY DAD'S WRONG, DR. YUHASZ. YOU KNOW THAT, RIGHT?
I AM A FREAK.
DON'T SAY THAT, JOHN. COLBERT'S JUST A BIT OF A JACKASS.
MAYBE. BUT HE'S NOT A LIAR.
I'D BE A TOTAL IDIOT NOT TO KNOW HOW WEIRD I LOOK COMPARED TO EVERYONE ELSE, NO MATTER HOW MUCH MY DAD TRIES TO SUGARCOAT IT.
I'M NOT GOING TO LIE—IT HURTS SOMETIMES... BEING THIS WAY. BUT THE THING IS, I ALSO KNOW IT'S NOT ALL I AM.
I'M SMART. I'M POWERFUL. AND WITH ABOMINATIONS LIKE THIS THING RUNNING LOOSE IN OUR WORLD, I'M NEEDED.
JUST LIKE YOU. JUST LIKE MY DAD. JUST LIKE THAT JERK COLBERT.
THE SUM'S GREATER THAN THE PARTS—MY DAD'S RIGHT ABOUT THAT.
I MAY BE A FREAK, BUT COMING TO THIS ROOM ALWAYS REMINDS ME THAT I'M STILL A HUMAN... AND THAT HUMANKIND IS IN DANGER.
SOMEBODY HAS TO SAVE US, DOCTOR. ALL OF US.
SOMEBODY HAS TO STOP THE REAL MONSTERS.

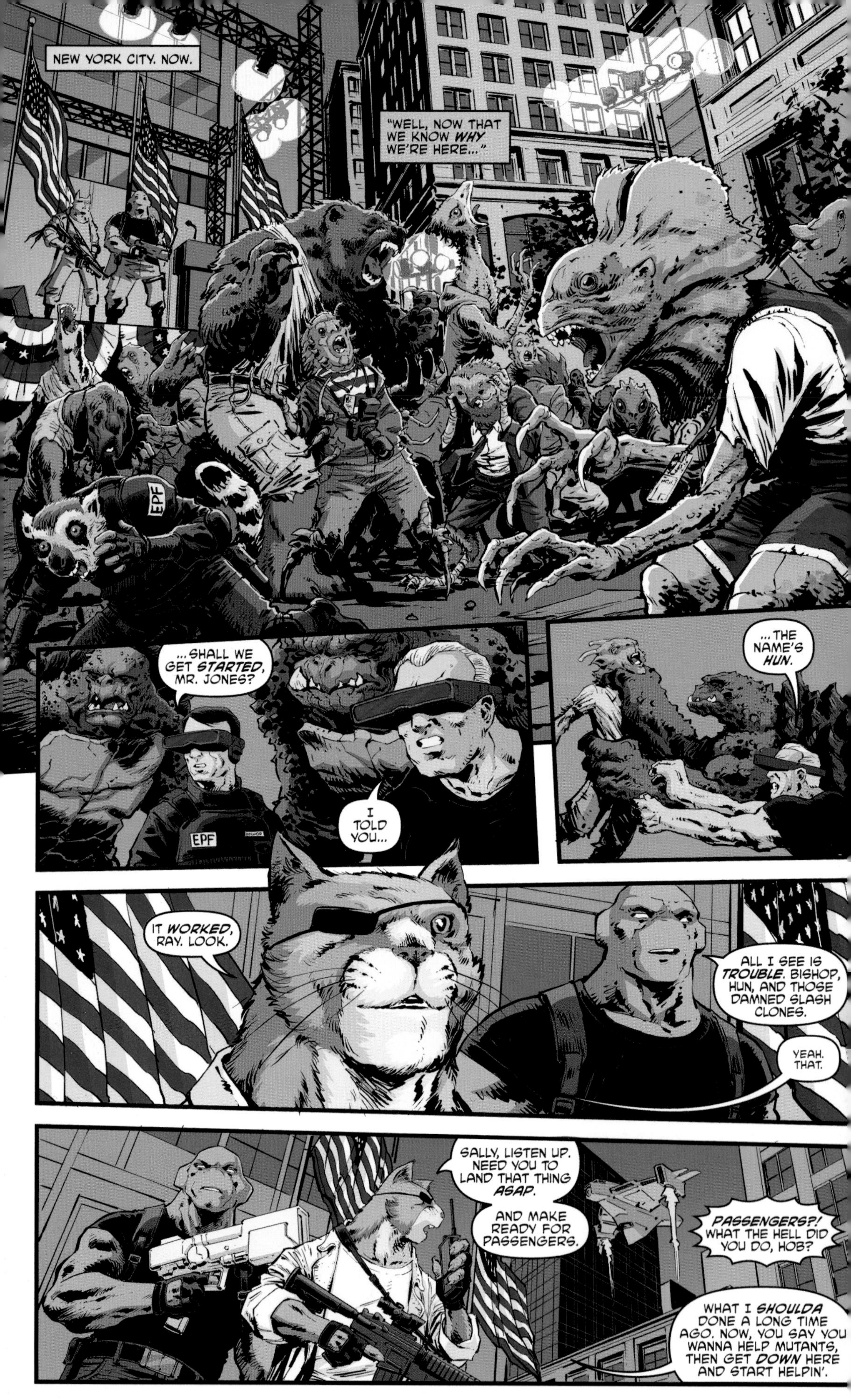

NEW YORK CITY. NOW.
"WELL, NOW THAT WE KNOW WHY WE'RE HERE..."
EPF
...SHALL WE GET STARTED, MR. JONES?
I TOLD YOU...
EPF
...THE NAME'S HUN.
IT WORKED, RAY. LOOK.
ALL I SEE IS TROUBLE. BISHOP, HUN, AND THOSE DAMNED SLASH CLONES.
YEAH. THAT.
SALLY, LISTEN UP. NEED YOU TO LAND THAT THING ASAP.
AND MAKE READY FOR PASSENGERS.
PASSENGERS?! WHAT THE HELL DID YOU DO, HOB?
WHAT I SHOULDA DONE A LONG TIME AGO. NOW, YOU SAY YOU WANNA HELP MUTANTS, THEN GET DOWN HERE AND START HELPIN'.

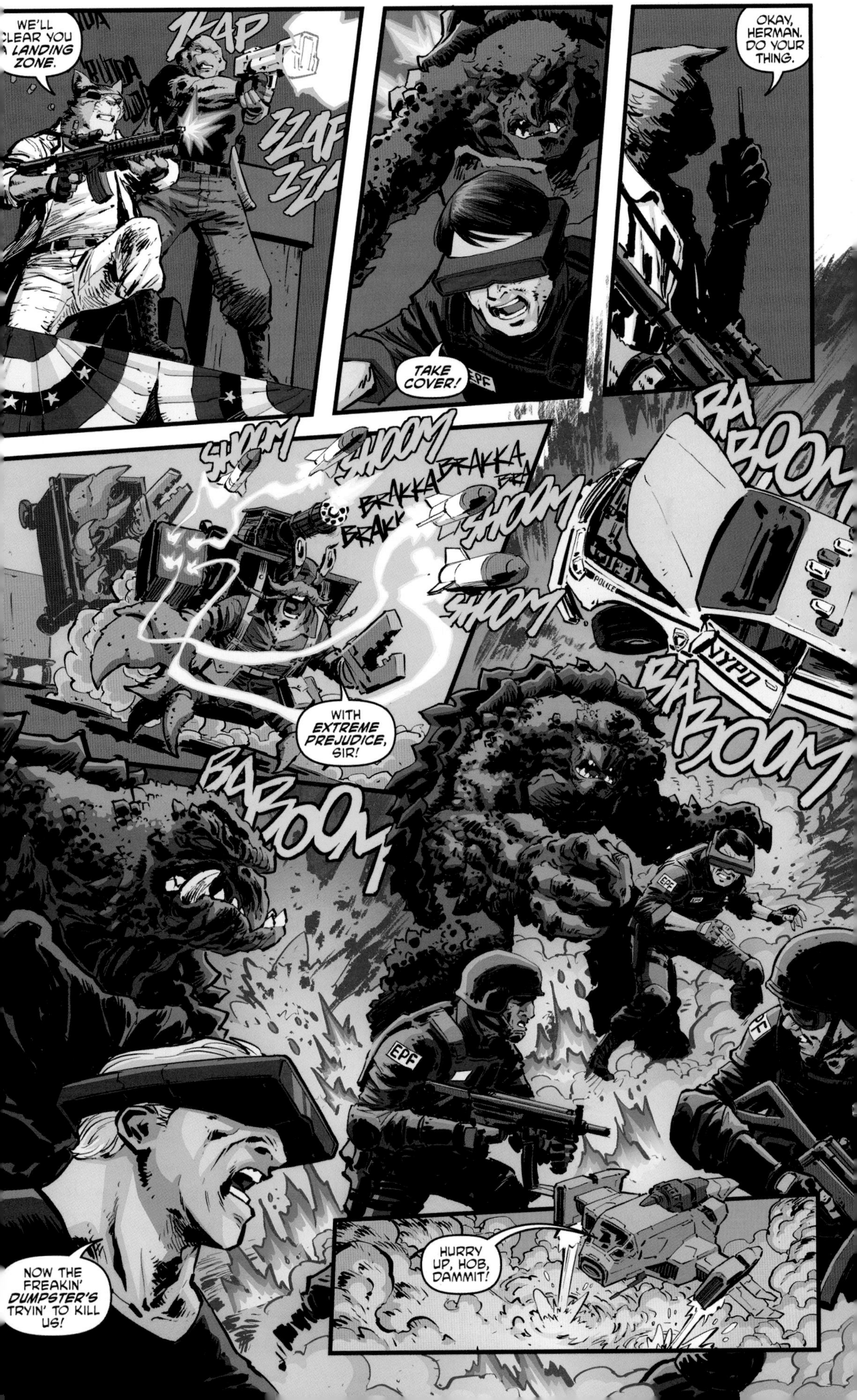
WE'LL CLEAR YOU A LANDING ZONE.
ZZAP
ZZAP ZZAP
TAKE COVER!
OKAY, HERMAN. DO YOUR THING.
SHOOM
SHOOM
BRAKKA
BRAKKA
BRAKK
SHOOM
SHOOM
BABOOM
WITH EXTREME PREJUDICE, SIR!
BABOOM
BABOOM
NOW THE FREAKIN' DUMPSTER'S TRYIN' TO KILL US!
HURRY UP, HOB, DAMMIT!

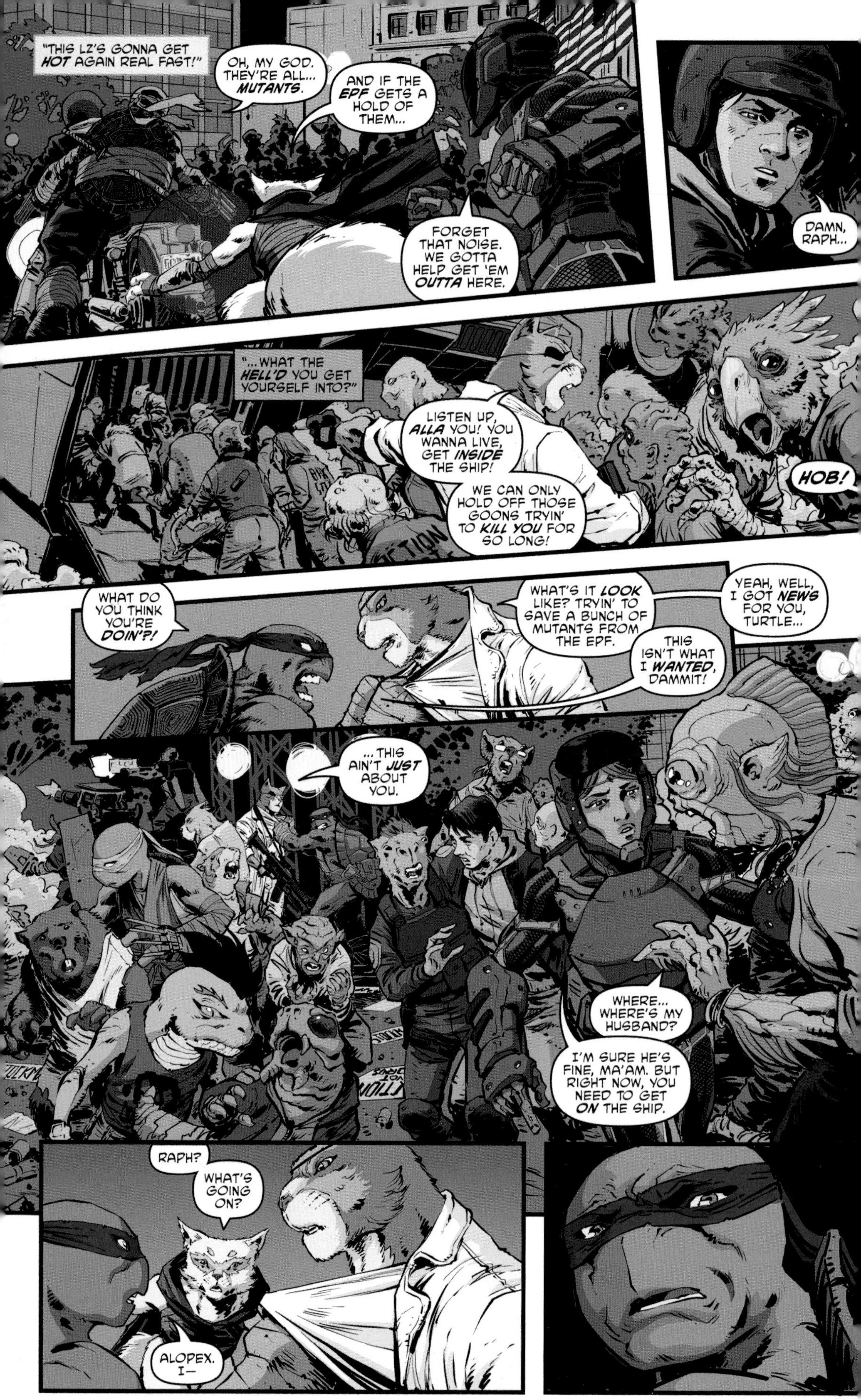

"THIS LZ'S GONNA GET HOT AGAIN REAL FAST!"
OH, MY GOD. THEY'RE ALL... MUTANTS.
AND IF THE EPF GETS A HOLD OF THEM...
FORGET THAT NOISE. WE GOTTA HELP GET 'EM OUTTA HERE.
DAMN, RAPH...
"...WHAT THE HELL'D YOU GET YOURSELF INTO?"
LISTEN UP, ALLA YOU! YOU WANNA LIVE, GET INSIDE THE SHIP!
WE CAN ONLY HOLD OFF THOSE GOONS TRYIN' TO KILL YOU FOR SO LONG!
HOB!
WHAT DO YOU THINK YOU'RE DOIN'?!
WHAT'S IT LOOK LIKE? TRYIN' TO SAVE A BUNCH OF MUTANTS FROM THE EPF.
YEAH, WELL, I GOT NEWS FOR YOU, TURTLE...
THIS ISN'T WHAT I WANTED, DAMMIT!
...THIS AIN'T JUST ABOUT YOU.
WHERE... WHERE'S MY HUSBAND?
I'M SURE HE'S FINE, MA'AM. BUT RIGHT NOW, YOU NEED TO GET ON THE SHIP.
RAPH?
WHAT'S GOING ON?
ALOPEX. I—

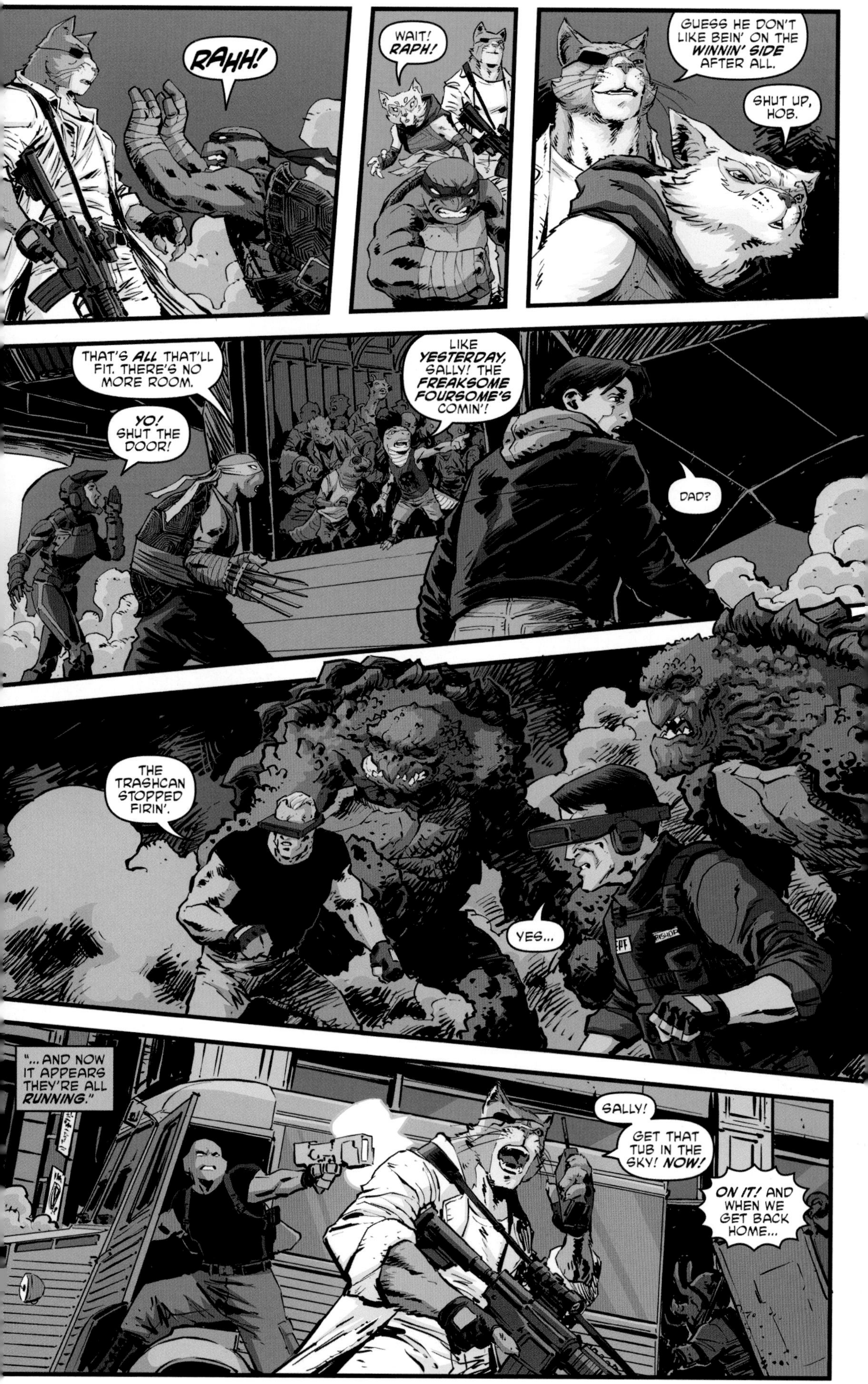
RAHH!
WAIT! RAPH!
GUESS HE DON'T LIKE BEIN' ON THE WINNIN' SIDE AFTER ALL.
SHUT UP, HOB.
THAT'S ALL THAT'LL FIT. THERE'S NO MORE ROOM.
YO! SHUT THE DOOR!
LIKE YESTERDAY, SALLY! THE FREAKSOME FOURSOME'S COMIN'!
DAD?
THE TRASHCAN STOPPED FIRIN'.
YES...
"...AND NOW IT APPEARS THEY'RE ALL RUNNING."
SALLY!
GET THAT TUB IN THE SKY! NOW!
ON IT! AND WHEN WE GET BACK HOME...

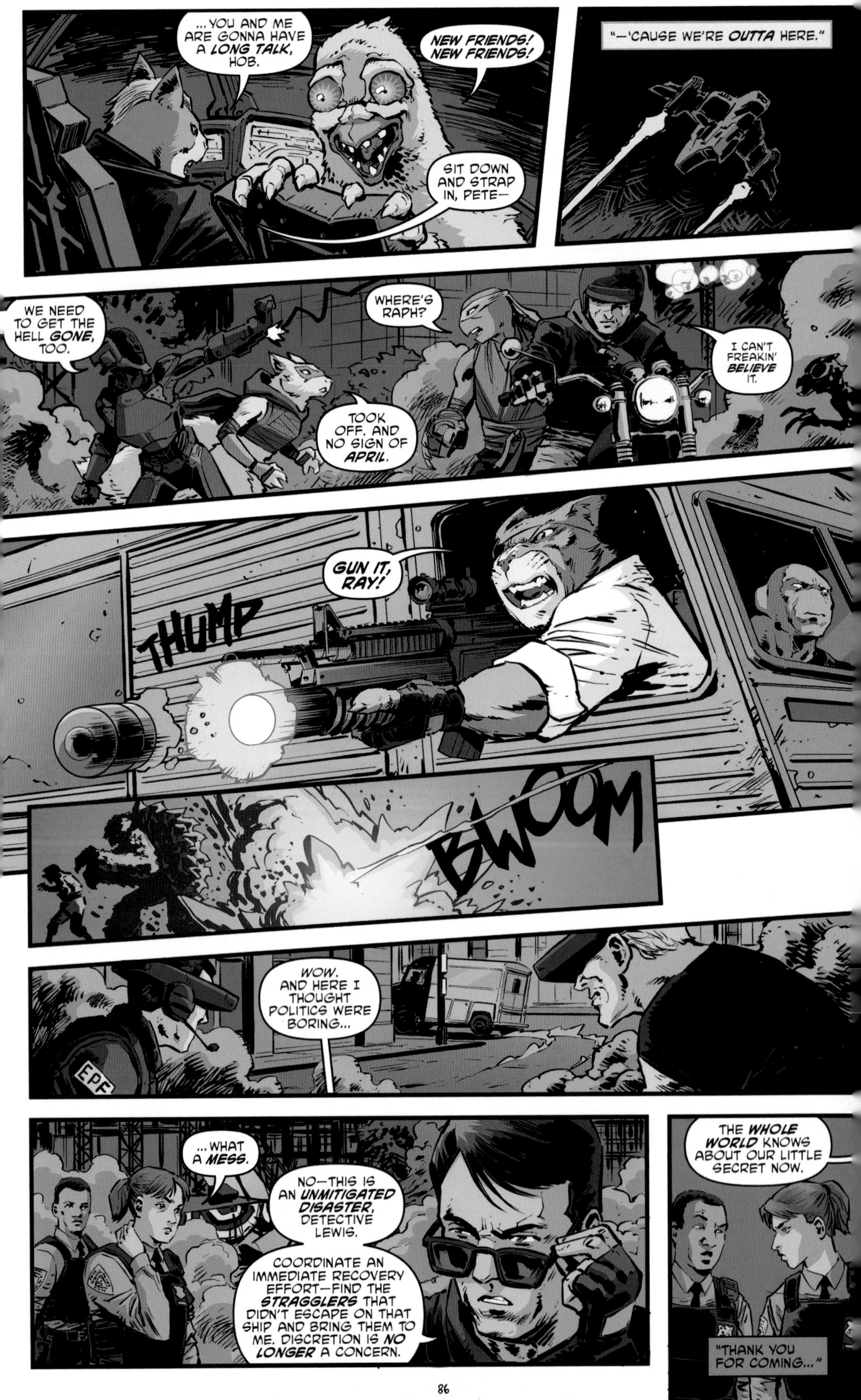
...YOU AND ME ARE GONNA HAVE A LONG TALK, HOB.
NEW FRIENDS! NEW FRIENDS!
SIT DOWN AND STRAP IN, PETE—
"—'CAUSE WE'RE OUTTA HERE."
WE NEED TO GET THE HELL GONE, TOO.
WHERE'S RAPH?
TOOK OFF. AND NO SIGN OF APRIL.
I CAN'T FREAKIN' BELIEVE IT.
GUN IT, RAY!
THUMP
BWOOM
WOW. AND HERE I THOUGHT POLITICS WERE BORING...
EPF
...WHAT A MESS.
NO—THIS IS AN UNMITIGATED DISASTER, DETECTIVE LEWIS.
COORDINATE AN IMMEDIATE RECOVERY EFFORT—FIND THE STRAGGLERS THAT DIDN'T ESCAPE ON THAT SHIP AND BRING THEM TO ME. DISCRETION IS NO LONGER A CONCERN.
THE WHOLE WORLD KNOWS ABOUT OUR LITTLE SECRET NOW.
"THANK YOU FOR COMING..."

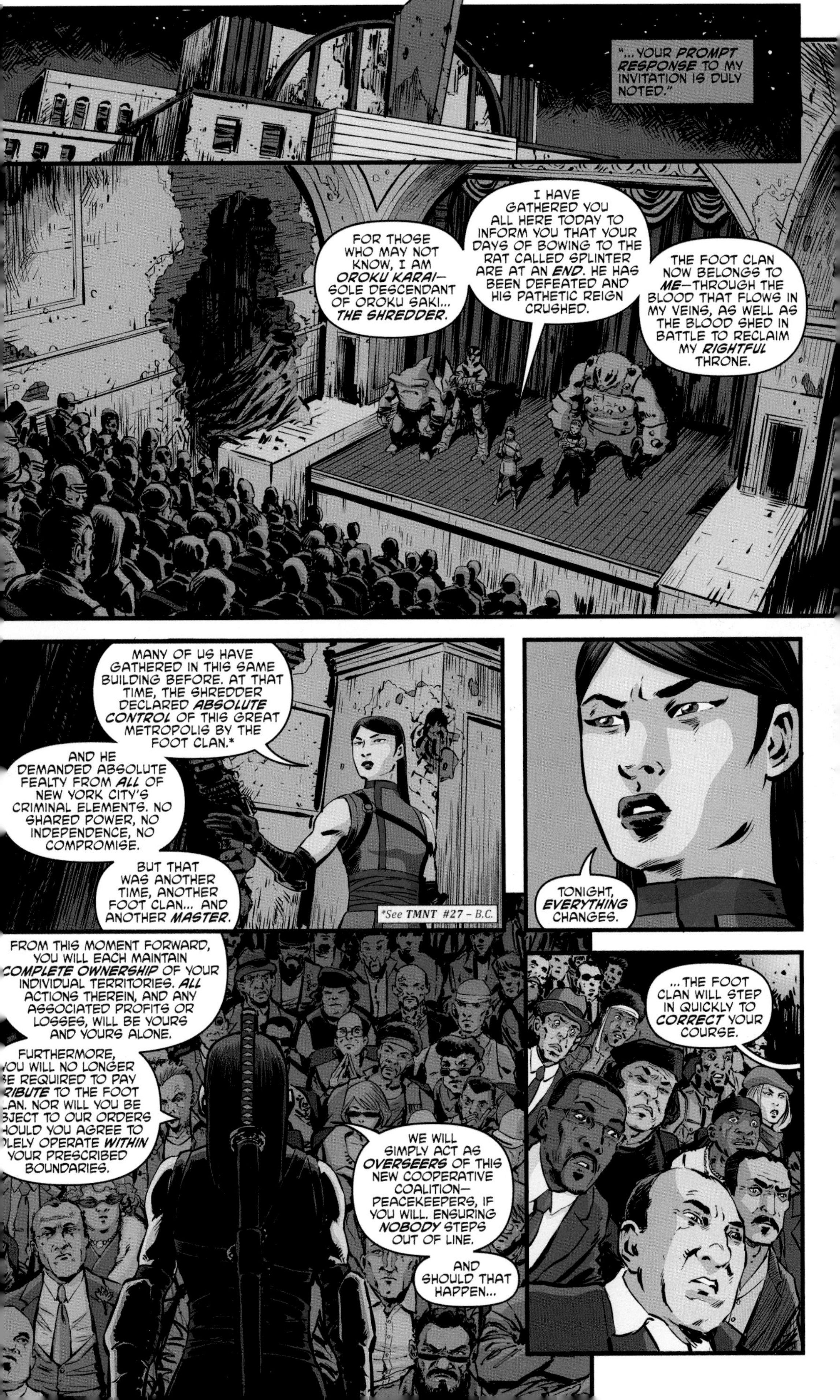
"...YOUR PROMPT RESPONSE TO MY INVITATION IS DULY NOTED."
FOR THOSE WHO MAY NOT KNOW, I AM OROKU KARAI—SOLE DESCENDANT OF OROKU SAKI... THE SHREDDER.
I HAVE GATHERED YOU ALL HERE TODAY TO INFORM YOU THAT YOUR DAYS OF BOWING TO THE RAT CALLED SPLINTER ARE AT AN END. HE HAS BEEN DEFEATED AND HIS PATHETIC REIGN CRUSHED.
THE FOOT CLAN NOW BELONGS TO ME—THROUGH THE BLOOD THAT FLOWS IN MY VEINS, AS WELL AS THE BLOOD SHED IN BATTLE TO RECLAIM MY RIGHTFUL THRONE.
MANY OF US HAVE GATHERED IN THIS SAME BUILDING BEFORE. AT THAT TIME, THE SHREDDER DECLARED ABSOLUTE CONTROL OF THIS GREAT METROPOLIS BY THE FOOT CLAN.*
AND HE DEMANDED ABSOLUTE FEALTY FROM ALL OF NEW YORK CITY'S CRIMINAL ELEMENTS. NO SHARED POWER, NO INDEPENDENCE, NO COMPROMISE.
BUT THAT WAS ANOTHER TIME, ANOTHER FOOT CLAN... AND ANOTHER MASTER.
*See TMNT #27 – B.C.
TONIGHT, EVERYTHING CHANGES.
FROM THIS MOMENT FORWARD, YOU WILL EACH MAINTAIN COMPLETE OWNERSHIP OF YOUR INDIVIDUAL TERRITORIES. ALL ACTIONS THEREIN, AND ANY ASSOCIATED PROFITS OR LOSSES, WILL BE YOURS AND YOURS ALONE.
FURTHERMORE, YOU WILL NO LONGER BE REQUIRED TO PAY TRIBUTE TO THE FOOT CLAN. NOR WILL YOU BE SUBJECT TO OUR ORDERS SHOULD YOU AGREE TO SOLELY OPERATE WITHIN YOUR PRESCRIBED BOUNDARIES.
WE WILL SIMPLY ACT AS OVERSEERS OF THIS NEW COOPERATIVE COALITION—PEACEKEEPERS, IF YOU WILL. ENSURING NOBODY STEPS OUT OF LINE.
AND SHOULD THAT HAPPEN...
...THE FOOT CLAN WILL STEP IN QUICKLY TO CORRECT YOUR COURSE.

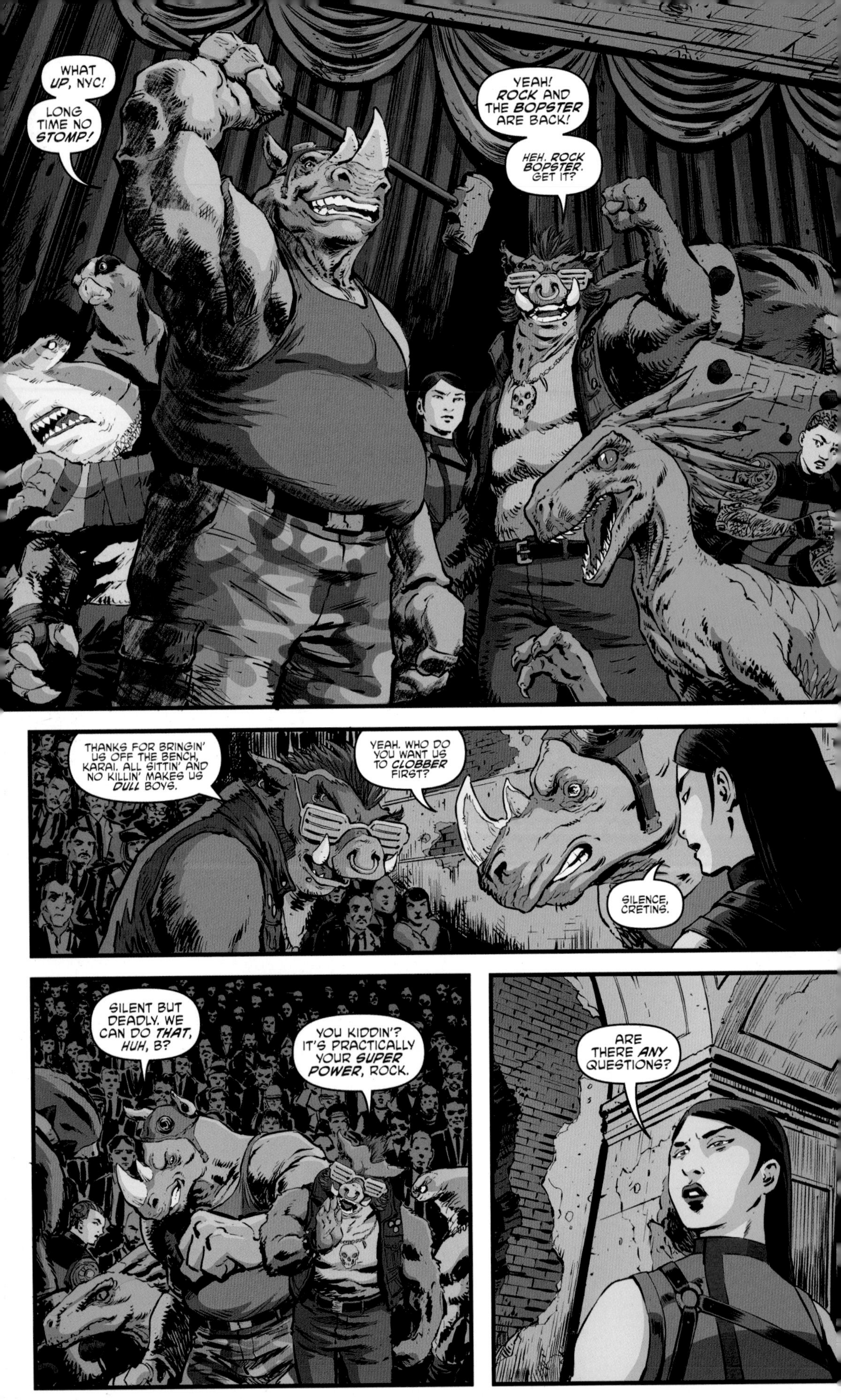
WHAT UP, NYC!
LONG TIME NO STOMP!
YEAH! ROCK AND THE BOPSTER ARE BACK!
HEH. ROCK BOPSTER. GET IT?
THANKS FOR BRINGIN' US OFF THE BENCH, KARAI. ALL SITTIN' AND NO KILLIN' MAKES US DULL BOYS.
YEAH. WHO DO YOU WANT US TO CLOBBER FIRST?
SILENCE, CRETINS.
SILENT BUT DEADLY. WE CAN DO THAT, HUH, B?
YOU KIDDIN'? IT'S PRACTICALLY YOUR SUPER POWER, ROCK.
ARE THERE ANY QUESTIONS?

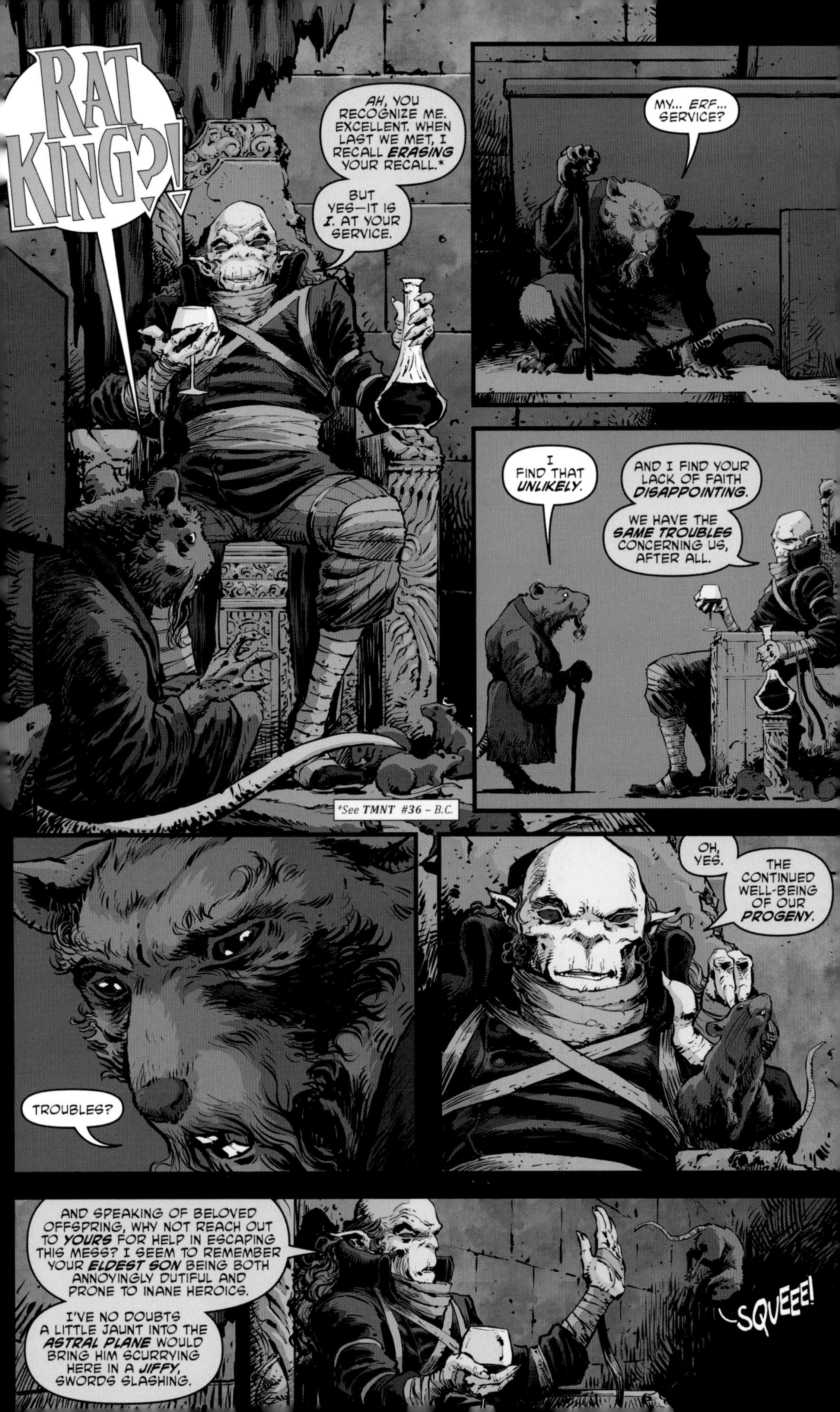
RAT KING?!
AH, YOU RECOGNIZE ME. EXCELLENT. WHEN LAST WE MET, I RECALL ERASING YOUR RECALL.*
BUT YES—IT IS I. AT YOUR SERVICE.
*See TMNT #36 – B.C.
MY... ERF... SERVICE?
I FIND THAT UNLIKELY.
AND I FIND YOUR LACK OF FAITH DISAPPOINTING.
WE HAVE THE SAME TROUBLES CONCERNING US, AFTER ALL.
TROUBLES?
OH, YES.
THE CONTINUED WELL-BEING OF OUR PROGENY.
AND SPEAKING OF BELOVED OFFSPRING, WHY NOT REACH OUT TO YOURS FOR HELP IN ESCAPING THIS MESS? I SEEM TO REMEMBER YOUR ELDEST SON BEING BOTH ANNOYINGLY DUTIFUL AND PRONE TO INANE HEROICS.
I'VE NO DOUBTS A LITTLE JAUNT INTO THE ASTRAL PLANE WOULD BRING HIM SCURRYING HERE IN A JIFFY, SWORDS SLASHING.
SQUEEE!

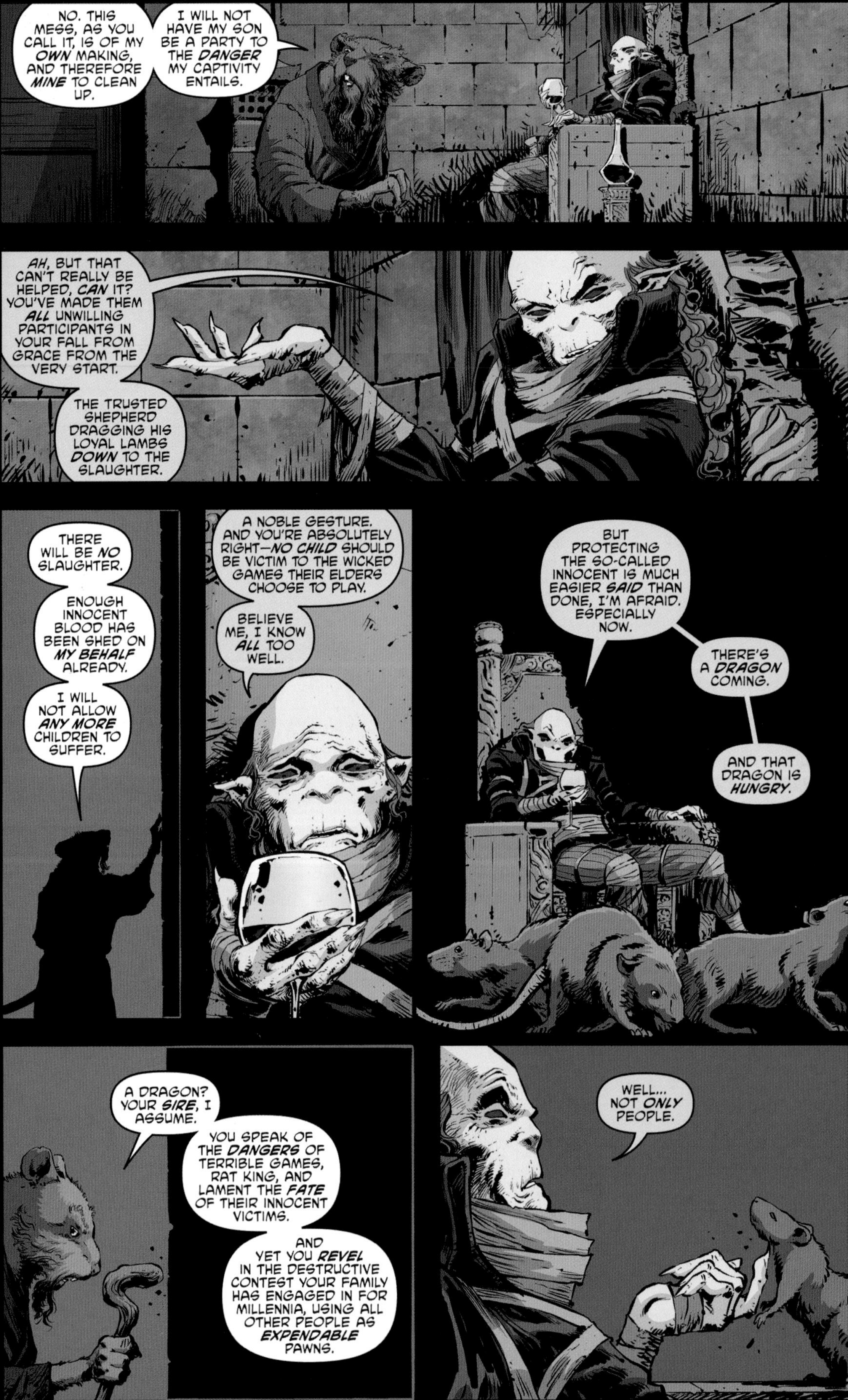
NO. THIS MESS, AS YOU CALL IT, IS OF MY OWN MAKING, AND THEREFORE MINE TO CLEAN UP.
I WILL NOT HAVE MY SON BE A PARTY TO THE DANGER MY CAPTIVITY ENTAILS.
AH, BUT THAT CAN'T REALLY BE HELPED, CAN IT? YOU'VE MADE THEM ALL UNWILLING PARTICIPANTS IN YOUR FALL FROM GRACE FROM THE VERY START.
THE TRUSTED SHEPHERD DRAGGING HIS LOYAL LAMBS DOWN TO THE SLAUGHTER.
THERE WILL BE NO SLAUGHTER.
ENOUGH INNOCENT BLOOD HAS BEEN SHED ON MY BEHALF ALREADY.
I WILL NOT ALLOW ANY MORE CHILDREN TO SUFFER.
A NOBLE GESTURE. AND YOU'RE ABSOLUTELY RIGHT—NO CHILD SHOULD BE VICTIM TO THE WICKED GAMES THEIR ELDERS CHOOSE TO PLAY.
BELIEVE ME, I KNOW ALL TOO WELL.
BUT PROTECTING THE SO-CALLED INNOCENT IS MUCH EASIER SAID THAN DONE, I'M AFRAID. ESPECIALLY NOW.
THERE'S A DRAGON COMING.
AND THAT DRAGON IS HUNGRY.
A DRAGON? YOUR SIRE, I ASSUME.
YOU SPEAK OF THE DANGERS OF TERRIBLE GAMES, RAT KING, AND LAMENT THE FATE OF THEIR INNOCENT VICTIMS.
AND YET YOU REVEL IN THE DESTRUCTIVE CONTEST YOUR FAMILY HAS ENGAGED IN FOR MILLENNIA, USING ALL OTHER PEOPLE AS EXPENDABLE PAWNS.
WELL... NOT ONLY PEOPLE.

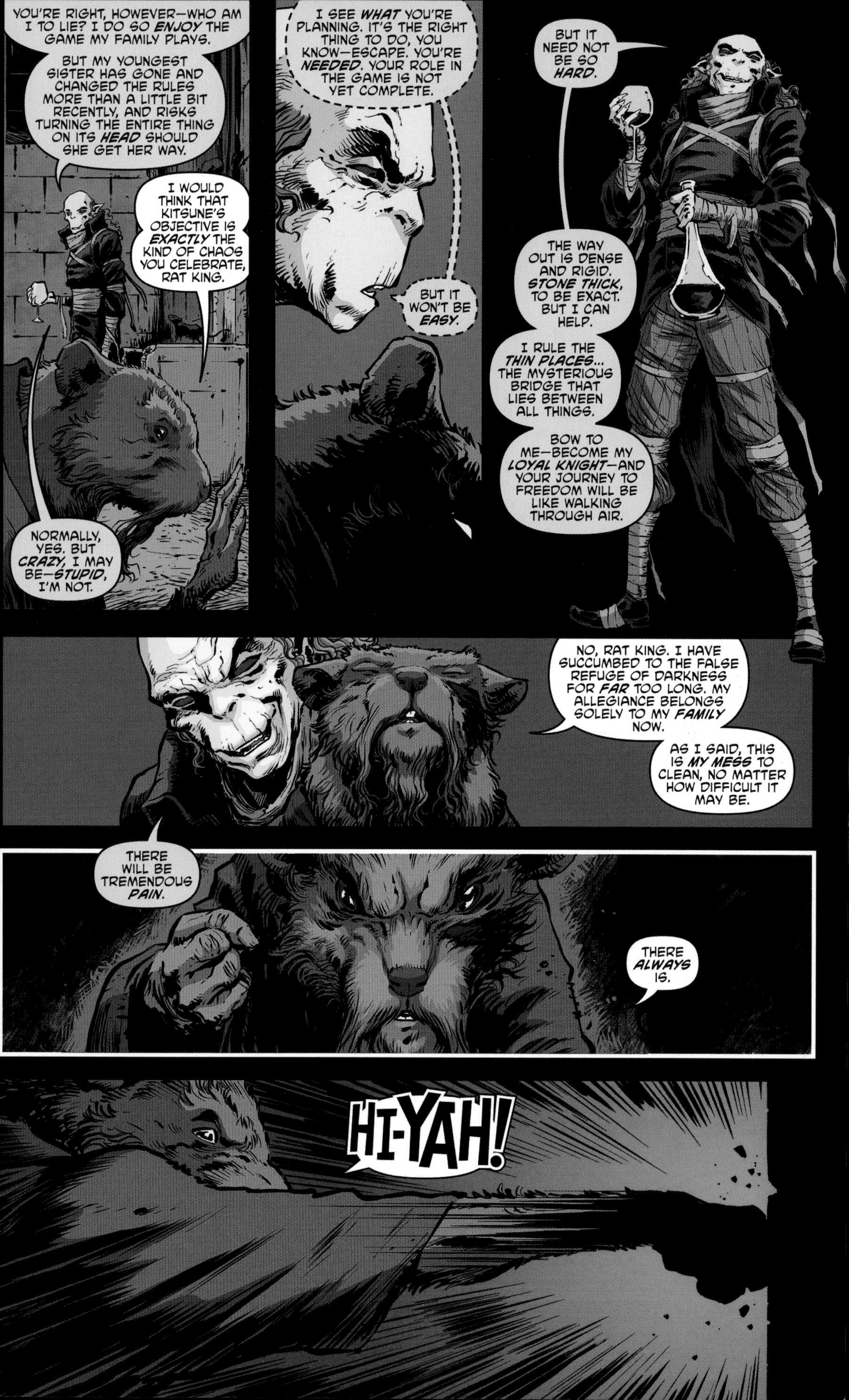
YOU'RE RIGHT, HOWEVER—WHO AM I TO LIE? I DO SO ENJOY THE GAME MY FAMILY PLAYS.
BUT MY YOUNGEST SISTER HAS GONE AND CHANGED THE RULES MORE THAN A LITTLE BIT RECENTLY, AND RISKS TURNING THE ENTIRE THING ON ITS HEAD SHOULD SHE GET HER WAY.
I WOULD THINK THAT KITSUNE'S OBJECTIVE IS EXACTLY THE KIND OF CHAOS YOU CELEBRATE, RAT KING.
NORMALLY, YES. BUT CRAZY, I MAY BE—STUPID, I'M NOT.
I SEE WHAT YOU'RE PLANNING. IT'S THE RIGHT THING TO DO, YOU KNOW—ESCAPE. YOU'RE NEEDED. YOUR ROLE IN THE GAME IS NOT YET COMPLETE.
BUT IT WON'T BE EASY.
BUT IT NEED NOT BE SO HARD.
THE WAY OUT IS DENSE AND RIGID. STONE THICK, TO BE EXACT. BUT I CAN HELP.
I RULE THE THIN PLACES... THE MYSTERIOUS BRIDGE THAT LIES BETWEEN ALL THINGS.
BOW TO ME—BECOME MY LOYAL KNIGHT—AND YOUR JOURNEY TO FREEDOM WILL BE LIKE WALKING THROUGH AIR.
NO, RAT KING. I HAVE SUCCUMBED TO THE FALSE REFUGE OF DARKNESS FOR FAR TOO LONG. MY ALLEGIANCE BELONGS SOLELY TO MY FAMILY NOW.
AS I SAID, THIS IS MY MESS TO CLEAN, NO MATTER HOW DIFFICULT IT MAY BE.
THERE WILL BE TREMENDOUS PAIN.
THERE ALWAYS IS.
HI-YAH!

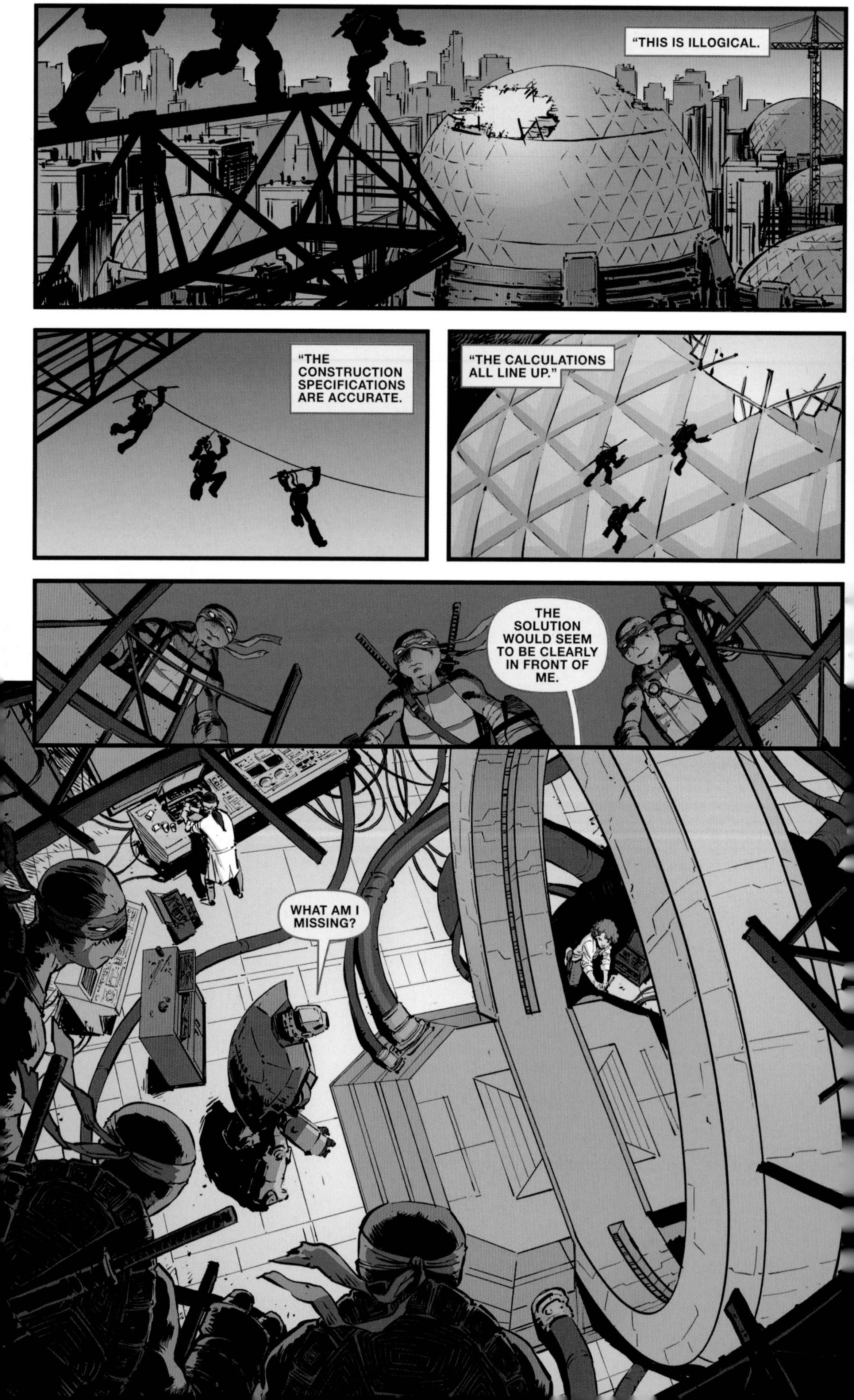
"THIS IS ILLOGICAL.
"THE CONSTRUCTION SPECIFICATIONS ARE ACCURATE.
"THE CALCULATIONS ALL LINE UP."
THE SOLUTION WOULD SEEM TO BE CLEARLY IN FRONT OF ME.
WHAT AM I MISSING?

WHAT ARE **YOU** KEEPING FROM ME?!

HEY, DON'T START ACCUSING **US** OF HOLDING BACK.

WE'VE BEEN WORKING *NON-STOP* EVER SINCE YOU GOT THE BLASTED IDEA IN THAT TIN CAN HEAD OF YOURS.

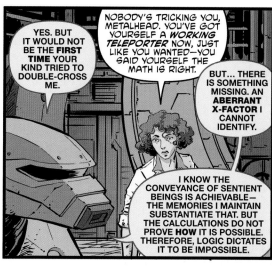

NOBODY'S TRICKING YOU, METALHEAD. YOU'VE GOT YOURSELF A *WORKING TELEPORTER* NOW, JUST LIKE YOU WANTED—YOU SAID YOURSELF THE MATH IS RIGHT.

YES. BUT IT WOULD NOT BE THE **FIRST TIME** YOUR KIND TRIED TO DOUBLE-CROSS ME.

BUT... THERE IS SOMETHING MISSING. AN **ABERRANT X-FACTOR** I CANNOT IDENTIFY.

I KNOW THE CONVEYANCE OF SENTIENT BEINGS IS ACHIEVABLE— THE MEMORIES I MAINTAIN SUBSTANTIATE THAT. BUT THE CALCULATIONS DO NOT PROVE **HOW** IT IS POSSIBLE. THEREFORE, LOGIC DICTATES IT TO BE IMPOSSIBLE.

GREAT. METALHEAD'S BUILDING A TELEPORTER— THAT'S *ALL* WE NEED.

MAYBE THIS IS A *GOOD* THING.

HOW?

NO TIME TO EXPLAIN. JUST DO YOUR BEST TO KEEP OUR *FRIENDS* SAFE—

"—I'LL DEAL WITH *METALHEAD*."

I WILL RUN THE TEST SCENARIO AGAIN. I **WILL** IDENTIFY THE ANOMALY.

HOW? NOTHING'S CHANGED. YOUR TESTING IS JUST *STUBBORN REDUNDANCY* AT THIS POINT.

I AM GROWING IMPATIENT WITH YOUR CONSTANT **SARCASM**, DR. LILJA.

PERHAPS IT IS TIME I SWAP OUT SIMULATION TESTING WITH A **LIVE** SUBJECT.

HAROLD?

WAIT, I—

DEFINITION OF INSANITY FOR 500, ALEX.

METALHEAD!

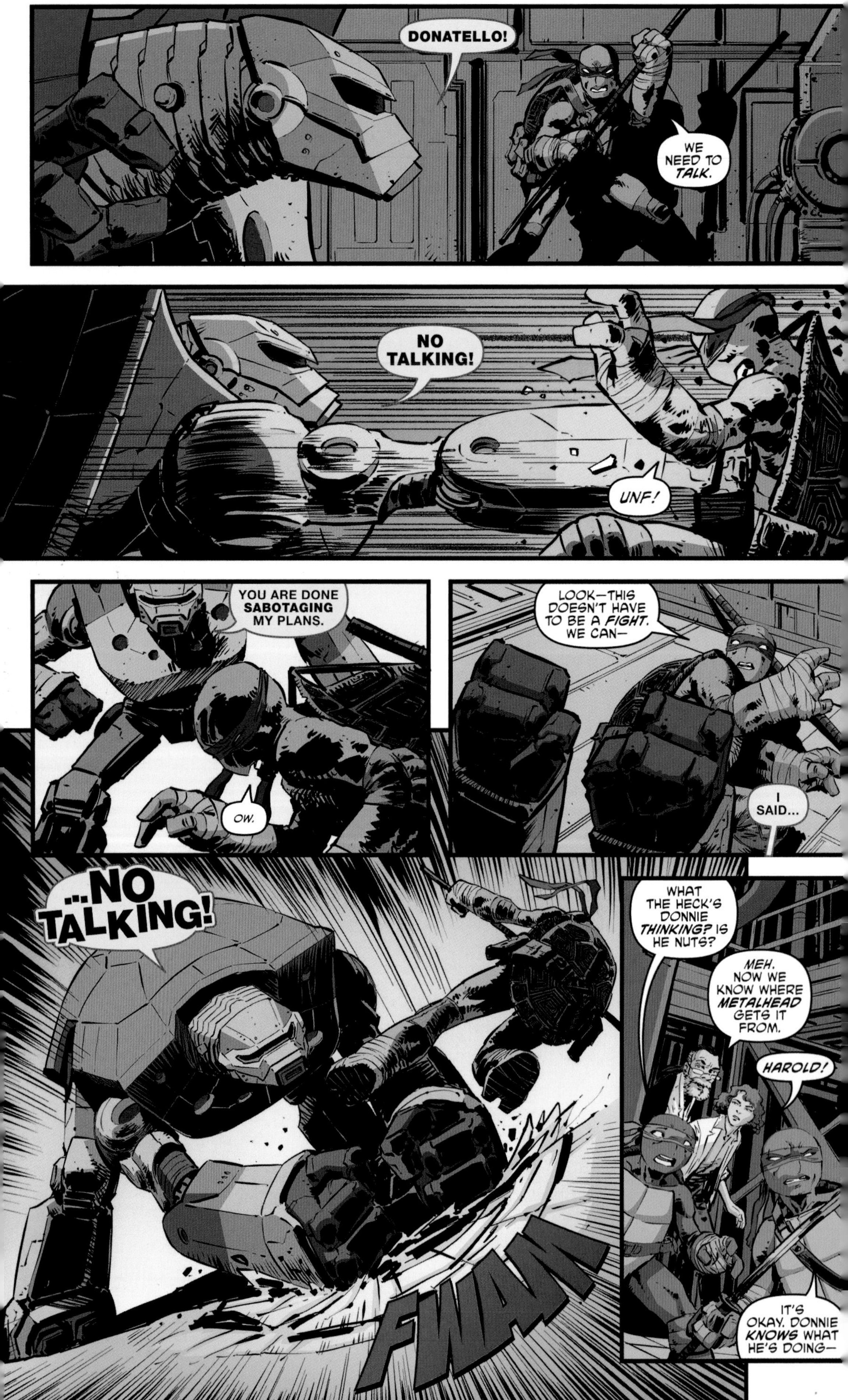
DONATELLO!
WE NEED TO TALK.
NO TALKING!
UNF!
YOU ARE DONE SABOTAGING MY PLANS.
OW.
LOOK—THIS DOESN'T HAVE TO BE A FIGHT. WE CAN—
I SAID...
...NO TALKING!
FWAM
WHAT THE HECK'S DONNIE THINKING? IS HE NUTS?
MEH. NOW WE KNOW WHERE METALHEAD GETS IT FROM.
HAROLD!
IT'S OKAY. DONNIE KNOWS WHAT HE'S DOING—

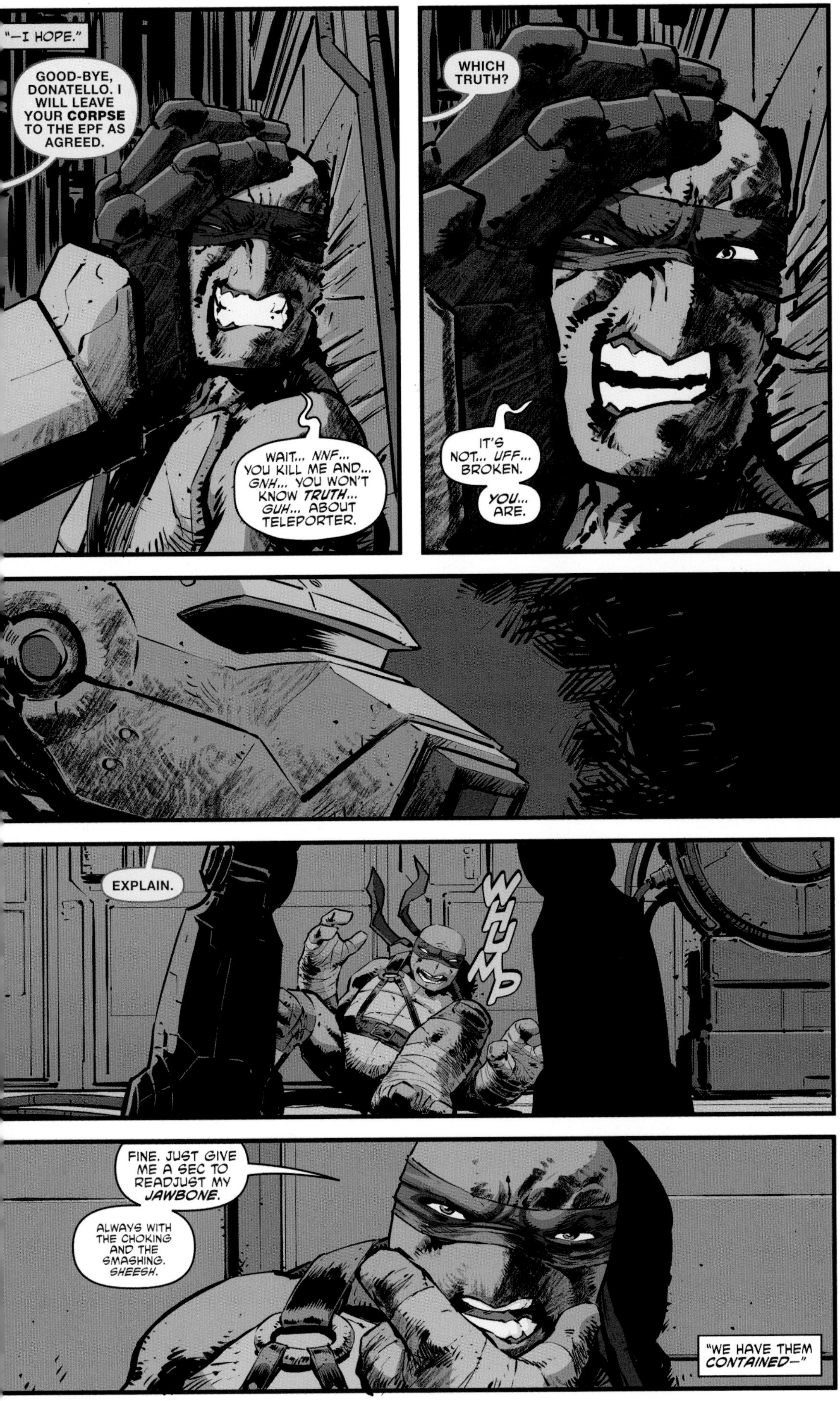
"—I HOPE."
GOOD-BYE, DONATELLO. I WILL LEAVE YOUR **CORPSE** TO THE EPF AS AGREED.
WAIT... *NNF*... YOU KILL ME AND... *GNH*... YOU WON'T KNOW ***TRUTH***... *GUH*... ABOUT TELEPORTER.
WHICH TRUTH?
IT'S NOT... *UFF*... BROKEN.
YOU... ARE.
EXPLAIN.
WHUMP
FINE. JUST GIVE ME A SEC TO READJUST MY ***JAWBONE***.
ALWAYS WITH THE CHOKING AND THE SMASHING. *SHEESH.*
"WE HAVE THEM ***CONTAINED***—"

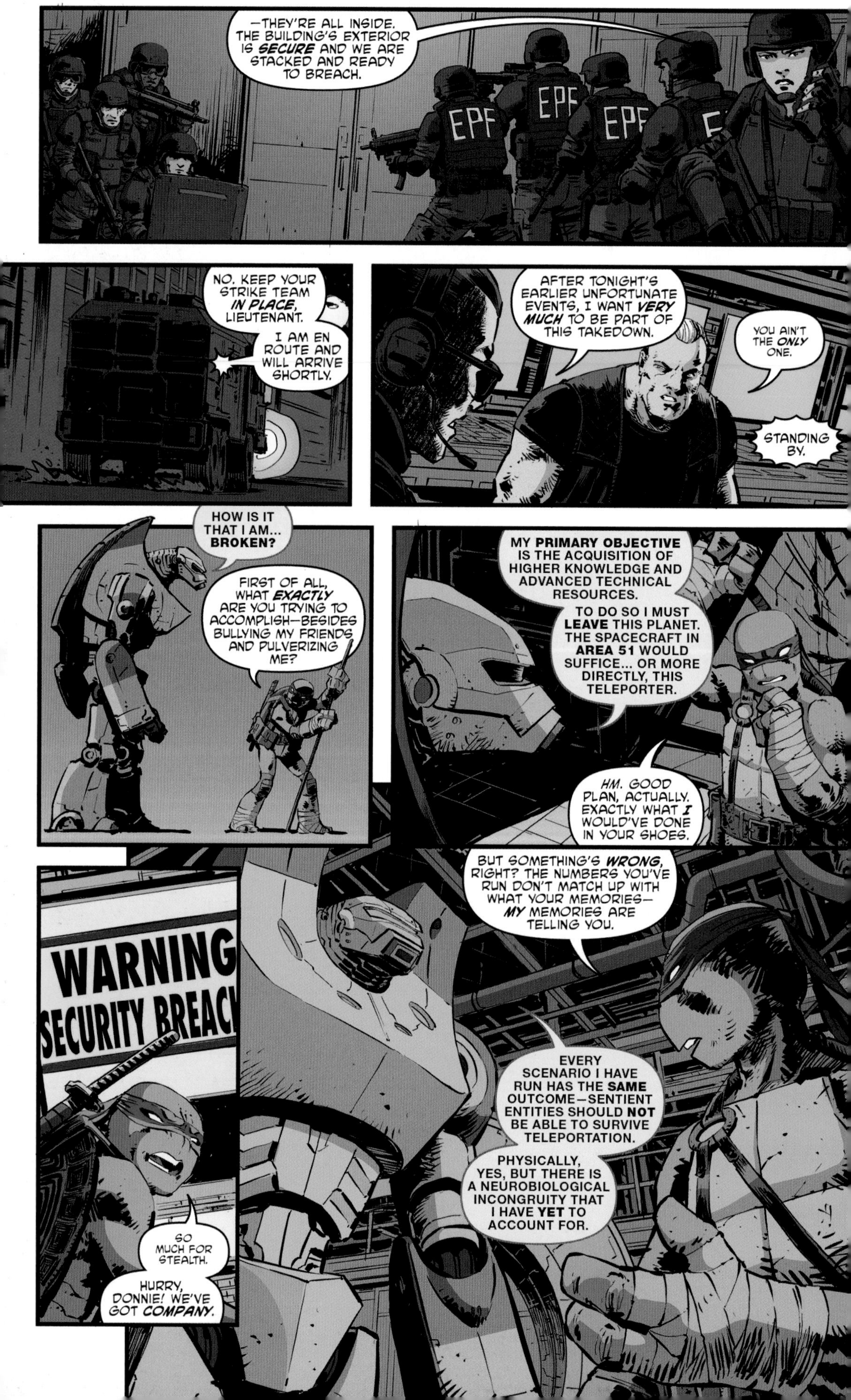
—THEY'RE ALL INSIDE. THE BUILDING'S EXTERIOR IS SECURE AND WE ARE STACKED AND READY TO BREACH.
EPF
EPF
EPF
NO. KEEP YOUR STRIKE TEAM IN PLACE, LIEUTENANT.
I AM EN ROUTE AND WILL ARRIVE SHORTLY.
AFTER TONIGHT'S EARLIER UNFORTUNATE EVENTS, I WANT VERY MUCH TO BE PART OF THIS TAKEDOWN.
YOU AIN'T THE ONLY ONE.
STANDING BY.
HOW IS IT THAT I AM... BROKEN?
FIRST OF ALL, WHAT EXACTLY ARE YOU TRYING TO ACCOMPLISH—BESIDES BULLYING MY FRIENDS AND PULVERIZING ME?
MY PRIMARY OBJECTIVE IS THE ACQUISITION OF HIGHER KNOWLEDGE AND ADVANCED TECHNICAL RESOURCES.
TO DO SO I MUST LEAVE THIS PLANET. THE SPACECRAFT IN AREA 51 WOULD SUFFICE... OR MORE DIRECTLY, THIS TELEPORTER.
HM. GOOD PLAN, ACTUALLY. EXACTLY WHAT I WOULD'VE DONE IN YOUR SHOES.
WARNING
SECURITY BREAC
SO MUCH FOR STEALTH.
HURRY, DONNIE! WE'VE GOT COMPANY.
BUT SOMETHING'S WRONG, RIGHT? THE NUMBERS YOU'VE RUN DON'T MATCH UP WITH WHAT YOUR MEMORIES—MY MEMORIES ARE TELLING YOU.
EVERY SCENARIO I HAVE RUN HAS THE SAME OUTCOME—SENTIENT ENTITIES SHOULD NOT BE ABLE TO SURVIVE TELEPORTATION.
PHYSICALLY, YES, BUT THERE IS A NEUROBIOLOGICAL INCONGRUITY THAT I HAVE YET TO ACCOUNT FOR.

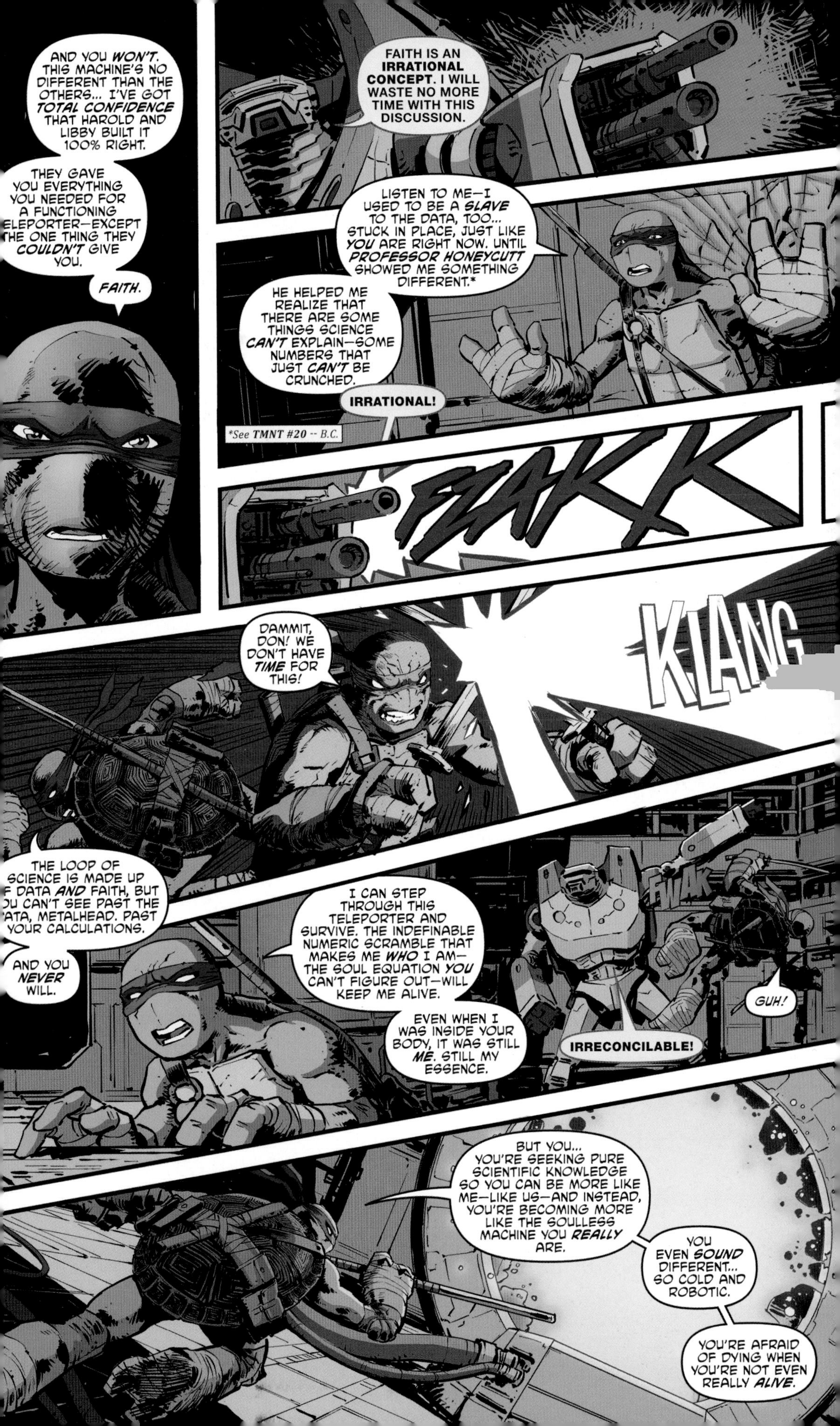
AND YOU *WON'T*. THIS MACHINE'S NO DIFFERENT THAN THE OTHERS... I'VE GOT *TOTAL CONFIDENCE* THAT HAROLD AND LIBBY BUILT IT 100% RIGHT.
THEY GAVE YOU EVERYTHING YOU NEEDED FOR A FUNCTIONING ELEPORTER—EXCEPT THE ONE THING THEY *COULDN'T* GIVE YOU.
FAITH.
FAITH IS AN **IRRATIONAL CONCEPT**. I WILL WASTE NO MORE TIME WITH THIS DISCUSSION.
LISTEN TO ME—I USED TO BE A *SLAVE* TO THE DATA, TOO... STUCK IN PLACE, JUST LIKE *YOU* ARE RIGHT NOW. UNTIL *PROFESSOR HONEYCUTT* SHOWED ME SOMETHING DIFFERENT.*
HE HELPED ME REALIZE THAT THERE ARE SOME THINGS SCIENCE *CAN'T* EXPLAIN—SOME NUMBERS THAT JUST *CAN'T* BE CRUNCHED.
IRRATIONAL!
*See TMNT #20 -- B.C.
FZAKK
KLANG
DAMMIT, DON! WE DON'T HAVE *TIME* FOR THIS!
THE LOOP OF SCIENCE IS MADE UP OF DATA *AND* FAITH, BUT YOU CAN'T SEE PAST THE DATA, METALHEAD. PAST YOUR CALCULATIONS.
AND YOU *NEVER* WILL.
I CAN STEP THROUGH THIS TELEPORTER AND SURVIVE. THE INDEFINABLE NUMERIC SCRAMBLE THAT MAKES ME *WHO* I AM—THE SOUL EQUATION *YOU* CAN'T FIGURE OUT—WILL KEEP ME ALIVE.
EVEN WHEN I WAS INSIDE YOUR BODY, IT WAS STILL *ME*. STILL MY ESSENCE.
FWAK
GUH!
IRRECONCILABLE!
BUT YOU... YOU'RE SEEKING PURE SCIENTIFIC KNOWLEDGE SO YOU CAN BE MORE LIKE ME—LIKE US—AND INSTEAD, YOU'RE BECOMING MORE LIKE THE SOULLESS MACHINE YOU *REALLY* ARE.
YOU EVEN *SOUND* DIFFERENT... SO COLD AND ROBOTIC.
YOU'RE AFRAID OF DYING WHEN YOU'RE NOT EVEN REALLY *ALIVE*.

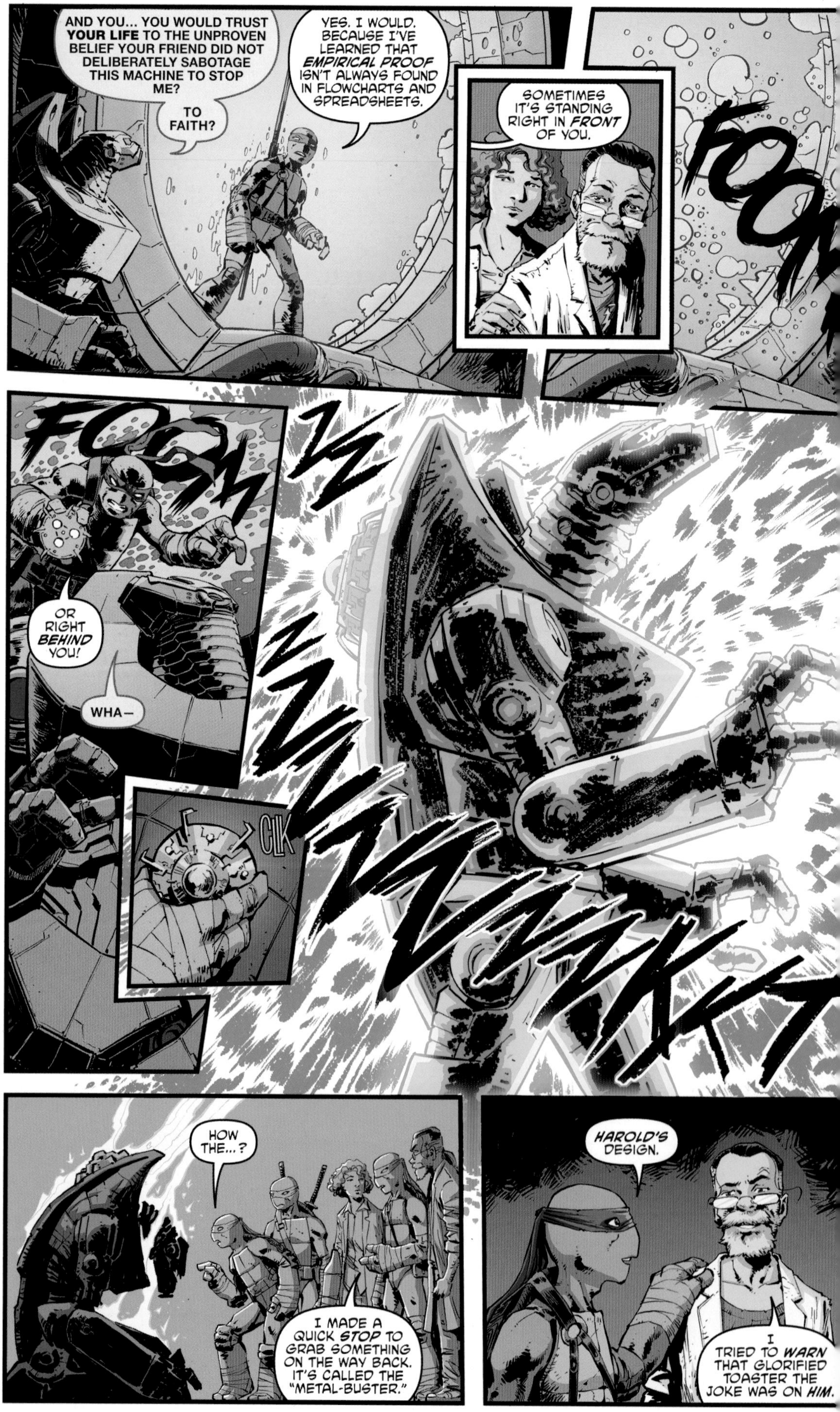

AND YOU... YOU WOULD TRUST YOUR LIFE TO THE UNPROVEN BELIEF YOUR FRIEND DID NOT DELIBERATELY SABOTAGE THIS MACHINE TO STOP ME?
TO FAITH?
YES. I WOULD. BECAUSE I'VE LEARNED THAT EMPIRICAL PROOF ISN'T ALWAYS FOUND IN FLOWCHARTS AND SPREADSHEETS.
SOMETIMES IT'S STANDING RIGHT IN FRONT OF YOU.
FOOM
FOOM
OR RIGHT BEHIND YOU!
WHA—
CLIK
ZZZZZZZZZAKKT
HOW THE...?
I MADE A QUICK STOP TO GRAB SOMETHING ON THE WAY BACK. IT'S CALLED THE "METAL-BUSTER."
HAROLD'S DESIGN.
I TRIED TO WARN THAT GLORIFIED TOASTER THE JOKE WAS ON HIM.

IT MIGHT BE ON *US*, TOO. BISHOP JUST SHOWED UP—AND HE'S GOT THAT IDIOT *HUN* WITH HIM.

NOT GOOD.

BUT *THIS* IS. APRIL JUST TEXTED THAT SHE'S *SAFE* WITH HER PARENTS.

ANGEL'S CHECKING IN, TOO, GUYS. THEY'RE *ALL* OKAY... 'CEPT STILL NO *RAPH*.

OKAY—WE NEED TO GET EVERYONE *OUT* OF HERE, AND I THINK WE CAN KILL TWO BIRDS DOING IT.

MAYBE *THREE*.

AND HOW EXACTLY DO YOU PROPOSE TO DO *THAT*?

FIRST, YOU AND HAROLD NEED TO *TELEPORT* AWAY TO SOMEPLACE SAFE.

THEN DONNIE'S GONNA SET IT UP TO GET US TO *FOOT HEADQUARTERS*... AND LEAVE THE TELEPORTER *RUNNING* AFTER WE'RE GONE.

AND MIKEY'S GONNA TEXT OUR FRIENDS TO *MEET* US THERE.

WE'LL JUST HAVE TO FIGURE OUT WHAT TO DO ABOUT *RAPH* LATER.

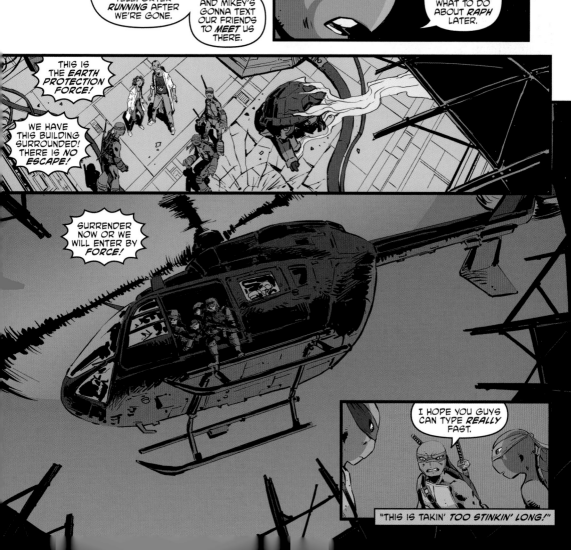

THIS IS THE *EARTH PROTECTION FORCE!*

WE HAVE THIS BUILDING SURROUNDED! THERE IS *NO ESCAPE!*

SURRENDER NOW OR WE WILL ENTER BY *FORCE!*

I HOPE YOU GUYS CAN TYPE *REALLY* FAST.

"THIS IS TAKIN' *TOO STINKIN' LONG!*"

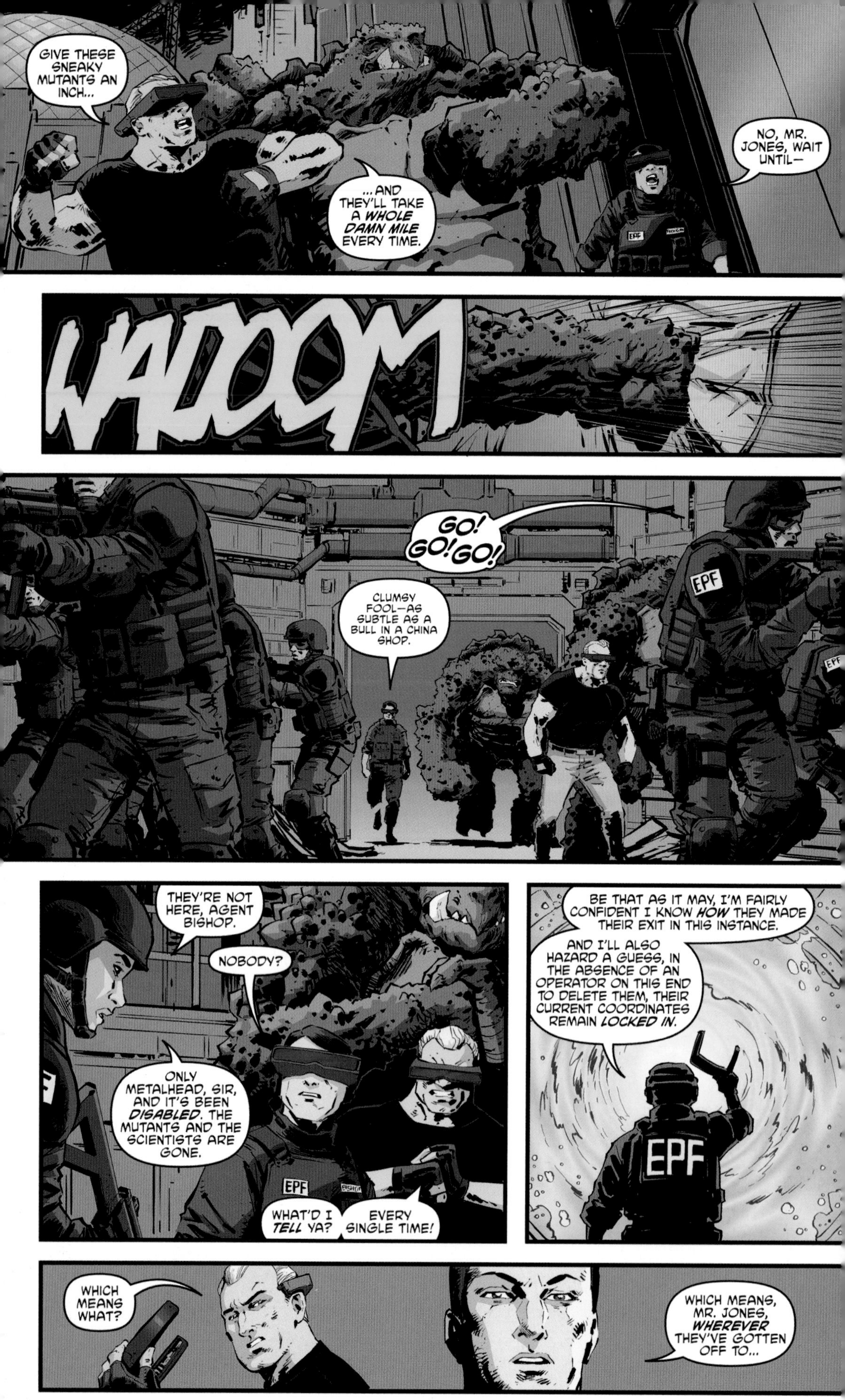

GIVE THESE SNEAKY MUTANTS AN INCH...
...AND THEY'LL TAKE A WHOLE DAMN MILE EVERY TIME.
NO, MR. JONES, WAIT UNTIL—
WADOOM
GO! GO! GO!
CLUMSY FOOL—AS SUBTLE AS A BULL IN A CHINA SHOP.
EPF
THEY'RE NOT HERE, AGENT BISHOP.
NOBODY?
ONLY METALHEAD, SIR, AND IT'S BEEN DISABLED. THE MUTANTS AND THE SCIENTISTS ARE GONE.
WHAT'D I TELL YA?
EVERY SINGLE TIME!
BE THAT AS IT MAY, I'M FAIRLY CONFIDENT I KNOW HOW THEY MADE THEIR EXIT IN THIS INSTANCE.
AND I'LL ALSO HAZARD A GUESS, IN THE ABSENCE OF AN OPERATOR ON THIS END TO DELETE THEM, THEIR CURRENT COORDINATES REMAIN LOCKED IN.
EPF
WHICH MEANS WHAT?
WHICH MEANS, MR. JONES, WHEREVER THEY'VE GOTTEN OFF TO...

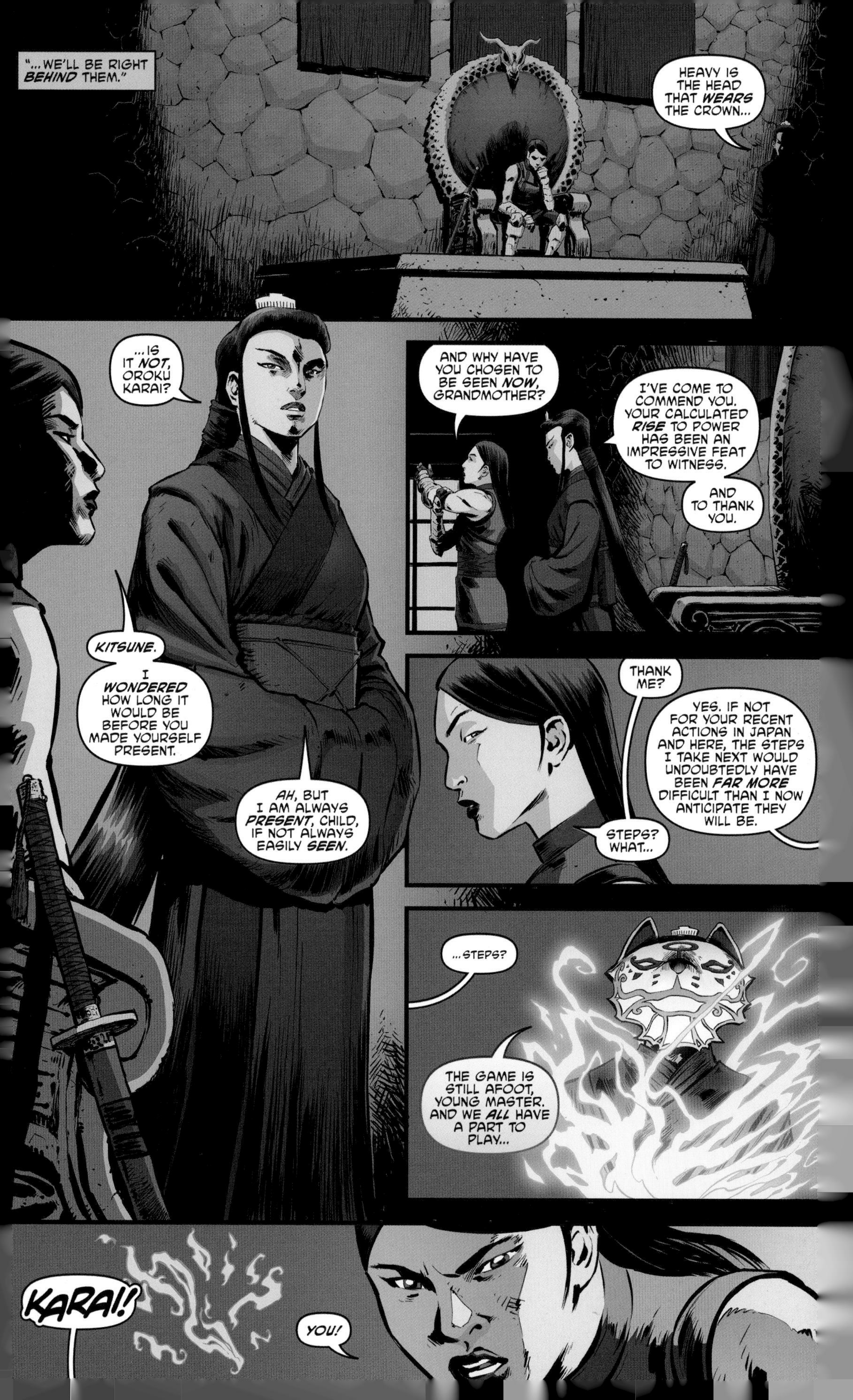
"...WE'LL BE RIGHT BEHIND THEM."
HEAVY IS THE HEAD THAT WEARS THE CROWN...
...IS IT NOT, OROKU KARAI?
AND WHY HAVE YOU CHOSEN TO BE SEEN NOW, GRANDMOTHER?
I'VE COME TO COMMEND YOU. YOUR CALCULATED RISE TO POWER HAS BEEN AN IMPRESSIVE FEAT TO WITNESS.
AND TO THANK YOU.
KITSUNE.
I WONDERED HOW LONG IT WOULD BE BEFORE YOU MADE YOURSELF PRESENT.
AH, BUT I AM ALWAYS PRESENT, CHILD, IF NOT ALWAYS EASILY SEEN.
THANK ME?
YES. IF NOT FOR YOUR RECENT ACTIONS IN JAPAN AND HERE, THE STEPS I TAKE NEXT WOULD UNDOUBTEDLY HAVE BEEN FAR MORE DIFFICULT THAN I NOW ANTICIPATE THEY WILL BE.
STEPS? WHAT...
...STEPS?
THE GAME IS STILL AFOOT, YOUNG MASTER. AND WE ALL HAVE A PART TO PLAY...
KARAI!
YOU!

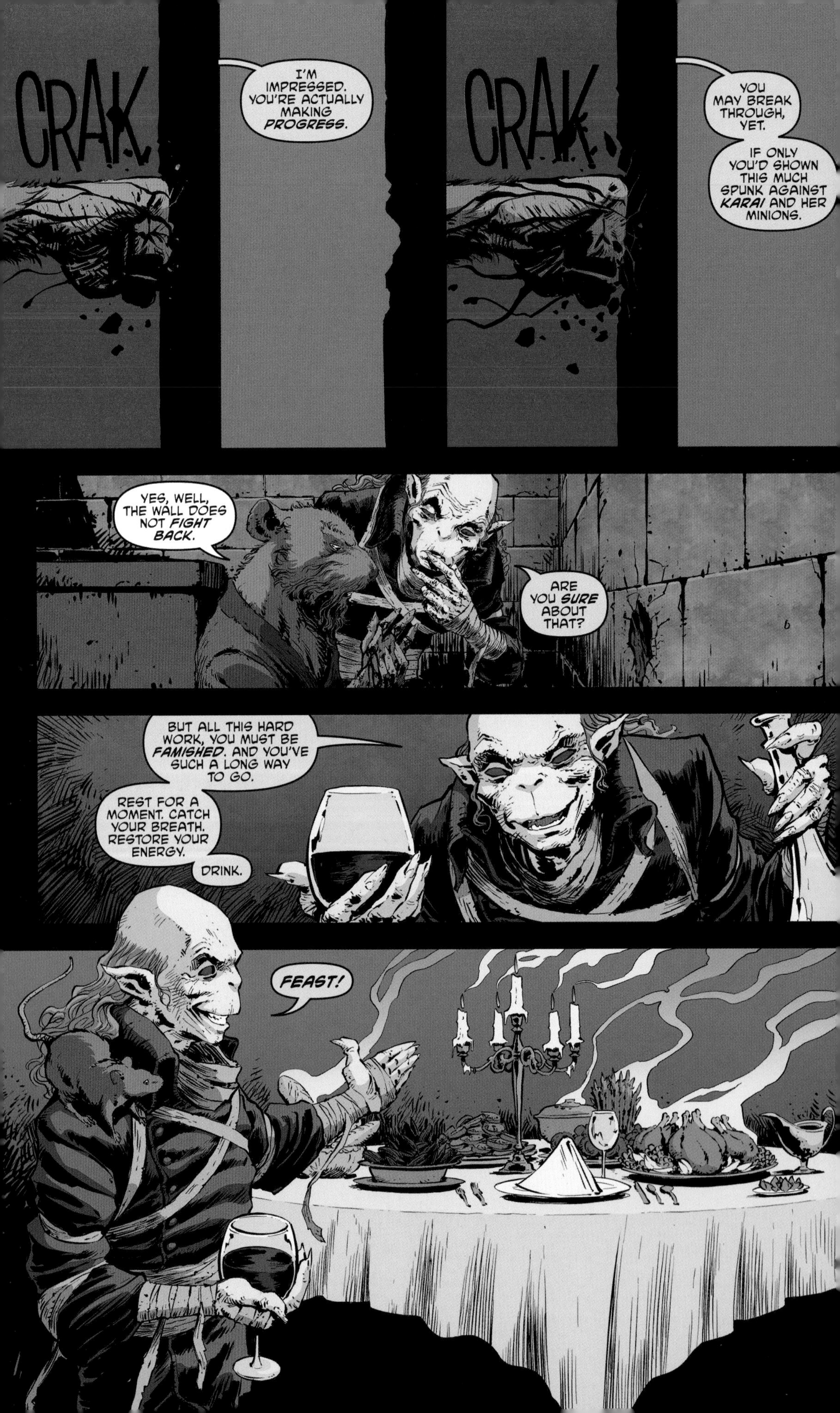
CRAK
I'M IMPRESSED. YOU'RE ACTUALLY MAKING PROGRESS.
CRAK
YOU MAY BREAK THROUGH, YET.
IF ONLY YOU'D SHOWN THIS MUCH SPUNK AGAINST KARAI AND HER MINIONS.
YES, WELL, THE WALL DOES NOT FIGHT BACK.
ARE YOU SURE ABOUT THAT?
BUT ALL THIS HARD WORK, YOU MUST BE FAMISHED. AND YOU'VE SUCH A LONG WAY TO GO.
REST FOR A MOMENT. CATCH YOUR BREATH. RESTORE YOUR ENERGY.
DRINK.
FEAST!

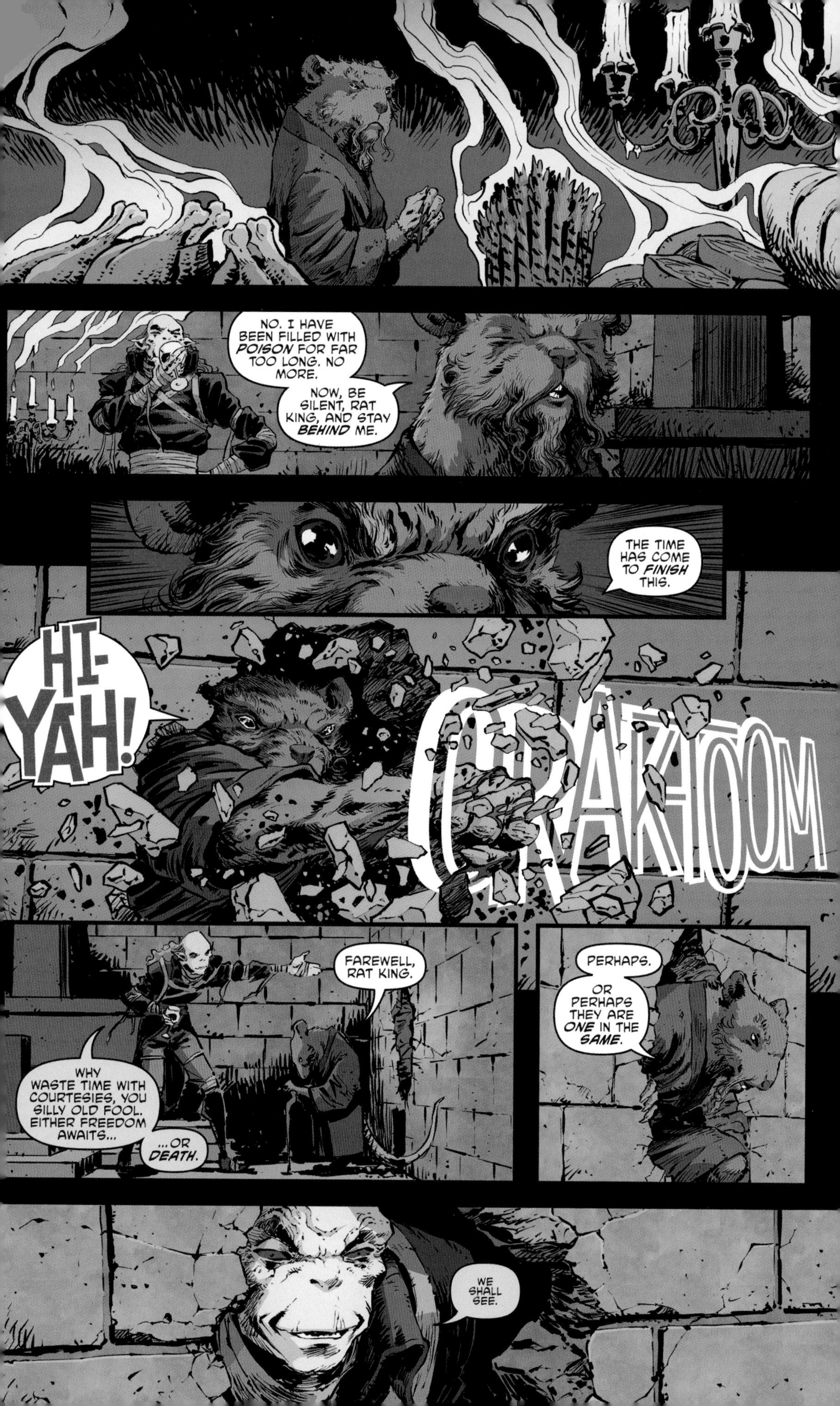
NO. I HAVE BEEN FILLED WITH POISON FOR FAR TOO LONG. NO MORE.
NOW, BE SILENT, RAT KING, AND STAY BEHIND ME.
THE TIME HAS COME TO FINISH THIS.
HI-YAH!
CRAKTOOM
FAREWELL, RAT KING.
WHY WASTE TIME WITH COURTESIES, YOU SILLY OLD FOOL. EITHER FREEDOM AWAITS...
...OR DEATH.
PERHAPS.
OR PERHAPS THEY ARE ONE IN THE SAME.
WE SHALL SEE.

SO, THE MUTANT COWARDS *RETURN.*

HAVE YOU COME TO SURRENDER OR TO DIE?

NEITHER. WE'RE *STILL* RUNNING.

FOOM

THE EARTH PROTECTION FORCE IS RIGHT BEHIND US, KARAI. IT'S NOT GONNA BE LONG BEFORE THEY COME *STORMING* THROUGH THAT PORTAL. WE'RE JUST TRYING TO GET AWAY BEFORE THEY ATTACK.

THE EPF WILL NOT ATTACK THE FOOT CLAN. THERE IS A *TRUCE* BETWEEN US.

YEAH—ONE THAT *MASTER SPLINTER* BROKERED, NOT YOU. I'M PRETTY SURE ALL BETS ARE *OFF* NOW.

YOU REALLY NEED TO CUT THIS *SHORT,* LEO.

YEAH, BRO-BISHOP'S COMING!

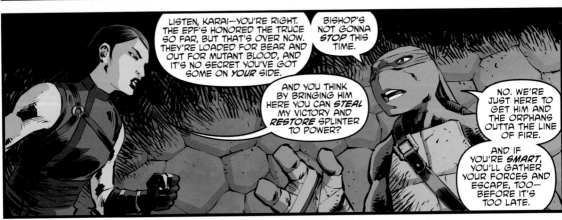

LISTEN, KARAI—YOU'RE RIGHT. THE EPF'S HONORED THE TRUCE SO FAR, BUT THAT'S OVER NOW. THEY'RE LOADED FOR BEAR AND OUT FOR MUTANT BLOOD, AND IT'S NO SECRET YOU'VE GOT SOME ON *YOUR* SIDE.

BISHOP'S NOT GONNA *STOP* THIS TIME.

AND YOU THINK BY BRINGING HIM HERE YOU CAN *STEAL* MY VICTORY AND *RESTORE* SPLINTER TO POWER?

NO. WE'RE JUST HERE TO GET HIM AND THE ORPHANS OUTTA THE LINE OF FIRE.

AND IF YOU'RE *SMART,* YOU'LL GATHER YOUR FORCES AND ESCAPE, TOO— BEFORE IT'S TOO LATE.

IT'S ALREADY TOO LATE. YOUR FATHER AND THOSE CHILDREN... THIS *CITY* BELONGS TO THE FOOT CLAN NOW, AND I WILL ALLOW *NOTHING* TO STAND IN OUR WAY.

I WILL—

THE *KIRA NO KEN*—GONE. HOW...

KITSUNE!

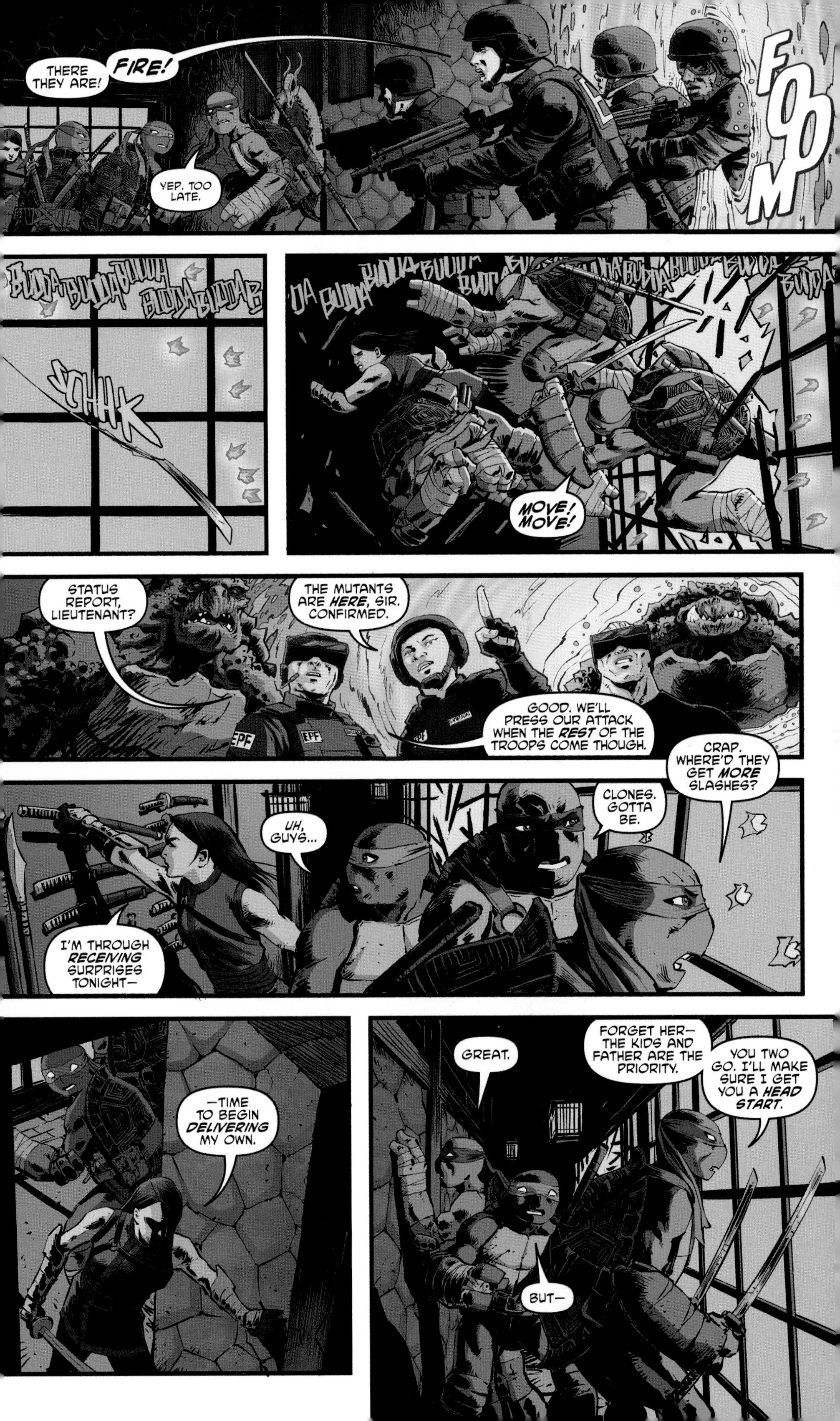
THERE THEY ARE!
FIRE!
YEP. TOO LATE.
FOOM
BUDDABUDDABUDDA BUDDABUDDAB
SCHHK
DA BUDDA BUDDA BUDDA BUDDA BUDDA BUDDA BUDDA BUDDA
MOVE! MOVE!
STATUS REPORT, LIEUTENANT?
THE MUTANTS ARE HERE, SIR. CONFIRMED.
GOOD. WE'LL PRESS OUR ATTACK WHEN THE REST OF THE TROOPS COME THOUGH.
EPF
UH, GUYS...
CLONES. GOTTA BE.
CRAP. WHERE'D THEY GET MORE SLASHES?
I'M THROUGH RECEIVING SURPRISES TONIGHT—
—TIME TO BEGIN DELIVERING MY OWN.
GREAT.
FORGET HER— THE KIDS AND FATHER ARE THE PRIORITY.
YOU TWO GO. I'LL MAKE SURE I GET YOU A HEAD START.
BUT—

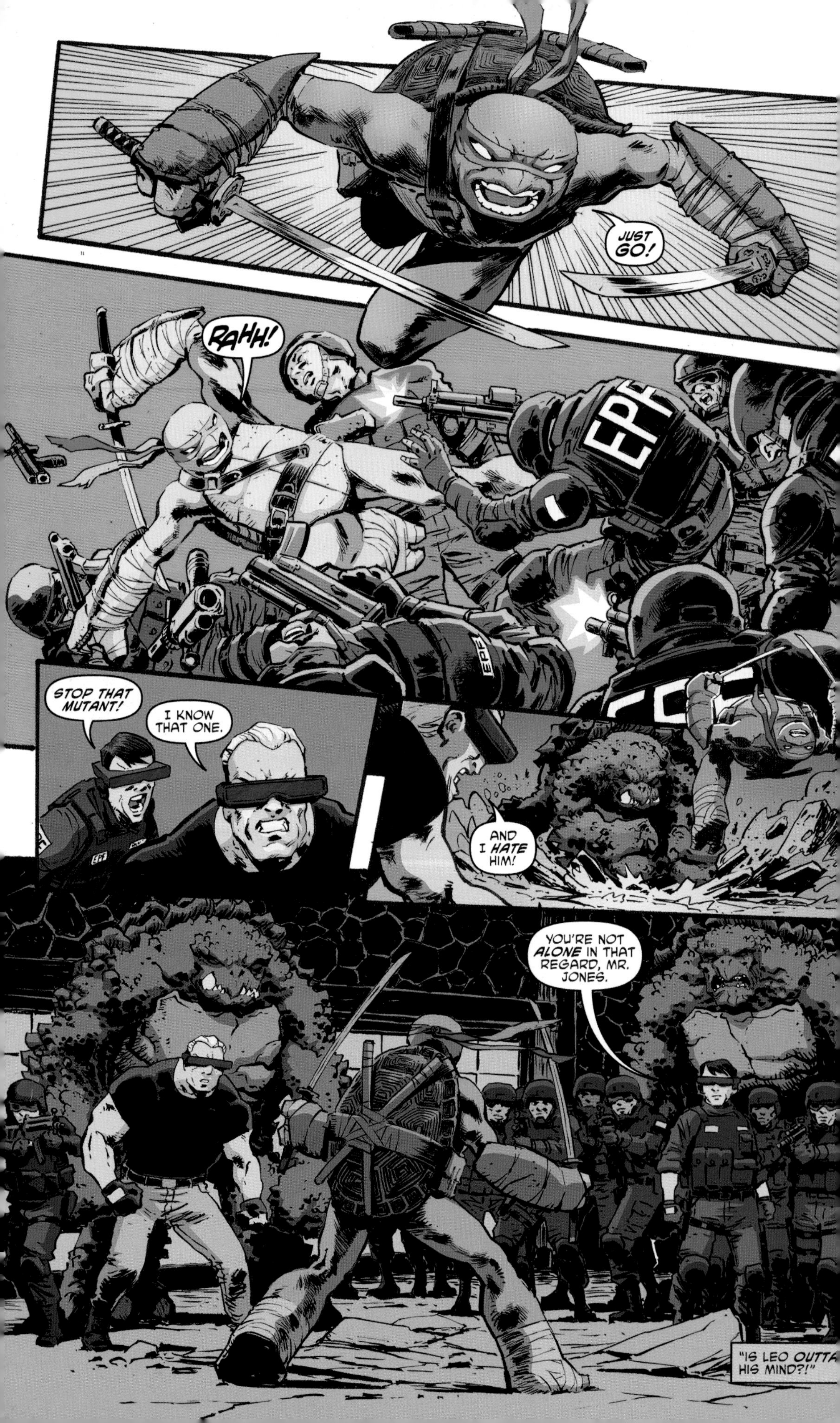
JUST GO!
RAHH!
EPF
STOP THAT MUTANT!
I KNOW THAT ONE.
AND I HATE HIM!
YOU'RE NOT ALONE IN THAT REGARD, MR. JONES.
"IS LEO OUTTA HIS MIND?!"

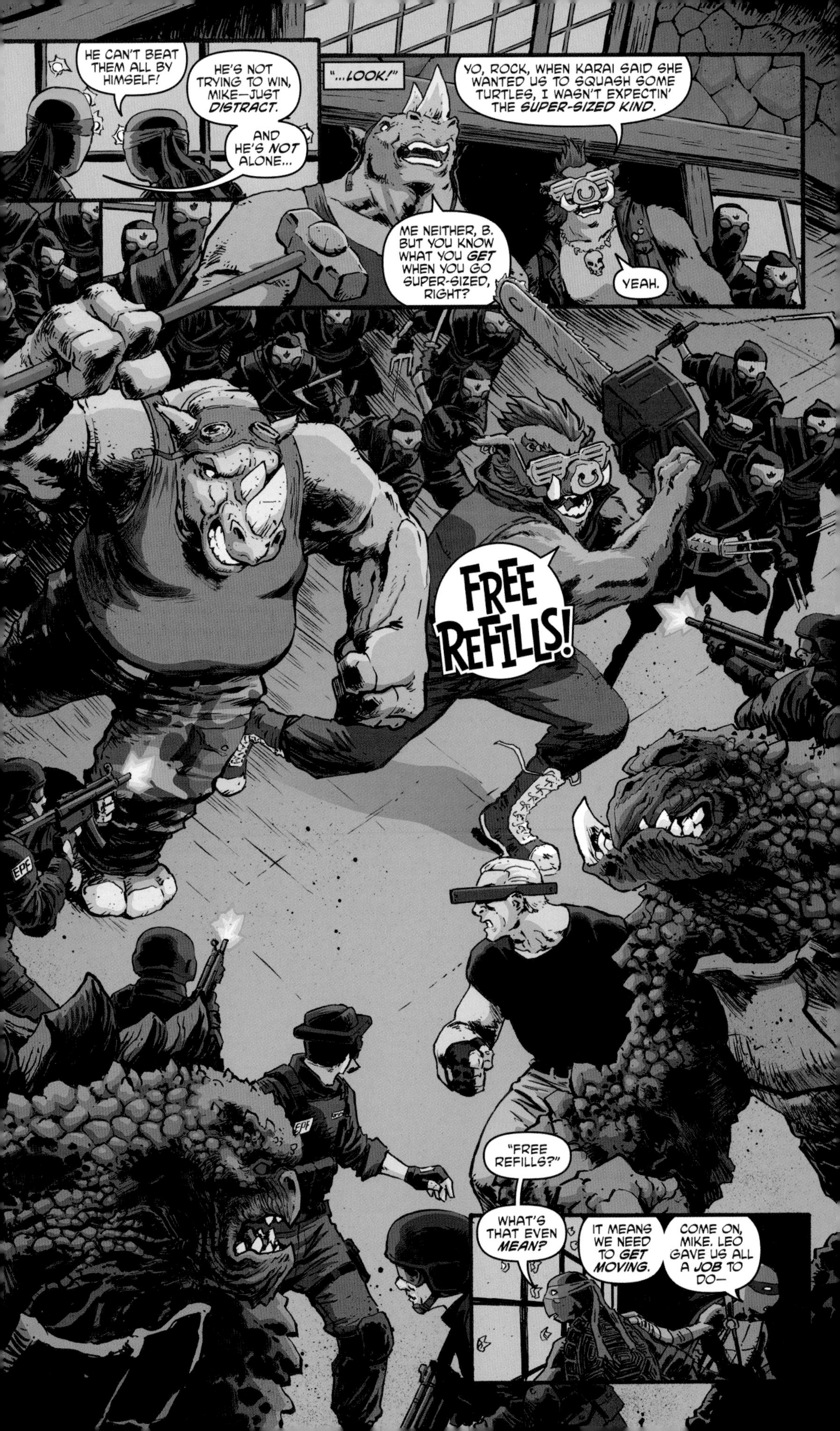
HE CAN'T BEAT THEM ALL BY HIMSELF!
HE'S NOT TRYING TO WIN, MIKE—JUST *DISTRACT*.
AND HE'S *NOT* ALONE...
"...*LOOK!*"
YO, ROCK, WHEN KARAI SAID SHE WANTED US TO SQUASH SOME TURTLES, I WASN'T EXPECTIN' THE *SUPER-SIZED KIND*.
ME NEITHER, B. BUT YOU KNOW WHAT YOU *GET* WHEN YOU GO SUPER-SIZED, RIGHT?
YEAH.
FREE REFILLS!
EPF
EPF
"FREE REFILLS?"
WHAT'S THAT EVEN *MEAN?*
IT MEANS WE NEED TO *GET MOVING*.
COME ON, MIKE. LEO GAVE US ALL A *JOB* TO DO—

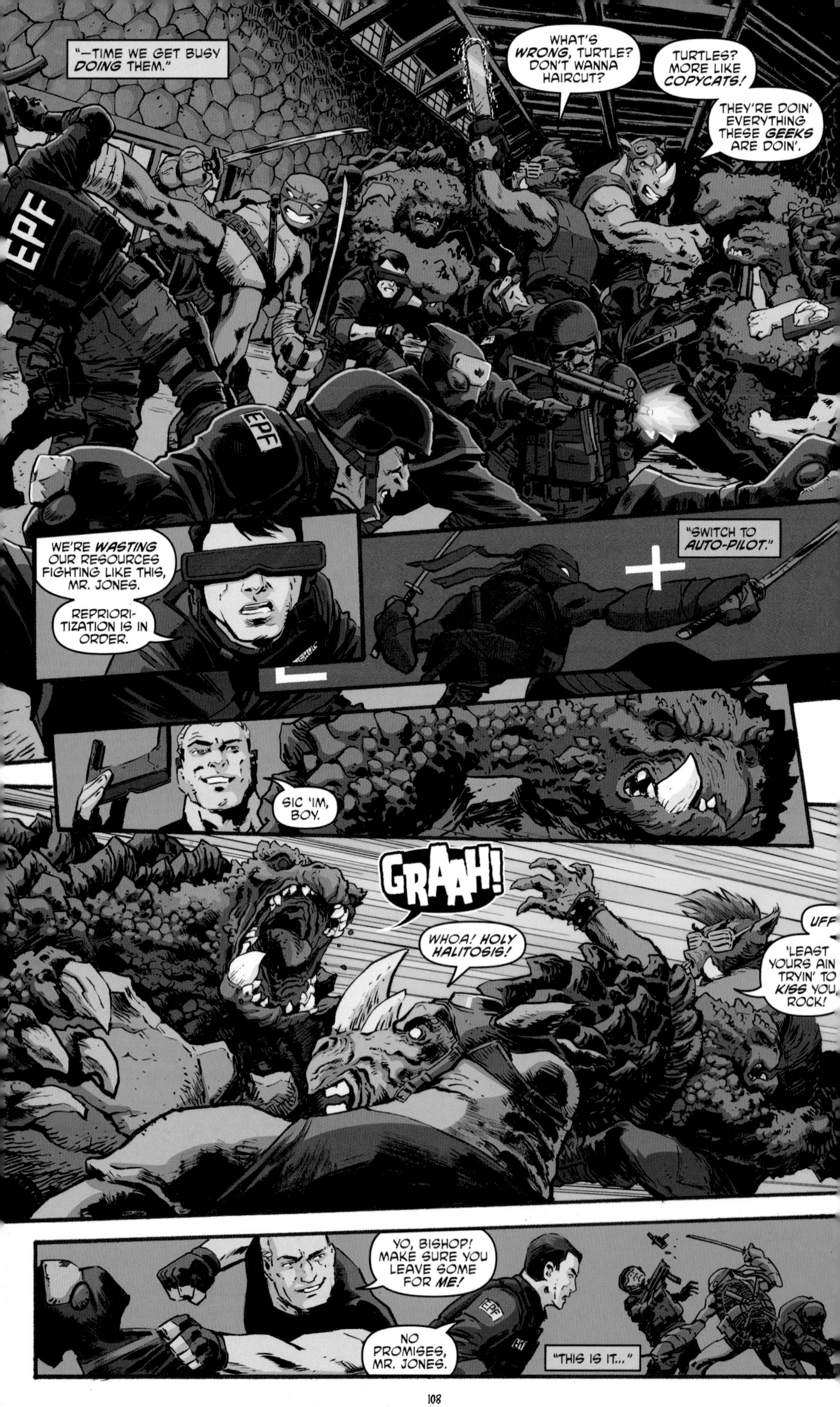

"—TIME WE GET BUSY DOING THEM."
WHAT'S WRONG, TURTLE? DON'T WANNA HAIRCUT?
TURTLES? MORE LIKE COPYCATS!
THEY'RE DOIN' EVERYTHING THESE GEEKS ARE DOIN'.
EPF
WE'RE WASTING OUR RESOURCES FIGHTING LIKE THIS, MR. JONES.
REPRIORI-TIZATION IS IN ORDER.
"SWITCH TO AUTO-PILOT."
SIC 'IM, BOY.
GRAAH!
WHOA! HOLY HALITOSIS!
UFF
'LEAST YOURS AIN TRYIN' TO KISS YOU, ROCK!
YO, BISHOP! MAKE SURE YOU LEAVE SOME FOR ME!
NO PROMISES, MR. JONES.
"THIS IS IT..."

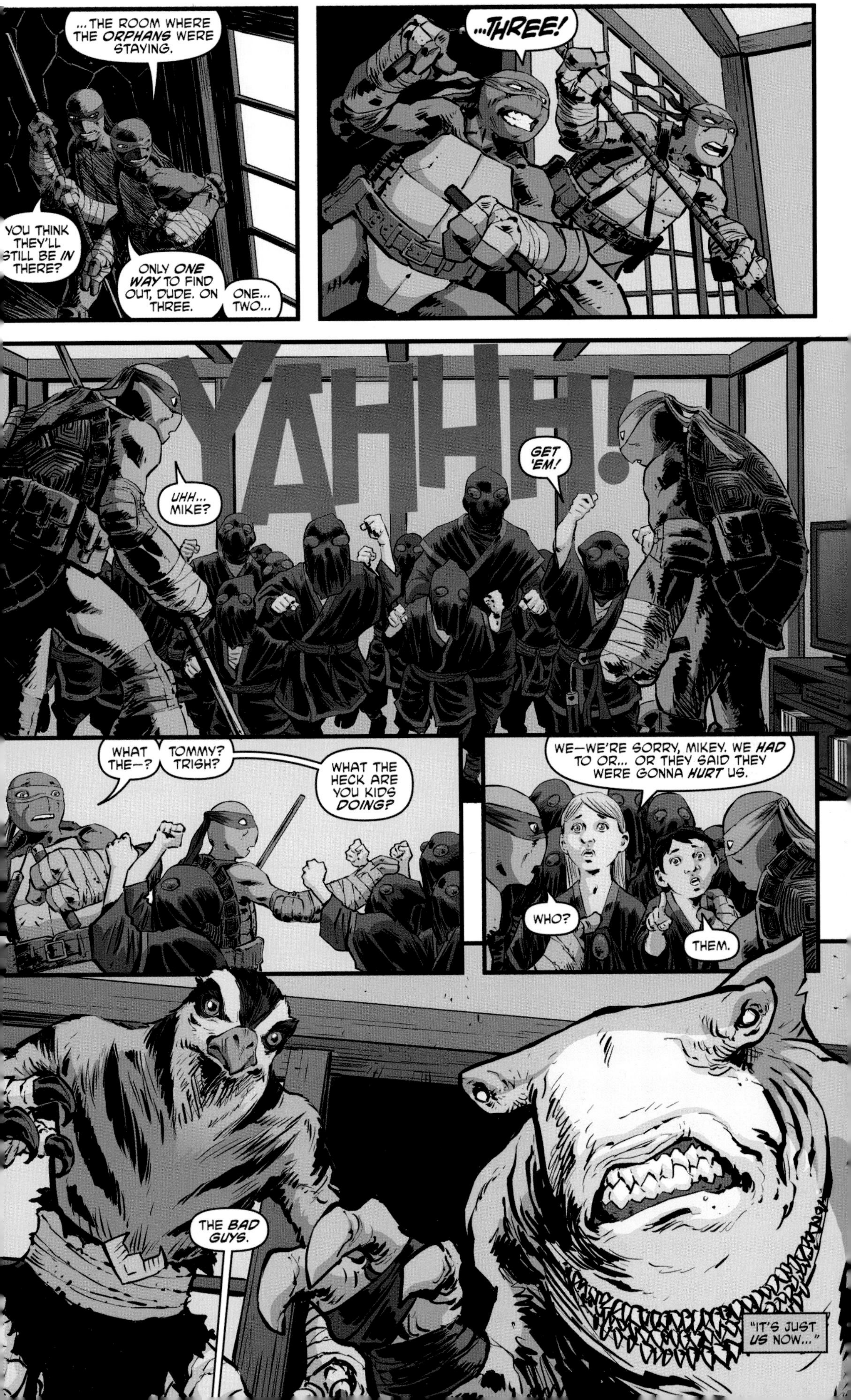
...THE ROOM WHERE THE ORPHANS WERE STAYING.
YOU THINK THEY'LL STILL BE IN THERE?
ONLY ONE WAY TO FIND OUT, DUDE. ON THREE.
ONE... TWO...
...THREE!
YAHHH!
UHH... MIKE?
GET 'EM!
WHAT THE--?
TOMMY? TRISH?
WHAT THE HECK ARE YOU KIDS DOING?
WE--WE'RE SORRY, MIKEY. WE HAD TO OR... OR THEY SAID THEY WERE GONNA HURT US.
WHO?
THEM.
THE BAD GUYS.
"IT'S JUST US NOW..."

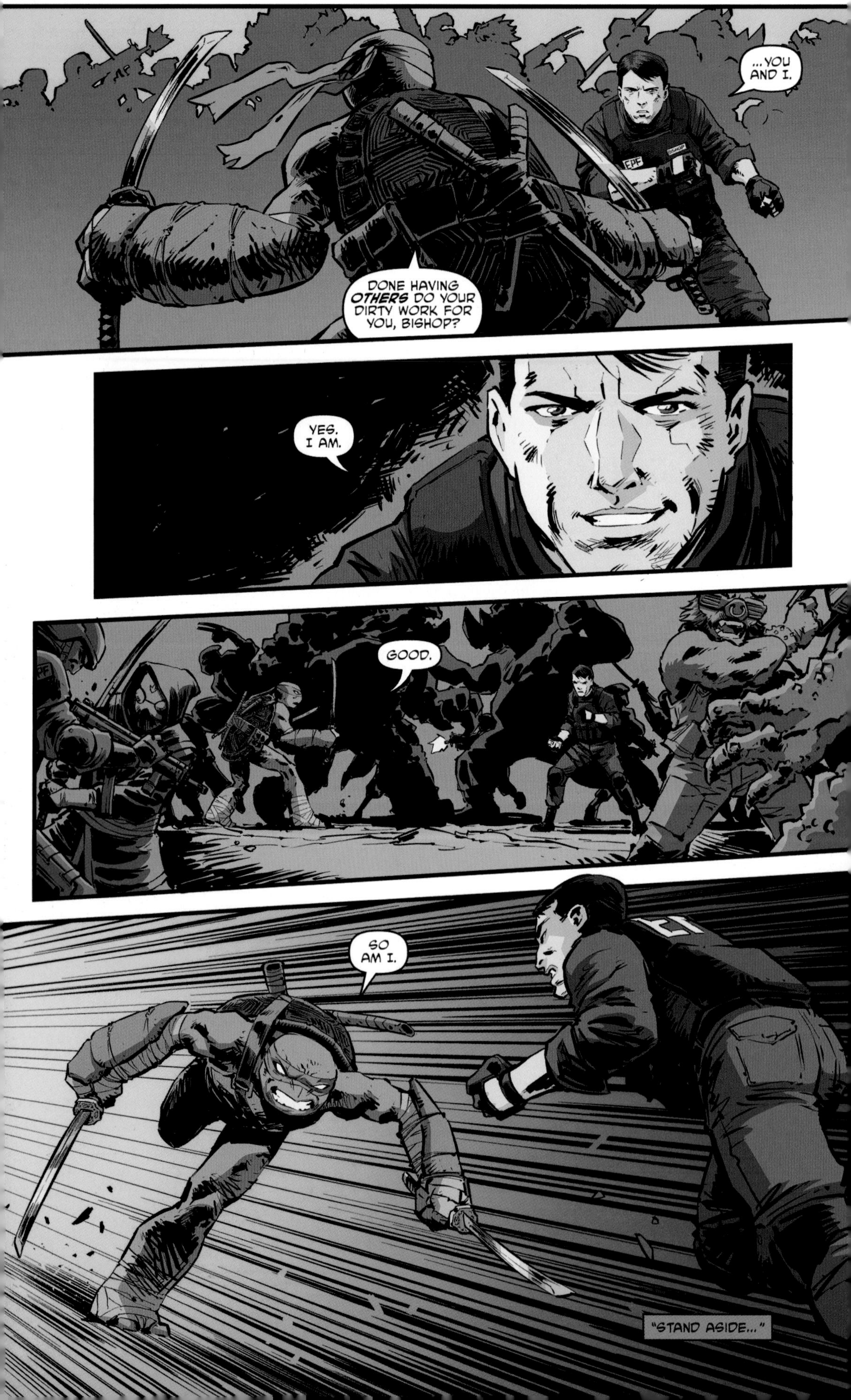
...YOU AND I.
DONE HAVING OTHERS DO YOUR DIRTY WORK FOR YOU, BISHOP?
YES. I AM.
GOOD.
SO AM I.
"STAND ASIDE..."

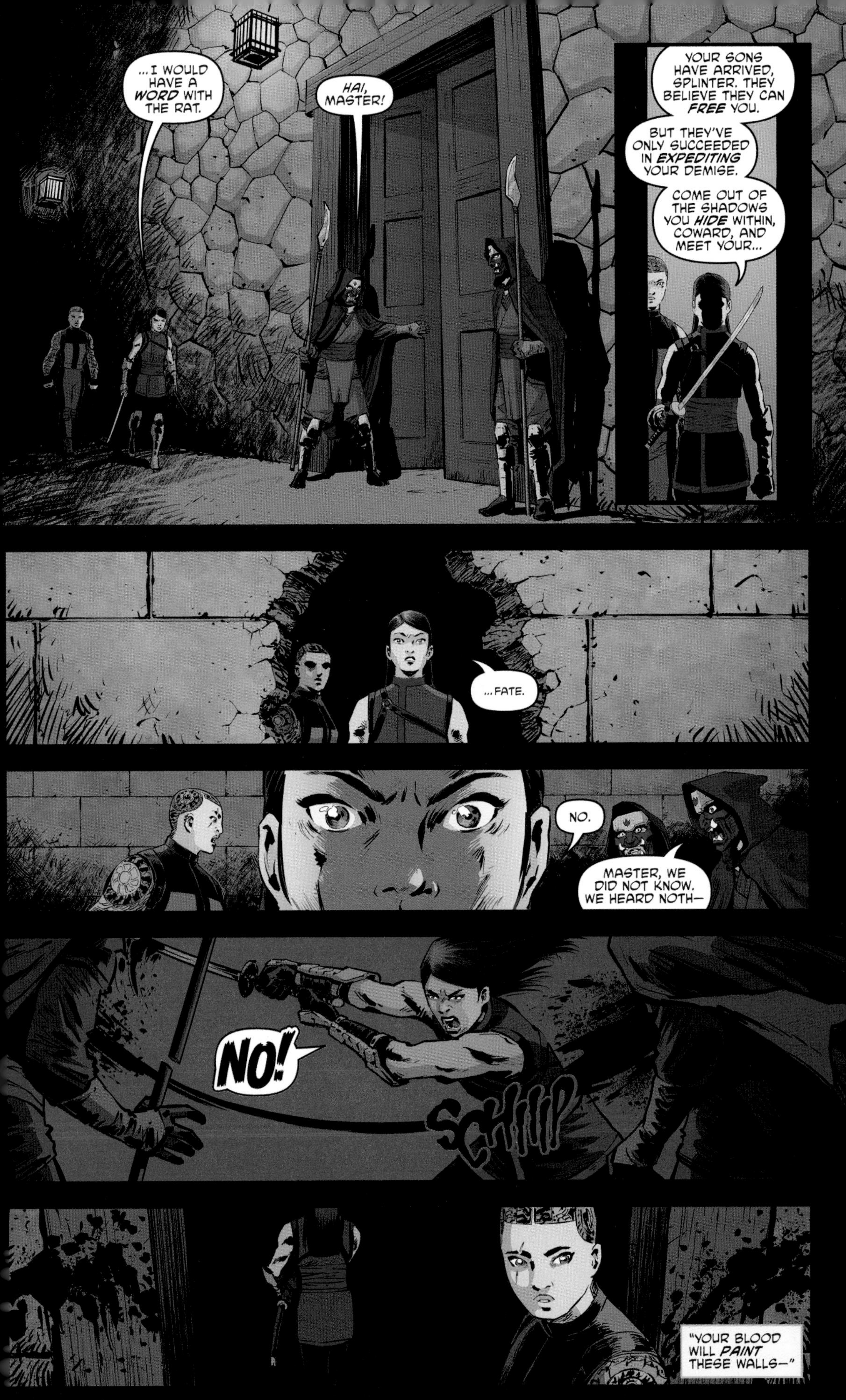
...I WOULD HAVE A WORD WITH THE RAT.
HAI, MASTER!
YOUR SONS HAVE ARRIVED, SPLINTER. THEY BELIEVE THEY CAN FREE YOU.
BUT THEY'VE ONLY SUCCEEDED IN EXPEDITING YOUR DEMISE.
COME OUT OF THE SHADOWS YOU HIDE WITHIN, COWARD, AND MEET YOUR...
...FATE.
NO.
MASTER, WE DID NOT KNOW. WE HEARD NOTH—
NO!
SCHHP
"YOUR BLOOD WILL PAINT THESE WALLS—"

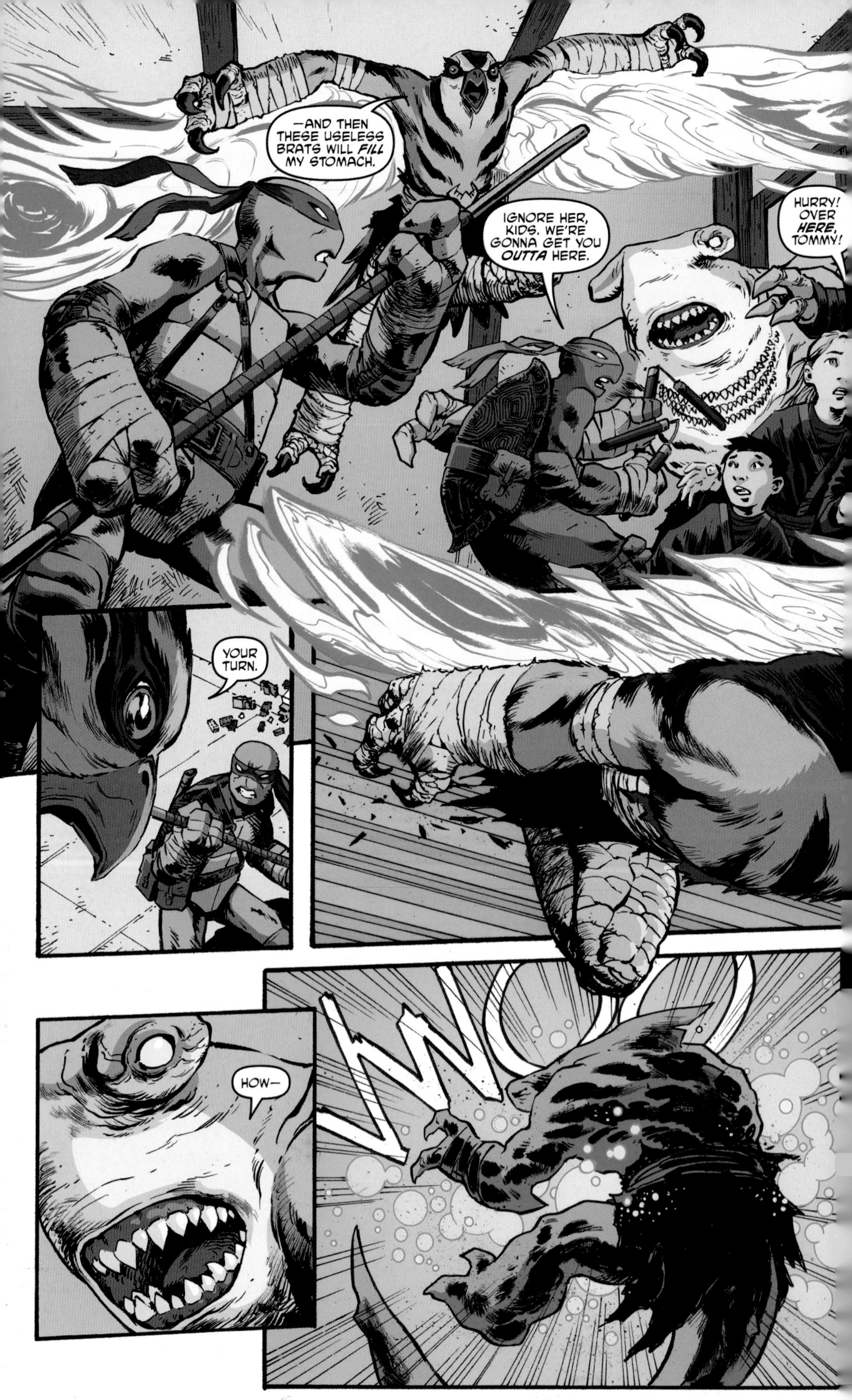

—AND THEN THESE USELESS BRATS WILL *FILL* MY STOMACH.
IGNORE HER, KIDS. WE'RE GONNA GET YOU *OUTTA* HERE.
HURRY! OVER *HERE*, TOMMY!
YOUR TURN.
HOW—

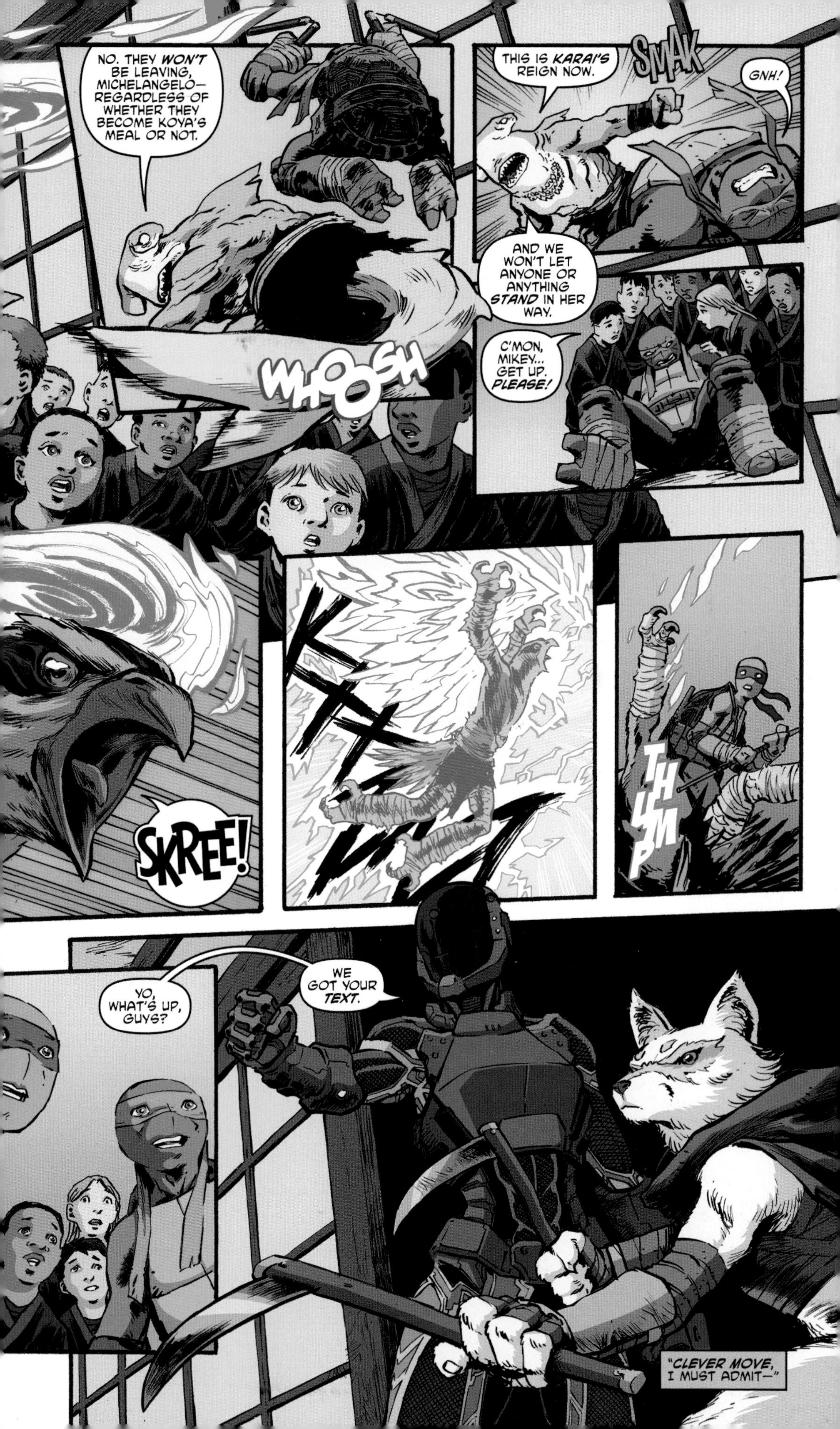
NO. THEY WON'T BE LEAVING, MICHELANGELO— REGARDLESS OF WHETHER THEY BECOME KOYA'S MEAL OR NOT.
WHOOSH
THIS IS KARAI'S REIGN NOW.
SMAK
GNH!
AND WE WON'T LET ANYONE OR ANYTHING STAND IN HER WAY.
C'MON, MIKEY... GET UP. PLEASE!
SKREE!
THUMP
YO, WHAT'S UP, GUYS?
WE GOT YOUR TEXT.
"CLEVER MOVE, I MUST ADMIT—"

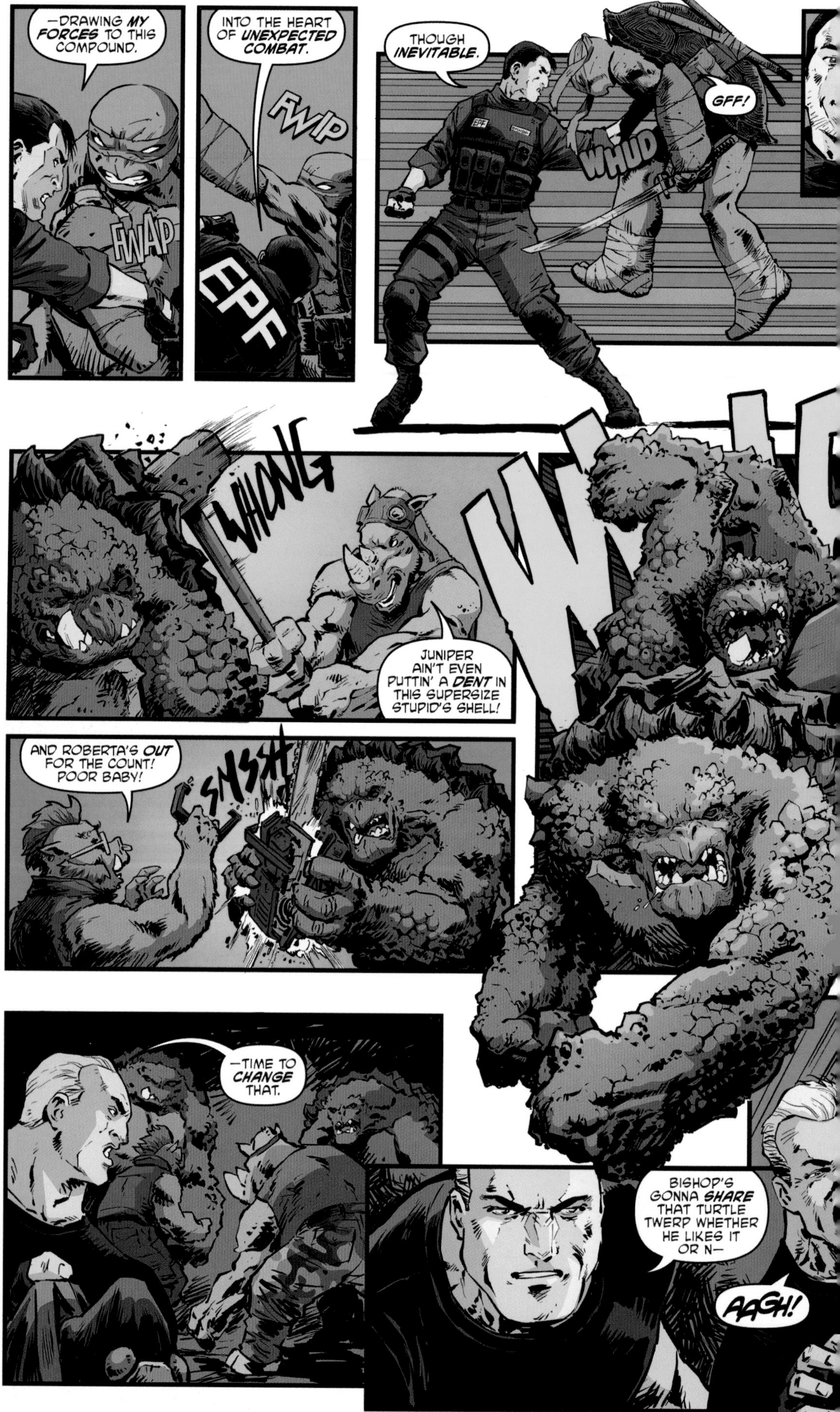

—DRAWING MY FORCES TO THIS COMPOUND.
FWAP
INTO THE HEART OF UNEXPECTED COMBAT.
FWIP
EPF
THOUGH INEVITABLE.
GFF!
WHUD
WHONG
JUNIPER AIN'T EVEN PUTTIN' A DENT IN THIS SUPERSIZE STUPID'S SHELL!
AND ROBERTA'S OUT FOR THE COUNT! POOR BABY!
CSHSSH
—TIME TO CHANGE THAT.
BISHOP'S GONNA SHARE THAT TURTLE TWERP WHETHER HE LIKES IT OR N—
AAGH!

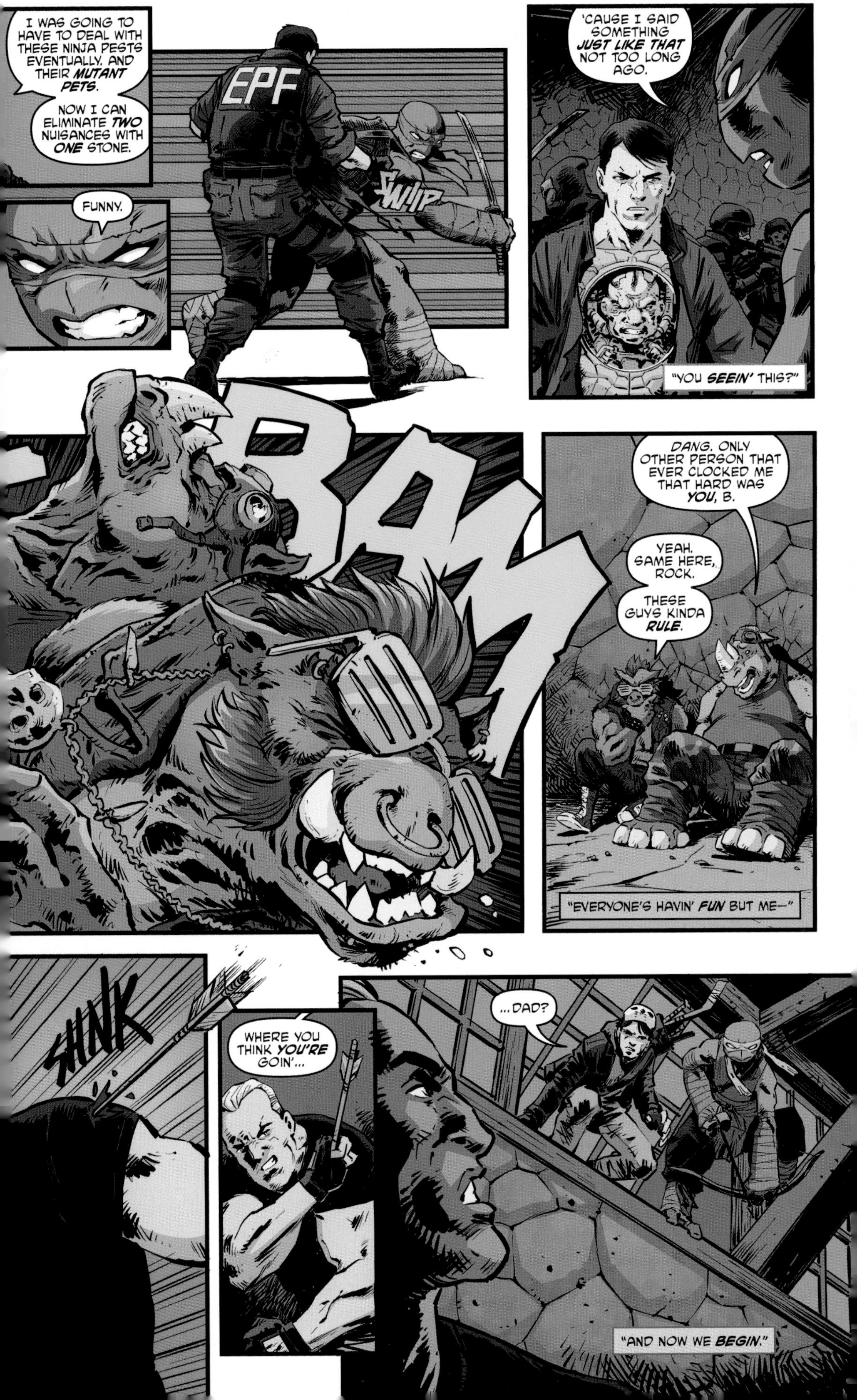

I WAS GOING TO HAVE TO DEAL WITH THESE NINJA PESTS EVENTUALLY. AND THEIR MUTANT PETS.
NOW I CAN ELIMINATE TWO NUISANCES WITH ONE STONE.
SWIP
FUNNY.
EPF
'CAUSE I SAID SOMETHING JUST LIKE THAT NOT TOO LONG AGO.
"YOU SEEIN' THIS?"
BAM
DANG. ONLY OTHER PERSON THAT EVER CLOCKED ME THAT HARD WAS YOU, B.
YEAH. SAME HERE, ROCK.
THESE GUYS KINDA RULE.
"EVERYONE'S HAVIN' FUN BUT ME–"
SHNK
WHERE YOU THINK YOU'RE GOIN'...
...DAD?
"AND NOW WE BEGIN."

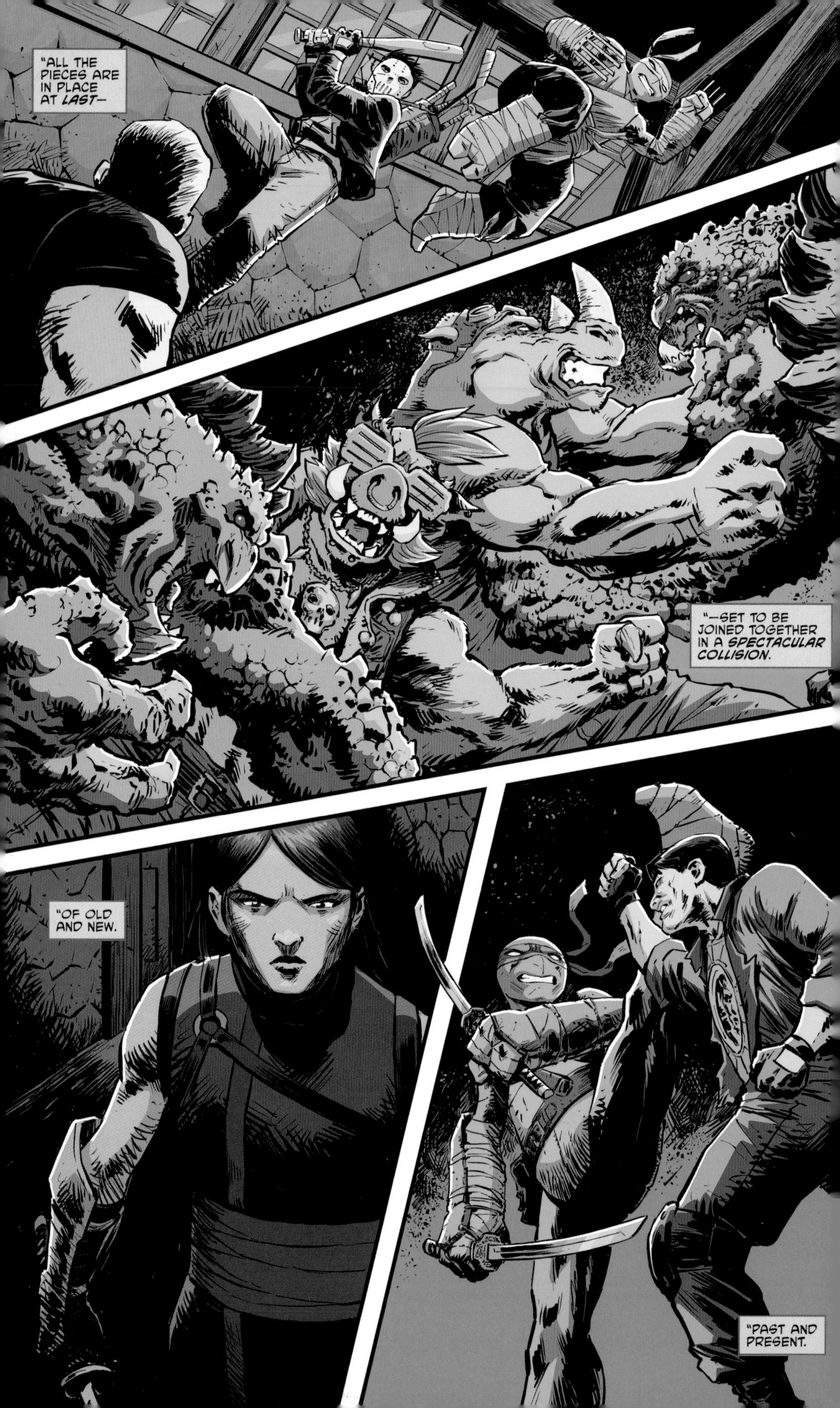
"ALL THE PIECES ARE IN PLACE AT *LAST*—
"—SET TO BE JOINED TOGETHER IN A *SPECTACULAR COLLISION*.
"OF OLD AND NEW.
"PAST AND PRESENT.

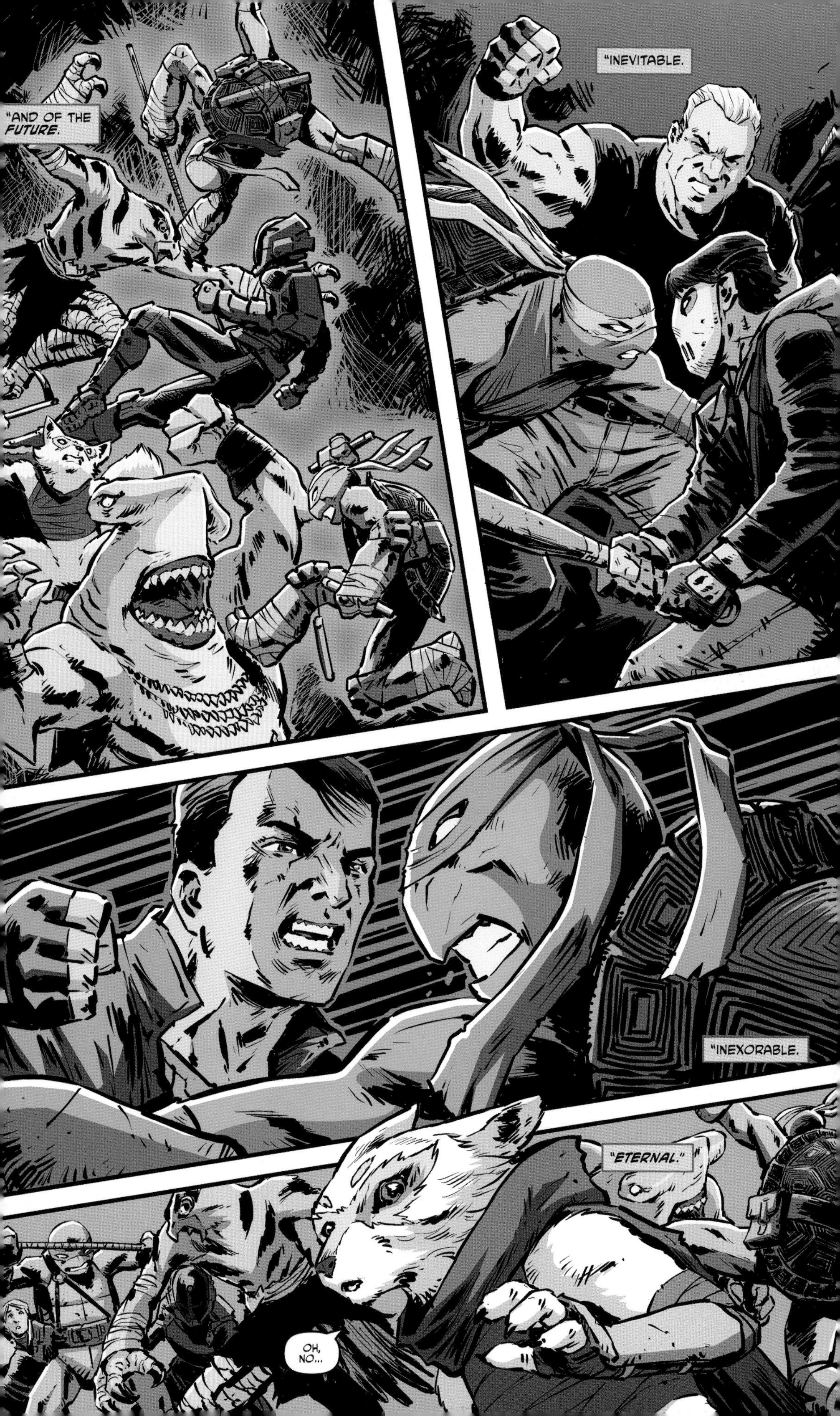
"AND OF THE FUTURE.
"INEVITABLE.
"INEXORABLE.
"ETERNAL."
OH, NO...

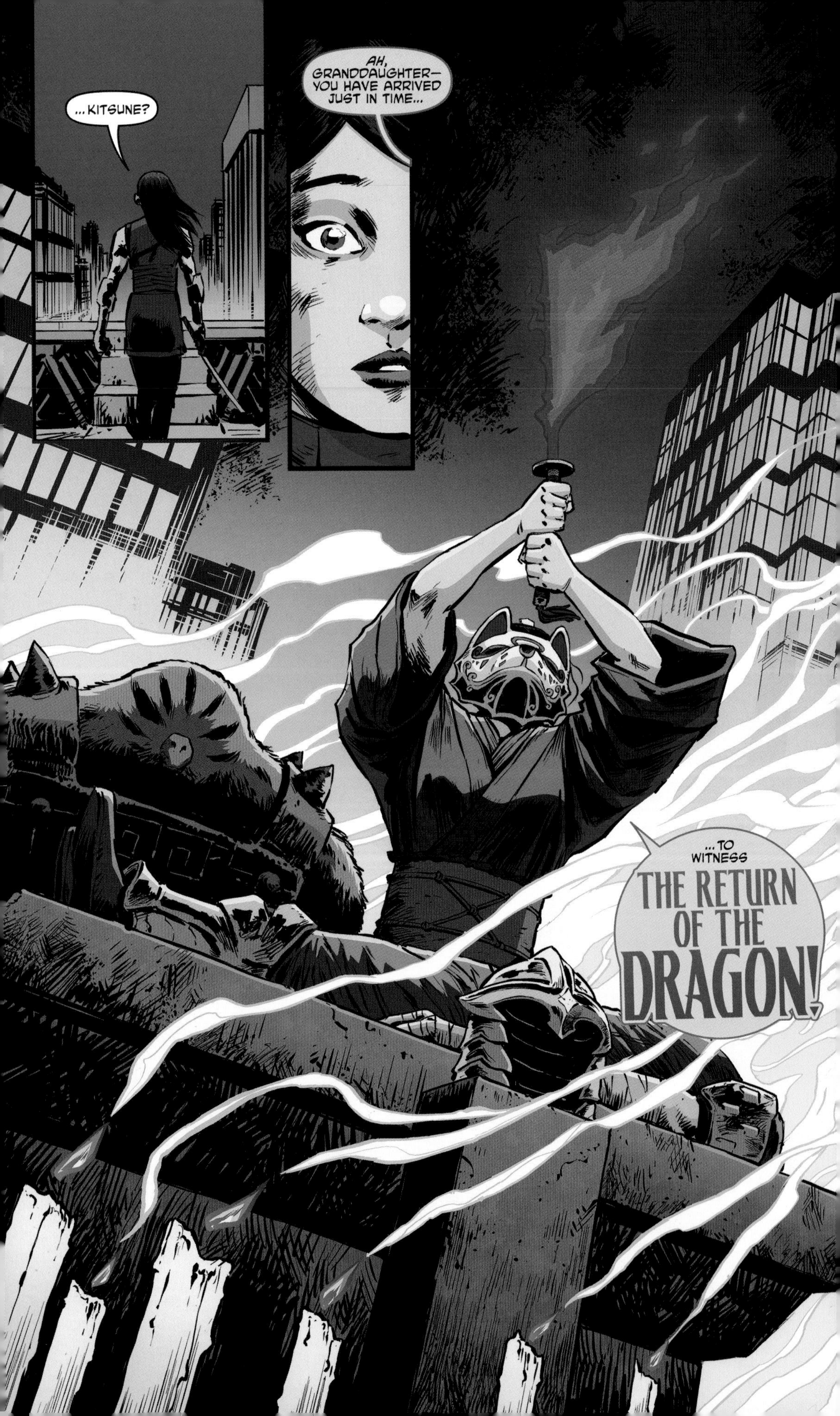
...KITSUNE?
AH, GRANDDAUGHTER— YOU HAVE ARRIVED JUST IN TIME...
...TO WITNESS THE RETURN OF THE DRAGON!

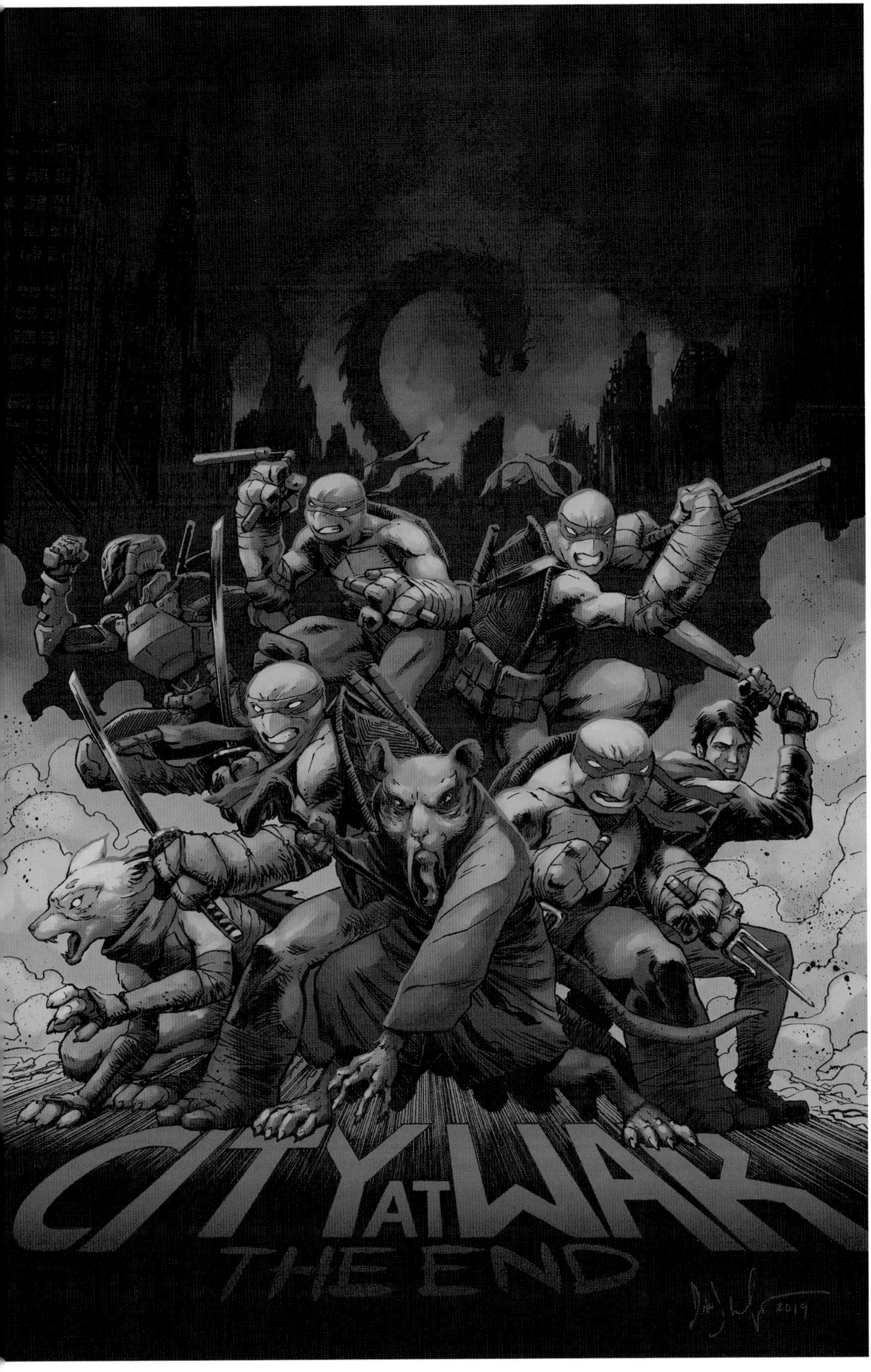
CITY AT WAR
THE END

ART BY DAVE WACHTER

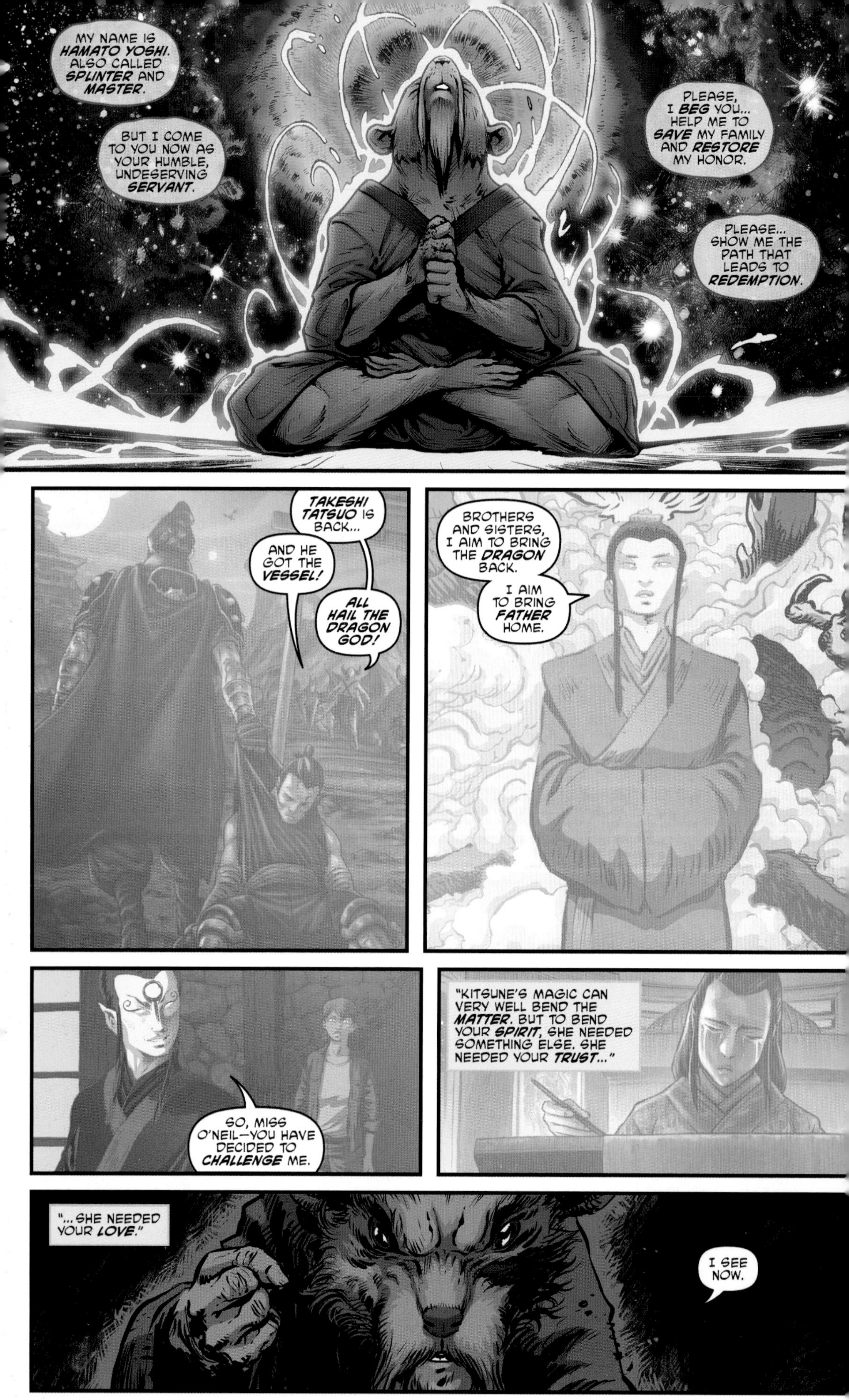
MY NAME IS HAMATO YOSHI. ALSO CALLED SPLINTER AND MASTER.
BUT I COME TO YOU NOW AS YOUR HUMBLE, UNDESERVING SERVANT.
PLEASE, I BEG YOU... HELP ME TO SAVE MY FAMILY AND RESTORE MY HONOR.
PLEASE... SHOW ME THE PATH THAT LEADS TO REDEMPTION.
TAKESHI TATSUO IS BACK...
AND HE GOT THE VESSEL!
ALL HAIL THE DRAGON GOD!
BROTHERS AND SISTERS, I AIM TO BRING THE DRAGON BACK.
I AIM TO BRING FATHER HOME.
SO, MISS O'NEIL—YOU HAVE DECIDED TO CHALLENGE ME.
"KITSUNE'S MAGIC CAN VERY WELL BEND THE MATTER. BUT TO BEND YOUR SPIRIT, SHE NEEDED SOMETHING ELSE. SHE NEEDED YOUR TRUST..."
"...SHE NEEDED YOUR LOVE."
I SEE NOW.

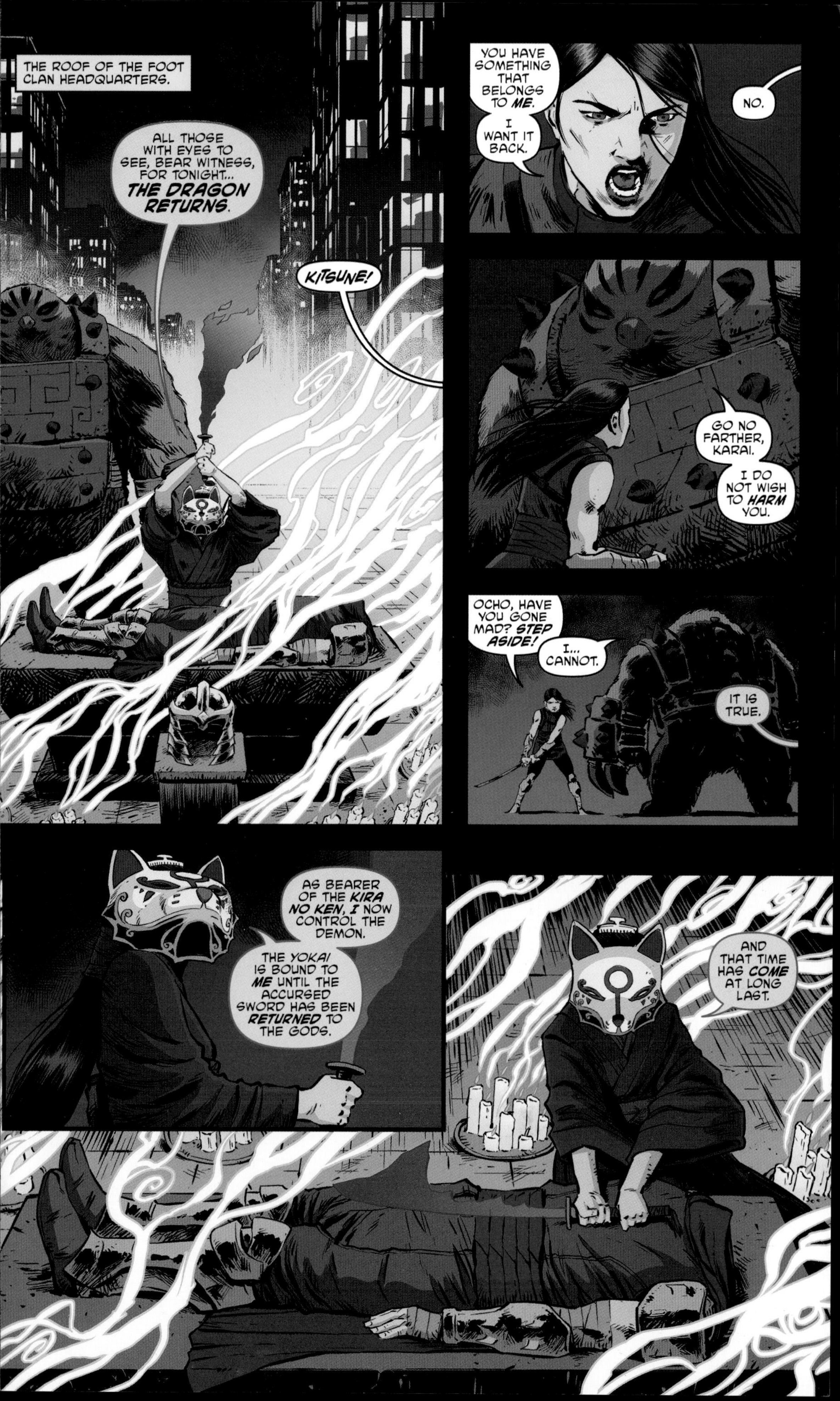
THE ROOF OF THE FOOT CLAN HEADQUARTERS.
ALL THOSE WITH EYES TO SEE, BEAR WITNESS, FOR TONIGHT... THE DRAGON RETURNS.
KITSUNE!
YOU HAVE SOMETHING THAT BELONGS TO ME.
I WANT IT BACK.
NO.
GO NO FARTHER, KARAI.
I DO NOT WISH TO HARM YOU.
OCHO, HAVE YOU GONE MAD? STEP ASIDE!
I... CANNOT.
IT IS TRUE.
AS BEARER OF THE KIRA NO KEN, I NOW CONTROL THE DEMON.
THE YOKAI IS BOUND TO ME UNTIL THE ACCURSED SWORD HAS BEEN RETURNED TO THE GODS.
AND THAT TIME HAS COME AT LONG LAST.

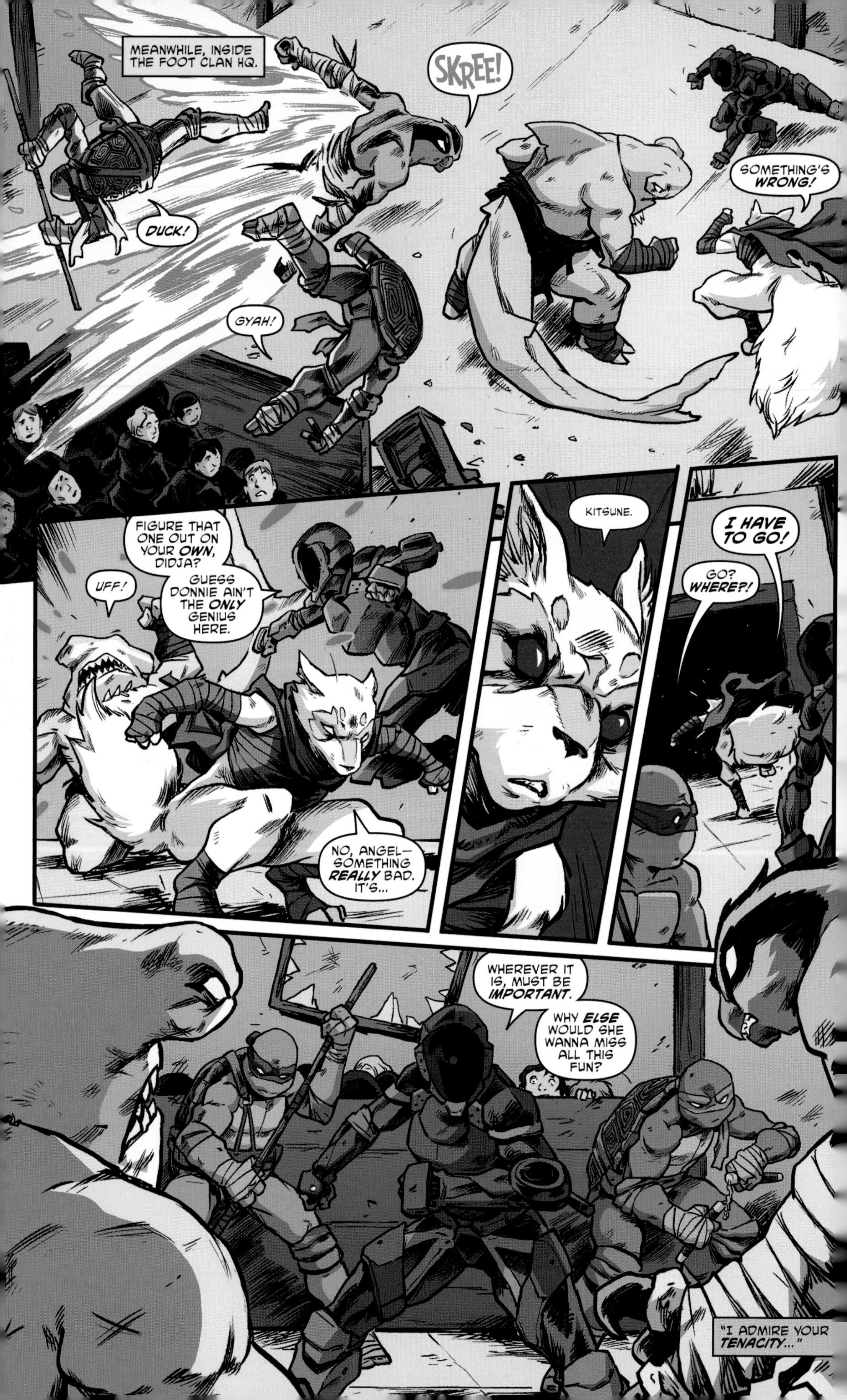
MEANWHILE, INSIDE THE FOOT CLAN HQ.
SKREE!
DUCK!
GYAH!
SOMETHING'S WRONG!
FIGURE THAT ONE OUT ON YOUR OWN, DIDJA?
GUESS DONNIE AIN'T THE ONLY GENIUS HERE.
UFF!
NO, ANGEL— SOMETHING REALLY BAD. IT'S...
KITSUNE.
I HAVE TO GO!
GO? WHERE?!
WHEREVER IT IS, MUST BE IMPORTANT.
WHY ELSE WOULD SHE WANNA MISS ALL THIS FUN?
"I ADMIRE YOUR TENACITY..."

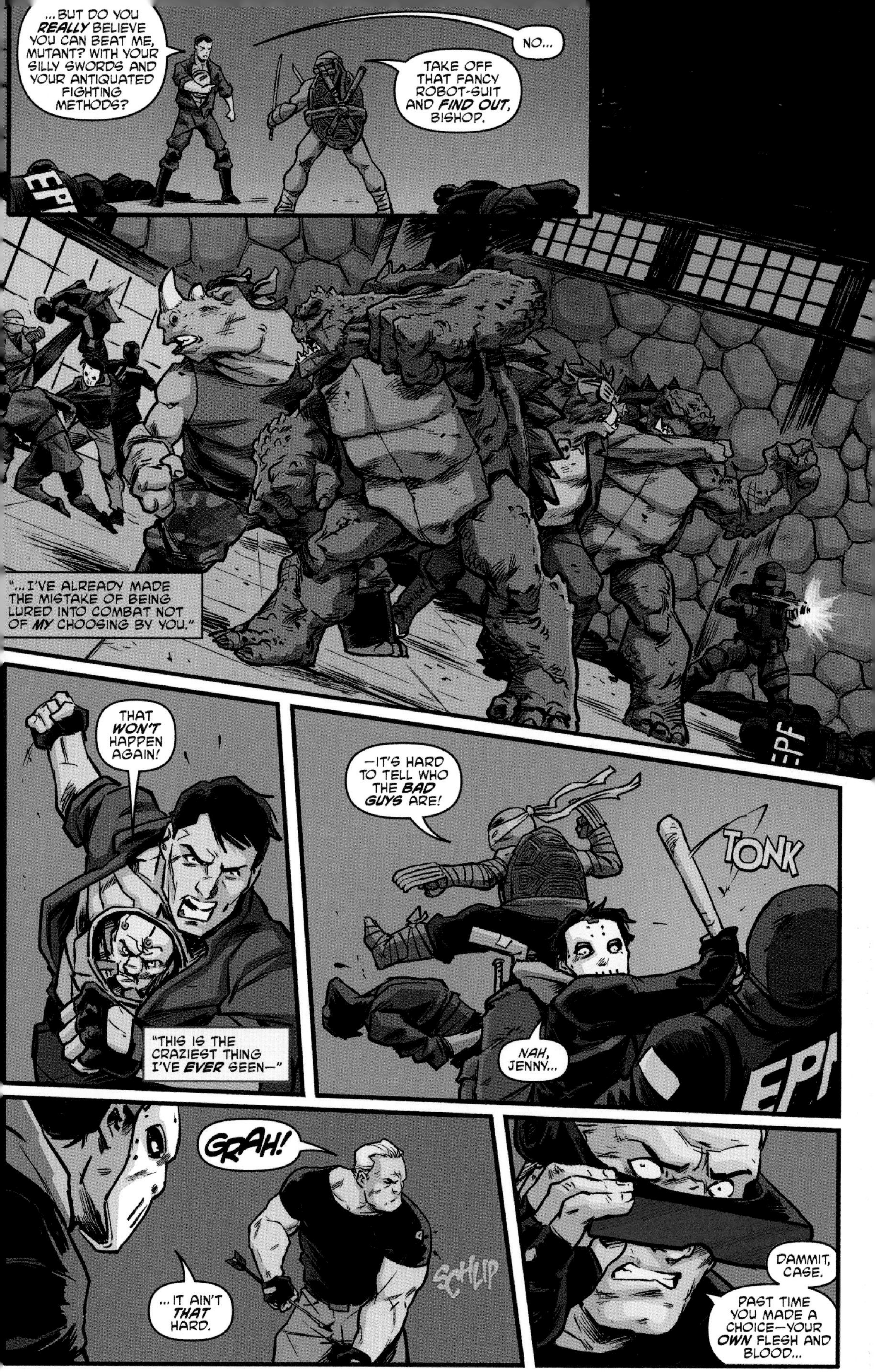
...BUT DO YOU REALLY BELIEVE YOU CAN BEAT ME, MUTANT? WITH YOUR SILLY SWORDS AND YOUR ANTIQUATED FIGHTING METHODS?
NO...
TAKE OFF THAT FANCY ROBOT-SUIT AND FIND OUT, BISHOP.
"...I'VE ALREADY MADE THE MISTAKE OF BEING LURED INTO COMBAT NOT OF MY CHOOSING BY YOU."
THAT WON'T HAPPEN AGAIN!
"THIS IS THE CRAZIEST THING I'VE EVER SEEN—"
—IT'S HARD TO TELL WHO THE BAD GUYS ARE!
TONK
NAH, JENNY...
GRAH!
...IT AIN'T THAT HARD.
SCHLIP
DAMMIT, CASE.
PAST TIME YOU MADE A CHOICE—YOUR OWN FLESH AND BLOOD...

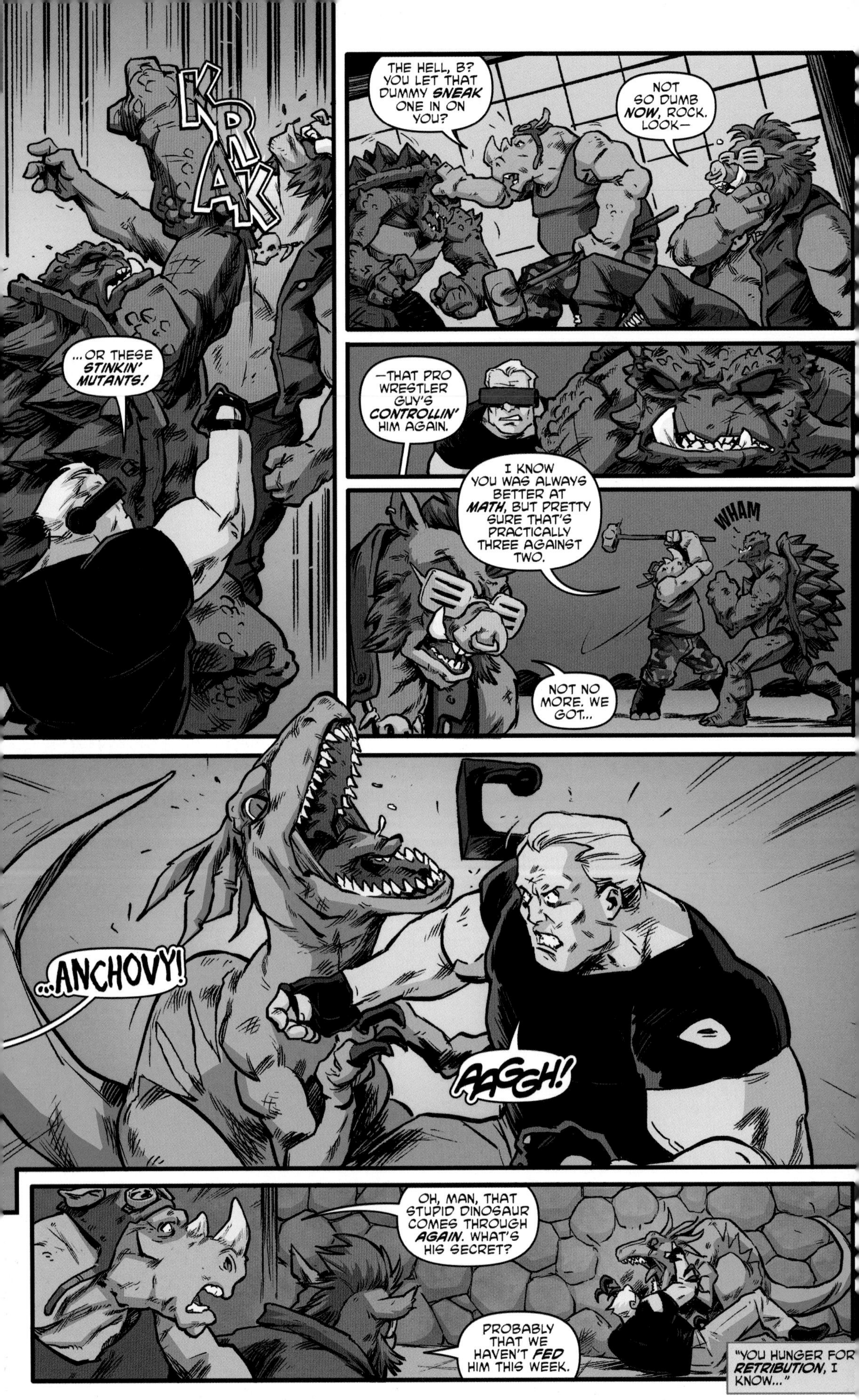
KRAK
...OR THESE STINKIN' MUTANTS!
THE HELL, B? YOU LET THAT DUMMY SNEAK ONE IN ON YOU?
NOT SO DUMB NOW, ROCK. LOOK—
—THAT PRO WRESTLER GUY'S CONTROLLIN' HIM AGAIN.
I KNOW YOU WAS ALWAYS BETTER AT MATH, BUT PRETTY SURE THAT'S PRACTICALLY THREE AGAINST TWO.
WHAM
NOT NO MORE. WE GOT...
...ANCHOVY!
AAGGH!
OH, MAN, THAT STUPID DINOSAUR COMES THROUGH AGAIN. WHAT'S HIS SECRET?
PROBABLY THAT WE HAVEN'T FED HIM THIS WEEK.
"YOU HUNGER FOR RETRIBUTION, I KNOW..."

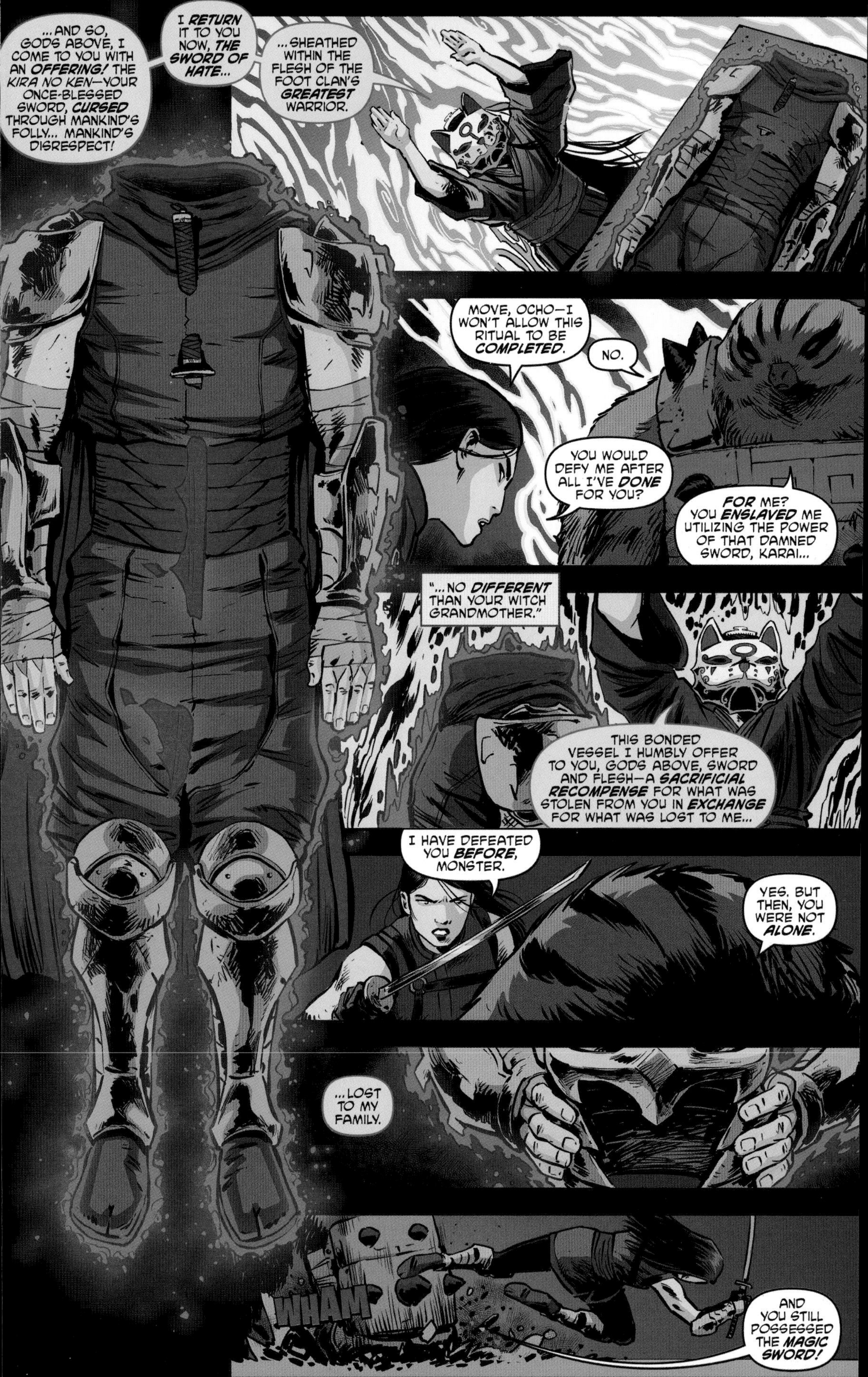
...AND SO, GODS ABOVE, I COME TO YOU WITH AN OFFERING! THE KIRA NO KEN—YOUR ONCE-BLESSED SWORD, CURSED THROUGH MANKIND'S FOLLY... MANKIND'S DISRESPECT!
I RETURN IT TO YOU NOW, THE SWORD OF HATE...
...SHEATHED WITHIN THE FLESH OF THE FOOT CLAN'S GREATEST WARRIOR.
MOVE, OCHO—I WON'T ALLOW THIS RITUAL TO BE COMPLETED.
NO.
YOU WOULD DEFY ME AFTER ALL I'VE DONE FOR YOU?
FOR ME? YOU ENSLAVED ME UTILIZING THE POWER OF THAT DAMNED SWORD, KARAI...
"...NO DIFFERENT THAN YOUR WITCH GRANDMOTHER."
THIS BONDED VESSEL I HUMBLY OFFER TO YOU, GODS ABOVE, SWORD AND FLESH—A SACRIFICIAL RECOMPENSE FOR WHAT WAS STOLEN FROM YOU IN EXCHANGE FOR WHAT WAS LOST TO ME...
I HAVE DEFEATED YOU BEFORE, MONSTER.
YES. BUT THEN, YOU WERE NOT ALONE.
...LOST TO MY FAMILY.
WHAM
AND YOU STILL POSSESSED THE MAGIC SWORD!

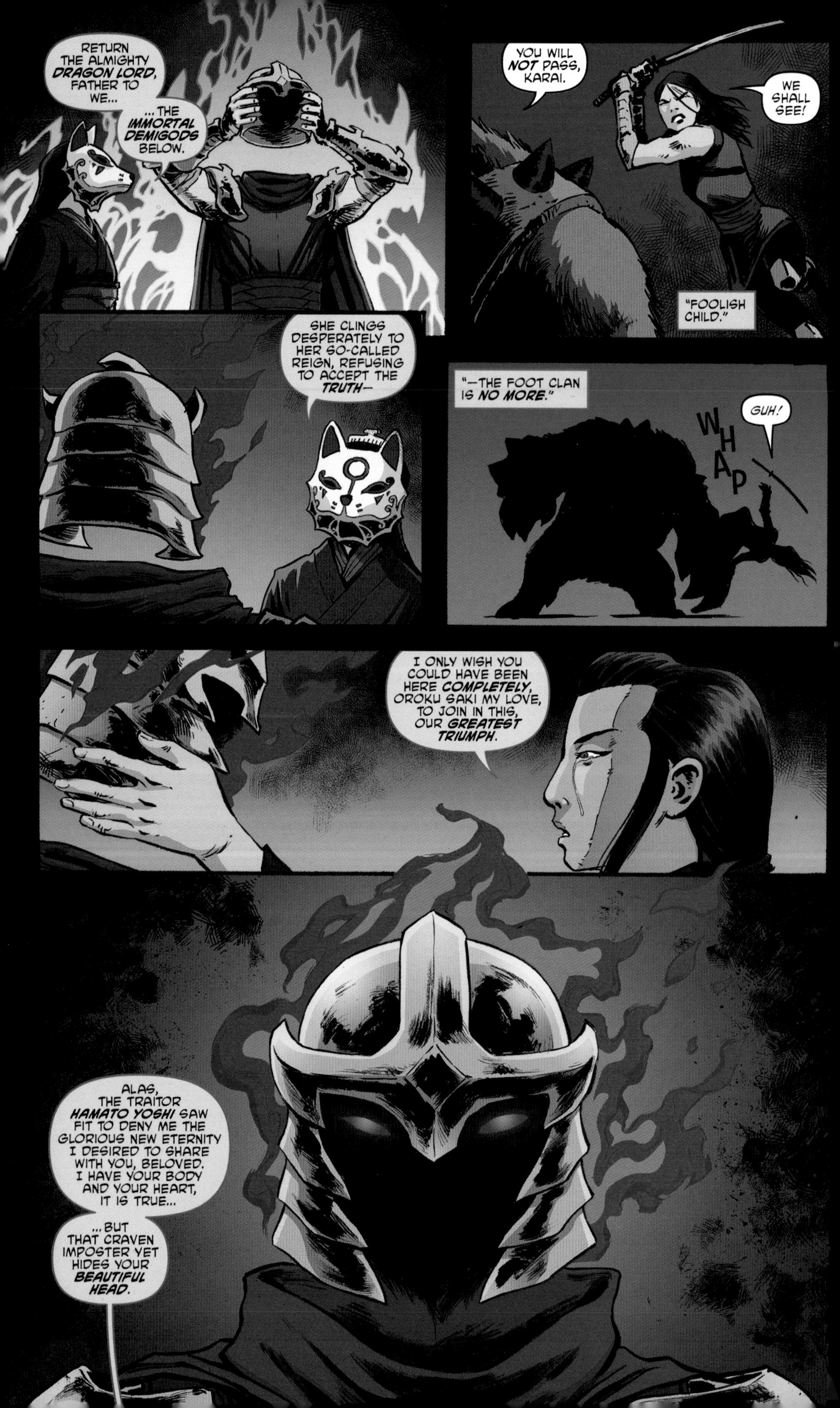

RETURN THE ALMIGHTY DRAGON LORD, FATHER TO WE...
...THE IMMORTAL DEMIGODS BELOW.
YOU WILL NOT PASS, KARAI.
WE SHALL SEE!
"FOOLISH CHILD."
SHE CLINGS DESPERATELY TO HER SO-CALLED REIGN, REFUSING TO ACCEPT THE TRUTH–
"–THE FOOT CLAN IS NO MORE."
WHAP
GUH!
I ONLY WISH YOU COULD HAVE BEEN HERE COMPLETELY, OROKU SAKI MY LOVE, TO JOIN IN THIS, OUR GREATEST TRIUMPH.
ALAS, THE TRAITOR HAMATO YOSHI SAW FIT TO DENY ME THE GLORIOUS NEW ETERNITY I DESIRED TO SHARE WITH YOU, BELOVED. I HAVE YOUR BODY AND YOUR HEART, IT IS TRUE...
...BUT THAT CRAVEN IMPOSTER YET HIDES YOUR BEAUTIFUL HEAD.

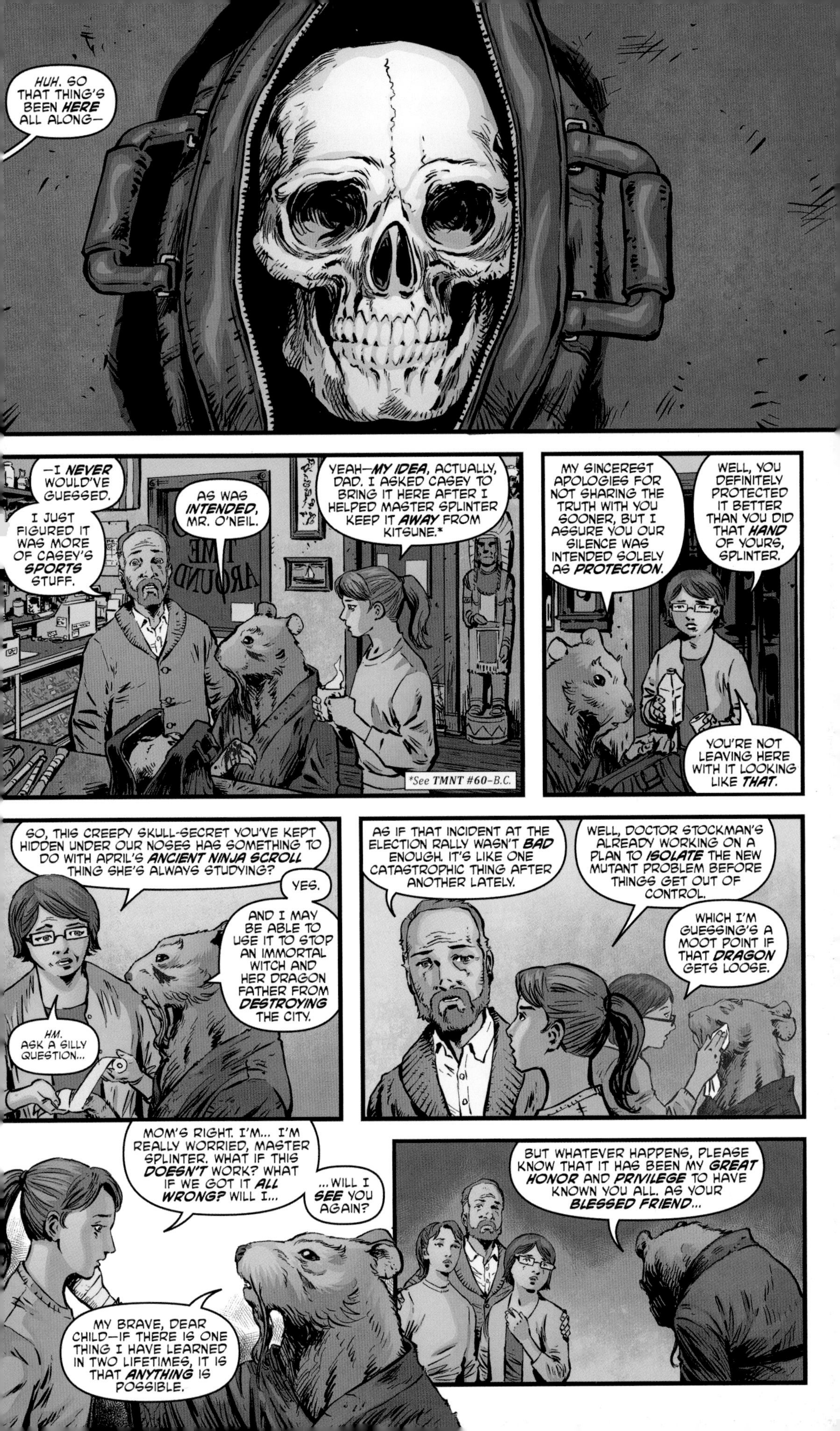

HUH. SO THAT THING'S BEEN *HERE* ALL ALONG—
—I *NEVER* WOULD'VE GUESSED.
I JUST FIGURED IT WAS MORE OF CASEY'S *SPORTS* STUFF.
AS WAS *INTENDED*, MR. O'NEIL.
YEAH—*MY IDEA*, ACTUALLY, DAD. I ASKED CASEY TO BRING IT HERE AFTER I HELPED MASTER SPLINTER KEEP IT *AWAY* FROM KITSUNE.*
*See TMNT #60–B.C.
MY SINCEREST APOLOGIES FOR NOT SHARING THE TRUTH WITH YOU SOONER, BUT I ASSURE YOU OUR SILENCE WAS INTENDED SOLELY AS *PROTECTION*.
WELL, YOU DEFINITELY PROTECTED IT BETTER THAN YOU DID THAT *HAND* OF YOURS, SPLINTER.
YOU'RE NOT LEAVING HERE WITH IT LOOKING LIKE *THAT*.
SO, THIS CREEPY SKULL-SECRET YOU'VE KEPT HIDDEN UNDER OUR NOSES HAS SOMETHING TO DO WITH APRIL'S *ANCIENT NINJA SCROLL* THING SHE'S ALWAYS STUDYING?
YES.
AND I MAY BE ABLE TO USE IT TO STOP AN IMMORTAL WITCH AND HER DRAGON FATHER FROM *DESTROYING* THE CITY.
HM. ASK A SILLY QUESTION...
AS IF THAT INCIDENT AT THE ELECTION RALLY WASN'T *BAD* ENOUGH. IT'S LIKE ONE CATASTROPHIC THING AFTER ANOTHER LATELY.
WELL, DOCTOR STOCKMAN'S ALREADY WORKING ON A PLAN TO *ISOLATE* THE NEW MUTANT PROBLEM BEFORE THINGS GET OUT OF CONTROL.
WHICH I'M GUESSING'S A MOOT POINT IF THAT *DRAGON* GETS LOOSE.
MOM'S RIGHT. I'M... I'M REALLY WORRIED, MASTER SPLINTER. WHAT IF THIS *DOESN'T* WORK? WHAT IF WE GOT IT *ALL WRONG?* WILL I...
...WILL I *SEE* YOU AGAIN?
MY BRAVE, DEAR CHILD—IF THERE IS ONE THING I HAVE LEARNED IN TWO LIFETIMES, IT IS THAT *ANYTHING* IS POSSIBLE.
BUT WHATEVER HAPPENS, PLEASE KNOW THAT IT HAS BEEN MY *GREAT HONOR* AND *PRIVILEGE* TO HAVE KNOWN YOU ALL. AS YOUR *BLESSED FRIEND*...

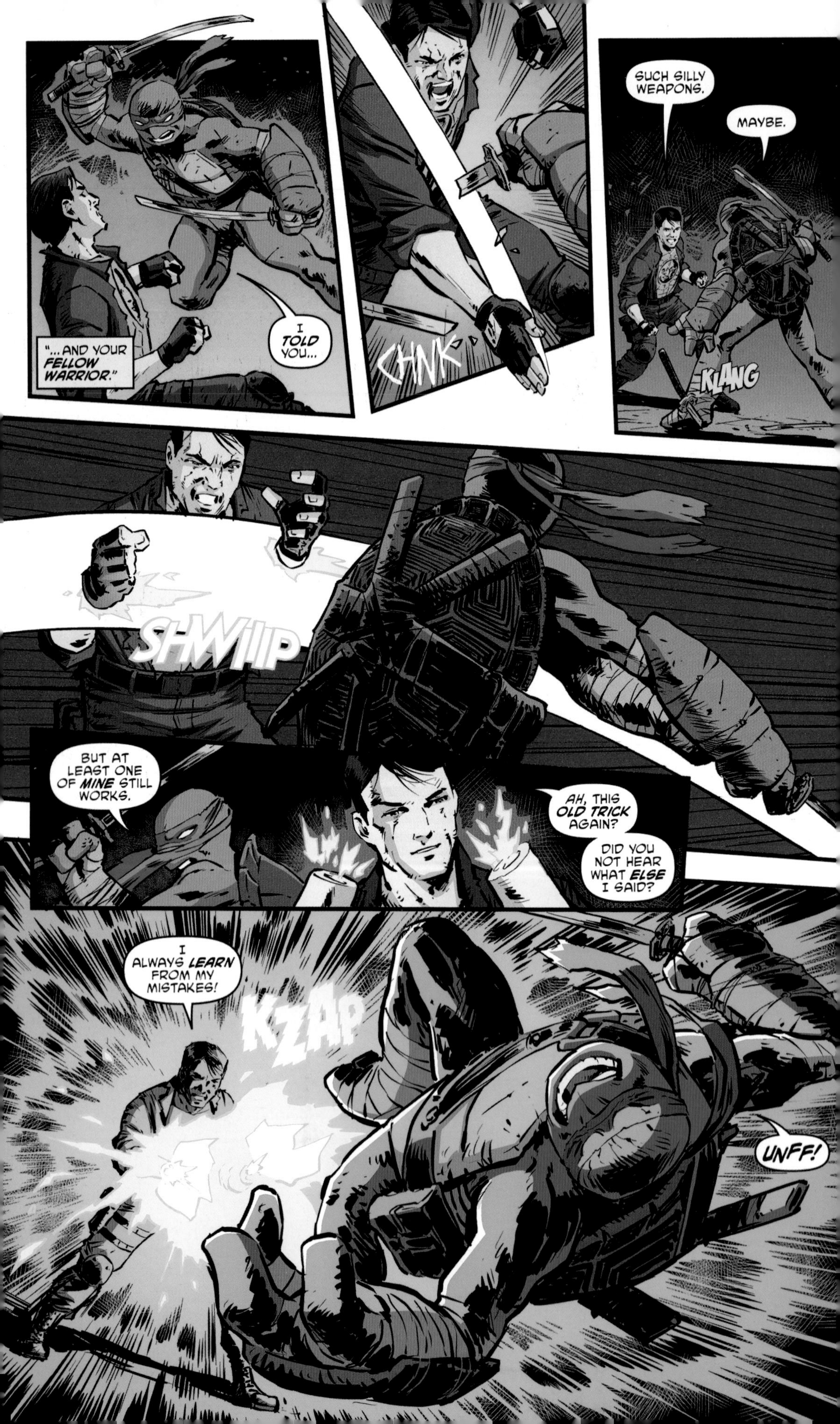

"...AND YOUR *FELLOW WARRIOR*."
I *TOLD* YOU...
CHNK
SUCH SILLY WEAPONS.
MAYBE.
KLANG
SHWIIP
BUT AT LEAST ONE OF *MINE* STILL WORKS.
AH, THIS OLD TRICK AGAIN?
DID YOU NOT HEAR WHAT *ELSE* I SAID?
I ALWAYS *LEARN* FROM MY MISTAKES!
KZAP
UNFF!

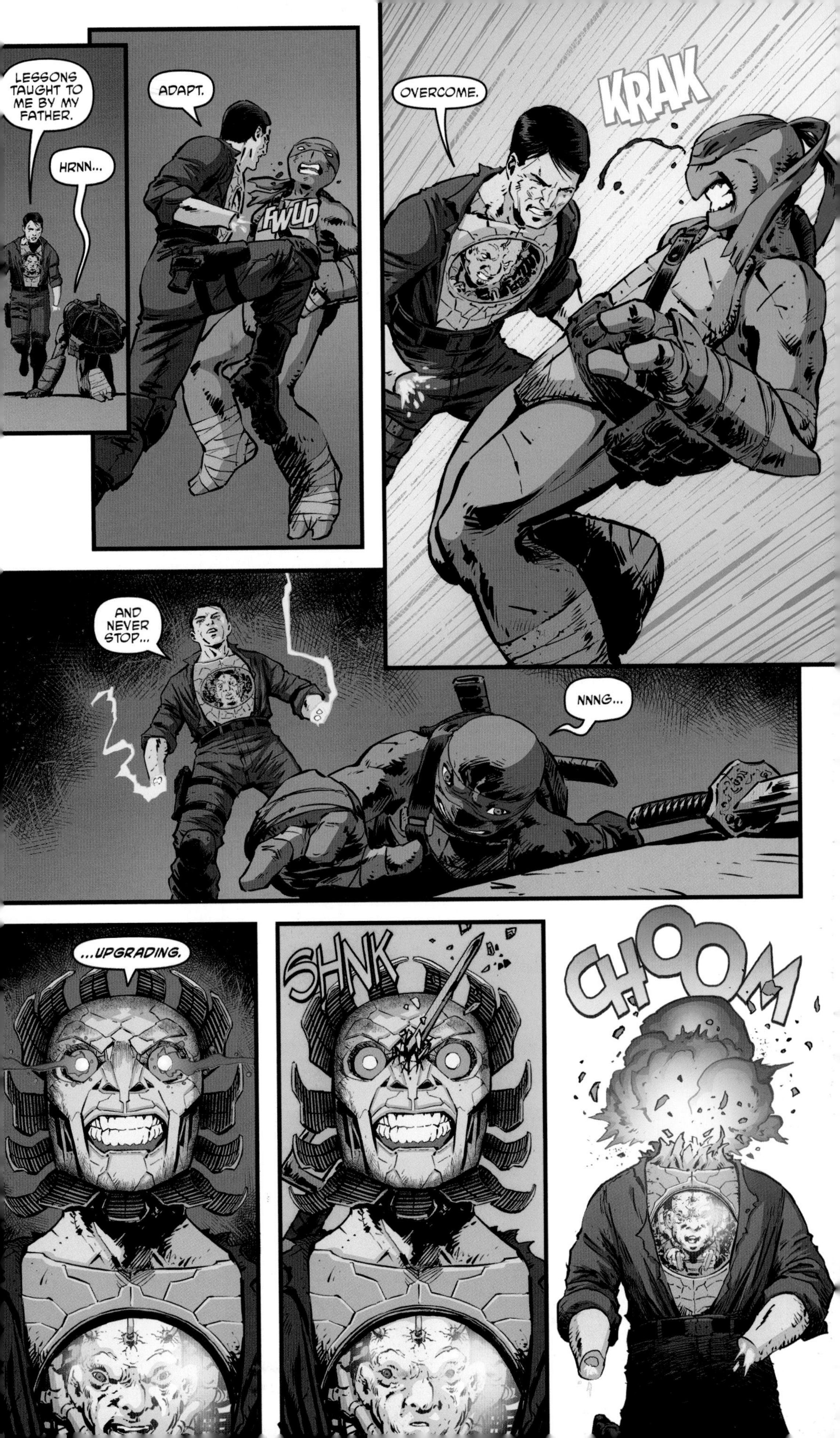
LESSONS TAUGHT TO ME BY MY FATHER.
HRNN...
ADAPT.
FWUD
OVERCOME.
KRAK
AND NEVER STOP...
NNNG...
...UPGRADING.
SHNK
CHOOM

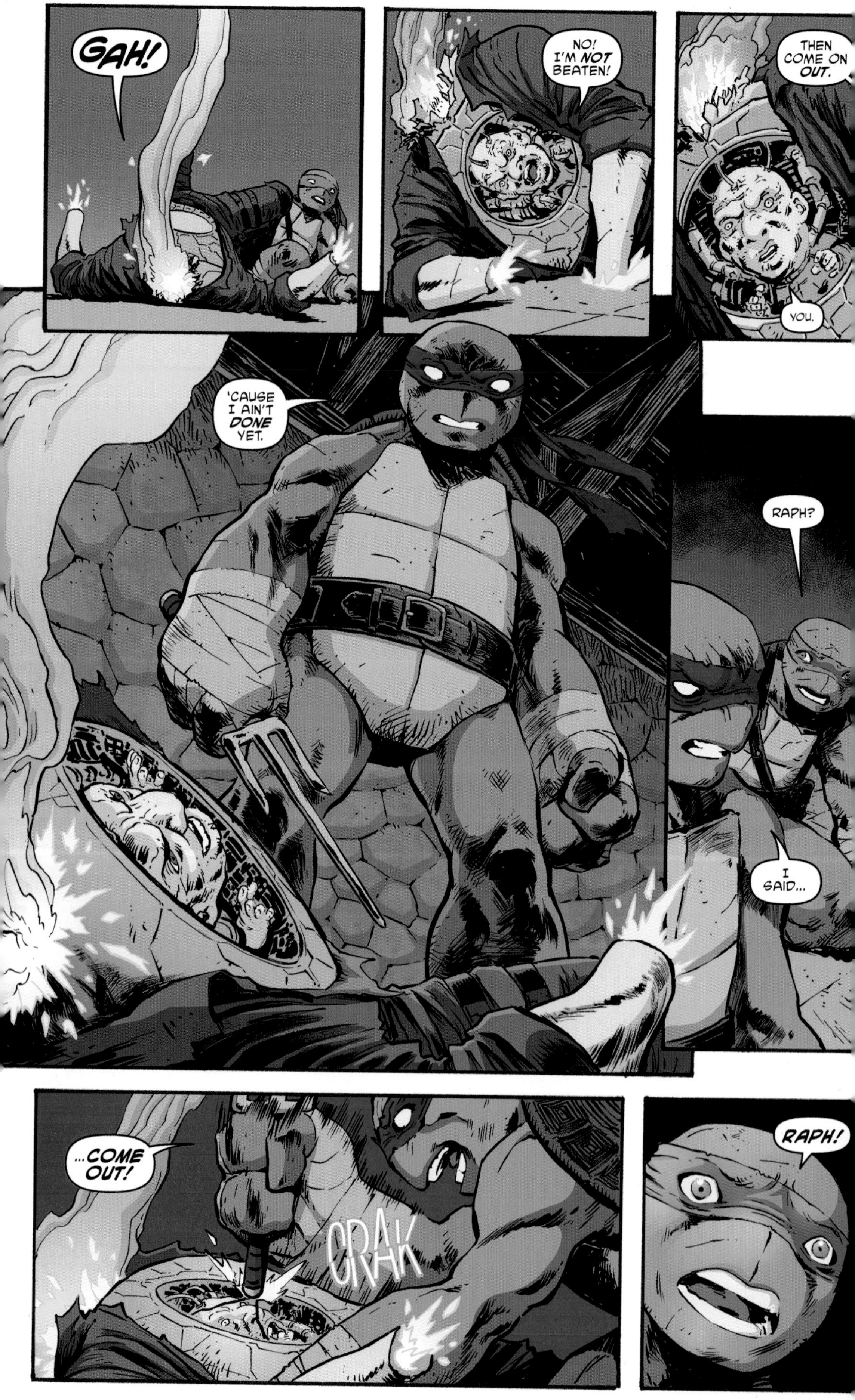
GAH!
NO! I'M NOT BEATEN!
THEN COME ON OUT.
YOU.
'CAUSE I AIN'T DONE YET.
RAPH?
I SAID...
...COME OUT!
CRAK
RAPH!

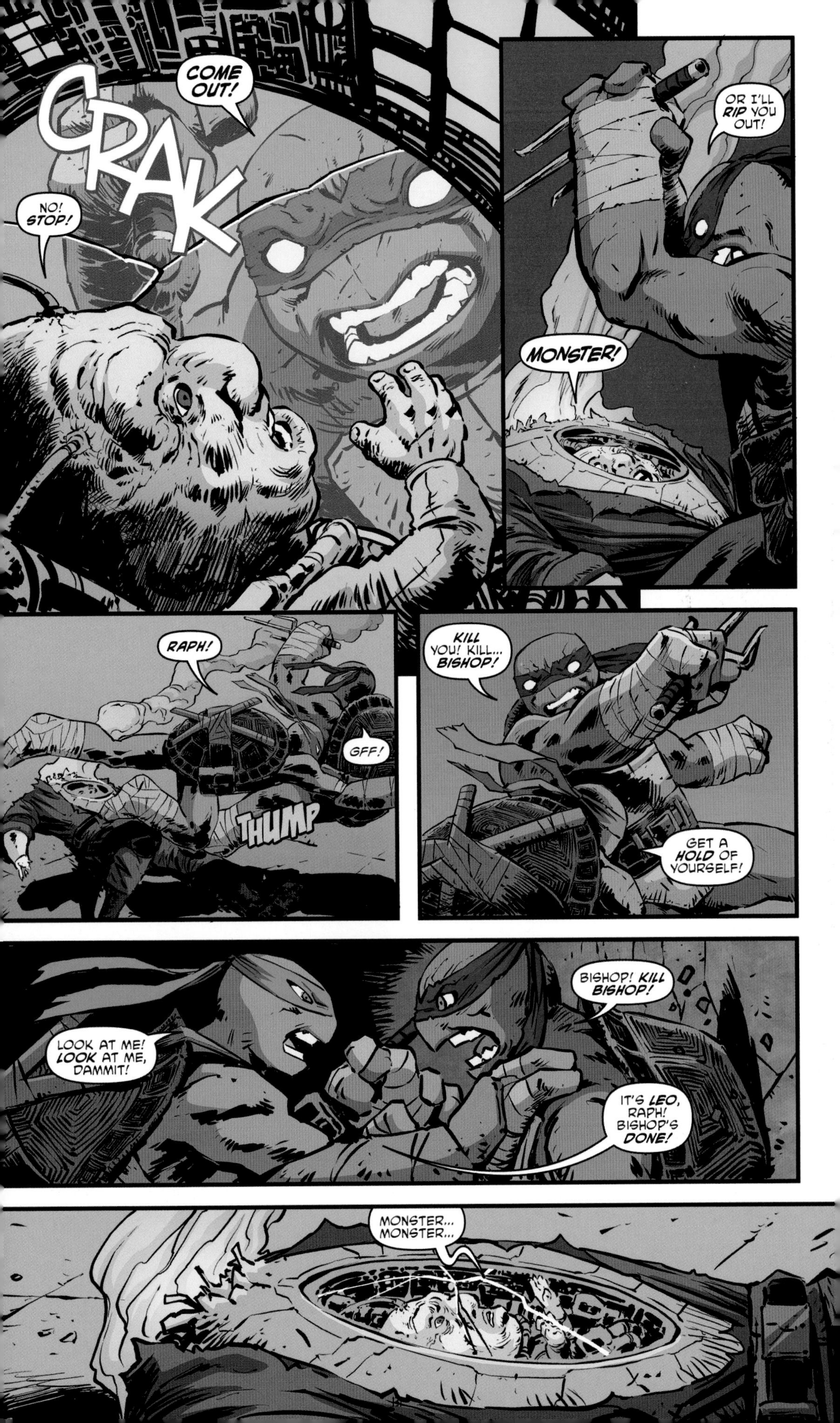
CRAK
COME OUT!
NO! STOP!
OR I'LL RIP YOU OUT!
MONSTER!
RAPH!
GFF!
THUMP
KILL YOU! KILL... BISHOP!
GET A HOLD OF YOURSELF!
BISHOP! KILL BISHOP!
LOOK AT ME! LOOK AT ME, DAMMIT!
IT'S LEO, RAPH! BISHOP'S DONE!
MONSTER... MONSTER...

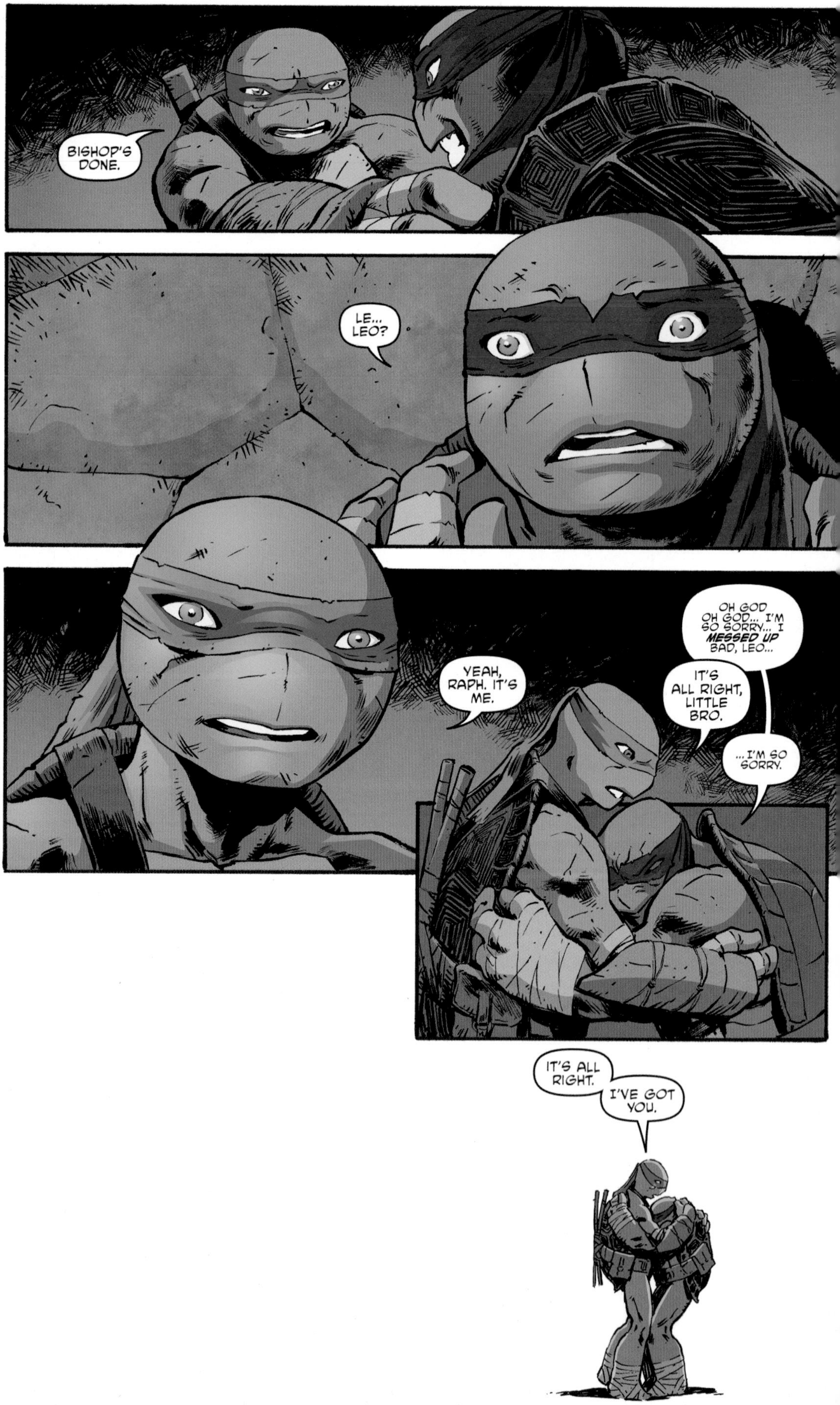
BISHOP'S DONE.
LE... LEO?
YEAH, RAPH. IT'S ME.
OH GOD OH GOD... I'M SO SORRY... I **MESSED UP** BAD, LEO...
IT'S ALL RIGHT, LITTLE BRO.
...I'M SO SORRY.
IT'S ALL RIGHT.
I'VE GOT YOU.

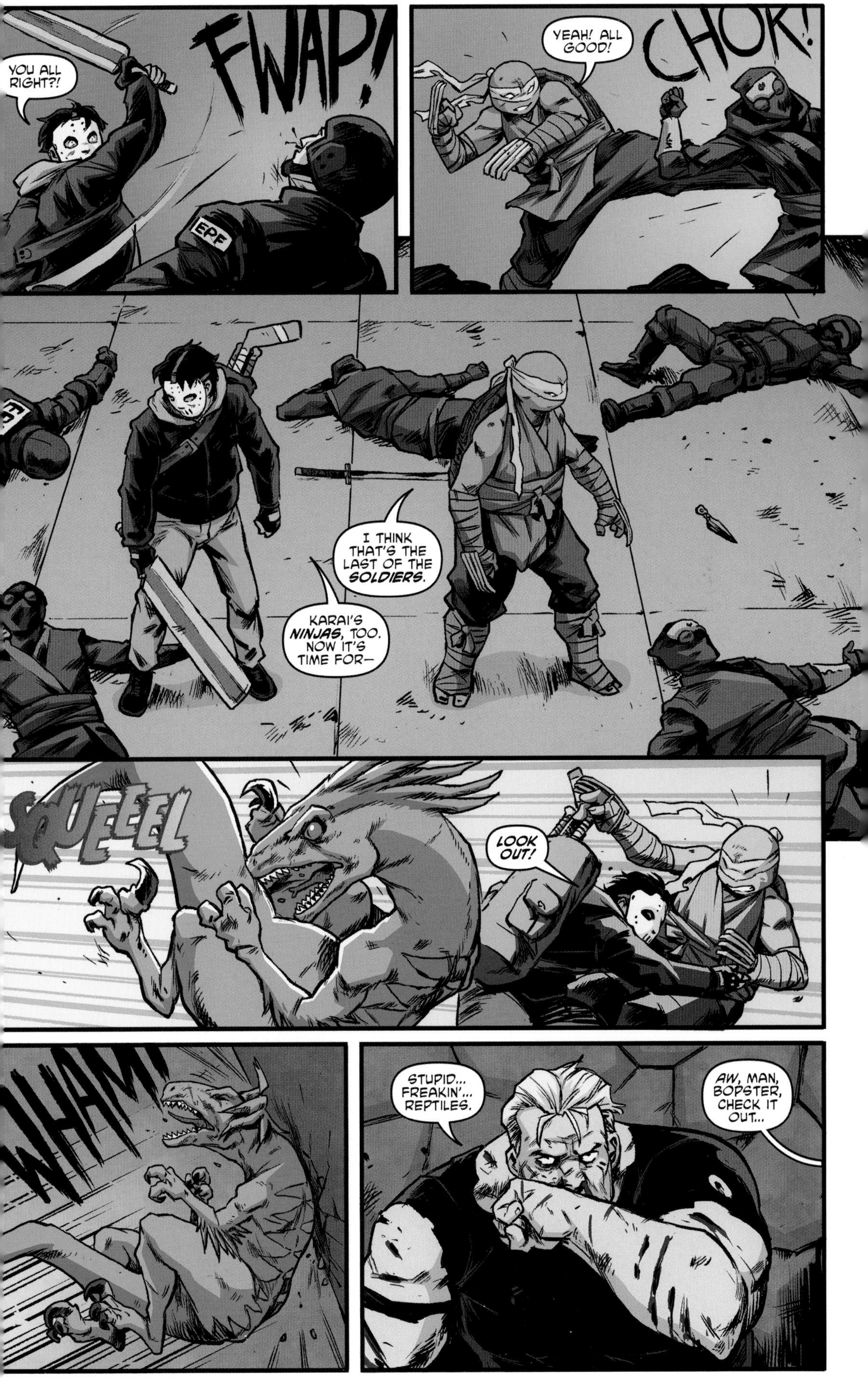
YOU ALL RIGHT?!
FWAP!
YEAH! ALL GOOD!
CHOK!
EPF
I THINK THAT'S THE LAST OF THE SOLDIERS.
KARAI'S NINJAS, TOO. NOW IT'S TIME FOR—
SQUEEEL
LOOK OUT!
WHAM!
STUPID... FREAKIN'... REPTILES.
AW, MAN, BOPSTER, CHECK IT OUT...

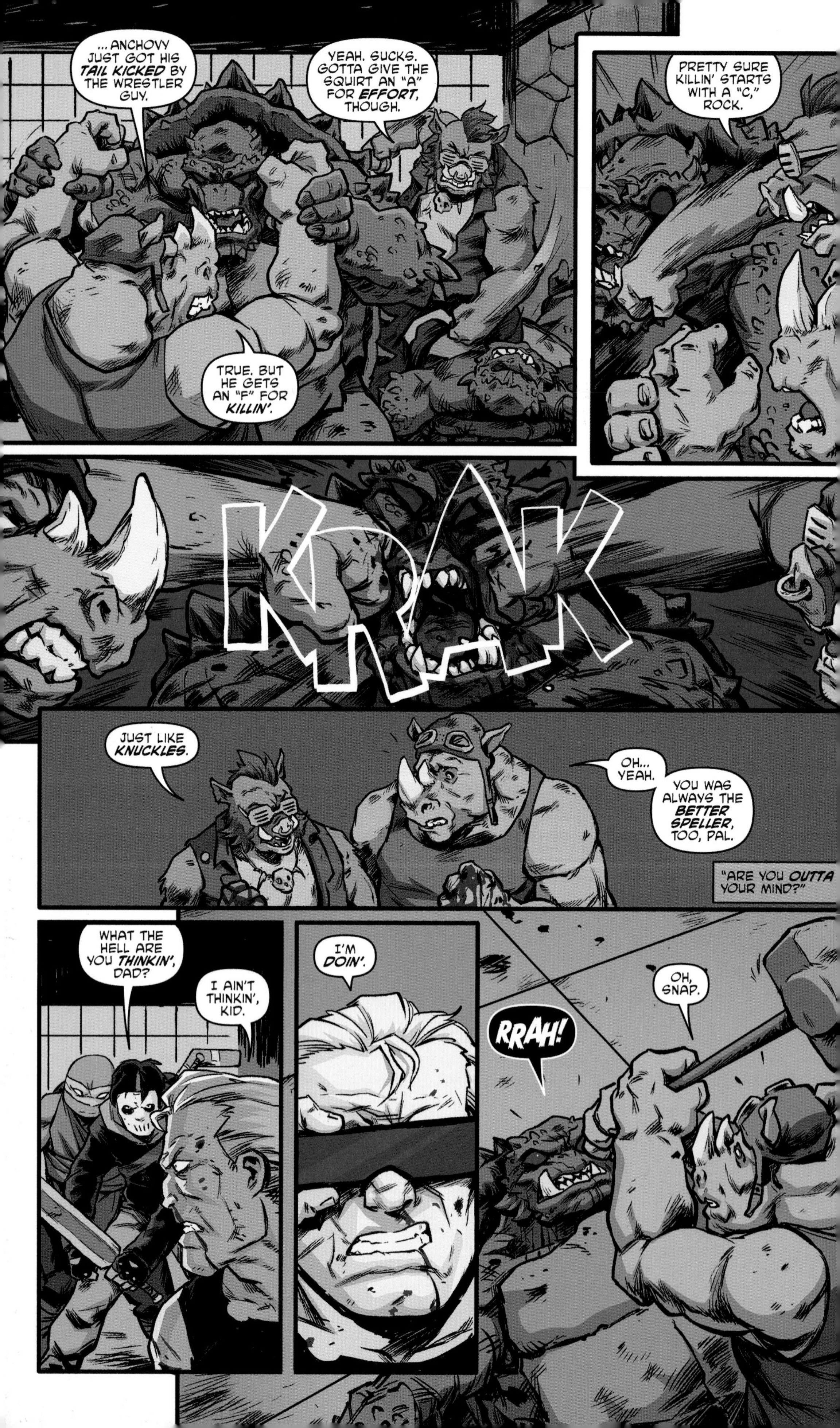
...ANCHOVY JUST GOT HIS TAIL KICKED BY THE WRESTLER GUY.
YEAH. SUCKS. GOTTA GIVE THE SQUIRT AN "A" FOR EFFORT, THOUGH.
TRUE. BUT HE GETS AN "F" FOR KILLIN'.
PRETTY SURE KILLIN' STARTS WITH A "C," ROCK.
KRAK
JUST LIKE KNUCKLES.
OH... YEAH.
YOU WAS ALWAYS THE BETTER SPELLER, TOO, PAL.
"ARE YOU OUTTA YOUR MIND?"
WHAT THE HELL ARE YOU THINKIN', DAD?
I AIN'T THINKIN', KID.
I'M DOIN'.
RRAH!
OH, SNAP.

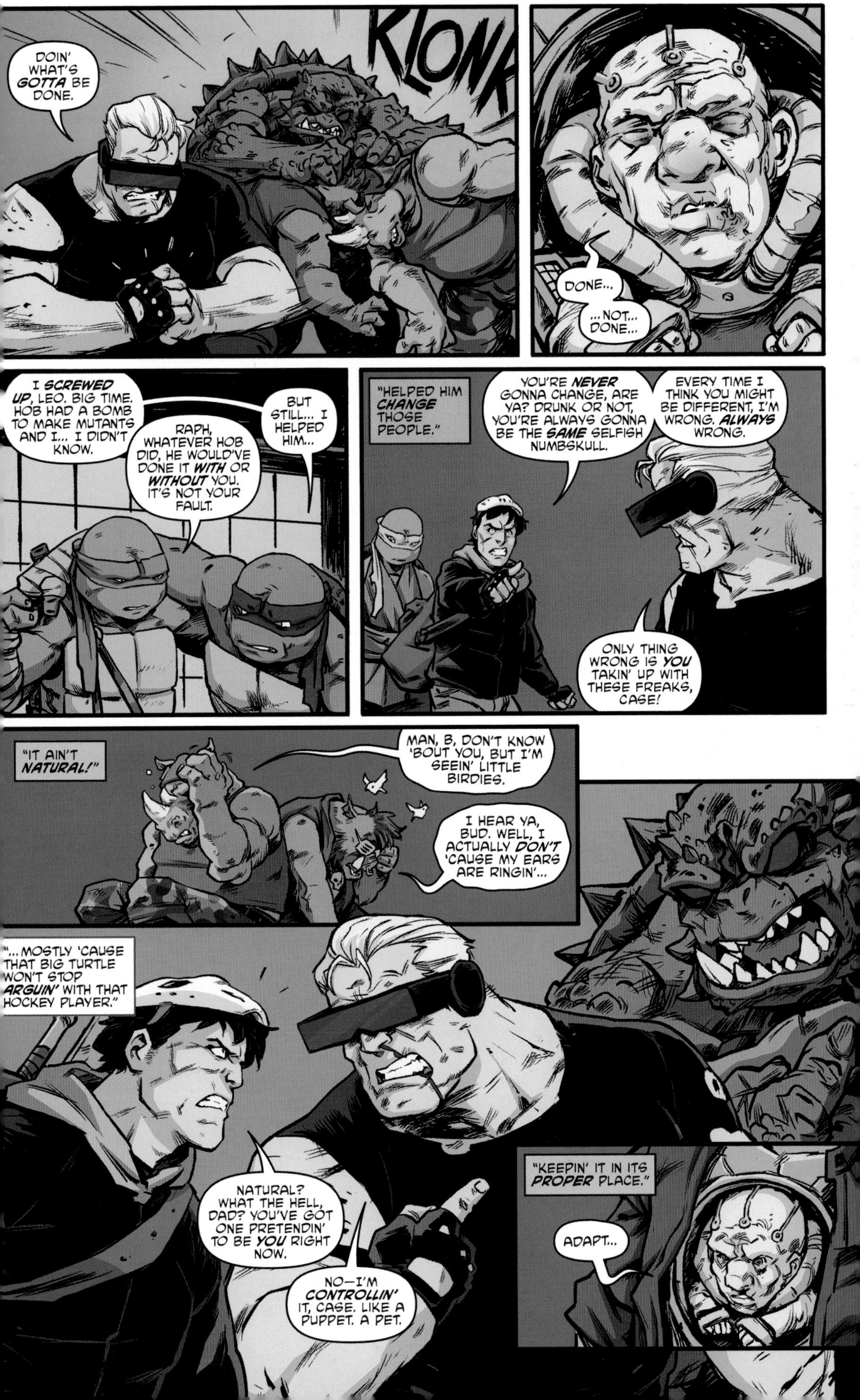
KLONK
DOIN' WHAT'S GOTTA BE DONE.
DONE...
...NOT... DONE...
I SCREWED UP, LEO. BIG TIME. HOB HAD A BOMB TO MAKE MUTANTS AND I... I DIDN'T KNOW.
BUT STILL... I HELPED HIM...
RAPH, WHATEVER HOB DID, HE WOULD'VE DONE IT WITH OR WITHOUT YOU. IT'S NOT YOUR FAULT.
"HELPED HIM CHANGE THOSE PEOPLE."
YOU'RE NEVER GONNA CHANGE, ARE YA? DRUNK OR NOT, YOU'RE ALWAYS GONNA BE THE SAME SELFISH NUMBSKULL.
EVERY TIME I THINK YOU MIGHT BE DIFFERENT, I'M WRONG. ALWAYS WRONG.
ONLY THING WRONG IS YOU TAKIN' UP WITH THESE FREAKS, CASE!
"IT AIN'T NATURAL!"
MAN, B, DON'T KNOW 'BOUT YOU, BUT I'M SEEIN' LITTLE BIRDIES.
I HEAR YA, BUD. WELL, I ACTUALLY DON'T 'CAUSE MY EARS ARE RINGIN'...
"...MOSTLY 'CAUSE THAT BIG TURTLE WON'T STOP ARGUIN' WITH THAT HOCKEY PLAYER."
NATURAL? WHAT THE HELL, DAD? YOU'VE GOT ONE PRETENDIN' TO BE YOU RIGHT NOW.
NO—I'M CONTROLLIN' IT, CASE. LIKE A PUPPET. A PET.
"KEEPIN' IT IN ITS PROPER PLACE."
ADAPT...

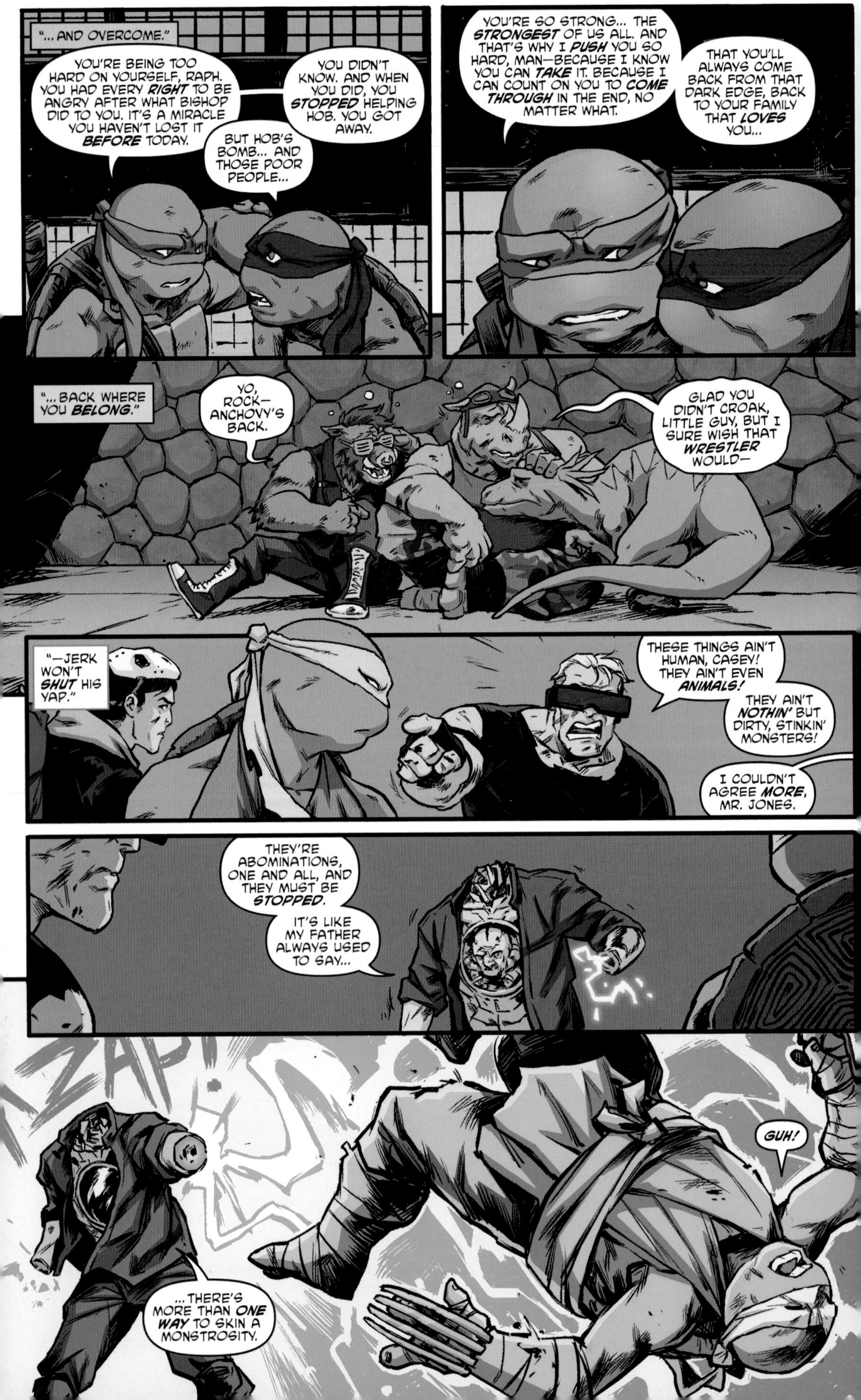
"...AND OVERCOME."
YOU'RE BEING TOO HARD ON YOURSELF, RAPH. YOU HAD EVERY RIGHT TO BE ANGRY AFTER WHAT BISHOP DID TO YOU. IT'S A MIRACLE YOU HAVEN'T LOST IT BEFORE TODAY.
BUT HOB'S BOMB... AND THOSE POOR PEOPLE...
YOU DIDN'T KNOW. AND WHEN YOU DID, YOU STOPPED HELPING HOB. YOU GOT AWAY.
YOU'RE SO STRONG... THE STRONGEST OF US ALL. AND THAT'S WHY I PUSH YOU SO HARD, MAN—BECAUSE I KNOW YOU CAN TAKE IT. BECAUSE I CAN COUNT ON YOU TO COME THROUGH IN THE END, NO MATTER WHAT.
THAT YOU'LL ALWAYS COME BACK FROM THAT DARK EDGE, BACK TO YOUR FAMILY THAT LOVES YOU...
"...BACK WHERE YOU BELONG."
YO, ROCK— ANCHOVY'S BACK.
GLAD YOU DIDN'T CROAK, LITTLE GUY, BUT I SURE WISH THAT WRESTLER WOULD—
"—JERK WON'T SHUT HIS YAP."
THESE THINGS AIN'T HUMAN, CASEY! THEY AIN'T EVEN ANIMALS!
THEY AIN'T NOTHIN' BUT DIRTY, STINKIN' MONSTERS!
I COULDN'T AGREE MORE, MR. JONES.
THEY'RE ABOMINATIONS, ONE AND ALL, AND THEY MUST BE STOPPED.
IT'S LIKE MY FATHER ALWAYS USED TO SAY...
ZAP!
GUH!
...THERE'S MORE THAN ONE WAY TO SKIN A MONSTROSITY.

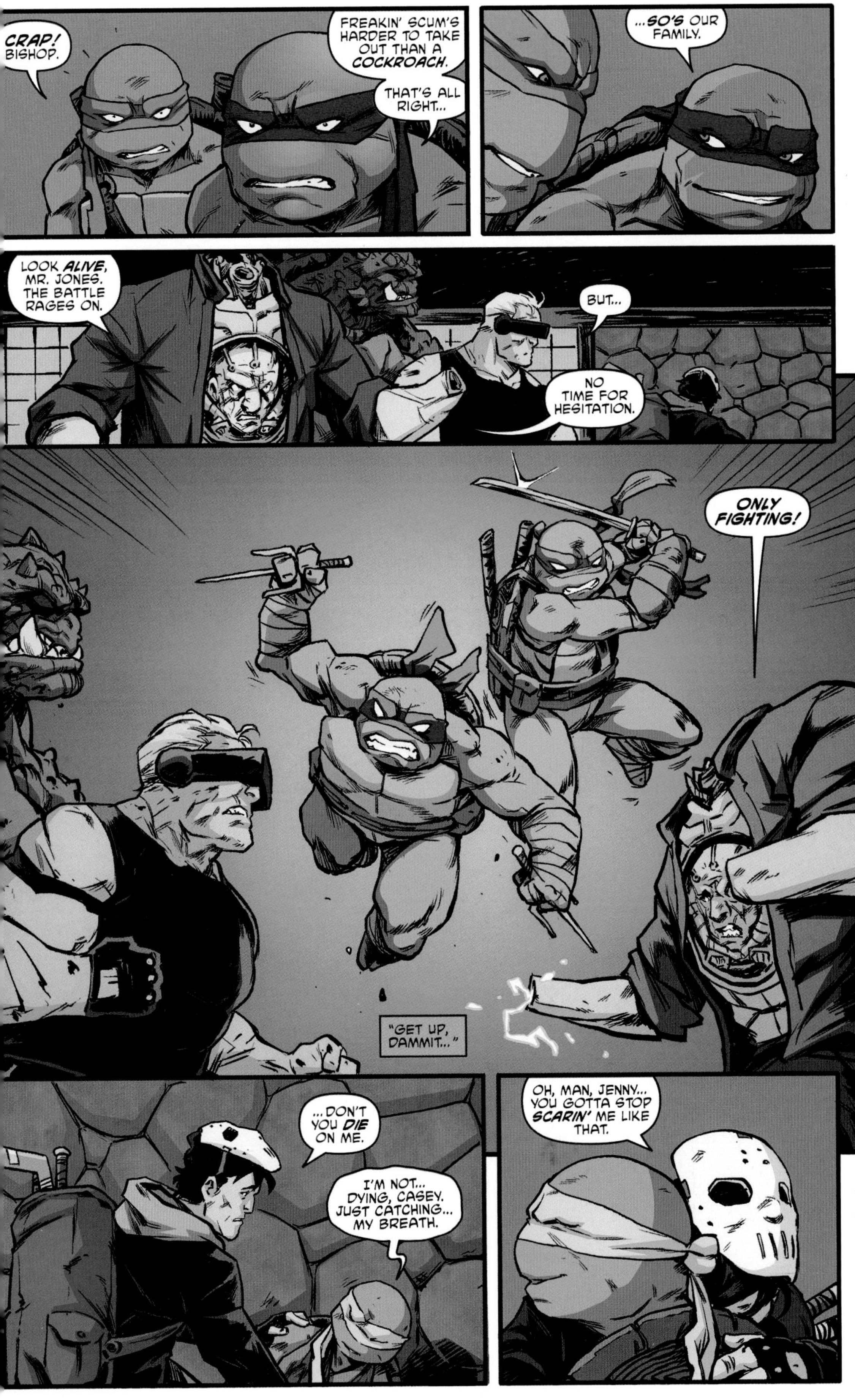
CRAP! BISHOP.
FREAKIN' SCUM'S HARDER TO TAKE OUT THAN A COCKROACH.
THAT'S ALL RIGHT...
...SO'S OUR FAMILY.
LOOK ALIVE, MR. JONES. THE BATTLE RAGES ON.
BUT...
NO TIME FOR HESITATION.
ONLY FIGHTING!
"GET UP, DAMMIT..."
...DON'T YOU DIE ON ME.
I'M NOT... DYING, CASEY. JUST CATCHING... MY BREATH.
OH, MAN, JENNY... YOU GOTTA STOP SCARIN' ME LIKE THAT.

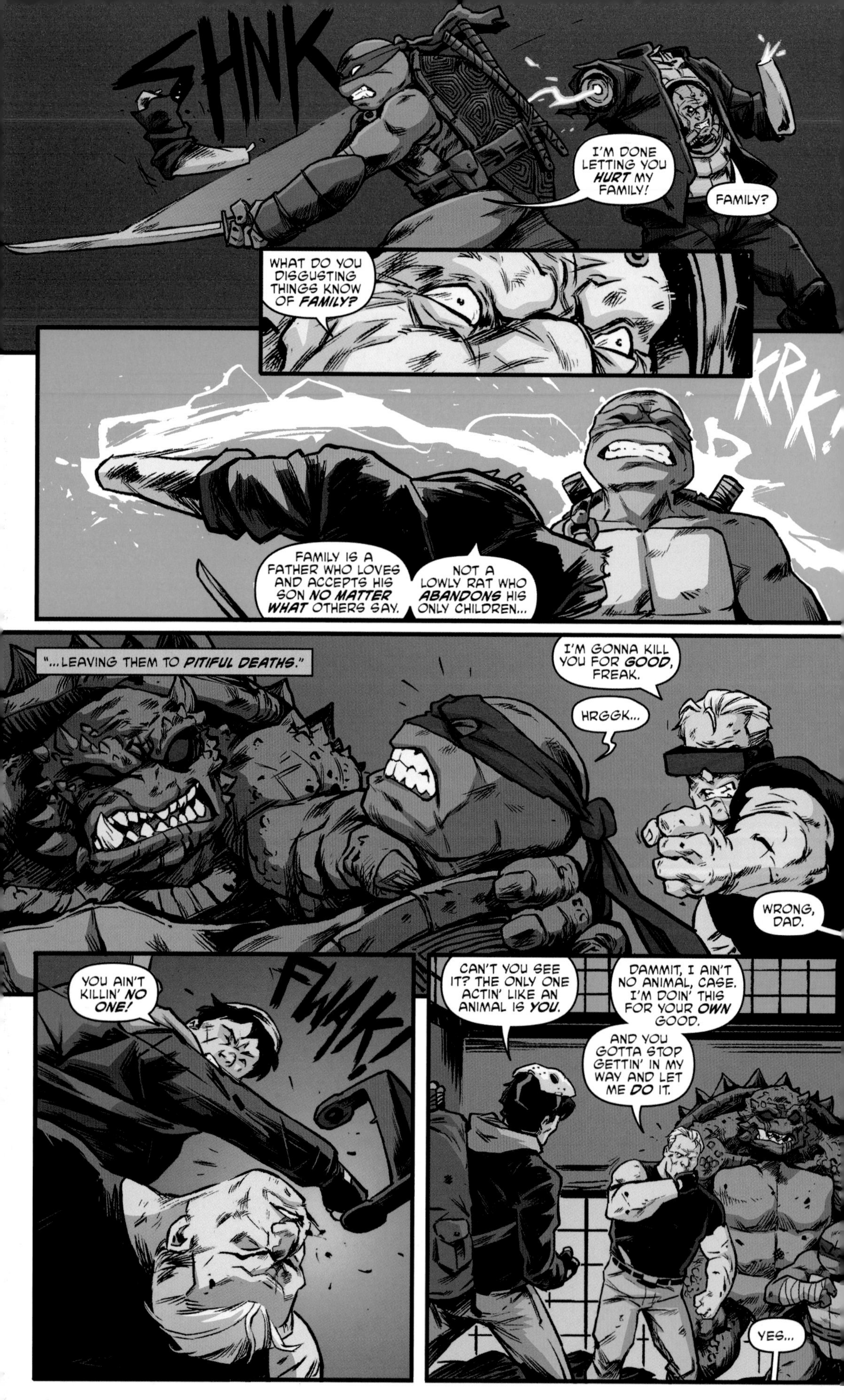
SHNK
I'M DONE LETTING YOU HURT MY FAMILY!
FAMILY?
WHAT DO YOU DISGUSTING THINGS KNOW OF FAMILY?
KRK!
FAMILY IS A FATHER WHO LOVES AND ACCEPTS HIS SON NO MATTER WHAT OTHERS SAY.
NOT A LOWLY RAT WHO ABANDONS HIS ONLY CHILDREN...
"...LEAVING THEM TO PITIFUL DEATHS."
I'M GONNA KILL YOU FOR GOOD, FREAK.
HRGGK...
WRONG, DAD.
YOU AIN'T KILLIN' NO ONE!
FWAK!
CAN'T YOU SEE IT? THE ONLY ONE ACTIN' LIKE AN ANIMAL IS YOU.
DAMMIT, I AIN'T NO ANIMAL, CASE. I'M DOIN' THIS FOR YOUR OWN GOOD.
AND YOU GOTTA STOP GETTIN' IN MY WAY AND LET ME DO IT.
YES...

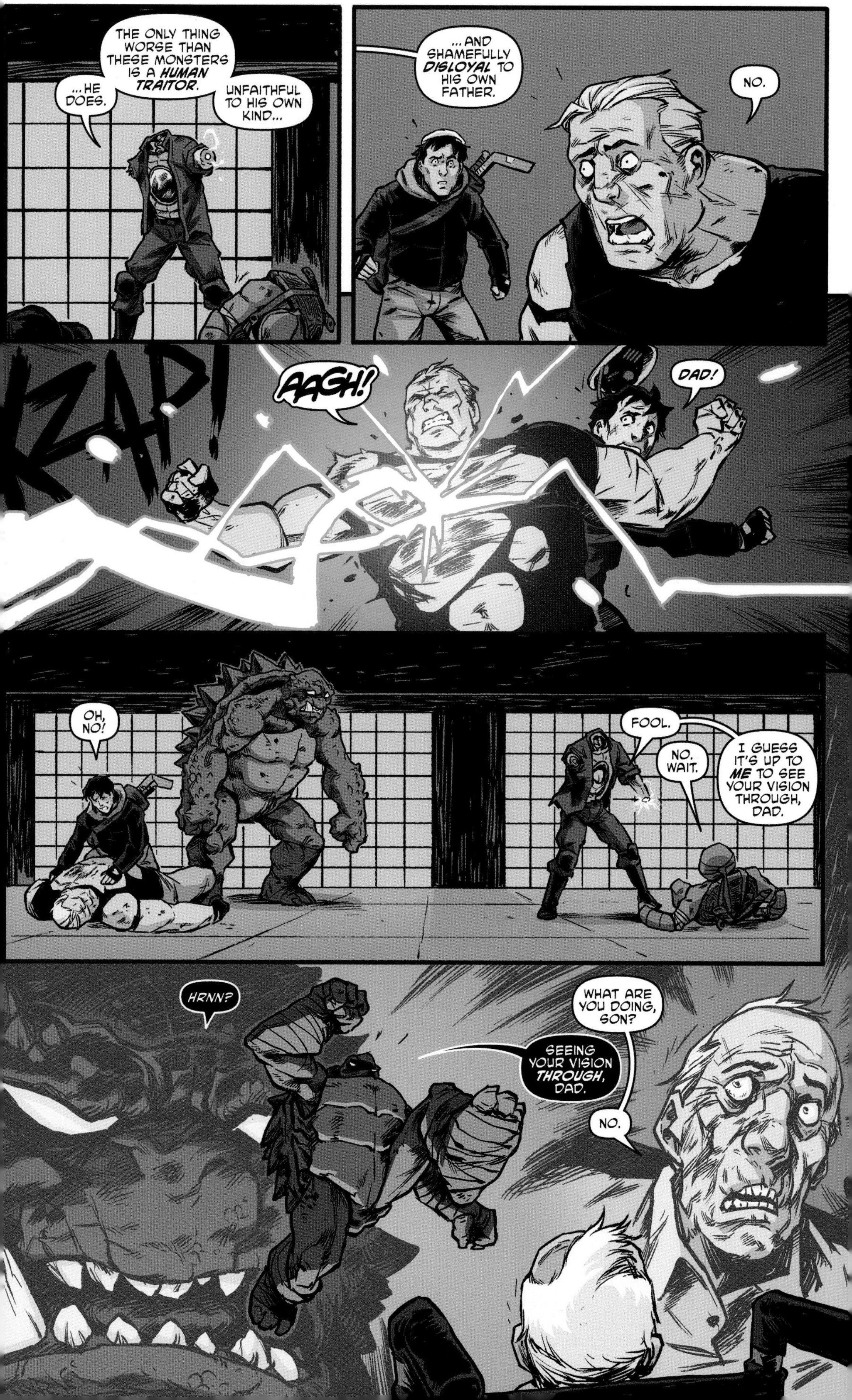
...HE DOES.
THE ONLY THING WORSE THAN THESE MONSTERS IS A HUMAN TRAITOR.
UNFAITHFUL TO HIS OWN KIND...
...AND SHAMEFULLY DISLOYAL TO HIS OWN FATHER.
NO.
ZAP!
AAGH!
DAD!
OH, NO!
FOOL.
NO. WAIT.
I GUESS IT'S UP TO ME TO SEE YOUR VISION THROUGH, DAD.
HRNN?
WHAT ARE YOU DOING, SON?
SEEING YOUR VISION THROUGH, DAD.
NO.

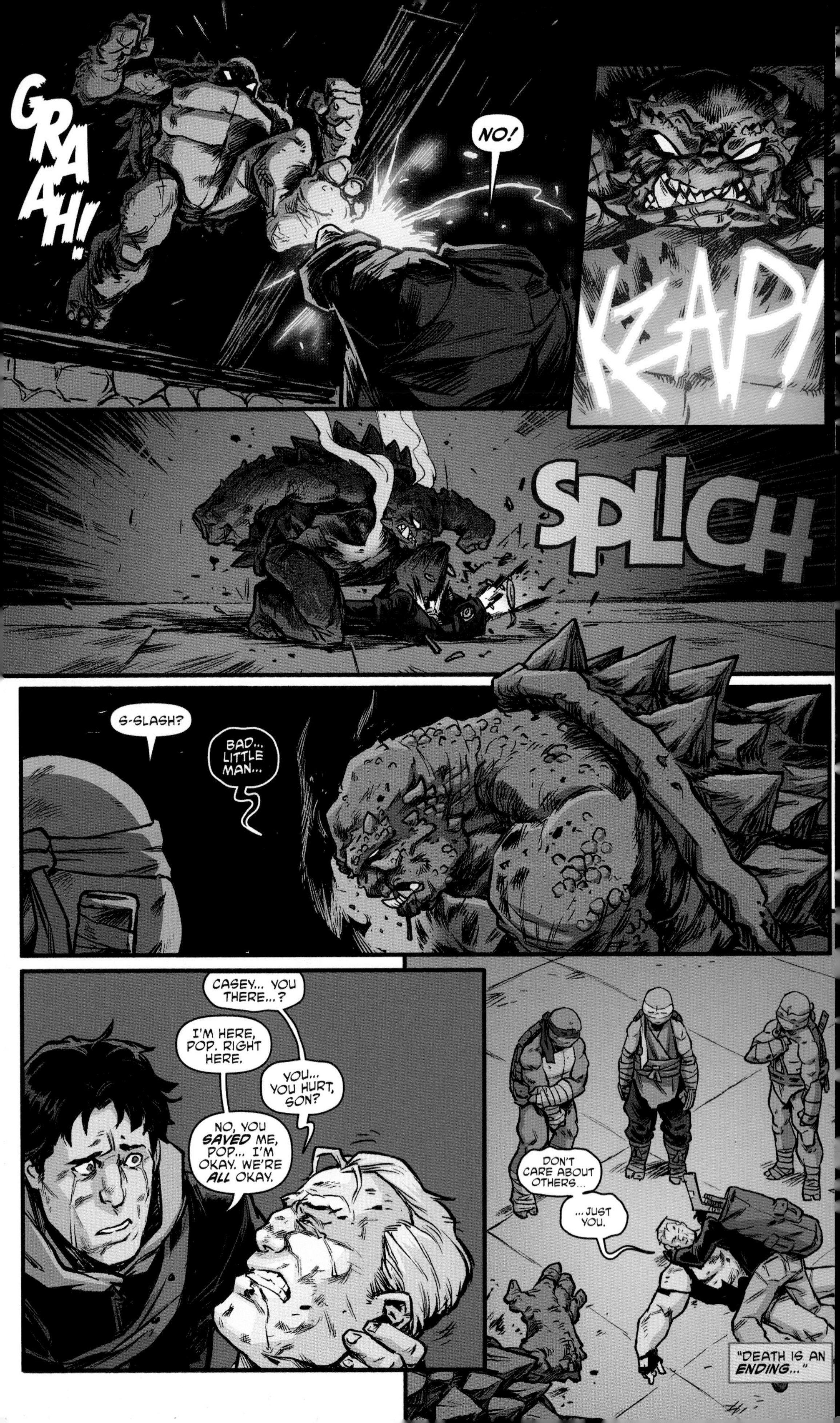
GRAAH!!
NO!
KZAP!
SPLICH
S-SLASH?
BAD... LITTLE MAN...
CASEY... YOU THERE...?
I'M HERE, POP. RIGHT HERE.
YOU... YOU HURT, SON?
NO, YOU SAVED ME, POP... I'M OKAY. WE'RE ALL OKAY.
DON'T CARE ABOUT OTHERS...
...JUST YOU.
"DEATH IS AN ENDING..."

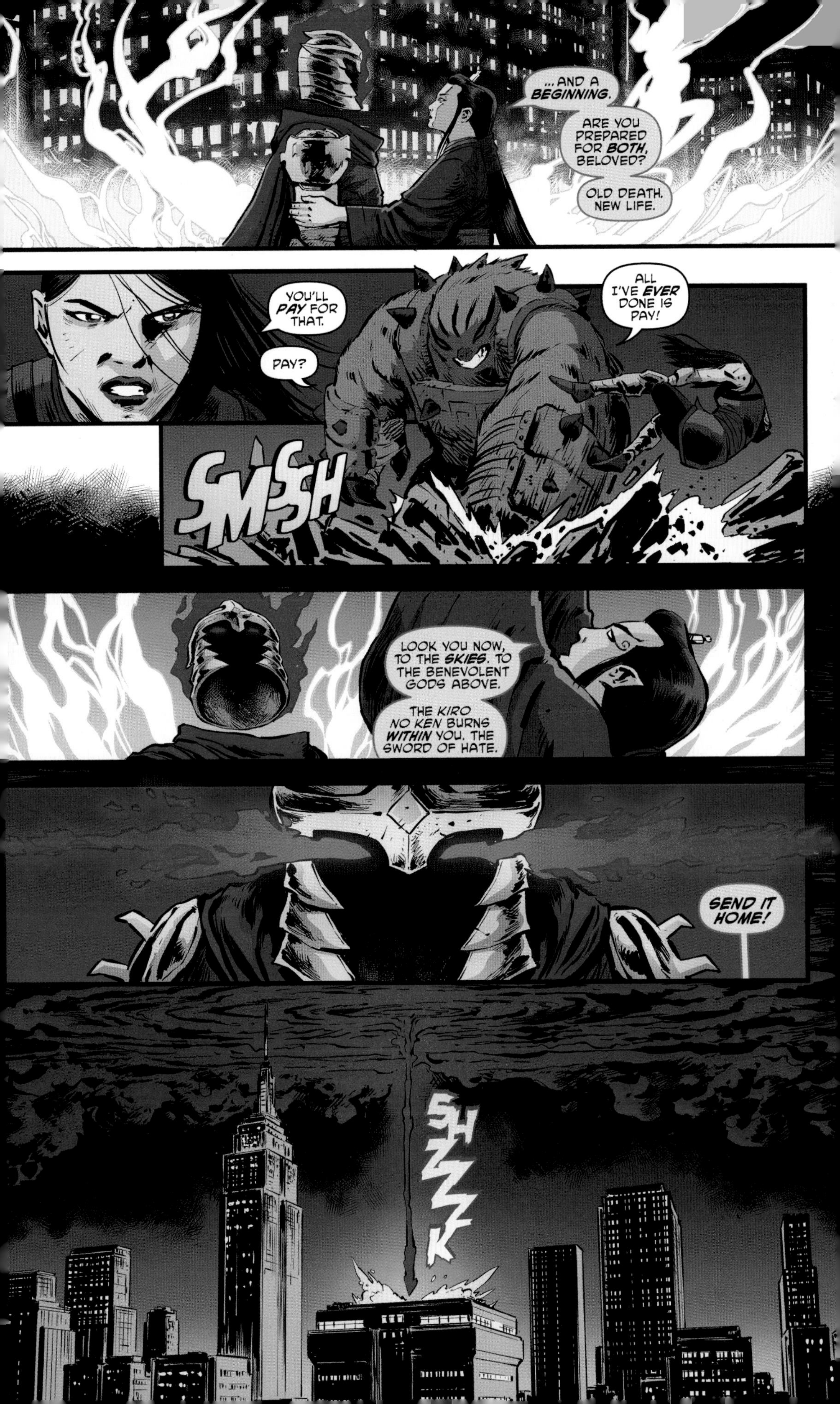
...AND A BEGINNING.
ARE YOU PREPARED FOR BOTH, BELOVED?
OLD DEATH. NEW LIFE.
YOU'LL PAY FOR THAT.
PAY?
ALL I'VE EVER DONE IS PAY!
SMESH
LOOK YOU NOW, TO THE SKIES. TO THE BENEVOLENT GODS ABOVE.
THE KIRO NO KEN BURNS WITHIN YOU. THE SWORD OF HATE.
SEND IT HOME!
SHZZK

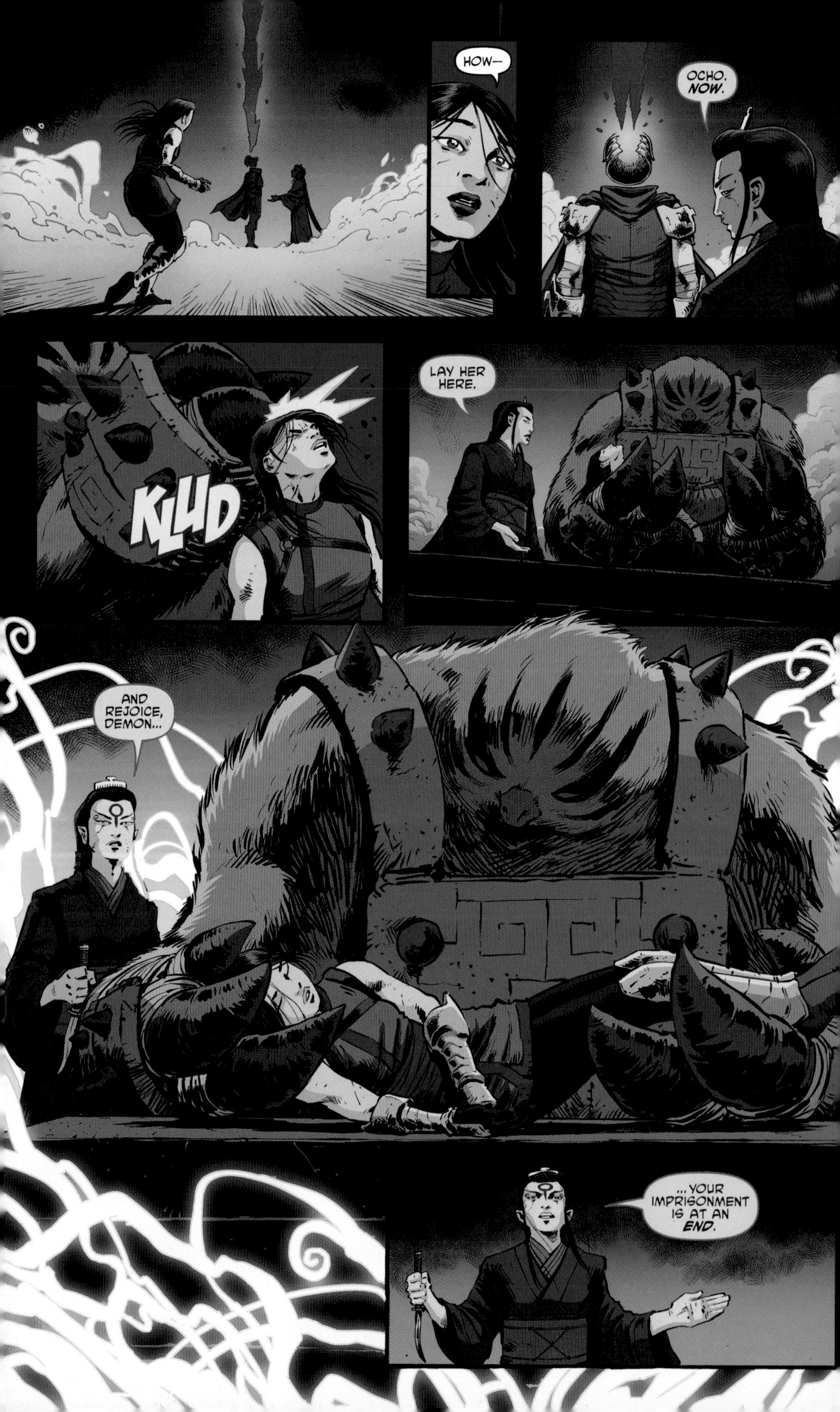
HOW—
OCHO. NOW.
KLUD
LAY HER HERE.
AND REJOICE, DEMON...
...YOUR IMPRISONMENT IS AT AN END.

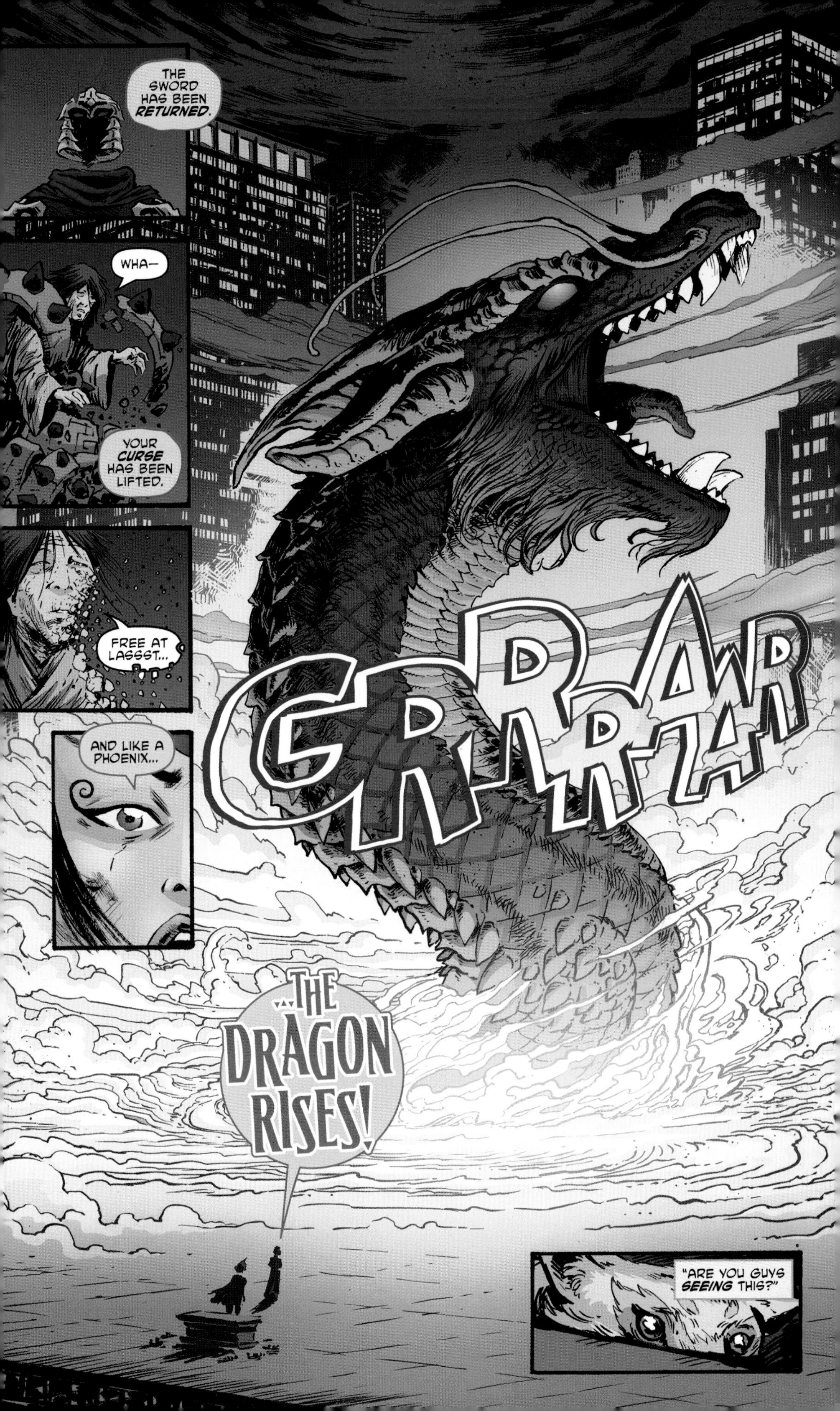
THE SWORD HAS BEEN *RETURNED*.
WHA—
YOUR *CURSE* HAS BEEN LIFTED.
FREE AT LASSST...
AND LIKE A PHOENIX...
GRRRAWR
...THE DRAGON RISES!
"ARE YOU GUYS *SEEING* THIS?"

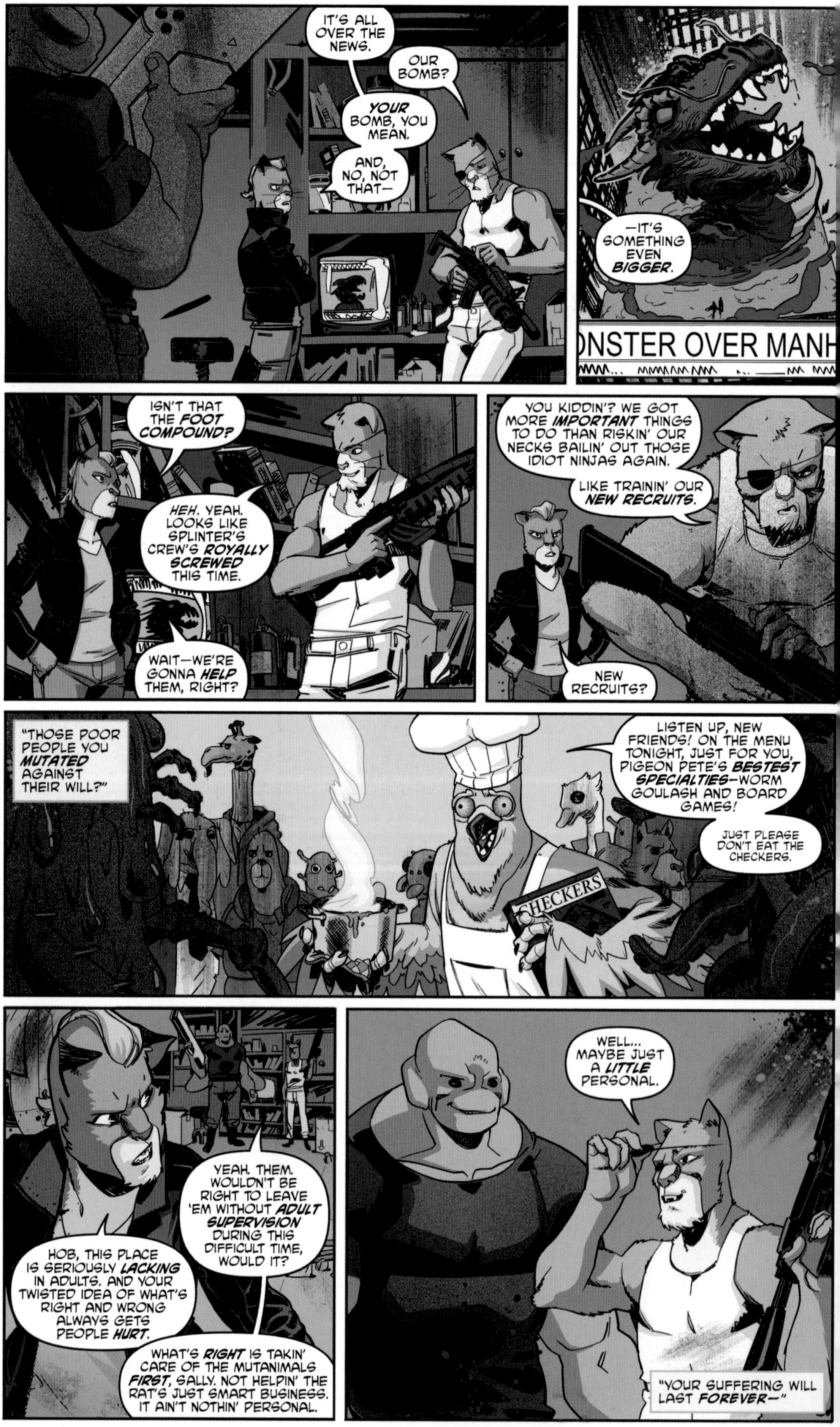
IT'S ALL OVER THE NEWS.
OUR BOMB?
YOUR BOMB, YOU MEAN.
AND, NO, NOT THAT—
—IT'S SOMETHING EVEN *BIGGER*.
NSTER OVER MANH
ISN'T THAT THE *FOOT COMPOUND?*
HEH. YEAH. LOOKS LIKE SPLINTER'S CREW'S *ROYALLY SCREWED* THIS TIME.
WAIT—WE'RE GONNA *HELP* THEM, RIGHT?
YOU KIDDIN'? WE GOT MORE *IMPORTANT* THINGS TO DO THAN RISKIN' OUR NECKS BAILIN' OUT THOSE IDIOT NINJAS AGAIN.
LIKE TRAININ' OUR *NEW RECRUITS*.
NEW RECRUITS?
"THOSE POOR PEOPLE YOU *MUTATED* AGAINST THEIR WILL?"
LISTEN UP, NEW FRIENDS! ON THE MENU TONIGHT, JUST FOR YOU, PIGEON PETE'S *BESTEST SPECIALTIES*—WORM GOULASH AND BOARD GAMES!
JUST PLEASE DON'T EAT THE CHECKERS.
CHECKERS
YEAH. THEM. WOULDN'T BE RIGHT TO LEAVE 'EM WITHOUT *ADULT SUPERVISION* DURING THIS DIFFICULT TIME, WOULD IT?
HOB, THIS PLACE IS SERIOUSLY *LACKING* IN ADULTS. AND YOUR TWISTED IDEA OF WHAT'S RIGHT AND WRONG ALWAYS GETS PEOPLE *HURT*.
WHAT'S *RIGHT* IS TAKIN' CARE OF THE MUTANIMALS *FIRST*, SALLY. NOT HELPIN' THE RAT'S JUST SMART BUSINESS. IT AIN'T NOTHIN' PERSONAL.
WELL... MAYBE JUST A *LITTLE* PERSONAL.
"YOUR SUFFERING WILL LAST *FOREVER*—"

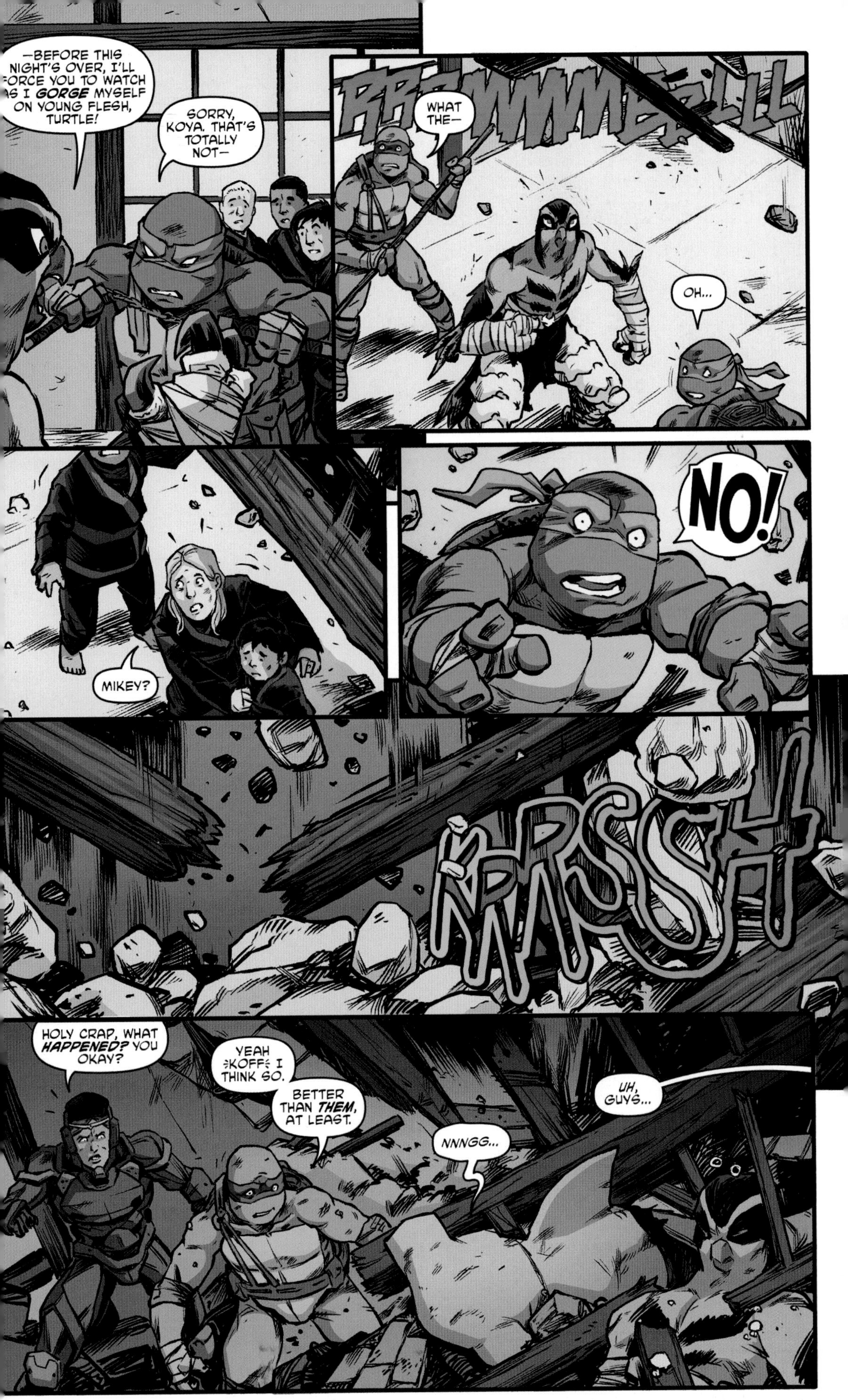
—BEFORE THIS NIGHT'S OVER, I'LL FORCE YOU TO WATCH AS I *GORGE* MYSELF ON YOUNG FLESH, TURTLE!
SORRY, KOYA. THAT'S TOTALLY NOT—
WHAT THE—
OH...
MIKEY?
NO!
KRSSH
HOLY CRAP, WHAT *HAPPENED?* YOU OKAY?
YEAH *KOFF* I THINK SO.
BETTER THAN *THEM*, AT LEAST.
NNNGG...
UH, GUYS...

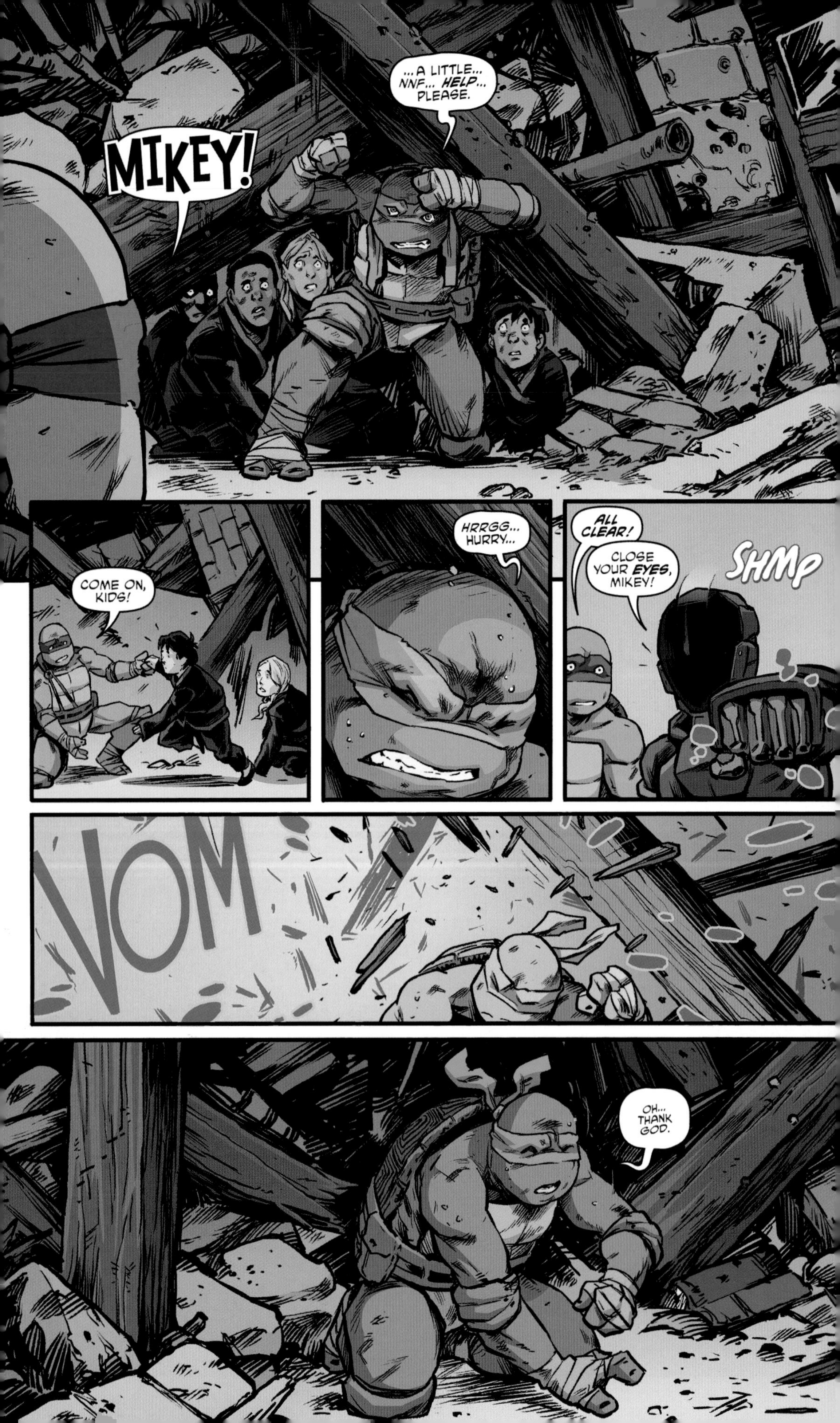

MIKEY!
...A LITTLE... NNF... HELP... PLEASE.
COME ON, KIDS!
HRRGG... HURRY...
ALL CLEAR!
CLOSE YOUR EYES, MIKEY!
SHMP
VOM
OH... THANK GOD.

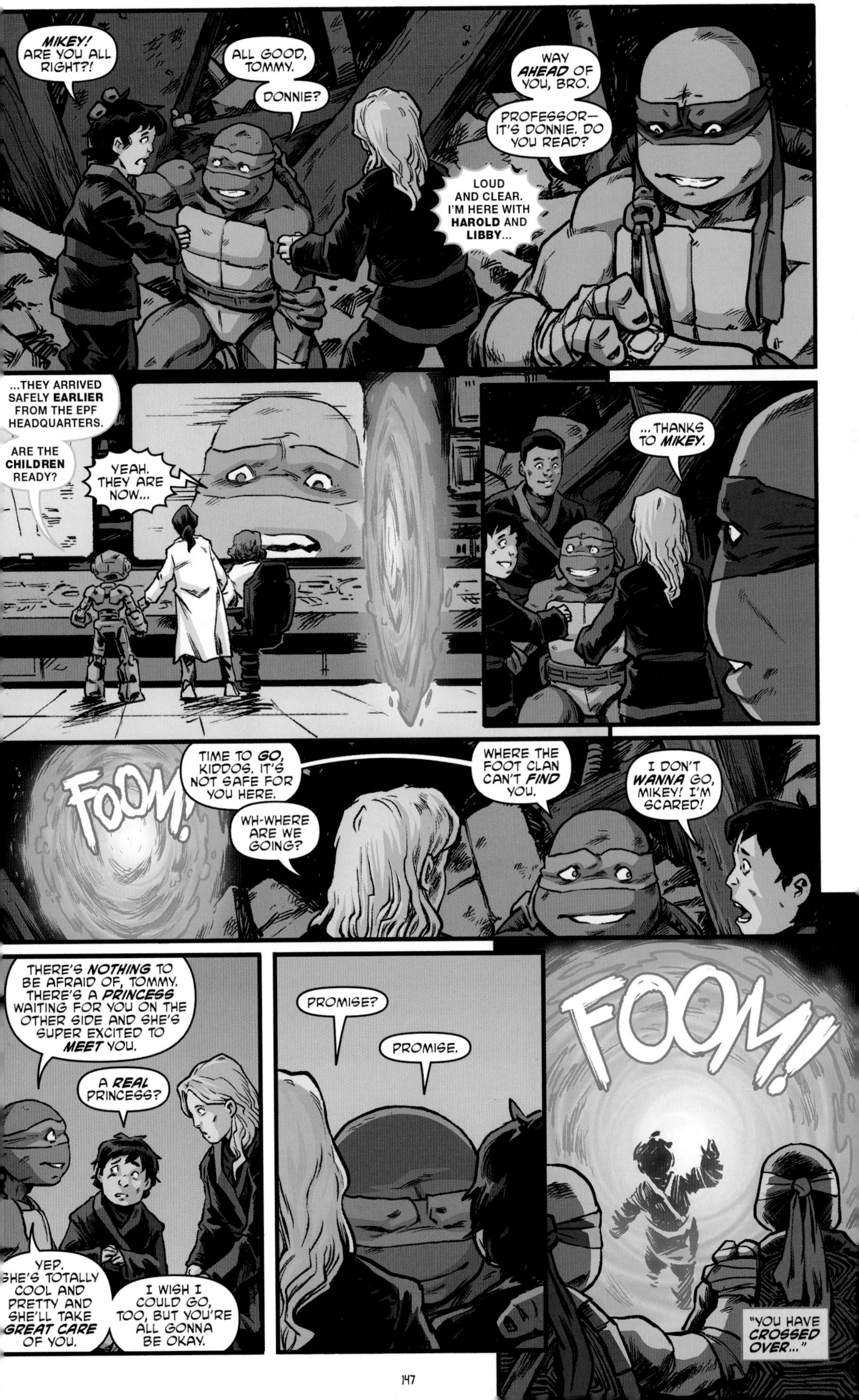
MIKEY! ARE YOU ALL RIGHT?!
ALL GOOD, TOMMY.
DONNIE?
WAY AHEAD OF YOU, BRO.
PROFESSOR— IT'S DONNIE. DO YOU READ?
LOUD AND CLEAR. I'M HERE WITH HAROLD AND LIBBY...
...THEY ARRIVED SAFELY EARLIER FROM THE EPF HEADQUARTERS.
ARE THE CHILDREN READY?
YEAH. THEY ARE NOW...
...THANKS TO MIKEY.
FOOM!
TIME TO GO, KIDDOS. IT'S NOT SAFE FOR YOU HERE.
WH-WHERE ARE WE GOING?
WHERE THE FOOT CLAN CAN'T FIND YOU.
I DON'T WANNA GO, MIKEY! I'M SCARED!
THERE'S NOTHING TO BE AFRAID OF, TOMMY. THERE'S A PRINCESS WAITING FOR YOU ON THE OTHER SIDE AND SHE'S SUPER EXCITED TO MEET YOU.
A REAL PRINCESS?
YEP. SHE'S TOTALLY COOL AND PRETTY AND SHE'LL TAKE GREAT CARE OF YOU.
I WISH I COULD GO, TOO, BUT YOU'RE ALL GONNA BE OKAY.
PROMISE?
PROMISE.
FOOM!
"YOU HAVE CROSSED OVER..."

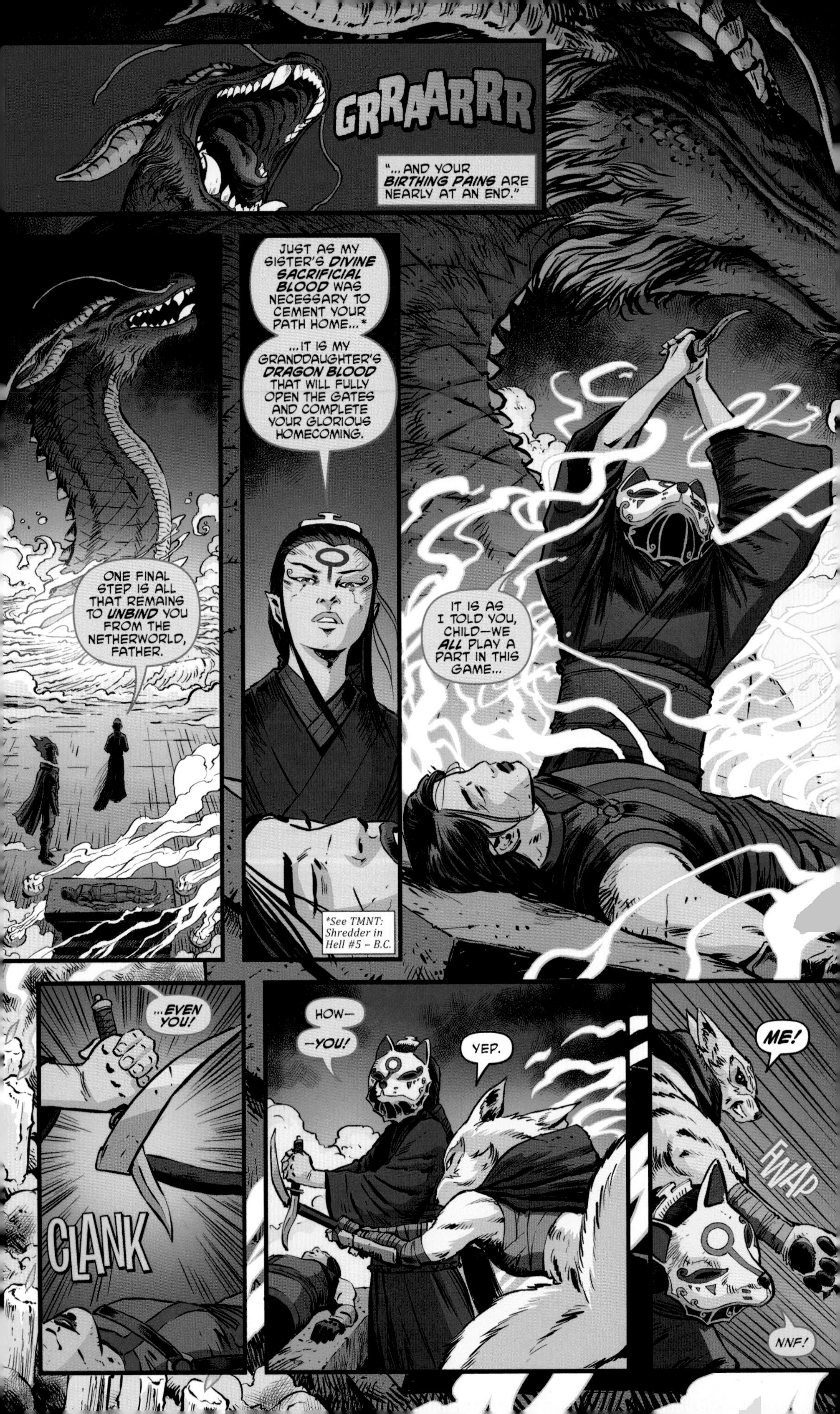
GRRAARRR
"...AND YOUR BIRTHING PAINS ARE NEARLY AT AN END."
JUST AS MY SISTER'S DIVINE SACRIFICIAL BLOOD WAS NECESSARY TO CEMENT YOUR PATH HOME...*
...IT IS MY GRANDDAUGHTER'S DRAGON BLOOD THAT WILL FULLY OPEN THE GATES AND COMPLETE YOUR GLORIOUS HOMECOMING.
ONE FINAL STEP IS ALL THAT REMAINS TO UNBIND YOU FROM THE NETHERWORLD, FATHER.
*See TMNT: Shredder in Hell #5 – B.C.
IT IS AS I TOLD YOU, CHILD—WE ALL PLAY A PART IN THIS GAME...
...EVEN YOU!
CLANK
HOW—
—YOU!
YEP.
ME!
FWAP
NNF!

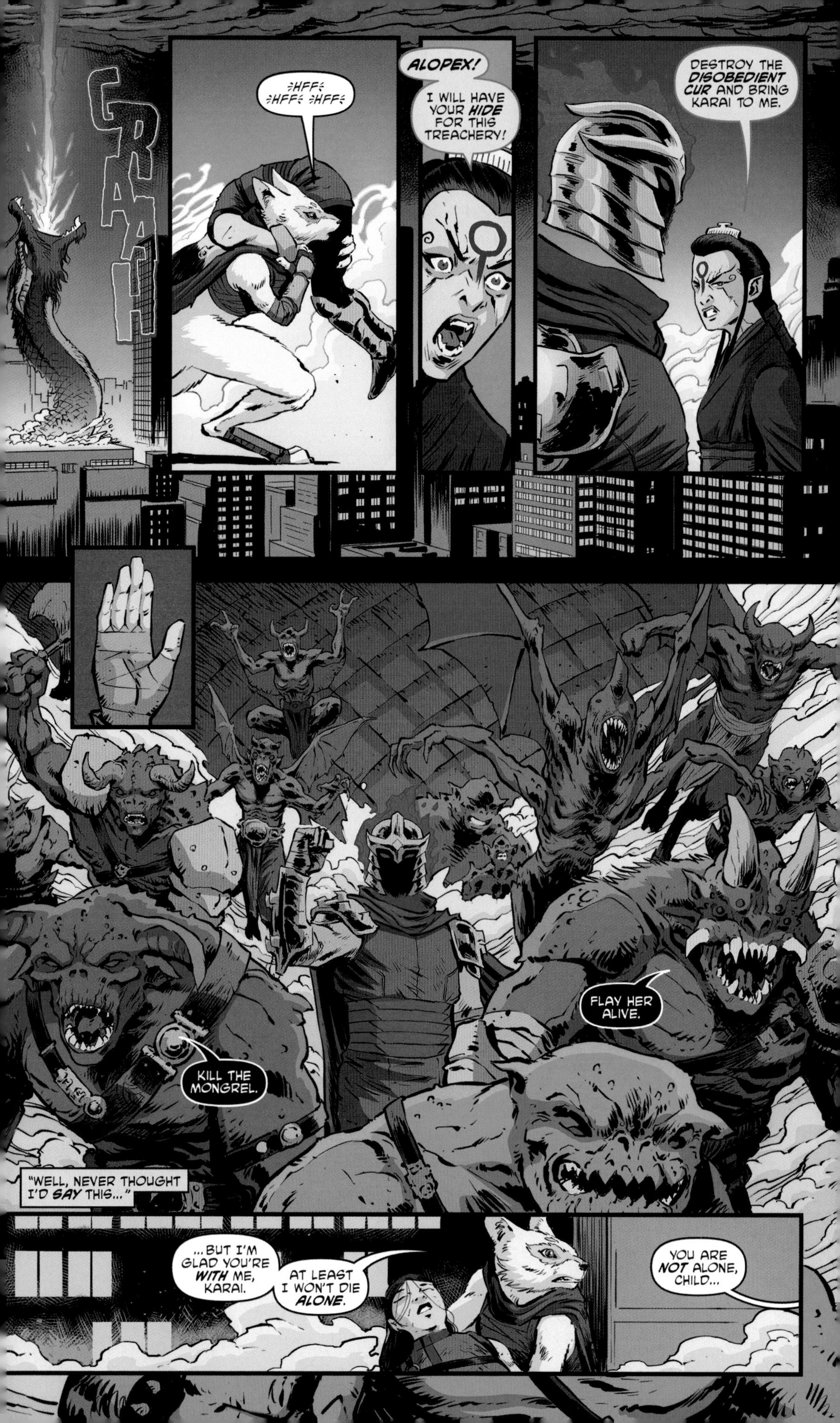
GRAAAH
HFF HFF HFF
ALOPEX!
I WILL HAVE YOUR HIDE FOR THIS TREACHERY!
DESTROY THE DISOBEDIENT CUR AND BRING KARAI TO ME.
FLAY HER ALIVE.
KILL THE MONGREL.
"WELL, NEVER THOUGHT I'D SAY THIS..."
...BUT I'M GLAD YOU'RE WITH ME, KARAI.
AT LEAST I WON'T DIE ALONE.
YOU ARE NOT ALONE, CHILD...

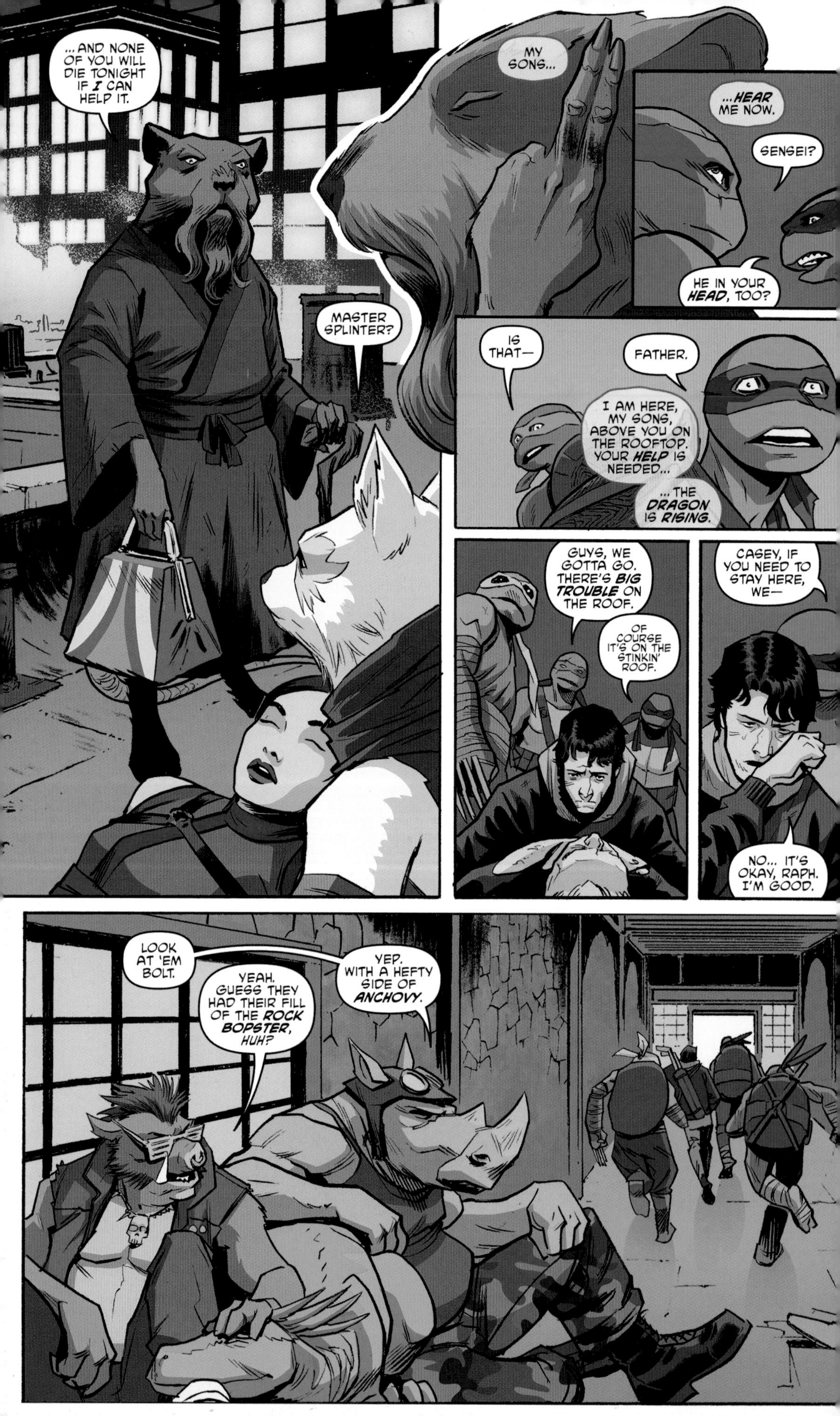
...AND NONE OF YOU WILL DIE TONIGHT IF *I* CAN HELP IT.
MASTER SPLINTER?
MY SONS...
...*HEAR* ME NOW.
SENSEI?
HE IN YOUR *HEAD*, TOO?
IS THAT—
FATHER.
I AM HERE, MY SONS, ABOVE YOU ON THE ROOFTOP. YOUR *HELP* IS NEEDED...
...THE *DRAGON* IS *RISING*.
GUYS, WE GOTTA GO. THERE'S *BIG TROUBLE* ON THE ROOF.
OF COURSE IT'S ON THE STINKIN' ROOF.
CASEY, IF YOU NEED TO STAY HERE, WE—
NO... IT'S OKAY, RAPH. I'M GOOD.
LOOK AT 'EM BOLT.
YEAH. GUESS THEY HAD THEIR FILL OF THE *ROCK BOPSTER*, HUH?
YEP. WITH A HEFTY SIDE OF *ANCHOVY*.

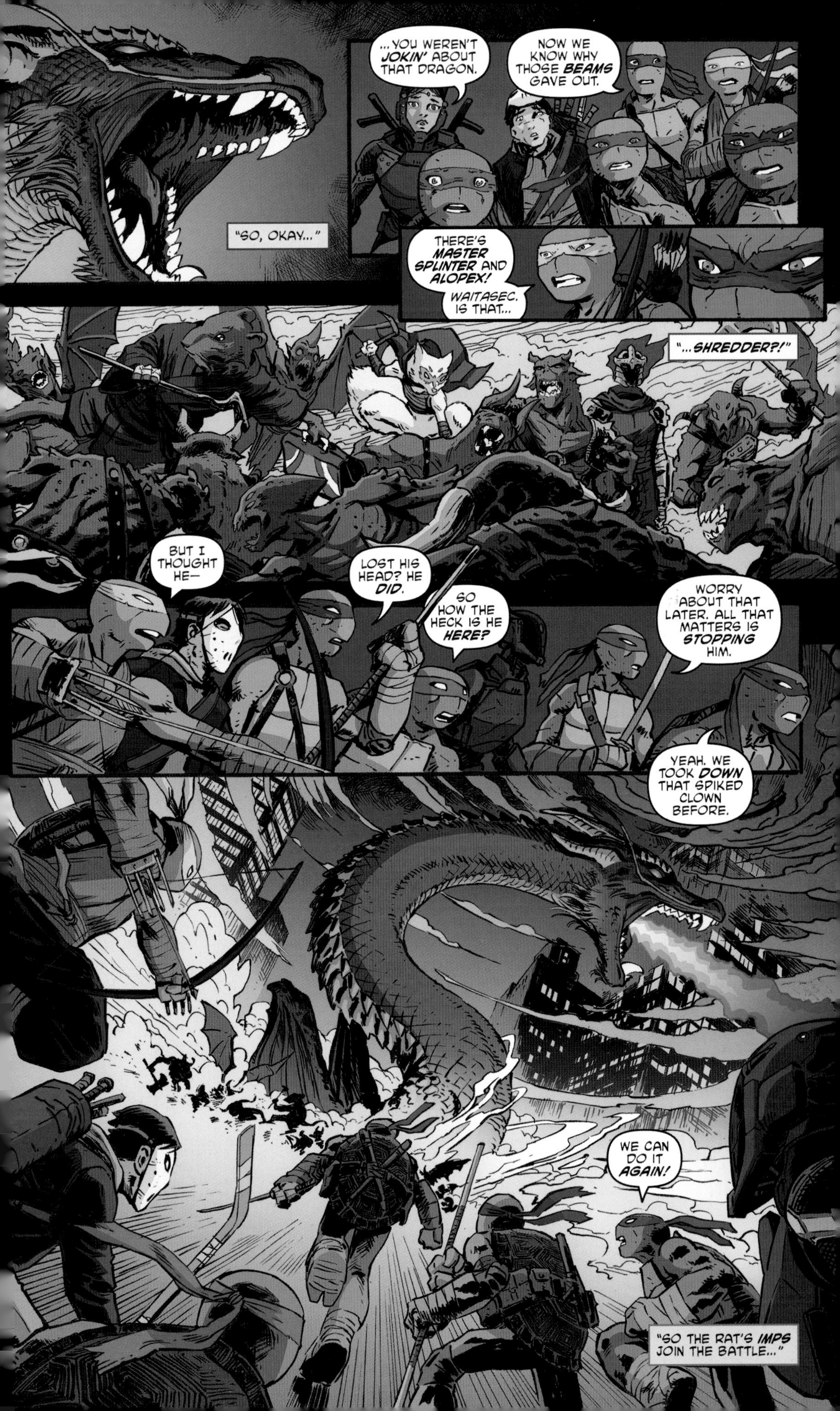
"SO, OKAY..."
...YOU WEREN'T JOKIN' ABOUT THAT DRAGON.
NOW WE KNOW WHY THOSE BEAMS GAVE OUT.
THERE'S MASTER SPLINTER AND ALOPEX!
WAITASEC. IS THAT...
"...SHREDDER?!"
BUT I THOUGHT HE—
LOST HIS HEAD? HE DID.
SO HOW THE HECK IS HE HERE?
WORRY ABOUT THAT LATER. ALL THAT MATTERS IS STOPPING HIM.
YEAH. WE TOOK DOWN THAT SPIKED CLOWN BEFORE.
WE CAN DO IT AGAIN!
"SO THE RAT'S IMPS JOIN THE BATTLE..."

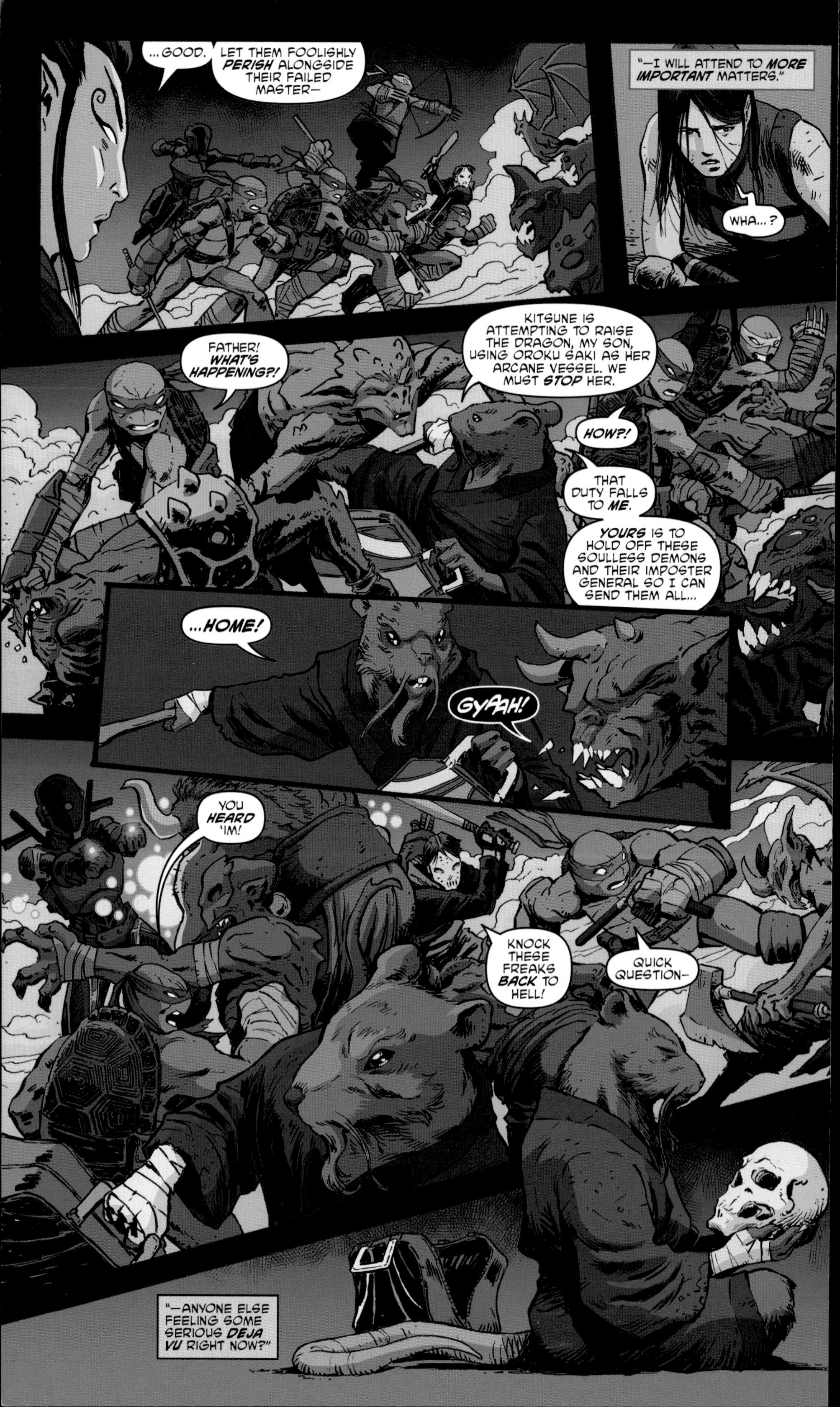
...GOOD.
LET THEM FOOLISHLY PERISH ALONGSIDE THEIR FAILED MASTER—
"—I WILL ATTEND TO MORE IMPORTANT MATTERS."
WHA...?
FATHER! WHAT'S HAPPENING?!
KITSUNE IS ATTEMPTING TO RAISE THE DRAGON, MY SON, USING OROKU SAKI AS HER ARCANE VESSEL. WE MUST STOP HER.
HOW?!
THAT DUTY FALLS TO ME.
YOURS IS TO HOLD OFF THESE SOULLESS DEMONS AND THEIR IMPOSTER GENERAL SO I CAN SEND THEM ALL...
...HOME!
GYAAH!
YOU HEARD 'IM!
KNOCK THESE FREAKS BACK TO HELL!
QUICK QUESTION—
"—ANYONE ELSE FEELING SOME SERIOUS DEJA VU RIGHT NOW?"

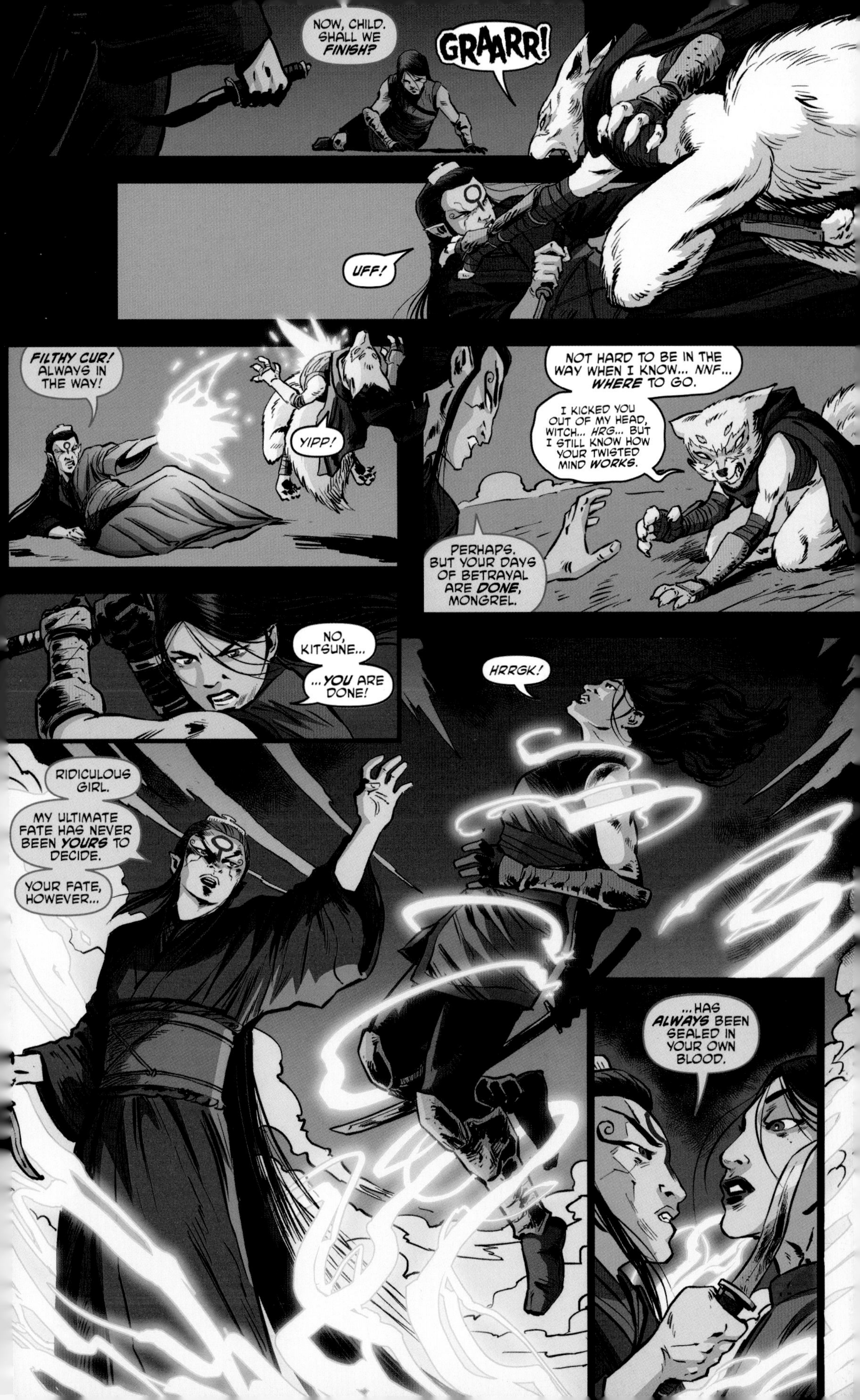
NOW, CHILD. SHALL WE FINISH?
GRAARR!
UFF!
FILTHY CUR! ALWAYS IN THE WAY!
YIPP!
NOT HARD TO BE IN THE WAY WHEN I KNOW... NNF... WHERE TO GO.
I KICKED YOU OUT OF MY HEAD, WITCH... HRG... BUT I STILL KNOW HOW YOUR TWISTED MIND WORKS.
PERHAPS. BUT YOUR DAYS OF BETRAYAL ARE DONE, MONGREL.
NO, KITSUNE...
...YOU ARE DONE!
HRRGK!
RIDICULOUS GIRL.
MY ULTIMATE FATE HAS NEVER BEEN YOURS TO DECIDE.
YOUR FATE, HOWEVER...
...HAS ALWAYS BEEN SEALED IN YOUR OWN BLOOD.

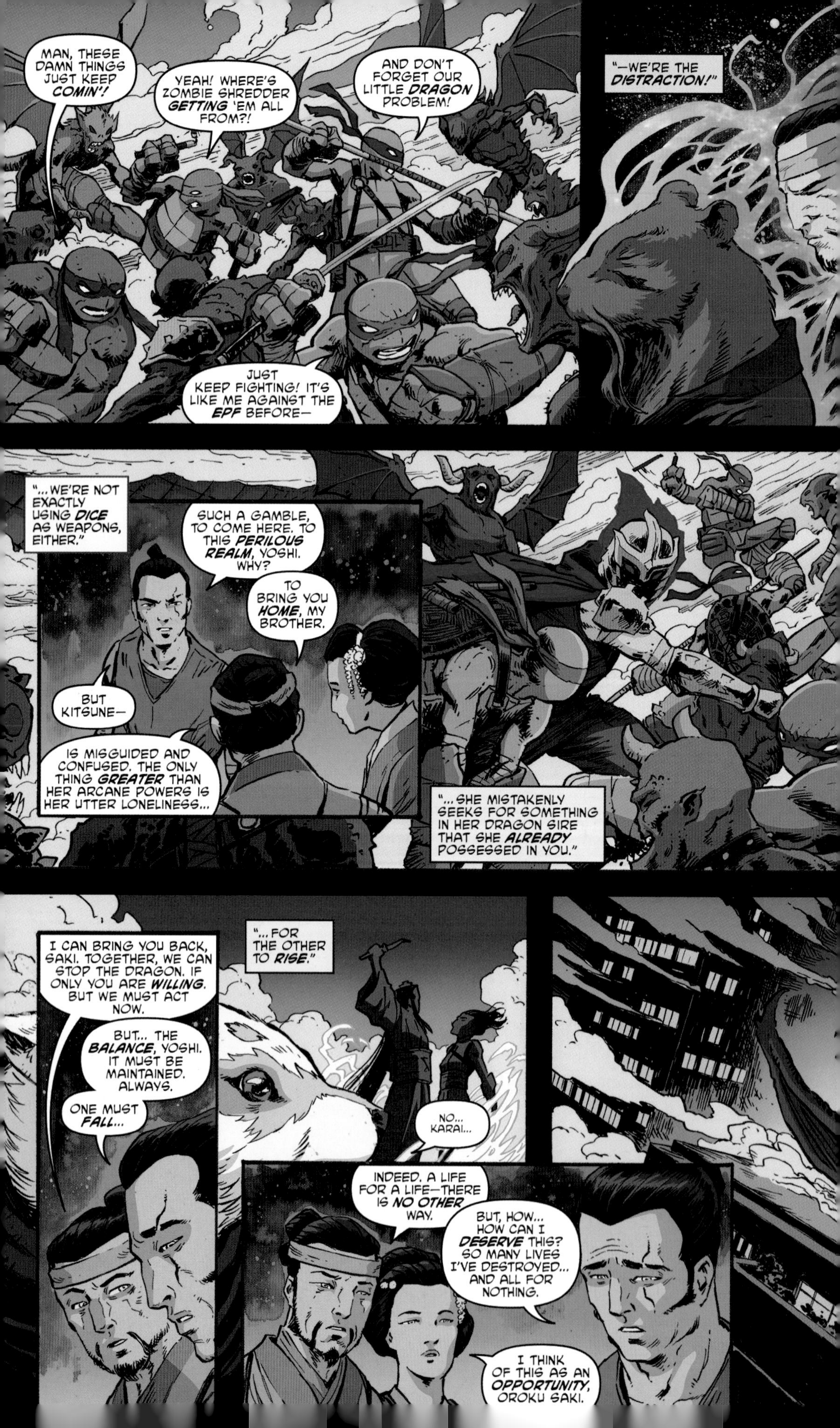
MAN, THESE DAMN THINGS JUST KEEP COMIN'!
YEAH! WHERE'S ZOMBIE SHREDDER GETTING 'EM ALL FROM?!
AND DON'T FORGET OUR LITTLE DRAGON PROBLEM!
JUST KEEP FIGHTING! IT'S LIKE ME AGAINST THE EPF BEFORE—
"—WE'RE THE DISTRACTION!"
"...WE'RE NOT EXACTLY USING DICE AS WEAPONS, EITHER."
SUCH A GAMBLE, TO COME HERE. TO THIS PERILOUS REALM, YOSHI. WHY?
TO BRING YOU HOME, MY BROTHER.
BUT KITSUNE—
IS MISGUIDED AND CONFUSED. THE ONLY THING GREATER THAN HER ARCANE POWERS IS HER UTTER LONELINESS...
"...SHE MISTAKENLY SEEKS FOR SOMETHING IN HER DRAGON SIRE THAT SHE ALREADY POSSESSED IN YOU."
I CAN BRING YOU BACK, SAKI. TOGETHER, WE CAN STOP THE DRAGON. IF ONLY YOU ARE WILLING. BUT WE MUST ACT NOW.
BUT... THE BALANCE, YOSHI. IT MUST BE MAINTAINED. ALWAYS.
ONE MUST FALL...
"...FOR THE OTHER TO RISE."
NO... KARAI...
INDEED. A LIFE FOR A LIFE—THERE IS NO OTHER WAY.
BUT, HOW... HOW CAN I DESERVE THIS? SO MANY LIVES I'VE DESTROYED... AND ALL FOR NOTHING.
I THINK OF THIS AS AN OPPORTUNITY, OROKU SAKI.

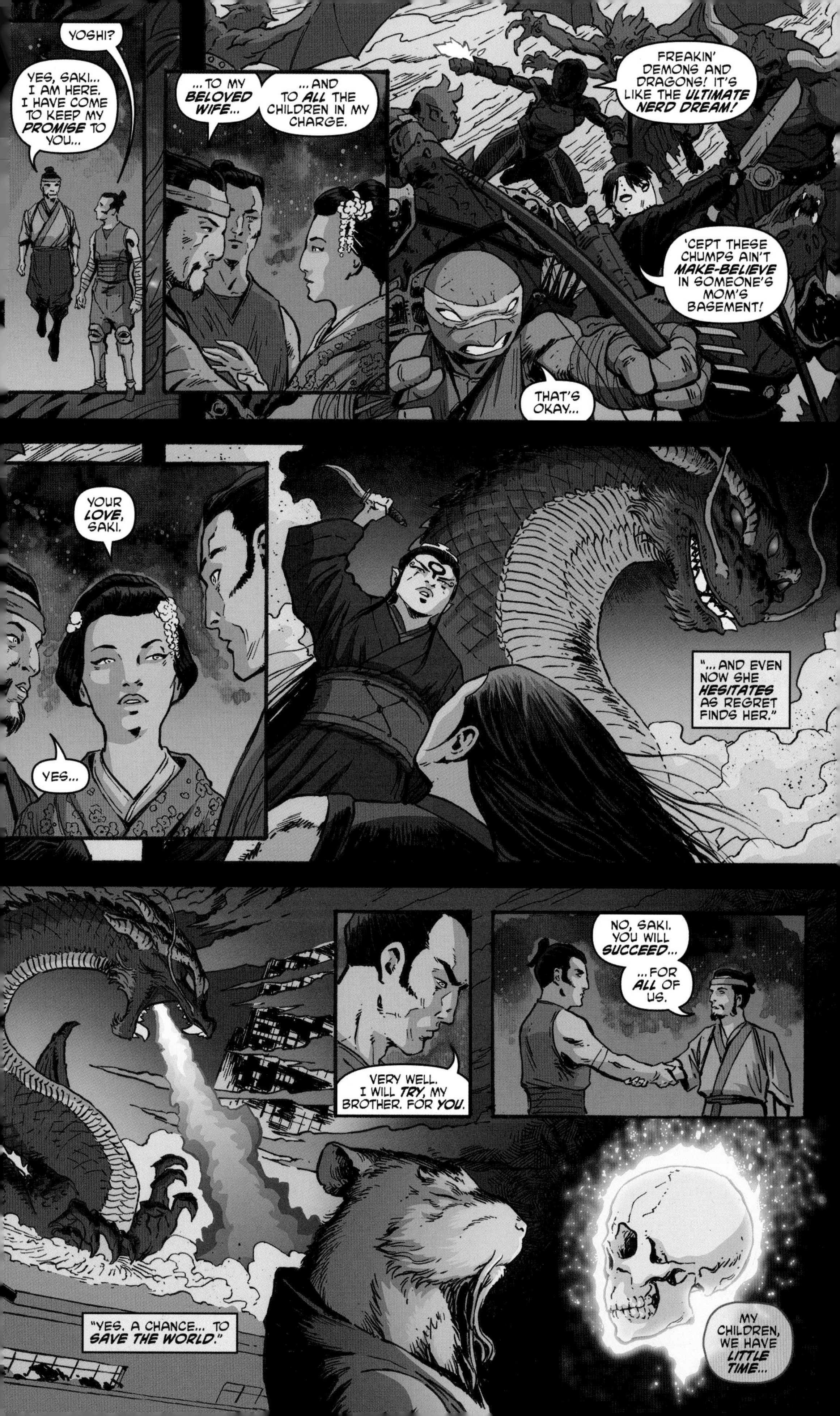
YOSHI?
YES, SAKI... I AM HERE. I HAVE COME TO KEEP MY PROMISE TO YOU...
...TO MY BELOVED WIFE...
...AND TO ALL THE CHILDREN IN MY CHARGE.
FREAKIN' DEMONS AND DRAGONS! IT'S LIKE THE ULTIMATE NERD DREAM!
'CEPT THESE CHUMPS AIN'T MAKE-BELIEVE IN SOMEONE'S MOM'S BASEMENT!
THAT'S OKAY...
YOUR LOVE, SAKI.
YES...
"...AND EVEN NOW SHE HESITATES AS REGRET FINDS HER."
VERY WELL. I WILL TRY, MY BROTHER. FOR YOU.
NO, SAKI. YOU WILL SUCCEED...
...FOR ALL OF US.
"YES. A CHANCE... TO SAVE THE WORLD."
MY CHILDREN, WE HAVE LITTLE TIME...

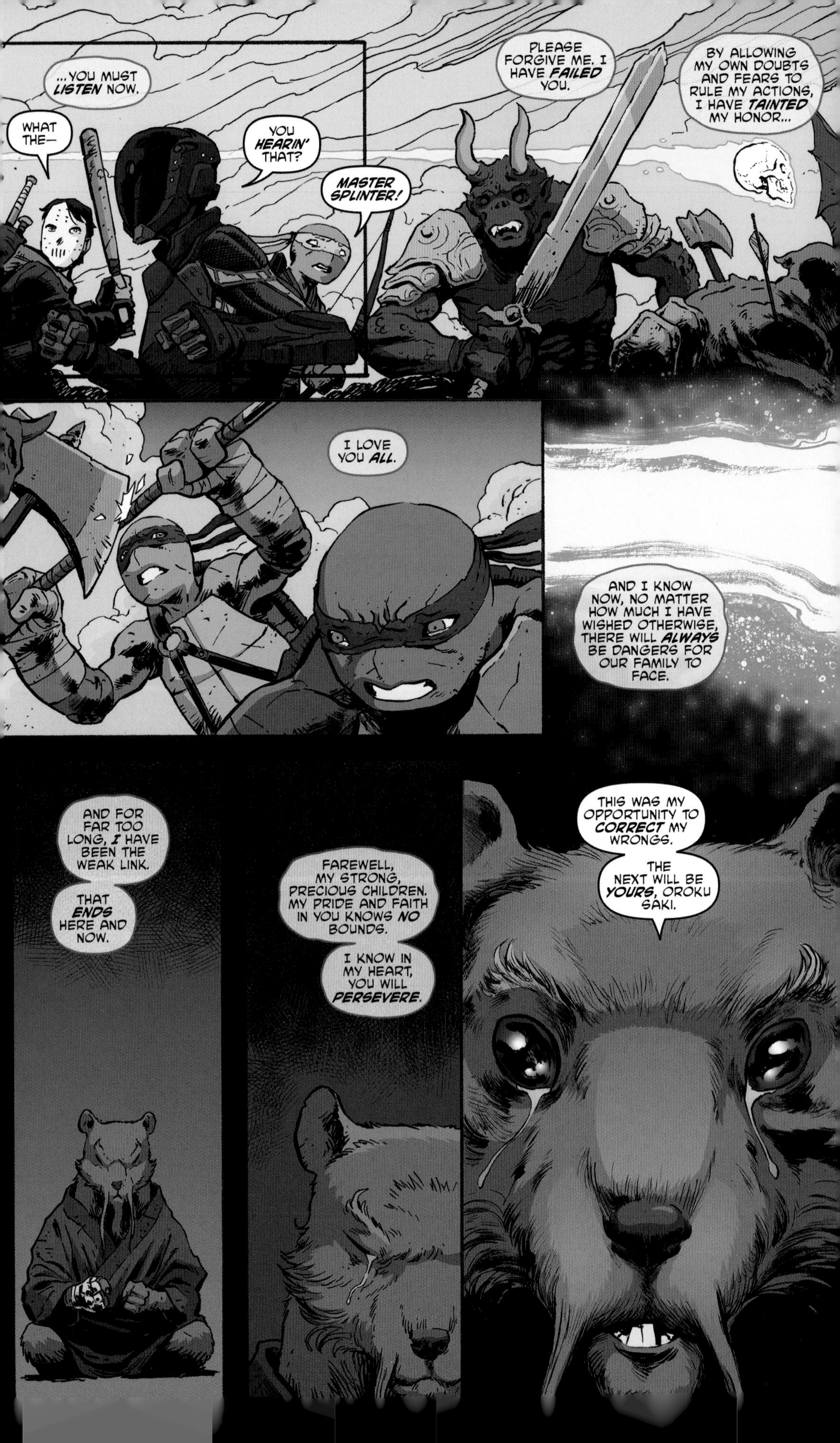
...YOU MUST LISTEN NOW.
WHAT THE—
YOU HEARIN' THAT?
MASTER SPLINTER!
PLEASE FORGIVE ME. I HAVE FAILED YOU.
BY ALLOWING MY OWN DOUBTS AND FEARS TO RULE MY ACTIONS, I HAVE TAINTED MY HONOR...
I LOVE YOU ALL.
AND I KNOW NOW, NO MATTER HOW MUCH I HAVE WISHED OTHERWISE, THERE WILL ALWAYS BE DANGERS FOR OUR FAMILY TO FACE.
AND FOR FAR TOO LONG, I HAVE BEEN THE WEAK LINK.
THAT ENDS HERE AND NOW.
FAREWELL, MY STRONG, PRECIOUS CHILDREN. MY PRIDE AND FAITH IN YOU KNOWS NO BOUNDS.
I KNOW IN MY HEART, YOU WILL PERSEVERE.
THIS WAS MY OPPORTUNITY TO CORRECT MY WRONGS.
THE NEXT WILL BE YOURS, OROKU SAKI.

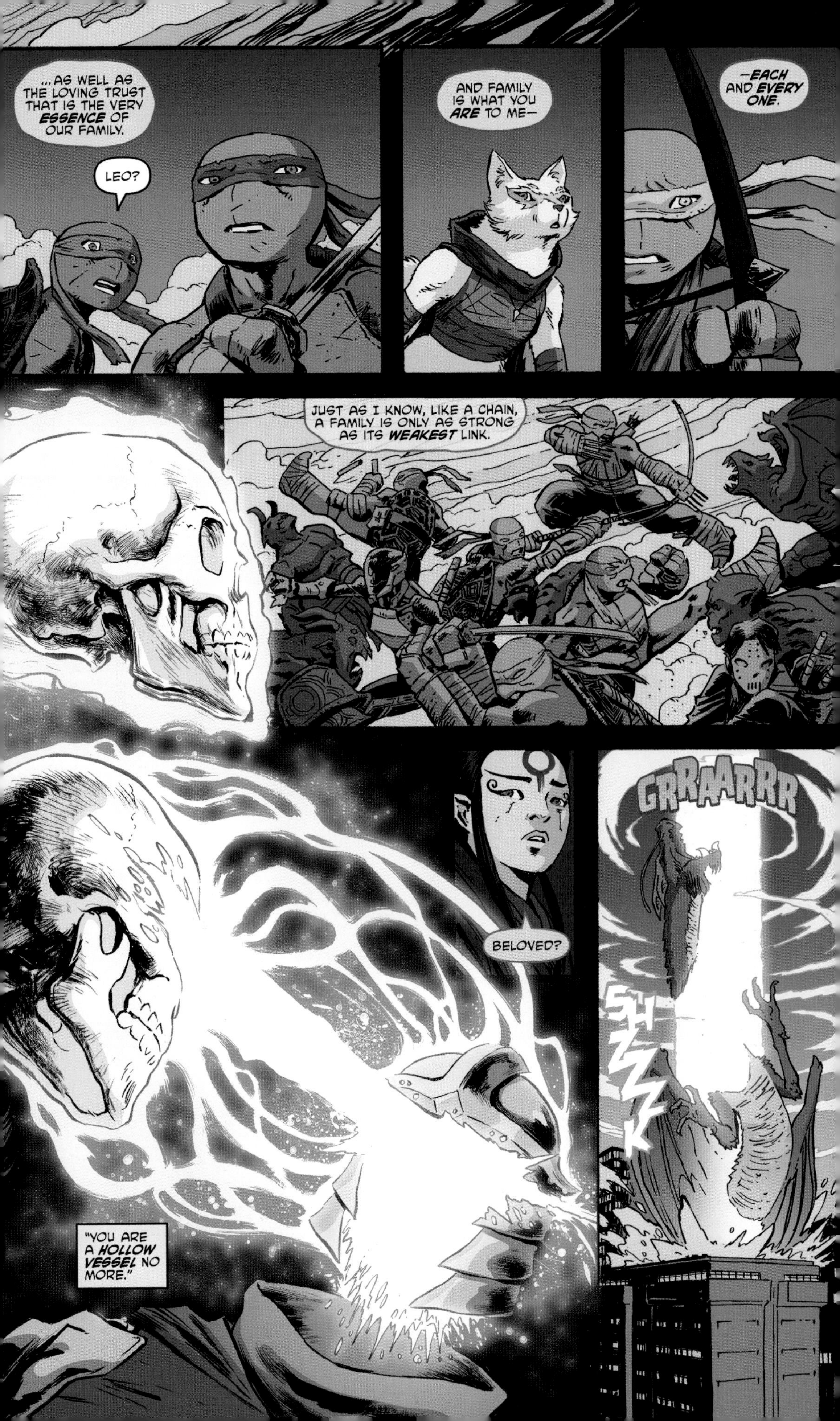
...AS WELL AS THE LOVING TRUST THAT IS THE VERY ESSENCE OF OUR FAMILY.
LEO?
AND FAMILY IS WHAT YOU ARE TO ME—
—EACH AND EVERY ONE.
JUST AS I KNOW, LIKE A CHAIN, A FAMILY IS ONLY AS STRONG AS ITS WEAKEST LINK.
BELOVED?
GRRAARRR
SHZZZK
"YOU ARE A HOLLOW VESSEL NO MORE."

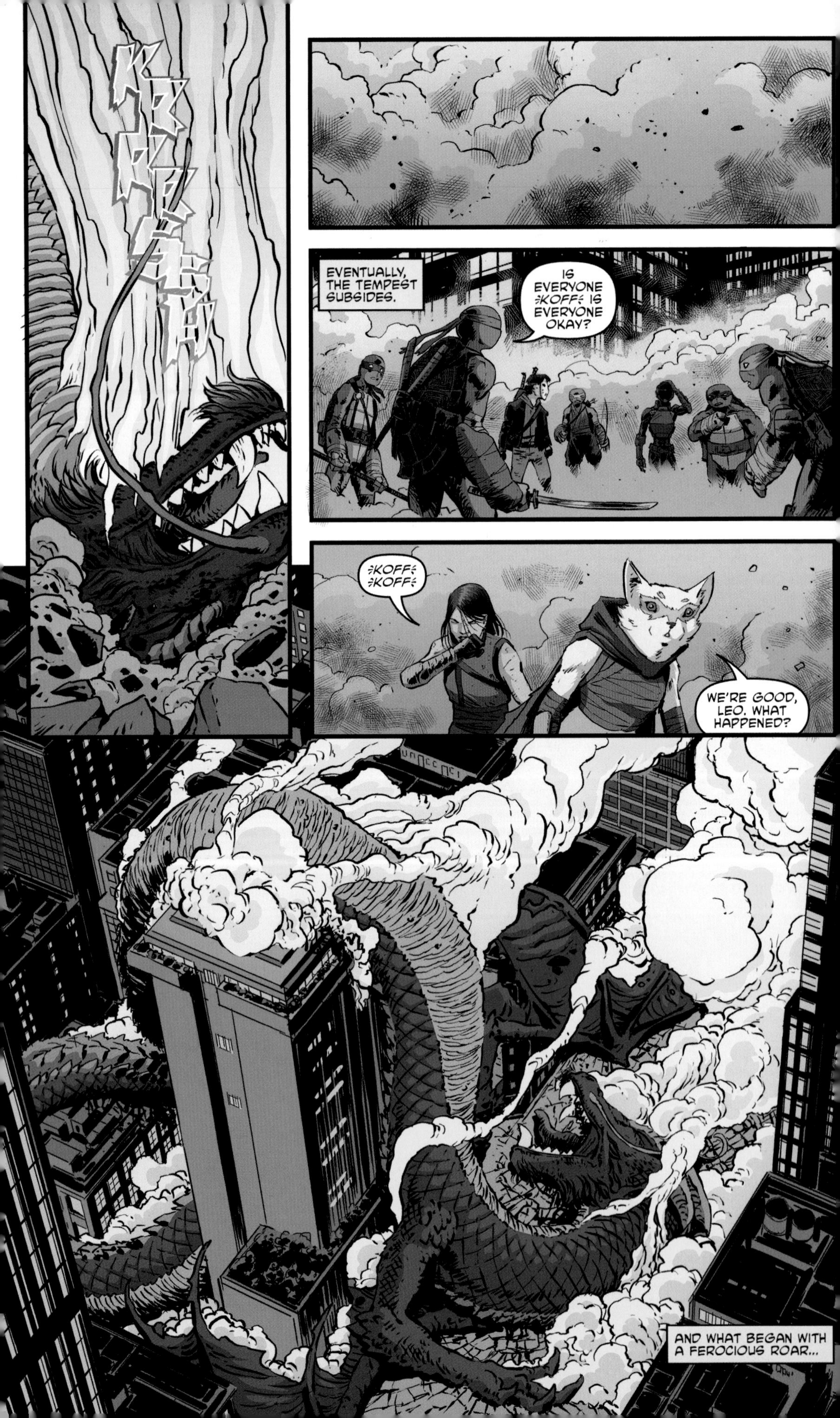
EVENTUALLY, THE TEMPEST SUBSIDES.
IS EVERYONE ≈KOFF≈ IS EVERYONE OKAY?
≈KOFF≈ ≈KOFF≈
WE'RE GOOD, LEO. WHAT HAPPENED?
AND WHAT BEGAN WITH A FEROCIOUS ROAR...

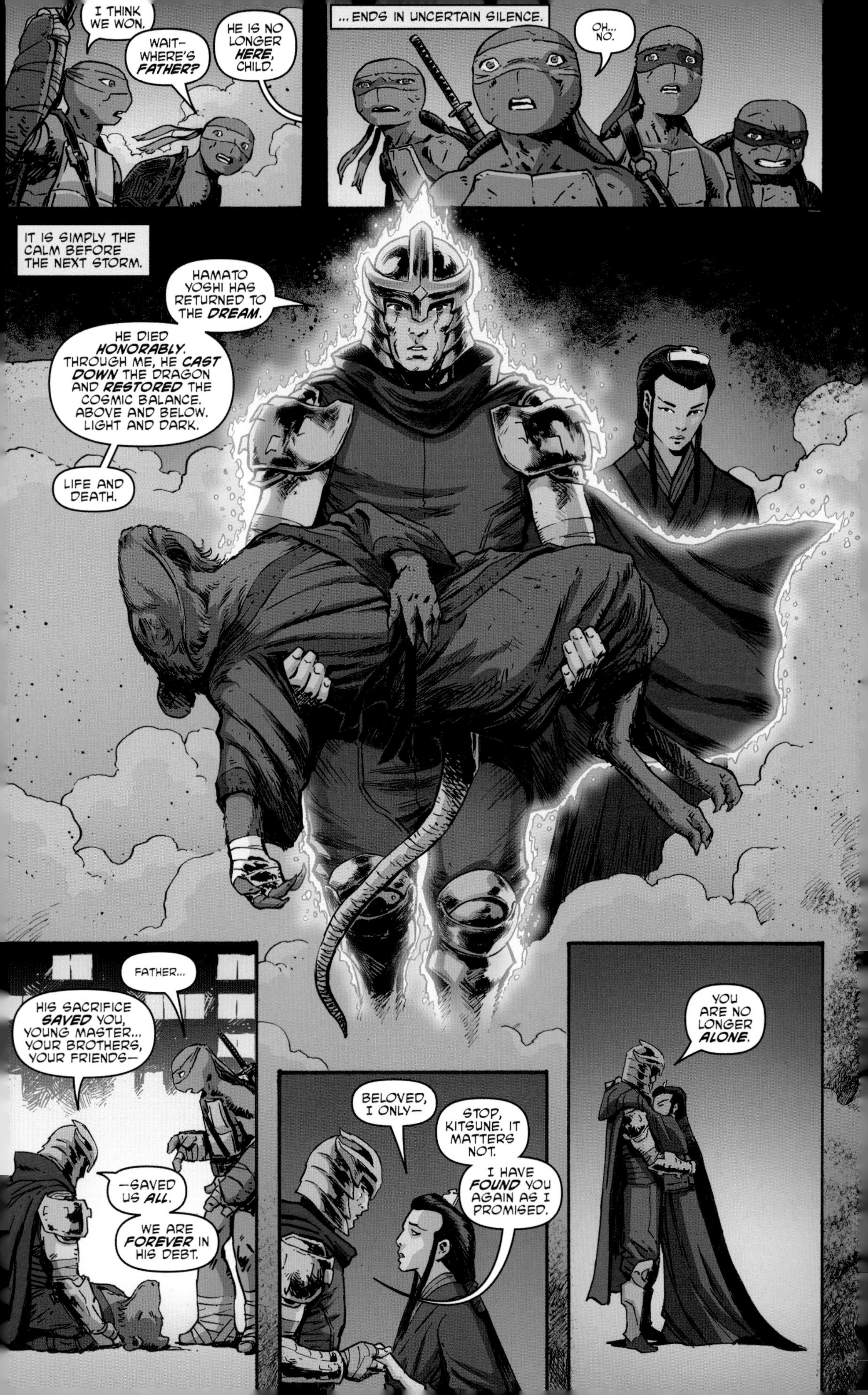
I THINK WE WON.
WAIT— WHERE'S FATHER?
HE IS NO LONGER HERE, CHILD.
...ENDS IN UNCERTAIN SILENCE.
OH... NO.
IT IS SIMPLY THE CALM BEFORE THE NEXT STORM.
HAMATO YOSHI HAS RETURNED TO THE DREAM.
HE DIED HONORABLY. THROUGH ME, HE CAST DOWN THE DRAGON AND RESTORED THE COSMIC BALANCE. ABOVE AND BELOW. LIGHT AND DARK.
LIFE AND DEATH.
FATHER...
HIS SACRIFICE SAVED YOU, YOUNG MASTER... YOUR BROTHERS, YOUR FRIENDS—
—SAVED US ALL.
WE ARE FOREVER IN HIS DEBT.
BELOVED, I ONLY—
STOP, KITSUNE. IT MATTERS NOT.
I HAVE FOUND YOU AGAIN AS I PROMISED.
YOU ARE NO LONGER ALONE.

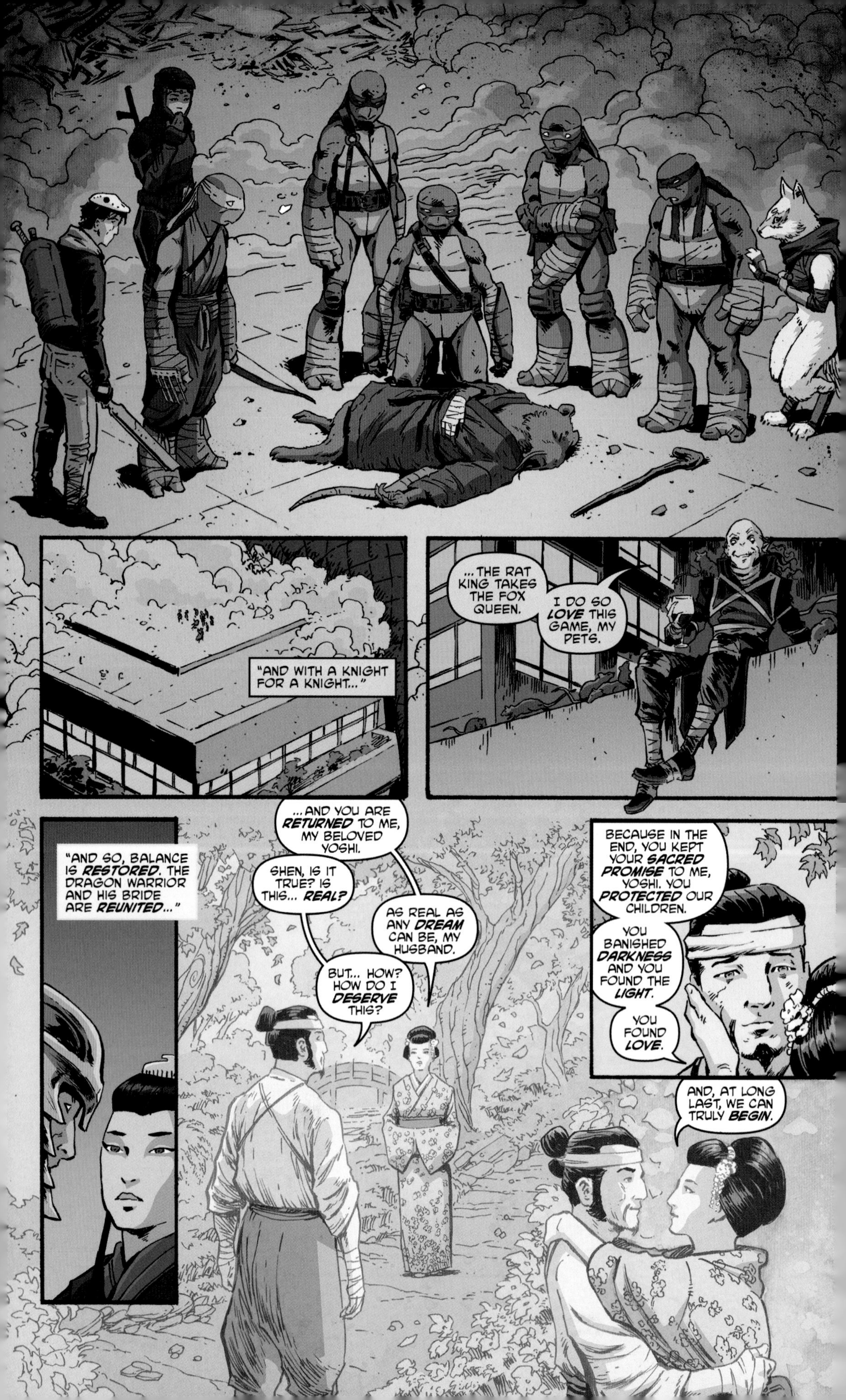
"AND WITH A KNIGHT FOR A KNIGHT..."
...THE RAT KING TAKES THE FOX QUEEN.
I DO SO LOVE THIS GAME, MY PETS.
"AND SO, BALANCE IS RESTORED. THE DRAGON WARRIOR AND HIS BRIDE ARE REUNITED..."
...AND YOU ARE RETURNED TO ME, MY BELOVED YOSHI.
SHEN, IS IT TRUE? IS THIS... REAL?
AS REAL AS ANY DREAM CAN BE, MY HUSBAND.
BUT... HOW? HOW DO I DESERVE THIS?
BECAUSE IN THE END, YOU KEPT YOUR SACRED PROMISE TO ME, YOSHI. YOU PROTECTED OUR CHILDREN.
YOU BANISHED DARKNESS AND YOU FOUND THE LIGHT.
YOU FOUND LOVE.
AND, AT LONG LAST, WE CAN TRULY BEGIN.

Fin.

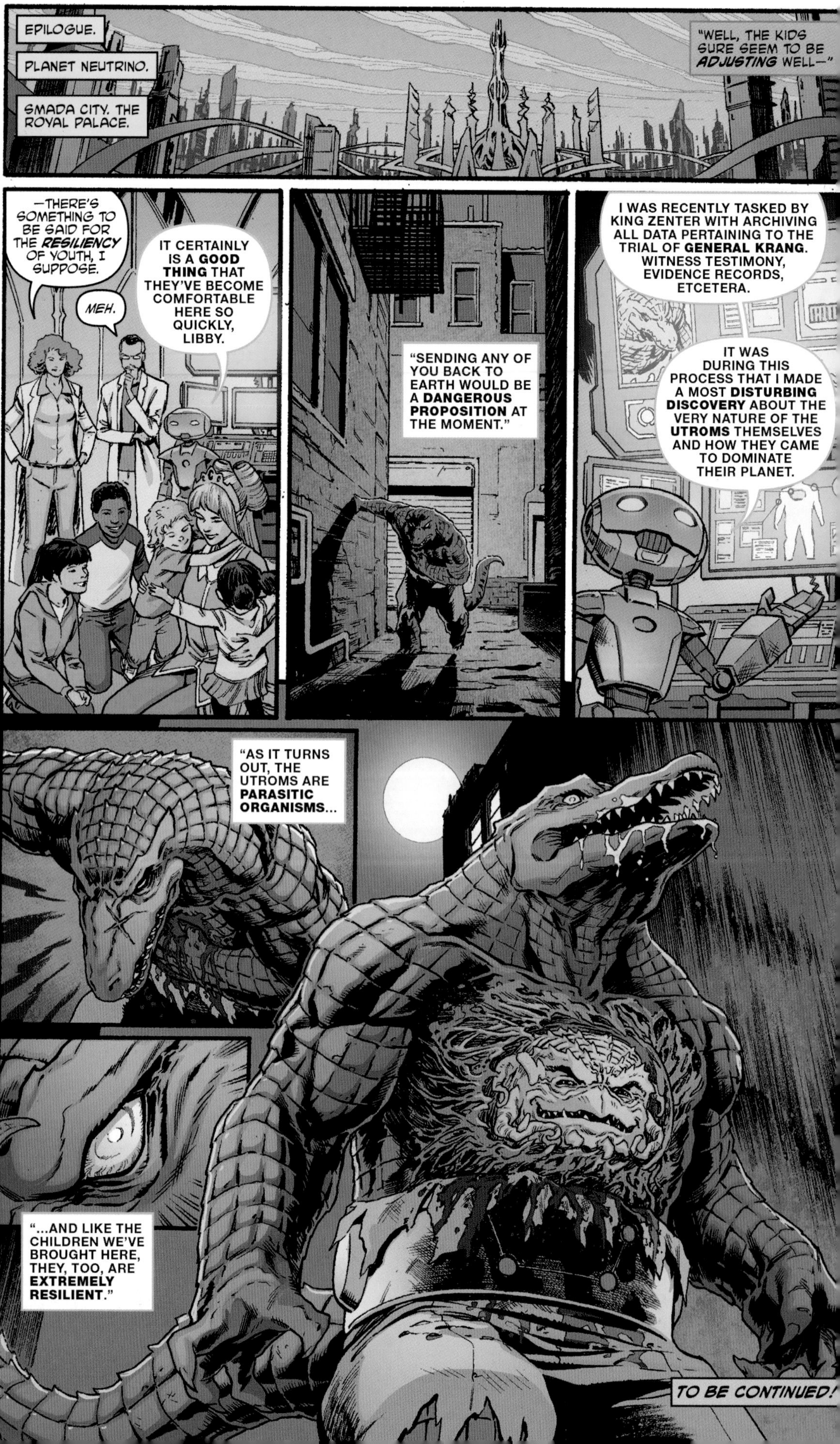
EPILOGUE.
PLANET NEUTRINO.
SMADA CITY. THE ROYAL PALACE.
"WELL, THE KIDS SURE SEEM TO BE ADJUSTING WELL—"
—THERE'S SOMETHING TO BE SAID FOR THE RESILIENCY OF YOUTH, I SUPPOSE.
MEH.
IT CERTAINLY IS A GOOD THING THAT THEY'VE BECOME COMFORTABLE HERE SO QUICKLY, LIBBY.
"SENDING ANY OF YOU BACK TO EARTH WOULD BE A DANGEROUS PROPOSITION AT THE MOMENT."
I WAS RECENTLY TASKED BY KING ZENTER WITH ARCHIVING ALL DATA PERTAINING TO THE TRIAL OF GENERAL KRANG. WITNESS TESTIMONY, EVIDENCE RECORDS, ETCETERA.
IT WAS DURING THIS PROCESS THAT I MADE A MOST DISTURBING DISCOVERY ABOUT THE VERY NATURE OF THE UTROMS THEMSELVES AND HOW THEY CAME TO DOMINATE THEIR PLANET.
"AS IT TURNS OUT, THE UTROMS ARE PARASITIC ORGANISMS...
"...AND LIKE THE CHILDREN WE'VE BROUGHT HERE, THEY, TOO, ARE EXTREMELY RESILIENT."
TO BE CONTINUED!

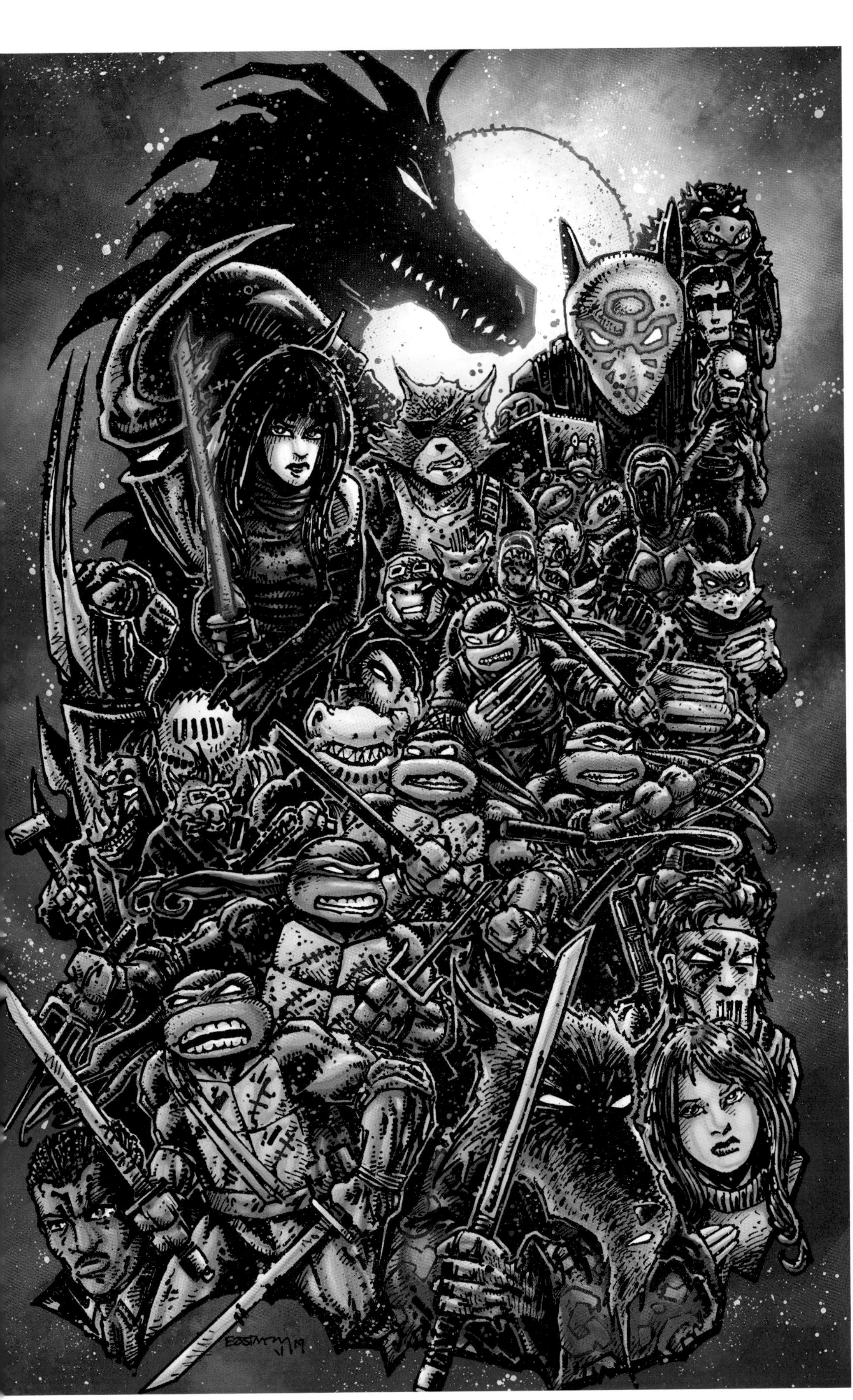

ART BY KEVIN EASTMAN · COLORS BY TOMI VARGA

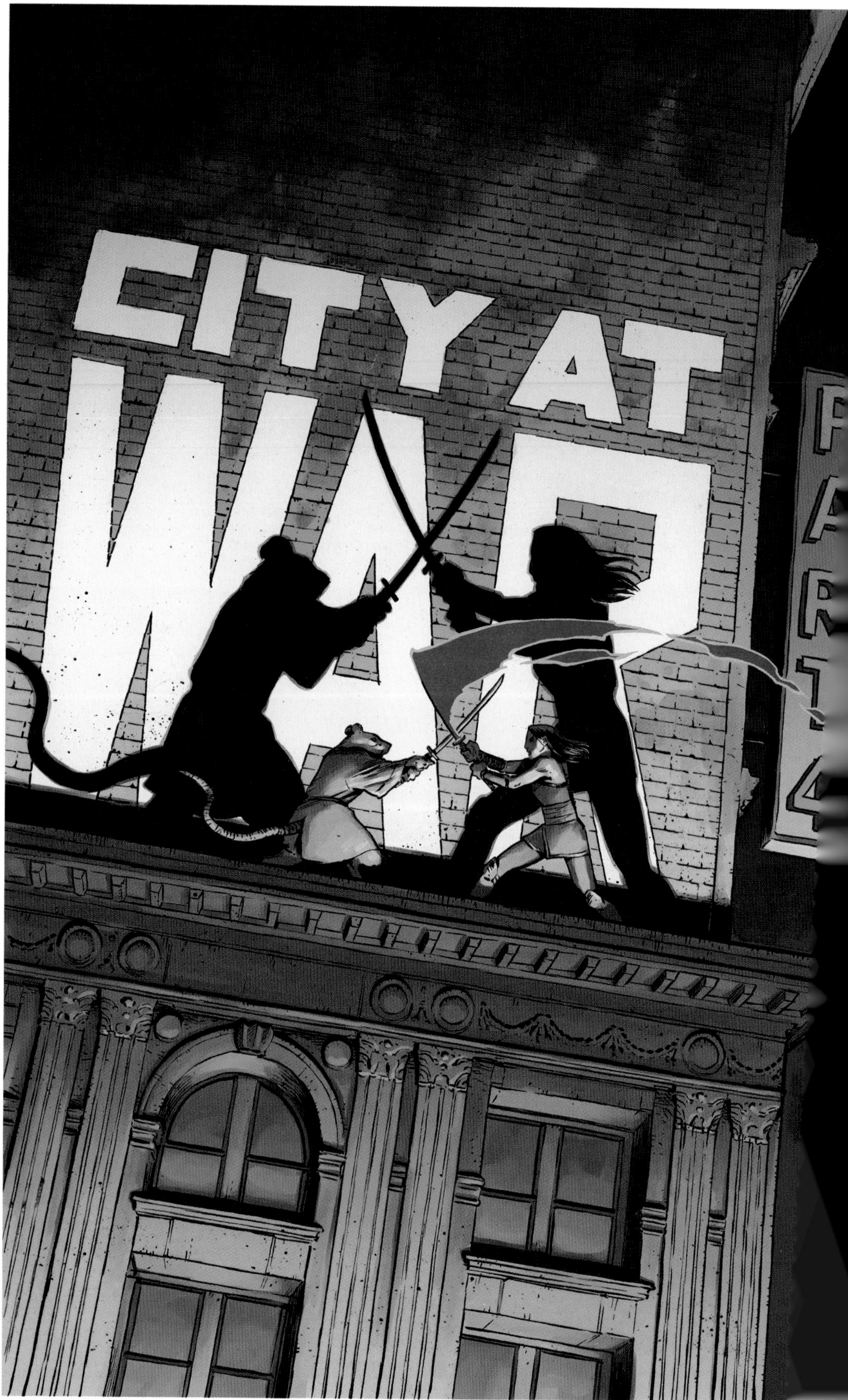
CITY AT
WAR
PART 4

ART BY DAVE WACHTER

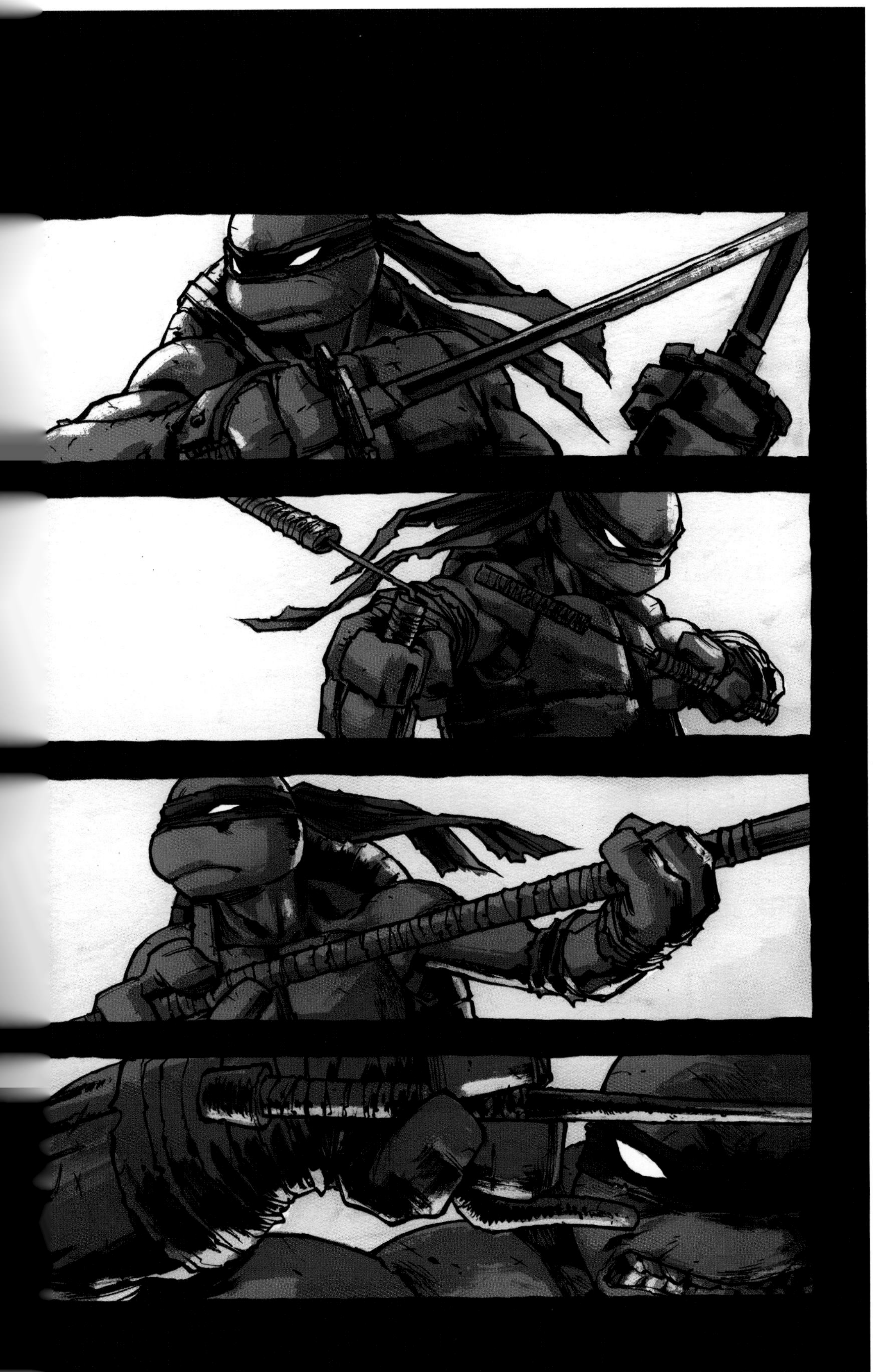

ART BY SOPHIE CAMPBELL

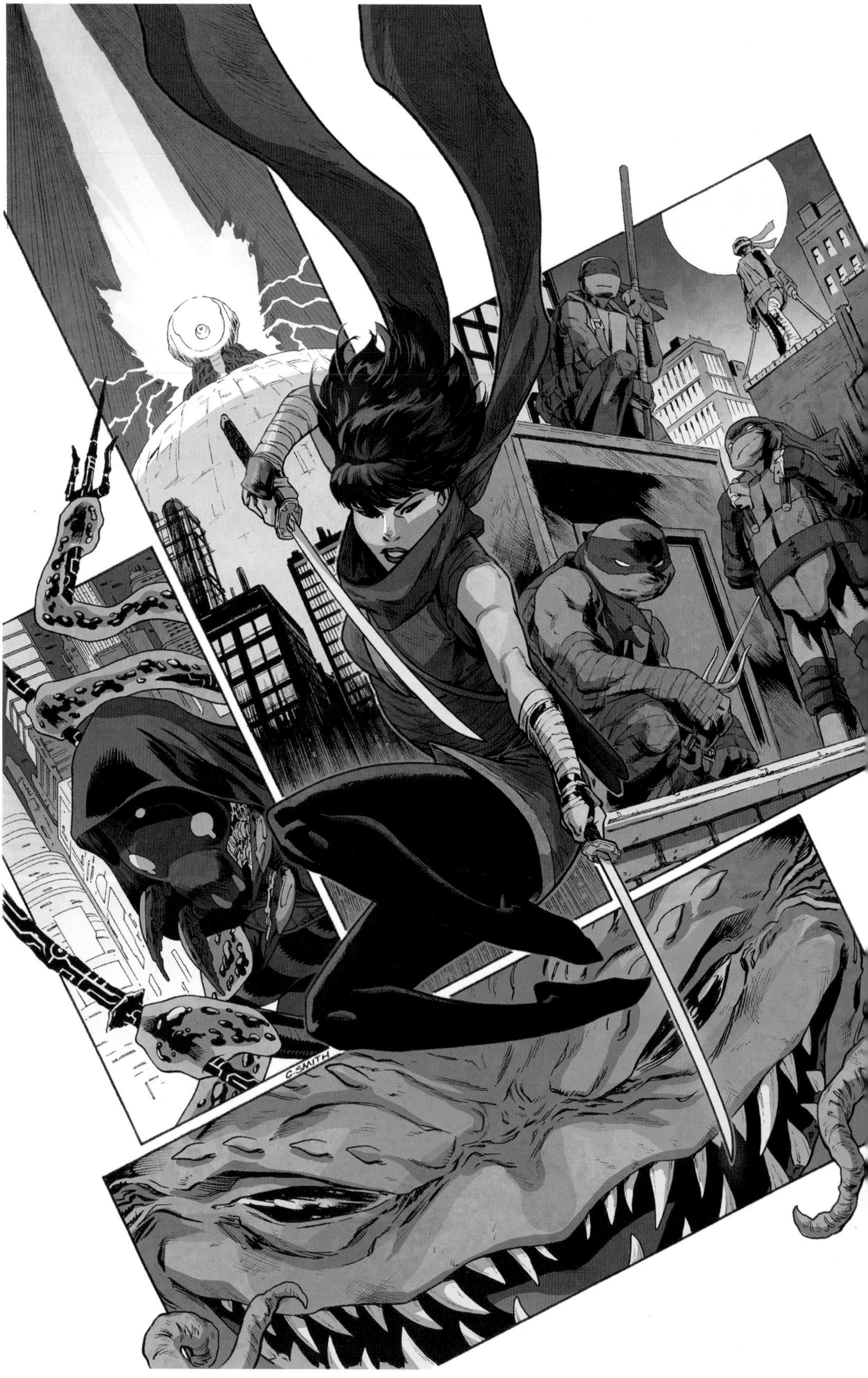
C.SMITH

ART BY CORY SMITH

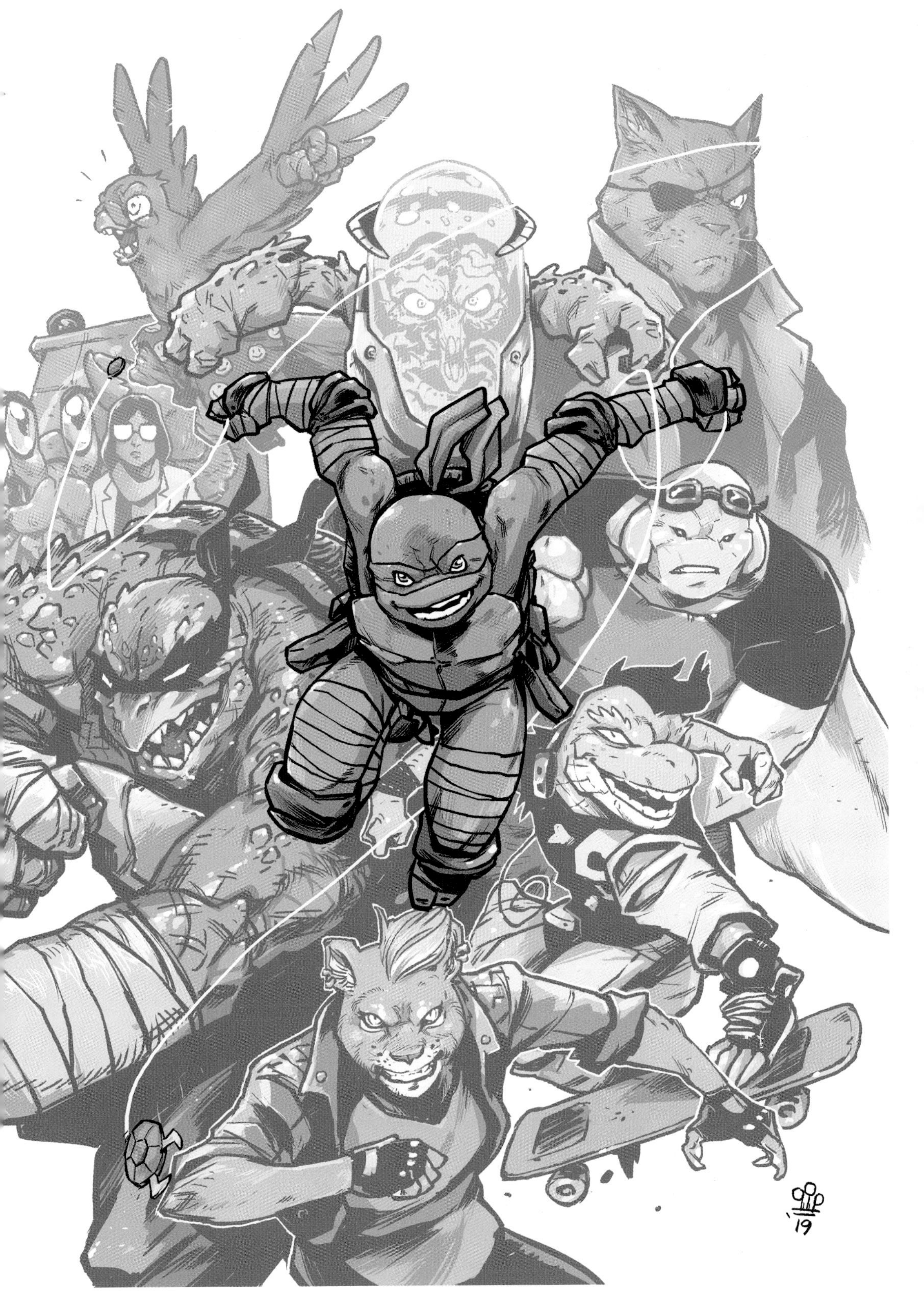

ART BY MICHAEL DIALYNAS

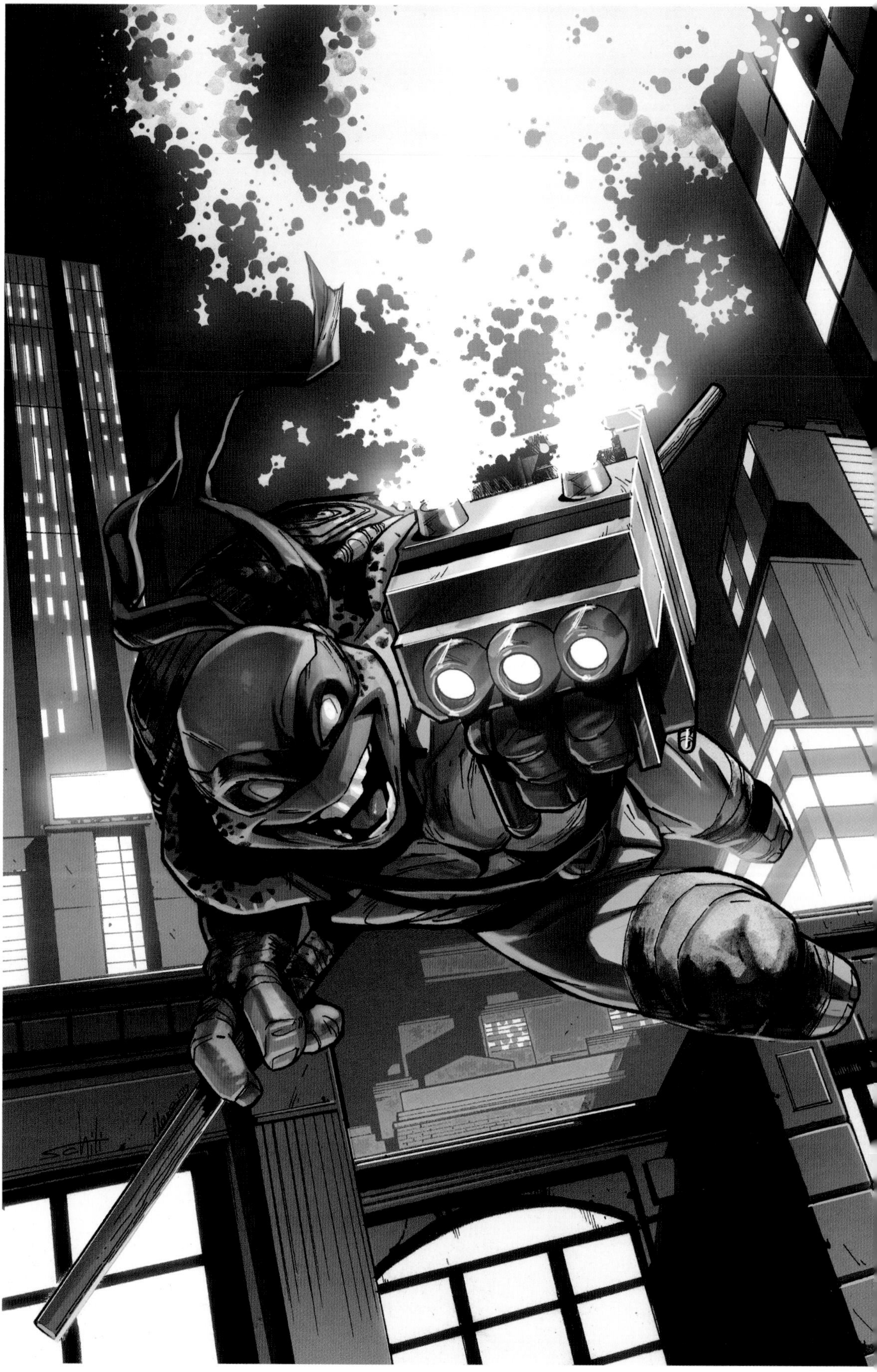

ART BY VALERIO SCHITI

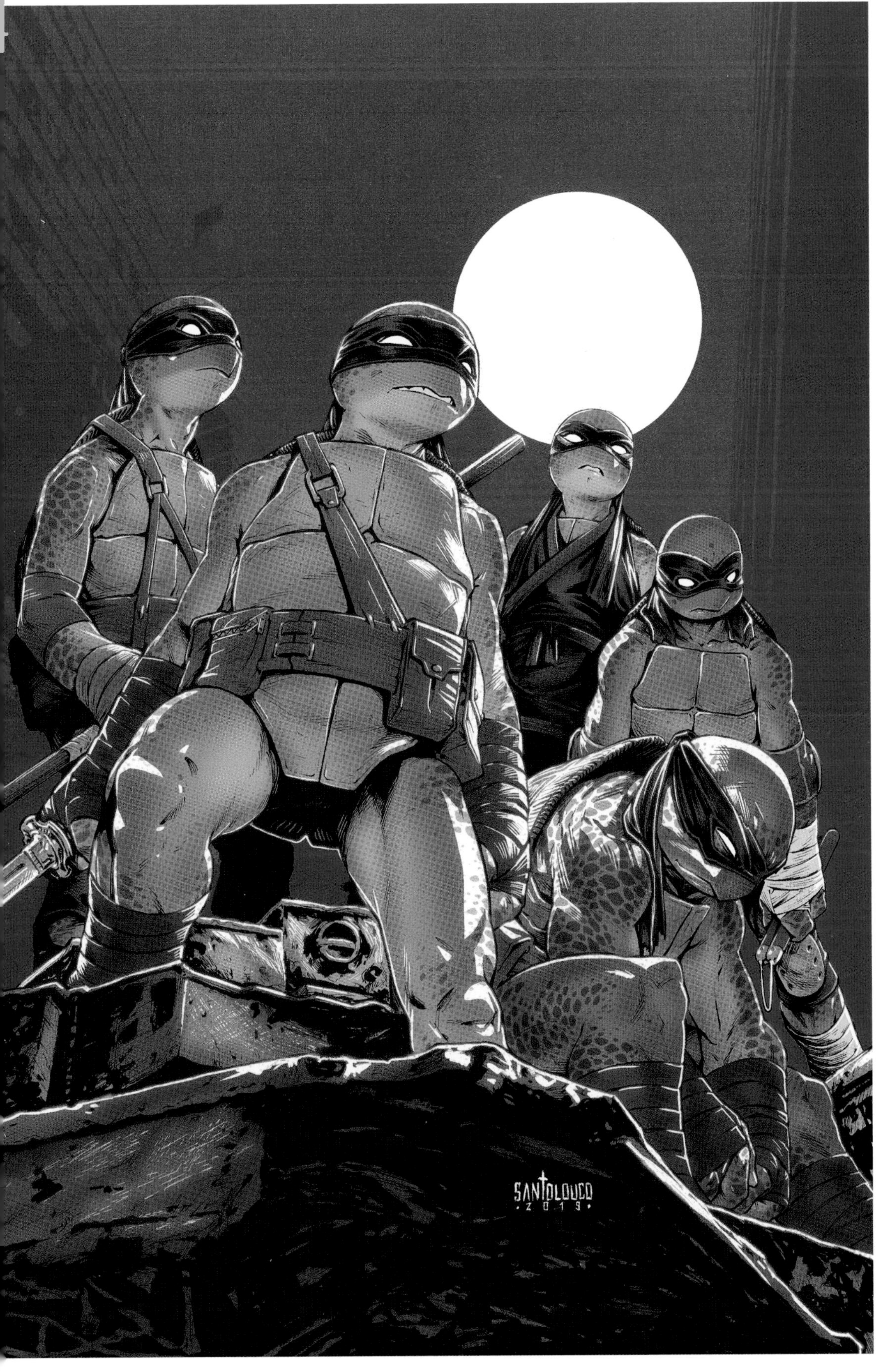
SANTOLOUCO
2019

ART BY MATEUS SANTOLOUCO

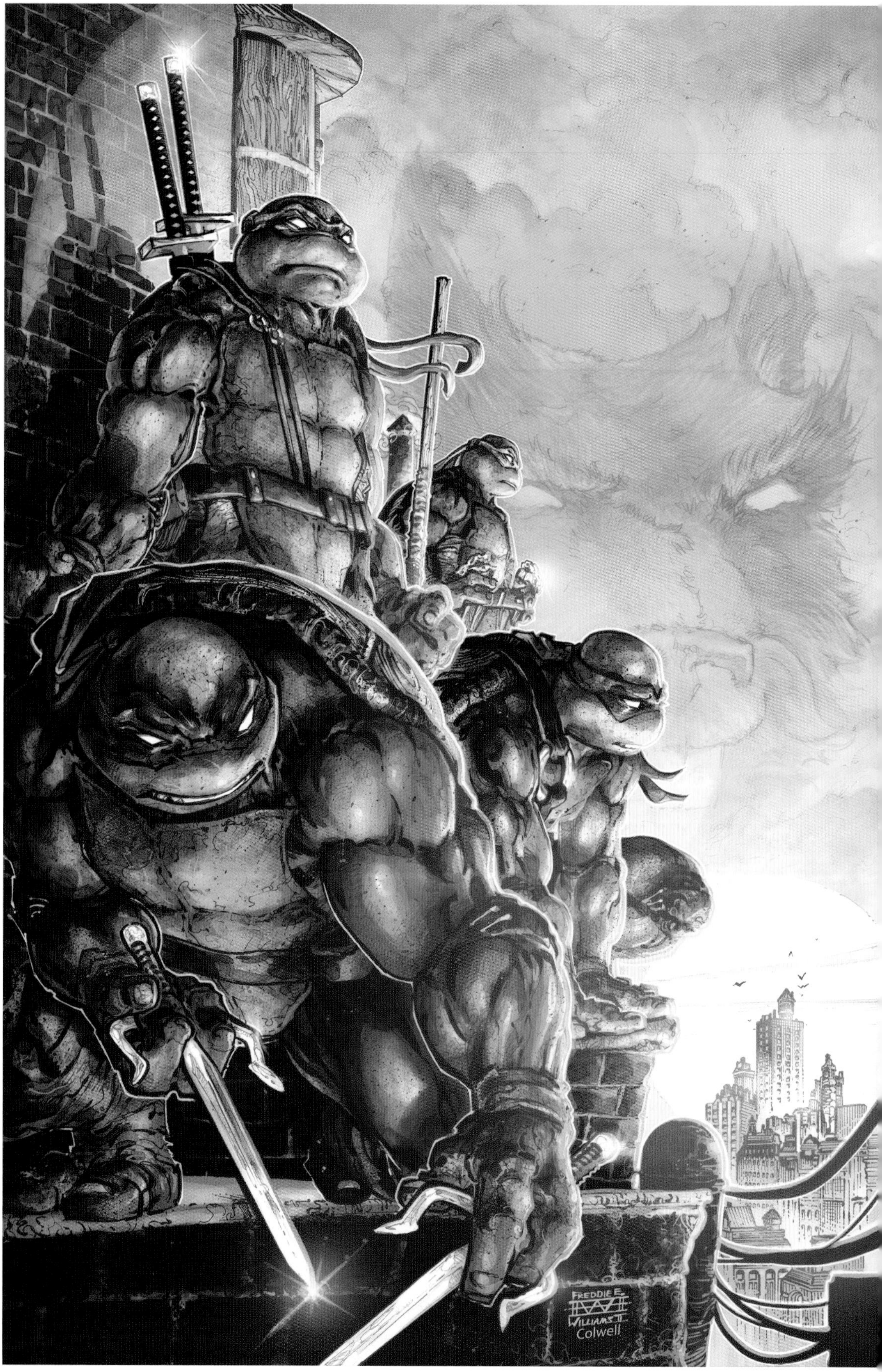
FREDDIE E.
WILLIAMS II
Colwell

ART BY FREDDIE WILLIAMS II

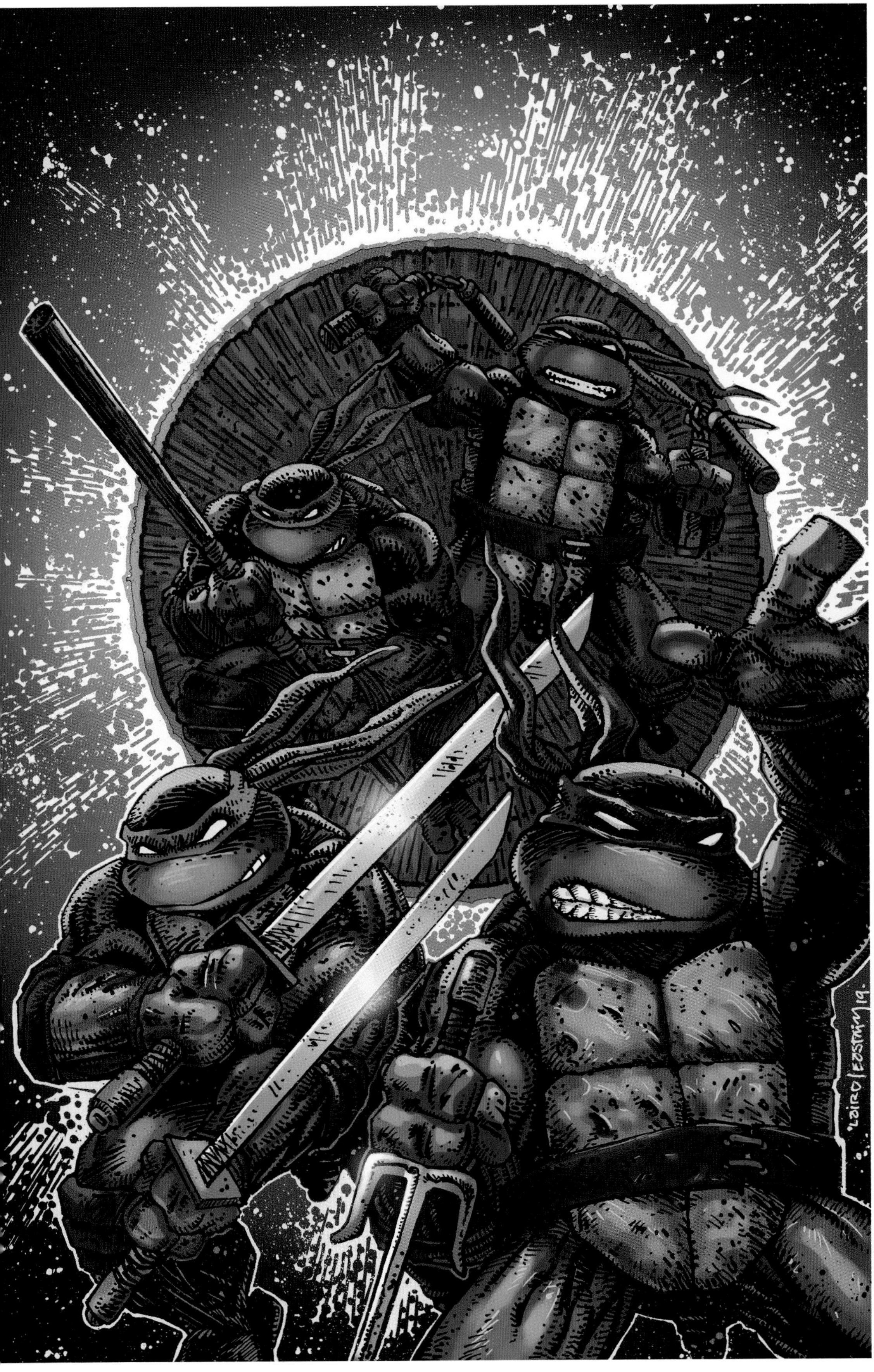

ART BY PETER LAIRD & KEVIN EASTMAN · COLORS BY FAHRIZA KAMAPUTRA

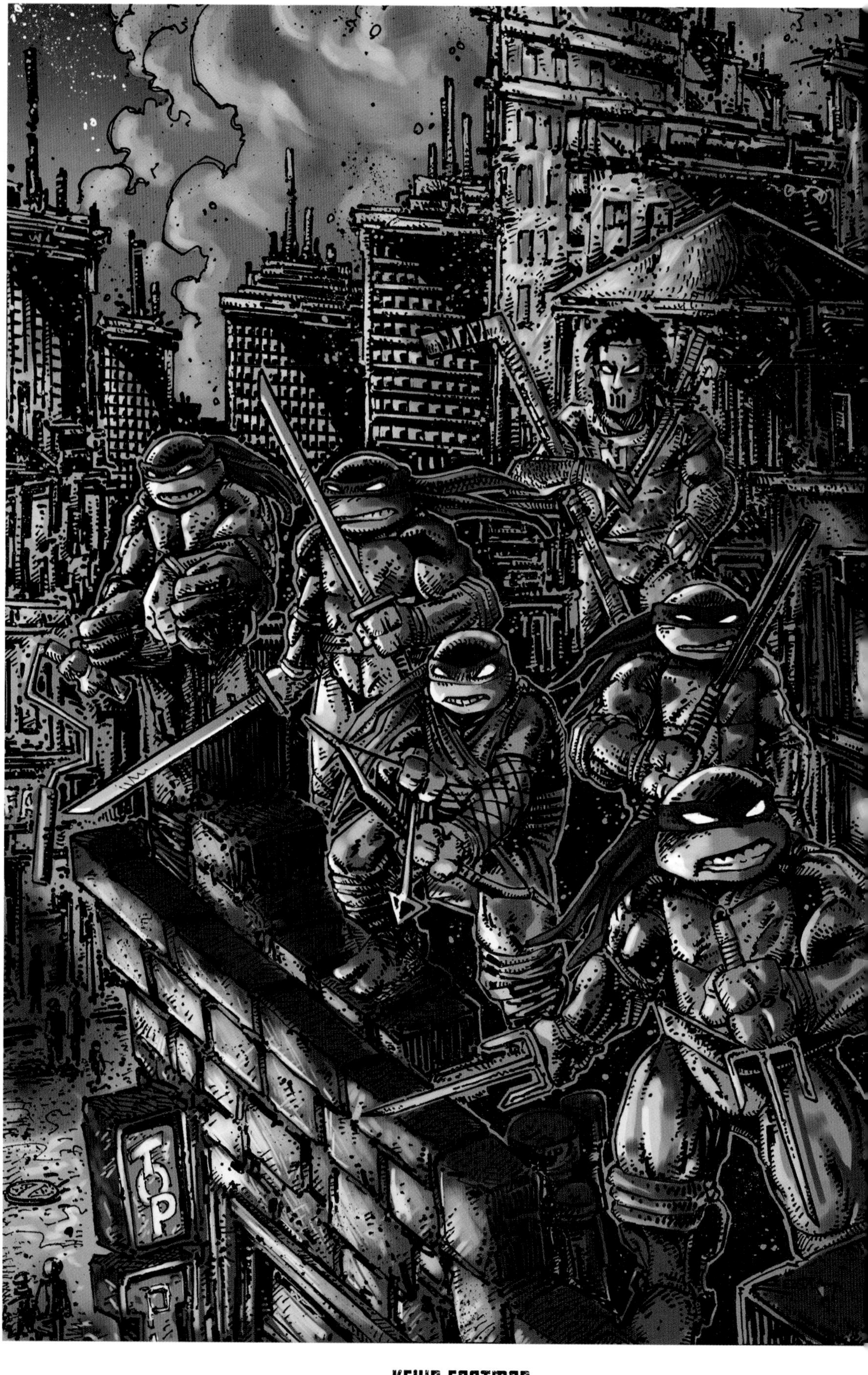
TOP

ART BY KEVIN EASTMAN

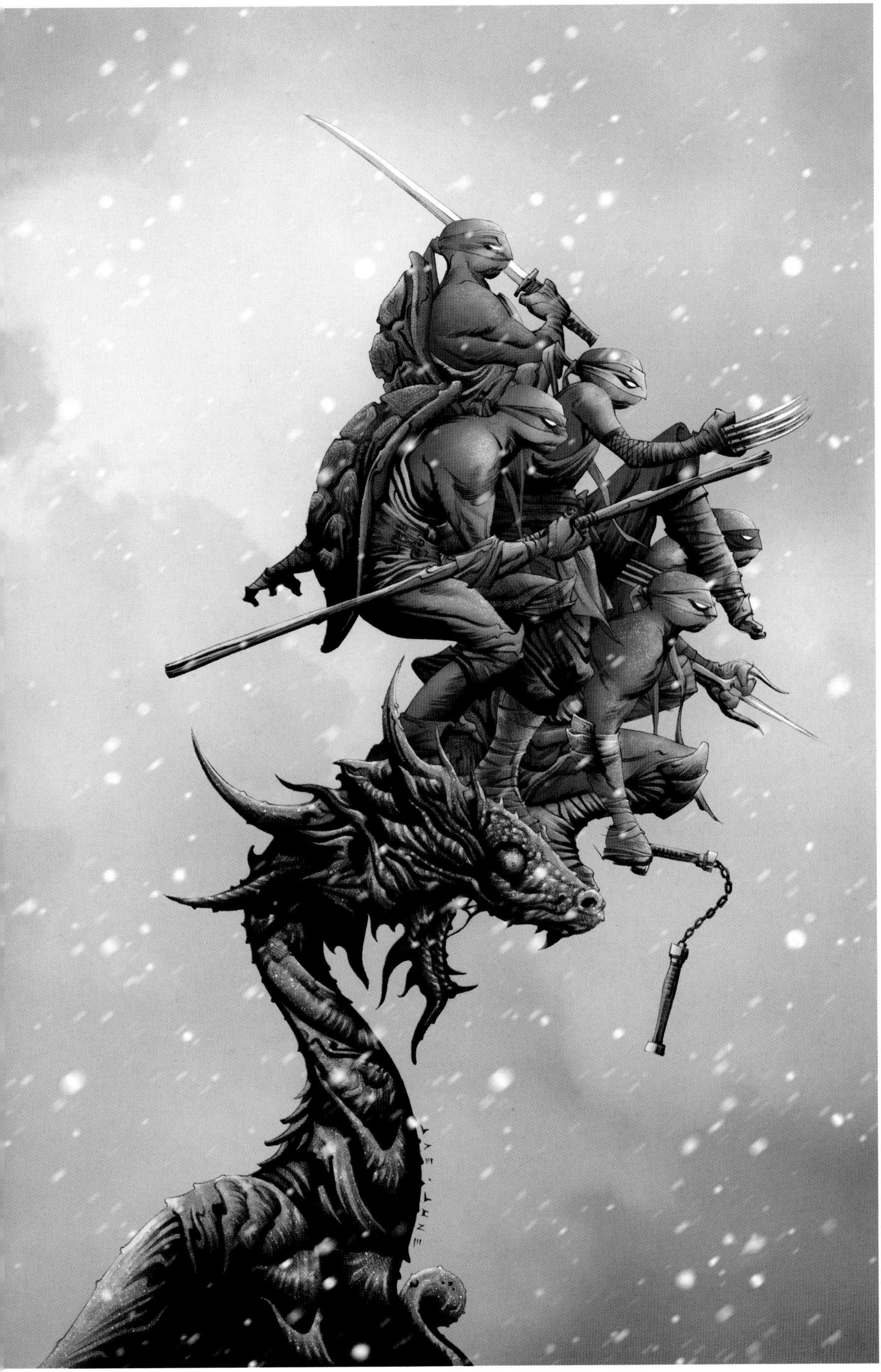

ART BY JAE LEE · COLORS BY JUNE CHUNG

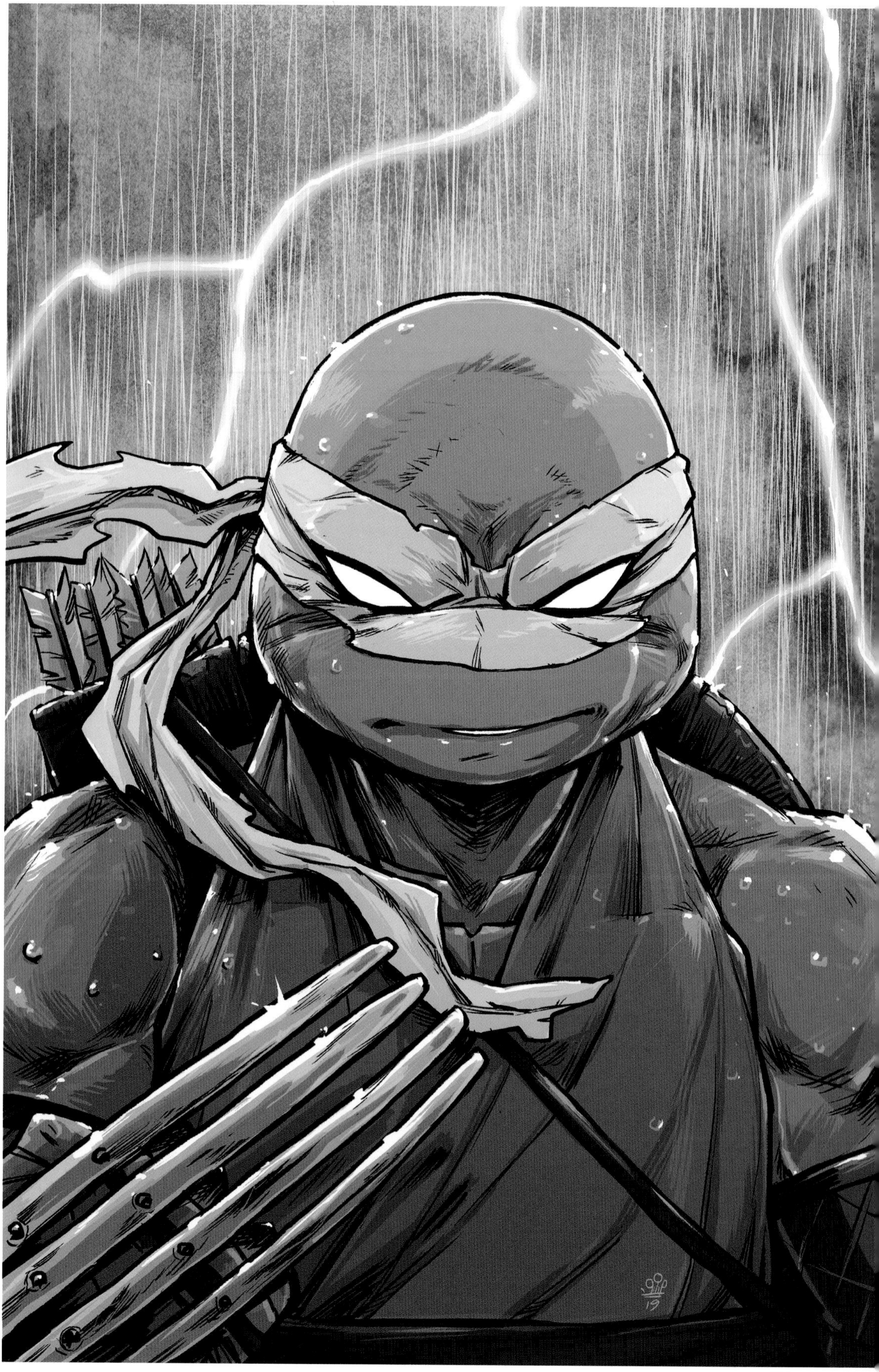

ART BY MICHAEL DIALYNAS

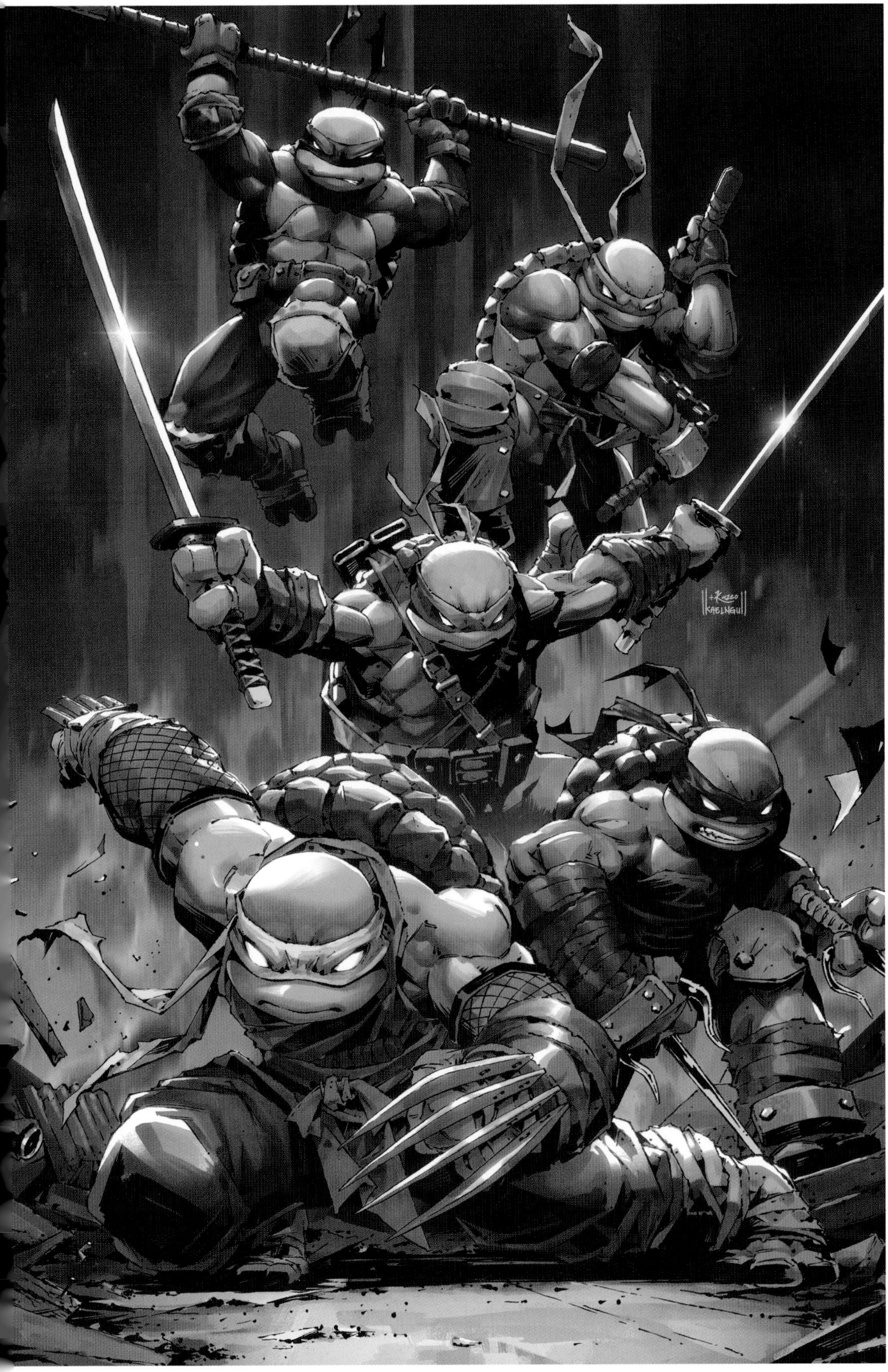

ART BY KAEL NGU

TEENAGE MUTANT NINJA TURTLES

CITY AT WAR, PT. 2 ▸ VOLUME 23

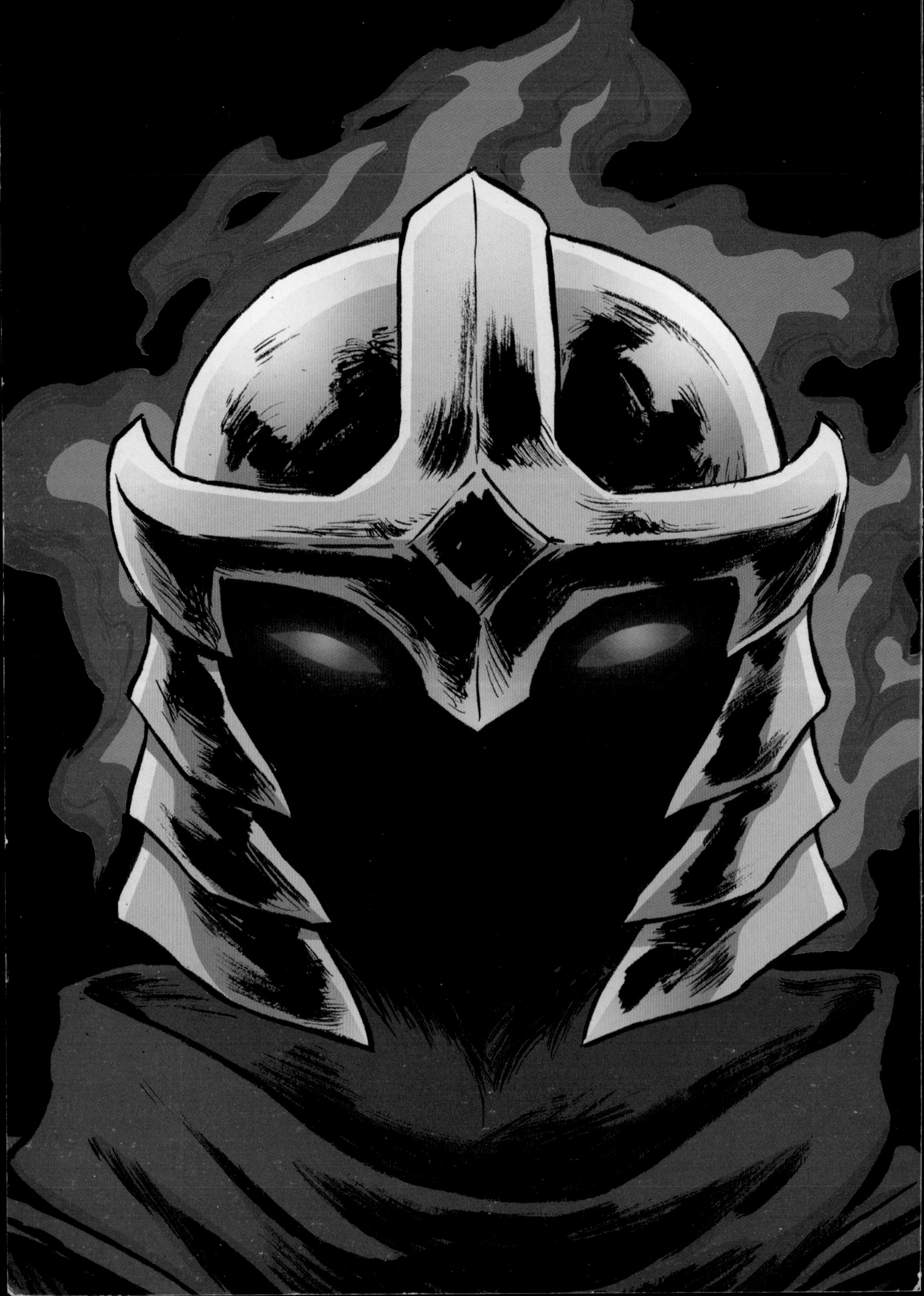